T0385475

PLANT GALLS
OF THE WESTERN UNITED STATES

RONALD A. RUSSO

CALIFORNIA WILDLIFE
FOUNDATION
CALIFORNIA OAKS FUND

PRINCETON UNIVERSITY PRESS
PRINCETON AND OXFORD

Published by Princeton University Press
41 William Street, Princeton, New Jersey 08540
6 Oxford Street, Woodstock, Oxfordshire OX20 1TR

press.princeton.edu

All photographs and illustrations by author unless noted otherwise.

All Rights Reserved
ISBN (pbk.) 9780691205762
ISBN (e-book) 9780691213408
Library of Congress Control Number: 2020949502

British Library Cataloging-in-Publication Data is available

Editorial: Robert Kirk and Abigail Johnson
Production Editorial: Karen Carter
Text Design: D & N Publishing, Wiltshire, UK
Jacket/Cover Design: Ruthie Rosenstock
Production: Steven Sears
Publicity: Caitlyn Robson and Matthew Taylor
Copyeditor: Amy Hughes

Publication of this book has been aided by the California Wildlife Foundation, California Oaks Fund

This book has been composed in Minion Pro (main text) and ITC Franklin Gothic (headings and captions)

Printed on acid-free paper. ∞

Printed in China

10 9 8 7 6 5 4 3 2 1

To my wife, Sheri

The act of discovery is one of the greatest joys;
it is a bright flash in the darkness,
with a reward not soon forgotten.

—H. E. Evans (1968)

CONTENTS

PREFACE

On a single blue oak in Chris and Ann Nelson's backyard in 1969, I found over 20 species of cynipid wasp galls. Thus began a journey that would take me, over the ensuing years, through most plant communities in the western United States. I had no idea at the time that this would become a lifelong passion. I have found galls nearly everywhere I looked. Immediately apparent throughout all of my searching was the startling fact that such extraordinary creations were so abundant, yet so collectively ignored. This guide represents a much more thorough field guide to galls induced on native and some ornamental plants than my previous book. This edition covers a broader region and includes 232 species not in the original book. Along with my own observations and field experience, I have worked to extract as much biological information from the literature—information that has to date been relatively hidden in obscure places inaccessible to most. While this guide encompasses 536 species of plant galls, including 231 species on oaks, it still remains incomplete and should be viewed as an **INTRODUCTION**, especially for Southwest oaks. For so many plant galls, their existence and the identities and biology of the causative organisms remain a mystery.

Over the past 35 years, researchers around the world have made great strides in understanding the complexities of host-inducer interactions. Someday, when the precise mechanisms are discovered that, for example, allow cynipid wasps to alter the expression of plant genes in specific ways to create galls unique to that species, we may find that such discoveries have applications to other sciences, especially in the medical field. Over 140 new species of gall organisms were discovered during the preparation of this guide. Each time I explore a new area, I find new species. You too may also find galls not described in this guide or any other reference. Please do not let that frustrate or discourage you. The earth is full of discoveries yet to be made. If nothing else, this single idea encourages me, and I hope you, to keep looking and exploring.

Whether about the ocean or the land, I have spent my entire career over the past 60 years trying to help people see that which they might not otherwise see, with the hope they would come to appreciate the great wonders of this planet. With this guide, I hope to open an entire universe that some may not have previously imagined possible. This earth has treasures beyond our wildest dreams, so get out into nature with your eyes, heart, and mind wide open.

Ronald A. Russo

ACKNOWLEDGMENTS

First and foremost, a special thanks to Harold Weidman, who ignited in me a lifelong passion for botany and plant taxonomy during my collegiate years, and to Chris Nelson, for bringing me a branch of urchin galls in 1969 that started this journey. Over the many years of my research and field collections that followed, I have enjoyed the assistance of several scientists, colleagues, and friends. I am indebted to John Tucker (oaks), Richard Goeden (tephritid flies), David Headrick (tephritid flies), Jim Wangberg (tephritid flies), Patrick Abbot (aphids), Raymond Gagné (gall midges), Jeffrey Joy (gall midges), Joseph Shorthouse (cynipid wasps), Bradford Hawkins (gall midges), Don Miller (manzanita aphids), Charles Dailey (cynipids), Jerry Powell (moths), Robert Raabe (forest pathology), and Sarah Rosenthal (cynipids) for their generous assistance that led to the *Field Guide to Plant Galls of California and Other Western States* (Russo 2006).

This updated and expanded guide would not have been possible without the continued assistance of Raymond Gagné (gall midges), James Zimmerman (Southwest cynipids), Gene Hall (Southwest insect collection), and Katherine Schick (cynipids). A special thanks to James Nicholls (cynipids) and Juli Pujade-Villar (cynipids) for sharing their recent research findings and graciously handling a variety of questions. I also appreciate May Chen for sharing galls she has found and Joyce Gross, not only for alerting me to galls she had found but also for the use of her incredible photographs in this guide. Also, I am so grateful that Ken, Tani and Jack Russo found needed samples for the Hair Charts. And a genuine thank you to Amy Hughes and Karen Carter for their brilliant editing of this guide.

I wish to extend my heartfelt gratitude to California Wildlife Foundation and particularly Janet Cobb, Executive Officer, for visionary dedication to protecting oak woodlands and unwavering support and contributions to this field guide.

Finally, I owe so much to my wife, Sheri, not only for her help with the manuscript but also for her enthusiastic hard work as an acute observer, finding many plant galls during our collecting trips, including new species.

If you have ever camped or hiked beneath oak trees or have oaks on your property or in the neighborhood, you probably have noticed peculiar swellings known as "oak apples" or mysterious colorful adornments on leaves or branches. Or you may have noticed projections, swellings, or pouches on the leaves of alder, willow, juniper, pine, manzanita, sage, creosote bush, wild plum, wood rose, rabbitbrush, or any number of native shrubs and trees in the western states. Welcome to the realm of plant galls!

The world of plant galls is a "Lilliputian realm" in which an organism, sometimes scarcely the size of a period on this page, can induce a plant to produce a swelling that provides food and shelter. Some of these galls, especially those of cynipid wasps, are so flamboyant in design and color they would challenge the wildest of architectural dreams. In their own right, gall organisms are nature's own miniature architects. Part of the magic of this little-known world is that plant galls are all around us: in forests, woodlands, marshlands, neighborhood parks, and even your garden.

This guide covers all the states west of the Rocky Mountains, including Alaska, and north of Mexico. (Any references to North America exclude Mexico.) Within this enormous geographic area there is a diverse variety of plant species that hosts a dazzling array of galls. Many of the gall-inducing organisms have been described and named by scientists. Many others are new species yet to be discovered, studied, and classified.

Plant galls are known for their incredible variety of shapes, sizes, and colors. They range from a gall the size of a pinhead on a leaf to a cankerous gall on the side of a tree trunk that exceeds 1.2 m in diameter. In color, they duplicate the full spectrum of the rainbow and then add blends of colors and patterns that tease the mind. Some galls are smooth and round. Others have wart-like bumps, spines, hairs, tubercles, or flared edges. Some look like balls, saucers, cups, bowls, sea urchins, caterpillars, spindles, clubs, teeth, donuts, or exploded twigs or buds. Some are quite noticeable because of their size or color. Others are nearly impossible to see because they look like normal buds or are so small that they escape detection.

Of all the galls and their host plants I have studied over the years, the blue, valley, and Oregon oaks of California and the white oaks of Utah, Arizona, and New Mexico produce the most intriguing and bizarre galls in shape and color. Few other insect-induced galls in North America, and perhaps anywhere else, can rival these "architectural wonders."

The purpose of this field guide is to introduce the reader to the causes, effects, and interrelationships of some of the galls and their inducers found in nearly all of the western states (except Texas). The book is divided into two major sections. The first covers the general biology of galls and gall-inducers, host plant effects, and broad ecological relationships with parasites and predators. The second, and larger, portion of this book covers the identification of galls and gall-inducing organisms based on host plants.

Out of necessity, this guide represents a **CATALOG OF GALLS** found in the West and is by no means a representation of all existing galls. I am certain that I will continue to find new galls, as will you, that are not described here. While I have collected galls from every western state, including Idaho, Wyoming, and Montana, much of my work over the past 50 years has been in Utah, Arizona, California, Nevada, Oregon, Washington, and Alaska. The usefulness of this guide extends to the entire West, with the ranges of several tree and shrub species extending across several states, as in the cases of Douglas-fir, several pines, aspens, cottonwoods, Great Basin sagebrush, *Baccharis* species, rabbitbrush, and creosote bush, among others, along with their respective galls.

This is not a book on insects, nor is it a book on plants. Instead, this is a guide that attempts to interpret a highly complex and evolved collection of rather challenging interrelationships between plants and plants, between plants and animals, and between animals and animals. In some instances, the galls that result from these highly refined relationships will capture the fancy of anyone who dares to focus attention on even a single, bizarre, brightly colored specimen. In taking time to study just a few such galls, you risk being captivated by the same mysterious fever that has lured countless other enthusiasts to birds, wildflowers, or mushrooms. Thanks to the widespread use of the internet, awareness is spreading. It takes only a dash of curiosity to explore, discover, and begin to understand the fascination of these strange creations, and, in so doing, the grand biodiversity of Earth itself.

About This Guide

WHY GALLS? Plant galls are in effect the signs of an organism's presence just as are the skulls, tracks, scratch marks, and droppings used to determine which animal made them. Gall-inducers are rarely visible, due to their small size and short life span. And since many galls tend to be "species-specific," possessing diagnostic features that are uniquely associated with a single gall-inducing species, great care has been taken to describe each gall's morphological characteristics, as subtle as they may seem. Unfortunately, we know little about the life cycles of the organisms that induce these galls, except in a relatively few cases.

PLANT IDENTIFICATION: Successful use of this field guide requires that you have a basic knowledge of taxonomy of native plants. In effect, you must know or be able to identify at least the genus, and in some cases the species, of the host plant to identify the gall organisms described. A number of fine field guides will help you identify plants in the western states. I have systematically used *The Jepson Manual of Vascular Plants* (2012) for taxonomic issues, along with several other recent regional guides. With some knowledge of plant identities, you can then go to the appropriate group or species and locate the gall(s) of interest. This guide provides as much detailed biological information as is available on each gall species covered, along with host plant and related details. Additionally, several tables list gall organisms known but not necessarily described within the text. Some galls that occur on ornamental plants, for example, are not described here but are referred to in the Ornamental Plant Galls section.

MUSEUM COLLECTIONS: I studied the cynipid wasp collections at the Bohart Museum of Entomology, University of California at Davis; the Essig Museum of Entomology, University of California at Berkeley; the Museum of Natural History, Sierra College at Rocklin; the California Academy of Sciences, San Francisco; and the University of Arizona Entomology Museum, Tucson.

COMMON NAMES: As with many organisms, plant galls have only scientific names, which apply to the gall-inducer. Common names in this guide have been created for the convenience of the reader and apply only to the physical characters of the gall itself—not the agent. The agents' formal scientific names come only from taxonomists who study the characteristics of the insect or other agent and publish a description and name in a scientific journal. These scientific names are always the binding element to clearly identify a gall-inducer's taxonomic position. The References section lists references I used to obtain scientific names and information for many species.

Unnamed Species

I have chosen to include in this guide a number of species that either I could not identify given available resources or that may be new to science and not yet classified in order to simply record their existence until such time as they can be identified. Even though in many cases the gall-inducer is known to be a midge or wasp, these species are listed here as **UNKNOWN**.

Many of the species listed in the 2006 guide as "Undescribed" have now been identified to genus and appear here with just the generic name, while a few have even been identified to species level. Since I am describing the gall as well as some aspects of the organism's life, I have changed the term from "Undescribed" to "Unknown." Thus, in the ensuing years after publication of this guide, my hope is that adult insects will be reared from Unknown species herein and will be formally described and named, as they have since publication of the 2006 guide.

Occasionally, the reader may find a scientific name that has "cf." between the genus and species names. This generally means that the described insect gall is "close to" the species named, with some differences. Some genus names are in quotation marks; this indicates that the organism is assigned to this genus provisionally, until further research confirms its classification.

It seems unfortunate to me that in our society, organisms without names seem to be less regarded than those with names, especially among smaller species. It is almost as if they don't exist if they don't have names. Between those species yet to be formally described and named and those already named and lost in 19th- or early 20th-century literature yet to be digitized, it seems that this "dark taxa" may never be completely uncovered. The earth is simply too vast, with incalculable refugia where new species exist that may never be found.

Galls in Nature

Plant galls represent just one facet, one platform, a single venue among tens of thousands of ways that plants and animals interact with each other in the world. By the very nature of the existence of galling organisms, thousands of other creatures are able to survive in the complicated, intricate, interdependent existence that drives life on this planet. The world of plant galls is but one among countless theatrical stages that exist where the "actors" perform specific roles in an ecological web that supports the rich biodiversity of our planet. As you will discover in this guide, their existence is important if for no other reason than they provide food and shelter to so many creatures.

Galls are tumorlike growths of plant tissue produced by host plants in response to chemical and/or mechanical stimuli of invading organisms (mainly bacteria, fungi, mites, insects), resulting in accelerated production of plant growth hormones (auxins, cytokinins, gibberellins, etc.). In effect, plant galls result from "reprogramming" the expression of the plant genome by an outside source. Galls are composed of cells that have undergone multiplication, reaching either abnormally high numbers or greater size than normal, on plant organs whose growth and development have been altered into forms not otherwise found on host plants, as in the case of some acorn, bud, and flower galls. The exact mechanism of gall formation may vary widely from one group of gall-inducers to another. There are so many variables, requirements, circumstances, and unknowns that no one universal method can apply to all gall-formers.

Based on what is known, at least of cynipid wasps, meristematic and parenchyma tissues are often involved in gall formation. It has been suggested that some gall wasps can convert relatively differentiated tissues back into meristematic tissue. This de-differentiation of host tissues prevents the normal expression of host characteristics and allows subsequent re-differentiation into specialized and varied tissue types observed in cynipid galls. For example, one aspect of this controlling influence is in the development of the concentric rings of tissue that surround the wasp larval chamber, which is usually lined with parenchymal nutritive tissue on which the larvae later feed.

Since galls of many insects (especially wasps and midges) are specific to their inducer species in size, shape, and color, there appears to be a hijacking of the normal expressions of genes to develop structures that serve the life cycle needs of individual gall-inducing organisms. The exact relationship between compounds provided by the adults or larvae and the resulting manifestation of plant cellular tissue into galls largely remains a mystery to this day. Something in the compounds provided by gall organisms directs, turns off, or reprograms the normal expression of plant genes during the development and expansion of the host plant's tissues. Scientists have been looking for a long time for the "blueprint" that seems to control gall characteristics. This has become the "holy grail" of gall research.

The Science of Gall Study

While the exact nature of galls has been the subject of much speculation and myth for centuries, the science of plant galls did not begin to develop until the 17th century. Gall science is divided into two separate fields: the study of plant galls and the arthropods that induce them, called **CECIDOLOGY**; and the study of how fungi and bacteria gall plants, which falls into plant pathology.

Cecidology brings together entomology, botany, and parasitology. Most gall-inducing insects are extremely selective in choosing their host plants. Because of this, a person can often identify the kind of plant by the species of gall organism, or the gall-inducer by the species or group of host plant(s). Galls are often so specific in shape, size, and often color to the species of gall-inducer (especially with cynipid wasps), the causative organism can be identified without ever seeing it. The scientific names attached to the photos and illustrations of galls in this guide are actually the names of the organisms that induce them.

A Brief History of Galls

Plant galls have been around for millions of years. I will forever wonder about early humans and their encounters with plant galls. What happened when the first hominids bit into large oak apples, thinking they were fruit, only to experience the high levels of tannin? How did they learn about galls as a source of dyes, eyewash, or decorations?

Some galls have been well known to industrial and agricultural interests as sources of tanning agents (tannin and gallic acid), printing ink, supplementary livestock feed, and in a few cases, the cause of major orchard damage, but their history goes well beyond modern times. Fossil evidence shows that fungi-induced galls existed 300–200 million years ago, during the Upper Paleozoic–Triassic period, in England. Suspected insect-induced galls existed about 225 million years ago, during the Triassic period, in France. The oldest confirmed insect-induced galls from North America are from the Upper Cretaceous, about 115 million years ago, and were taken from fossil beds in Maryland. The oldest known cynipid galls are from the late Eocene, about 34 million years ago, in Florissant, Colorado. Plant galls and gall organisms represent ancient relationships in the evolution of our planet. Today, many of these gall organism–host plant relationships reveal sophisticated and highly evolved organization and development.

Galls are an integral part of the natural landscape; they played a role in sustaining Native Americans. Evidence exists that Native Americans relied on galls for medicinal and other uses. Several groups located in California's Central Valley ground the galls of the California gall wasp (*Andricus quercuscalifornicus*) into a powder used for making eyewash and treating cuts, burns, and sores. The "raspberry gall" (in this guide referred to as the urchin gall) caused by the wasp *Antron quercusechinus* was also ground for use as a wash for inflamed eyes. Other galls were ground for use in dyes and hair coloring. Native peoples from the British Columbia coast reportedly ate the fungus galls found on false azalea (*Menziesia ferruginea*). Certain spring galls, loaded with tannic acid, were chewed to clean teeth. Native Americans from Arizona reportedly smoked the large round galls most likely caused by the stem-gall midge *Asphondylia auripila*, found on creosote bush (*Larrea tridentata*). What other uses for galls existed that we may never know about?

One of the first people to write about galls was the Greek naturalist Theophrastus (372–286 BC), who wrote about the famous "gall nuts" of Syria. Pliny, the Roman naturalist (AD 23–79), recorded 23 medical remedies made with plant galls, including a hair-restoration product. For centuries, the production of figs for animal and human consumption has relied on tiny gall wasps.

In 1861, over 800 tons of "Aleppo" galls (induced by a cynipid wasp, *Cynips gallaetinctoriae*, on a European oak, *Quercus infectoria*) were imported into England for commercial use. Aleppo galls, primarily from Turkey, were the most-used galls in medicine for many years. In the United States, over 550,000 pounds of galls were imported annually from Turkey as late as 1945 for commercial use. Later, a Texas gall, the "mealy-oak gall," became commercially popular due to its high tannin level of 40%. Galls have been used for dyeing wool, leather, and fur and for skin tattooing in East Africa. Galls (*Dryocosmus deciduus*) have even been used as supplemental livestock feed in Missouri and Arkansas. In Mexico, large oak galls (*Disholcaspis weldi*) were occasionally sold in fruit stands because of their reported sweetness.

Because of the lasting quality of ink produced from European oak galls, gall-based ink, called iron-gall ink, has been used for centuries. Monks used gall-based ink in the transcription of manuscripts nearly 1,000 years ago. Later, gall-based ink became the preferred ink used by the United States Treasury, Bank of England, German Chancellery, and the Danish government. Many important and well-known documents, including Book of Kells, Magna Carta, Dead Sea Scrolls, Declaration of Independence, as well as drawings by Rembrandt and Van Gogh and the compositions of Bach, Beethoven, Mozart, and others, were created using gall-based ink.

Plant galls have a long-standing place in the evolution of our landscape and our human history, and what we know has just scratched the surface of their importance to nature and the well-being of humankind.

Where Galls Form

Galls can form on every plant part: roots, trunks, branches, buds, flowers, fruits, and leaves. While some plants such as oaks support galls on all these parts, other plants, such as sage (*Salvia* spp.) and manzanita (*Arctostaphylos* spp.), may support galls only on their leaves. In one analysis in Europe involving oaks, a scientist found that of the cynipid wasp galls known, 2% were on flowers, 4% on acorns, 5% on roots, 5% on buds, 22% on branches, and about 62% on leaves. He also reported that over 80% of galls on members of the rose family (Rosaceae) developed on leaves. The reason for such a disproportionately high gall incidence on leaves is because the leaf is the part of the plant that undergoes the highest metabolic activity during a relatively short growth period. Galls can, therefore, develop relatively quickly in spring and summer. The normal photosynthetic activity of leaves contributes greatly to rapid development and nutrition of galls and the larvae growing in them.

As you go through this guide, you will notice that some species and groups of host plants support more gall-inducers than other plants. Nineteen host plant species or groups host more than 78% of the gall-inducers in this guide; 55% of these are found on oak trees, while only a few occur on roses (Table 1). When you ponder the enormous populations of these species

TABLE 1. MAJOR HOST PLANTS IN THIS GUIDE WITH FIVE OR MORE SPECIES OF GALL ORGANISMS

Host Plant Species or Group	Number of Gall Species
Alder (*Alnus* spp.)	6
Aspen, Cottonwood, Poplar (*Populus* spp.)	24
Ceanothus (*Ceanothus* spp.)	5
Cheesebush (*Ambrosia* spp.)	7
Coyote brush, Desert broom (*Baccharis* spp.)	14
Creosote bush (*Larrea tridentata*)	15
Honeysuckle (*Lonicera* spp.)	5
Incense cedar (*Calocedrus decurrens*)	5
Juniper (*Juniperus* spp.)	8
Oak (*Quercus* spp.)	231
Pine (*Pinus* spp.)	6
Plum, cherry (*Prunus* spp.)	6
Rabbitbrush (*Chrysothamnus* and *Ericameria* spp.)	15
Ragweed (*Ambrosia* spp.)	7
Rose (*Rosa* spp.)	10
Sagebrush (*Artemisia* spp.)	15
Saltbush (*Atriplex* spp.)	8
Service-berry (*Amelanchier* spp.)	7
Willow (*Salix* spp.)	24
Total	**418**

and their associated inquilines, parasites, and hyperparasites, the ecological ramifications and importance of such hosts as creosote bush (*Larrea tridentata*), wild roses (*Rosa* spp.), sagebrush (*Artemisia* spp.), oaks (*Quercus* spp.), and willows (*Salix* spp.), among others, are staggering.

Gall-Inducers at a Glance

Aside from insects and mites, the guide includes a broad spectrum of galls that develop as a result of the biological activity of invading organisms such as bacteria, rusts, sac fungi, and mistletoes. These galls are swellings from which reproductive products or agents are released. Some botanists regard the swellings that result from invasion of parasitic mistletoes (*Arceuthobium* spp.) as a reaction to irritation and not true galls. Mistletoe-induced witches' brooms are included as galls in this guide. The bulk of gall-inducers in this guide are mites and insects that create a dazzling array of galls within which their offspring are nourished.

Evolutionary Paths

During millions of years of evolution and adaptation among insects, natural selection influenced the biological paths that each group and species followed. As a result, each species found specific niches within which it operated for the purposes of survival and procreation. Some insects became woodborers, pollinators, or carrion eaters, while others rolled dung, captured spiders, or parasitized other animals. Somewhere along this evolutionary line, many species of insects and mites evolved intimate relationships with plants, resulting in the development of galls. These evolving gall-inducers became extreme specialists. Worldwide, there are an estimated 13,000 species of gall-inducing arthropods, a number that is slowly increasing with continued research. Among them there are at least 21 separate groups, but for our purposes we shall consider only 12: eriophyid mites (Eriophyidae), psyllids (Psyllidae), coccids (Kermesidae), aphids and adelgids (Aphididae and Adelgidae), beetles (Cerambycidae), moths (Gelechiidae, Tortricidae, Cosmopterigidae), leaf-mining flies (Agromyzidae), tephritid fruit flies (Tephritidae), and gall midges (Cecidomyiidae), and three families of wasps: tanaostigmatids (Eupelmidae), sawflies (Tenthredinidae), and cynipid gall wasps (Cynipidae).

The United States has over 2,000 known species of gall-inducing insects. Nearly 700 of these species are cynipid wasps. There are also more than 800 species of gall midges. Next in prominence are tephritid fruit flies. While an accurate number of gall-inducing tephritids north of Mexico is not available, several species are common in the West. Eriophyid mites are responsible for a considerable number of galls. Several aphids, two adelgids, and many moths induce galls in the West, even though there are far more than are listed in this guide. At least two leaf-mining flies and three tanaostigmatid wasps are known to gall western plants. Only one gall-inducing beetle is included here, even though many beetles are inquilines in galls. The only

TABLE 2. GALL-INDUCING SPECIES COVERED IN THIS GUIDE

Agent	Number of Species	
	On Native Plants	On Ornamental Plants
Bacteria	4	2
Fungi		
Rust	8	
Sac	10	1
Mildew	1	
Mistletoes (Viscaceae)	5	
Mites (Eriophyidae)	28	5
Aphids (Aphididae and Adelgidae)	16	1
Psyllids (Psyllidae)		2
Coccids (Kermesidae)	1	
Moths (Gelechiidae, Tortricidae, Cosmopterigidae)	16	
Beetles (Cerambycidae)	1	
Leaf-mining flies (Agromyzidae)	2	
Tephritid fruit flies (Tephritidae)	13	
Gall midges (Cecidomyiidae)	150	1
Tanaostigmatid wasps (Eupelmidae)	2	
Sawflies (Tenthredinidae)	14	
Cynipid wasps (Cynipidae)	242	2

Note: This does not include species referred to within a species' description.

coccid known to induce galls in the United States is found in the Southwest. The only psyllids included here occur on ornamentals (see Ornamental Plant Galls).

The second group of gall-inducers includes numerous species of bacteria, fungi, and mistletoes that stimulate the production of root, stem, and leaf galls. Unlike some insect galls, these agents often produce much less specificity in size, shape, and color of galls, making identification using these characteristics difficult and sometimes impossible. For some, identification is possible based on identity of the host and location and type of gall. Some bacterial galls (nitrogen-fixing nodules) appear on roots of host plants such as lupines (*Lupinus* spp.), alders (*Alnus* spp.), and the group of shrubs generally referred to as ceanothus (*Ceanothus* spp.). These galls are rare examples of situations in which the host plant and the gall-inducers mutually benefit. Other bacterial galls appear just below the soil surface of fruit trees and ornamental roses and are sometimes detrimental to the host plants. Fungus galls are associated with stems, leaves, flowers, and fruits of cottonwood (*Populus* spp.), alder (*Alnus* spp.), choke cherry and plum (*Prunus* spp.), and wood fern (*Dryopteris arguta*). Mistletoes almost always induce stem swellings and sometimes witches' brooms on host plants (pines [*Pinus* spp.], firs [*Abies* spp.], incense cedar [*Calocedrus decurrens*], among others). See Table 2 for a listing of the gall-inducing organisms covered in this guide.

Another group of gall-like structures appears on trees such as buckeyes (*Aesculus* spp.), California bay (*Umbellularia californica*), coast redwood (*Sequoia sempervirens*), and the ornamental pepper tree (*Schinus molle*), and are actually genetic anomalies or simply adventitious buds, not true galls resulting from invading organisms. See "Redwood False Galls" in the Tree Galls species accounts. The biology of each major group of gall-inducers is discussed later.

Common Types of Galls

Most galls occur on leaves, petioles, stems, and branches. Leaf galls are divided into specific types based on their general structure. Leaves support roll galls, fold galls, erineum pockets (also called "erinea" or "filzgalls"), pouch and bead galls, and mark or spangle galls. On stems and branches, we see either integral swellings or detachable outgrowths. Two other forms of galls include fasciations and witches' brooms. Other swellings, usually at the base of a tree trunk or high along the main trunk, called "burls," are often mistaken for galls.

ROLL GALLS: These galls are characterized by the outer edge of the leaf rolling inward, encompassing the gall organism (Figure 1). The rolled leaf tissues are either slightly or noticeably swollen and may be much harder than surrounding tissues. Mites, moths, and some midges generally produce roll galls.

Figure 1. Roll gall.

FOLD GALLS: These galls involve either the outer edge of the leaf simply folding over one time inwardly to encompass the gall organism, or the leaf folding along the midrib, creating a pouch on one side of the leaf (Figure 2). Swelling and distortion of leaf tissues are also characteristic of these galls. Aphids, moths, and midges usually induce fold galls.

Figure 2. Fold gall.

ERINEUM POCKETS: Erineum pockets (or erinea or filzgalls) are hair-lined pockets or depressions on leaves (Figure 3). These pockets are usually noticeable on one side of the leaf, with a corresponding bump on the opposite side. Eriophyid mites usually induce erineum galls. A sac fungus (*Taphrina populisalicis*) is also known to create spore-producing pockets on cottonwood leaves.

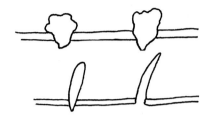

Figure 3. Erineum pocket.

BEAD AND POUCH GALLS: This group of galls can be shaped like small pouches, beads, clubs, spikes, shallow pits or blisters on the leaf surface and are often seen on willow and sage

Figure 4. Bead galls (top), pouch galls (bottom).

(Figure 4). All forms have an opening at the base, which allows escape of the mites or gall midges when mature. Eriophyid mites and some gall midges induce pouch and bead galls.

MARK AND SPANGLE GALLS: In most cases these leaf galls completely enclose the insect and have no openings, with the exception of some cecidomyiid galls. Mark and spangle galls are either detachable or are an integral part of the leaf, and both tend to be the most flamboyant among the galls in color and shape (Figure 5).

Figure 5. Mark and spangle galls.

Cynipid wasps and a few cecidomyiids (gall midges) induce most mark and spangle galls on leaves. Some cecidomyiid galls have openings leading to the larval chambers, but others do not.

FASCIATIONS: In these galls, the terminal buds of numerous plants are stimulated to fan out, creating extraordinarily flattened and rather striking shapes, often resembling elk or moose antlers (Figure 6). Sometimes bacteria, fungi, or mites are involved in these structures. The majority of fasciations, however, are thought by geneticists to be associated with broken DNA repair genes and are usually referred to as "noninfectious fasciations." Fasciations occur commonly on ornamental plants, as well as on a few native species (Table 3).

WITCHES' BROOMS: These are common on conifers but also occur on many native shrubs (Table 4). Brooms usually involve a dense collection of small branches and shoots emanating from a common focal point (Figure 7). Often these die after one season.

Figure 6. Fasciation.

Figure 7. Witches' broom.

TABLE 3. PARTIAL LIST OF HOST PLANTS THAT DEVELOP FASCIATIONS

Aloe (*Aloe* spp.)

Australian brush-cherry (*Eugenia myrtifolia*)

Chocolate lily (*Fritillaria lanceolata*)

Cotoneaster spp.

Cryptomeria spp.

Evening primrose (*Oenothera* spp.)

Mugwort (*Artemisia douglasiana*)

Mullein (*Verbascum thapsus*)

Poison oak (*Toxicodendron diversilobum*)

Sagebrush (*Artemisia* spp.)

Saguaro (*Carnegiea gigantea*)

Note: The saguaro, from Arizona, is an individual plant that has become famous, attracting photographers from throughout the West.

Large brooms exceeding 1.5 m in diameter have been found on Douglas-fir (*Pseudotsuga menziesii*) and western hemlock (*Tsuga heterophylla*). Witches' brooms usually involve bacteria, fungi, mistletoes, or mites. Broom-like clusters of shoots that originate from external mechanical injury not associated with an internal organism are not true galls. For example, porcupines have the habit of repeatedly chewing the same area of a conifer trunk or branch, which results in a broom-like cluster of shoots. From a distance, these dense clusters of branches might look like any other normal mistletoe-induced witches' broom.

STEM AND BRANCH GALLS: These galls involve a variety of causative agents including rust fungi, mistletoes, flies, moths, beetles, and wasps. Galls are either integral or protrude from the branch and are detachable (Figure 8). Integral stem galls can disrupt the flow of nutrients to outer regions, thereby killing the branch beyond the gall. Common curios from Central America sold

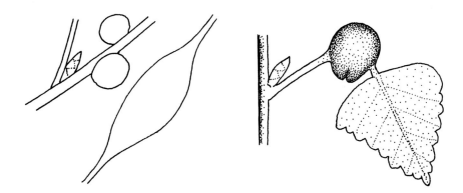

Figure 8. Detachable stem gall (left), integral stem gall (center), integral petiole gall (right)

TABLE 4. WITCHES' BROOM GALL-INDUCERS

Agent	Host Plant
Mildew	
Witches'-broom Fungus (*Sphaerotheca lanestris*)	Coast live oak (*Quercus agrifolia*)
Mycoplasma-like	
Unknown	Willow (*Salix* spp.)
Rust Fungus	
Puccinia evadens	Coyote brush (*Baccharis pilularis*)
Chrysomyxa arctostaphyli	Colorado blue spruce (*Picea pungens*)
Gymnosporangium confusum	Juniper (*Juniperus* spp.)
G. nidus-avis	Juniper
G. libocedri	Incense cedar (*Calocedrus decurrens*)
Pucciniastrum goeppertianum	Huckleberry (*Vaccinium* spp.)
Melampsorella caryophyllacearum	Fir (*Abies* spp.)
Endocronartium harknessii	Pine (*Pinus* spp.)
Sac Fungus	
Apiosporina collinsii	Service-berry (*Amelanchier* spp.)
Elytroderma deformans	Pine (*Pinus* spp.)
Exobasidium vaccinii	Manzanita (*Arctostaphylos* spp.), Rhododendron (*Rhododendron* spp.) and related other hosts
Taphrina amelanchierii	Service-berry (*Amelanchier* spp.)
T. aesculi	Buckeye (*Aesculus* spp.)
T. confusa	Choke cherry (*Prunus virginiana*), Sierra plum (*P. subcordata*)
T. thomasii	Holly-leafed cherry (*P. ilicifolia*)
Virus	
Nanus holodisci	Ocean spray (*Holodiscus discolor*)
Mistletoe	
Arceuthobium americanum	Lodgepole pine (*Pinus contorta* subsp. *murrayana*)
A. apachecum	White pine (*P. strobus*) (Arizona)
A. californicum	Sugar pine (*P. lambertiana*)
A. campylopodum	Coulter pine (*P. coulteri*), Jeffrey pine (*P. jeffreyi*), Knobcone pine (*P. attenuata*), ponderosa pine (*P. ponderosa*)
A. cyanocarpum	Limber pine (*P. flexilis*), western white pine (*P. monticola*)
A. occidentale	Bishop pine (*P. muricata*), Coulter pine (*P. coulteri*), Monterey pine (*P. radiata*)
A. laricis	Larch (*Larix* spp.)
A. tsugense	Hemlock (*Tsuga* spp.)
A. vaginatum	Ponderosa pine (*P. ponderosa*)
A. douglasii	Douglas-fir (*Pseudotsuga menziesii*)

in tourist shops in California and elsewhere are insect galls carved into lizards and birds (Plate 1). These galls look like an exploded branch, creating a fan-shaped natural art form, which allows easy escape of the adult wasps.

BURLS: These are knobby outgrowths with unusual grain, often at the bases of trees. Redwood burls are often sold as curios or for wood furniture. Even though burls have been referred to as "trunk galls," they usually do not involve invading organisms that stimulate their development. Rather, burls are the manifestations of dormant buds or adventitious buds and are not true galls. California bays, redwoods, buckeyes, sycamores, and pepper trees often sport large, knobby swellings or burls along their bases.

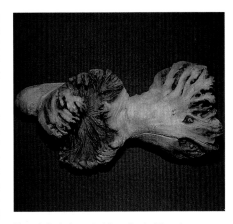

Plate 1. Curio imported from Central America made from branch anomaly probably caused by an interaction between a gall wasp and the host branch.

CANKERS: Several viruses, bacteria, and fungi induce massive eruptions and swellings of trunks and branches. These eruptions do not always have a gall-like form, although some are fissured swellings that ooze sap. For the purpose of this guide, most cankers on trees have been ignored, except for those prominent swellings induced by certain bacteria and rust fungi.

ROOT NODULES: A number of native plants have evolved a symbiotic relationship with **NITRO-GEN-FIXING BACTERIA.** Many of these **PIONEER PLANTS** tend to grow in nutrient-poor soils, particularly where the presence of nitrogen is low. As a result of this relationship, nodules form on the taproot, root hairs, and lateral roots that concentrate nitrogen from the air in usable form. In effect, these nodules are bacterial root galls and are considered as such in this guide. Nitrogen-fixing bacteria of the genera *Frankia* or *Rhizobium* in the soil are responsible for most nodules with specific host plants. Ultimately this nitrogen becomes available to other plants, thus allowing establishment of plants in terrain otherwise unsuitable to most species. See Table 5 for the species on which these nodules are known to occur.

TABLE 5. NITROGEN-FIXING BACTERIA AND COMMON HOST PLANTS

Bacteria	Host Plants
Frankia spp.	Alder (*Alnus* spp.)
	Antelope brush (*Purshia tridentata*)
	Bayberry (*Myrica pensylvanica*)
	Buffalo berry (*Shepherdia argentea*)
	Ceanothus (*Ceanothus* spp.)
	Mountain-mahogany (*Cercocarpus* spp.)
	Wax myrtle (*Myrica californica*)
Rhizobium spp.	Most legumes: peas, alfalfa, vetch, lupines

Seasonal Appearance and Growth Rate

The appearance of plant galls in nature is influenced by many factors but generally coincides with the season of greatest plant growth. In the Pacific States, galls normally develop on their host plants between spring and late summer. Some midge and fruit fly galls develop on rabbit-brush during winter. In the Southwest, the extreme temperatures of summer dictate that most gall growth (especially on oaks) occurs from fall through spring.

Generally, the insects that are successful are those whose emergence (from old galls or the duff under their host plant) coincides within a week or so of the development and optimal condition of their preferred host's gall organs (swelling buds, new shoots, and leaves). If they emerge too early or too late, they may miss the optimal period for reproduction and egg-laying. Some insects remain in **DIAPAUSE** for one to four years before they complete metamorphosis into adults. While the advantage of producing longer generations is not well understood, multiyear life cycles may represent a mechanism that helps stabilize the population, given availability of preferred galling sites and variability of weather, predation, and potential for environmental hardships.

In spring and summer, depending on elevation and location, vast amounts of food energy are directed into the production or expansion of buds, new shoots, branches, and leaves. During these seasons, many galls seem to appear overnight. Actually, their growth requires much more time. In summer at low elevations or in desert areas, most plant growth slows down, yet during this period, when nutrients would normally be used to sustain already existing plant organs, energy can be redirected into the production of a second flush of galls (as seen on oaks with cynipid wasps). The growth of these summer galls normally proceeds at a slower rate than that of spring galls. Any individual oak may produce both a spring and a summer crop of galls. Many species of cynipid wasps exhibit two alternating generations that induce different galls, often on different plant parts, at separate times of the year (see the discussion on cynipids in "The Gall-Inducers" section of the guide).

There are so many diverse species of gall organisms with complicated life requirements, we cannot apply a simple rule of thumb to all. The cynipid and tenthredinid wasps discussed here are among the most highly evolved and complex.

Environmental Factors

If you walk through an oak woodland, an aspen forest, or a manzanita **CHAPARRAL** community, you will find some trees and shrubs covered with plant galls, while others nearby appear to lack galls. The reasons for these sharp variations involve many environmental factors, as well as specific micro-environmental requirements of the gall organisms, much of which is still unknown.

Environmental factors such as exposure to sun and high temperatures, shade, humidity, soil characteristics, and host chemistry may play a significant role in the physiology and stress levels of the host plant and therefore its suitability as an egg-laying site. A willow growing in a warm, southwesterly exposure may not support the diversity and abundance of gall organisms as the same species of willow growing in a cooler, shaded, northeasterly location, or vice versa. The thickness of the leaf epidermis, the presence of high volumes of terpenes, and other chemical and physiological elements may impact the suitability of host plants. A gall insect must not only locate the right species of host plant during its short lifetime, it must find one in the proper physiological condition that is suitable for egg deposition.

Because so many gall insects are tiny and not strong flyers, their success in finding the proper host may be seriously influenced by conditions on the days these insects emerge. Many questions revolve around wind dispersal and **EDGE EFFECT**. Whether plants at the edge of established stands are more likely to support higher populations of gall insects than those protected from wind in the interior of the community needs further study. However, some assumptions are worth considering. Trees and shrubs upslope and separated from related patches downwind are likely to catch weak flyers blown off course on the day of emergence. Conversely, interior trees that do support gall-inducers and are more protected from wind are more likely to maintain several generations of the same species that come up from the duff below. Assuming that conditions for gall development and gall insect survival are suitable, an individual tree or shrub can support generation after generation of the same species, regardless of its location. I have found a single, small (less than 4 m tall) blue oak (*Q. douglasii*) growing alone in the midst of expansive grassland that supported nine species of cynipids and their galls. These wasp generations most likely used the same host tree year after year, by moving directly from the ground up into the tree, rather than migrating laterally from a neighboring tree some distance away (see discussion on *Heteroecus* spp. B and C, canyon live oak).

Populations of gall-inducing insects may vary dramatically from season to season and year to year depending on a variety of factors. Unusually harsh winters with colder temperatures; high winds on emergence days; large populations of competitors, parasites, and predators; wildfire; high summer temperatures; and drought impacts on the host plant, among other factors that are unknown, may influence population levels within a species.

One example of interspecies competition is seen in the relationship and concurrent cycles of the moth known as the California oak worm (*Phryganidia californica*) and the two-horned-gall wasp (*Dryocosmus dubiosus*). Both insects require leaves of coast live oak (*Quercus agrifolia*). When caterpillars of the oak moth defoliate live oaks, they eliminate the egg-laying sites for the wasps. About every seven years, when the moth reaches a peak in its population cycle, entire woodland areas can be defoliated. Without leaves, the wasps face serious problems. Conversely, at the peak of the population of two-horned-gall wasps, each live oak leaf can bear dozens of galls attached to the ventral midrib and lateral veins on leaves. Such a presence deprives outer leaf tissues of the nutrients required to sustain photosynthesis, resulting in massive browning of leaf margins, called SCORCH. Under these conditions, the low palatability of what is left may impact the feeding success and survival of moth caterpillars. So, potentially, each species may negatively impact the other. While there are no empirical data on this relationship, I suspect that the peaks in population levels for each species occur when the other is at its lowest level, and yet both species coexist in the same woodland decade after decade. So far, it does not appear that either population stresses host oaks beyond recovery.

Research on creosote bush in desert regions that extend to Texas has shown that plants growing under stressful conditions (with less water and nutrients, along with physiological impacts) on talus slopes supported higher numbers of galls and gall-inducing species than those plants growing on desert flats. In this same study, only two of the eight species of gall midges studied were more abundant on non-stressed plants. Stressed plants apparently produced more terminal branches compared to those on flats, where plant growth occurred primarily through the lengthening of the existing branches. This research points not only to the increased availability of potential galling sites as a key factor, but also to the potential of host chemistry as a key determinant in gall and gall-inducing species numbers.

Damage to Host Plants

Generally, the overall vigor and health of a shrub or tree is not significantly affected by the seasonal production of galls. Localized damage may be sustained if a branch, group of leaves, or a single leaf produces either a large number of galls, such as those of the gall wasp *Dryocosmus dubiosus* on coast live oak, or galls of a particular type, such as the witches' brooms of incense cedar rust (*Gymnosporangium libocedri*) on incense cedar. Significant damage to a host plant, as a result of gall production, would depend on several factors. Variables include the size of the host plant, the soil and exposure conditions under which it is growing, and the degree of infestation or infection by a particular gall organism. Severe damage can occur to a weakened tree if it is induced to produce, for example, large numbers of giant oak apples, such as those induced by the California gall wasp (*Andricus quercuscalifornicus*) or integral stem galls, consistently over successive years. Stunted valley oaks (*Quercus lobata*) can be found growing in nutrient-poor soil and heavily laden with oak apples. Looks can be deceiving, however, because these oak apples may remain on the host tree for three to four years. The wasps generally complete all growth and activity within the first year and then sleep from one to four years in diapause prior to pupation and emergence. A massive number of these galls on a stunted tree could be the accumulation of several years, making it look as if the tree is severely stressed by the galls, when soil and water or other environmental conditions may be more important influences.

The two-horned-gall wasp (*D. dubiosus*) is responsible for damage that draws the attention of homeowners. The galls of this wasp develop on the midrib and lateral veins on the underside of coast live oak leaves. With a dozen or more of these galls rerouting nutrients within a single leaf into the gall tissues, the outer leaf tissues beyond the galls are deprived and ultimately die, turning brown. In years when the population of this gall wasp is peaking, the coast live oaks look like they are dying (see the earlier discussion regarding this wasp and California oak worms in the "Environmental Factors" section). This condition is seasonal, as the live oaks bounce back the following season with new spring leaves.

Another situation that draws public attention involves a bacterial attack on the young acorns of coast live oak and interior live oak (*Q. wislizenii*) trees that have been galled by an acorn-gall wasp (*Melikaiella flora*). The adult wasps puncture the acorns with their ovipositors to lay eggs. The bacterium *Erwinia quercina* enters the acorns through these holes. After a while, frothy ooze develops and begins dripping from the acorns, landing on everything under the trees including cars and driveways, to the consternation of many people. Without the presence of the bacteria, people would scarcely notice the activities of these tiny acorn gall wasps. What effect the bacteria have on the gall larvae is unknown.

A common landscape shrub, Australian brush-cherry (*Eugenia myrtifolia*), in California often supports a psyllid that causes severe leaf deformities and branch-tip fasciations. Galled leaves are usually covered with dark red, bump-like, pit galls. Heavy pruning seems to be effective in controlling this gall pest. Even though a plant appears heavily infested, it can live for many years with its psyllid pests.

Another major concern is PEACH LEAF CURL, caused by the sac fungus *Taphrina deformans* (see Plate 586), which is widespread and results in significant swelling and distortion of leaves and loss of flowers and fruit. The fungus is common among ornamental peaches and nectarines. The leaves are often light green or reddish in color but eventually become completely white due to spore production by the fungus. Another species, the leaf-curl fungus *T. flectans*, induces leaf curl in wild cherries (*Prunus* spp.). Because of the extensive cell multiplication induced by these sac fungi, they should be considered gall-inducing organisms in the West, as they are in England.

Orchardists and nursery workers are quite familiar with CROWN GALL, associated with the bacterium *Agrobacterium tumefaciens*. This widespread soil bacterium attacks fruit, nut, and shade trees, commercial roses, and other ornamental plants, as well as a number of native plants. This bacterium creates large, swollen galls at the soil surface at the base of trees or shrubs and sometimes on aerial parts of the plants. These crown galls can exceed a foot in diameter, impair the flow of nutrients, and serve as an opening for damaging fungi.

The balsam woolly adelgid (*Adelges piceae*) is responsible for stunting and killing thousands of trees with its gouty terminal bud galls. It is a serious pest on tree farms in the Northwest. Another serious problem involves the dwarf mistletoe *Arceuthobium douglasii*, which induces huge witches' brooms on Douglas-fir throughout the West. Heavily broomed trees can become weakened and die.

The absolute worst, most destructive galling I have ever seen was in Hawaii. The tiny *Erythrina* gall wasp (*Quadrastichus erythrinae*) had escaped from Southeast Asia, arriving in Oahu in 2005. Within two years, it killed nearly every willi-willi tree (*Erythrina variegata*) on Oahu and Maui. I first found the bud and leaf galls in 2006, and by the next year all the native host trees I had examined were dead, an unusual occurrence for the victims of a galling insect.

While the above galls and their related secondary invaders can be serious health threats to their host plants, the vast majority of gall organisms in nature cause little long-term damage to their host plants. When you consider that most gall-inducing wasps, midges, and mites use the same host shrubs and trees year after year, taking only relatively insignificant amounts of plant nutrients, and also take into account natural parasite and predator controls, there seems to be relatively little damage to host plants.

Galls as Nutrient Sinks

There is growing evidence that as some galls develop, particularly those of cynipid wasps, macronutrients and micronutrients are redirected from roots and leaves into gall tissues, creating **NUTRIENT SINKS** within the host plant. These sinks contain higher concentrations of several nutrients than are normally found in other non-galled plant tissues of roots, stems, leaves, and fruit. Within cynipid gall tissues, **PARENCHYMA** cells form a nutritive layer around the larval chamber and sequester both macronutrients (e.g., nitrogen, phosphorus, magnesium) and micronutrients (e.g., iron, manganese, zinc). In fact, several researchers have documented the relocation and concentration of carbohydrates, lipids, proteins, and other nutrients into gall tissues. Galled leaves undergo increased photosynthetic rates, the by-products of which are intercepted by the galls. In this light, galls are viewed as the delivery mechanisms of superior food resources to larvae, in contrast to the nutritional quality of non-galled tissues that are consumed by leaf-eating caterpillars or beetles.

Galls can act as interceptors to either block the normal flow of resources or redirect the translocation of nutrients from various plant parts. In this manner, galls would draw nutrients from tissues beyond those that would normally carry the flow through the attacked organ. The position of the gall on the plant may determine whether the gall acts as an interceptor or redirector. Active concentration of nutrients within galls seems to be higher during the growth phase of galls rather than after the galls have matured and the larvae are further developed.

In Canada, researchers focused on lowbush blueberry (*Vaccinium angustifolium*) growing near an ore smelter. They found that the roots nearest the smelter contained the highest concentrations of copper and nickel, and that the concentrations logarithmically declined with distance from the smelter. When the team looked at blueberries near the smelter galled by the chalcid wasp *Hemadas nubilipennis*, they found that the greatest concentrations of copper and nickel were in the gall tissues and not the roots.

In another Canadian study, researchers found that some gall-inducers can apparently regulate the amount of nutrients within gall tissues or at least take only what they need. The galls of the cynipid wasp *Diplolepis triforma* on *Rosa* spp. had greater concentrations of nitrogen and most mineral nutrients than those of *D. spinosa*. Similarly, the larvae of *D. triforma* and the parasites feeding on the larvae contained higher concentrations of nitrogen and other nutrients than those of *D. spinosa*. Interestingly, the parasites of both species were similar in mineral composition to their hosts. Yet, in this case the galls of both species contained less nitrogen and minerals than ungalled tissues on the same hosts. Although this may appear to be in contrast to the nutrient sink concept, it does suggest that these two species, unlike others in the genus, are mobilizers of their host's resources utilizing only those elements essential to their development.

In yet another study, two researchers looked at the concentration of water in gall tissues from four-wing saltbush (*Atriplex canescens*), a small shrub growing in arid regions of the Southwest. They found that certain cecidomyiid galls (*Asphondylia* spp.) concentrated water in the gall tissues at the expense of the stems and branches. Furthermore, they found that shrubs growing near a spring supported significantly higher numbers of galls than those shrubs in a drier habitat, which suggested that the quantity of water available to the gall and larvae was a prime determinant in the ability of the host plant to support gall midges. Moreover, these results were reversed in a study of roses and the pincushion-gall wasp (*Diplolepis rosae*), where plants suffering from a lack of water actually supported more galls.

Clearly, each species may require different levels of water and various minerals and other nutrients to complete its development. Therefore, the concentrations of nutrients in galled compared to non-galled tissues may vary widely from species to species and host plant to host plant. The story of these highly complex chemical relationships is only now beginning to unfold, and many questions and years of research remain.

The Gall Community

No plant or animal in nature stands alone. Each is connected to other living creatures in one form or another. The world of even a single gall-inducing insect can be so convoluted and interwoven with its environment it could drive you crazy trying to unravel it. If the galls lying under a blue oak (*Q. douglasii*) or Gambel oak (*Q. gambelii*), for example, are not destroyed in winter by fungi, bacteria, or freezing conditions and not eaten by birds or mice, and the adult insects emerge, they face an onslaught of predatory lizards, spiders, flies, wasps, and birds before they find a suitable site to lay eggs. Some gall insects, especially the wasps, do not eat as adults and live for only a week or so. This increases the pressure on these insects to find suitable egg-laying sites as soon as possible. If a gall-inducer makes it this far, having laid eggs, and if the eggs hatch, the larvae and resulting galls can attract: **INQUILINES**, those insects (mostly vegetarian) that eat gall tissues; **PARASITES** that attack the gall-inducer's larvae; and **HYPERPARASITES** that attack the larvae of the parasites. As if all this were not difficult enough to follow, sometimes even the seemingly innocuous inquilines can switch tactics and kill any other insect they encounter within the gall while feeding on gall tissue. And finally, some insects simply prey on whatever insects they find inside the galls.

Over a two-year period, one study showed that the inquiline *Periclistus pirata* accounted for between 55% and 65% mortality in the stem-gall wasp *Diplolepis nodulosa*, a cynipid, on roses in Ontario, Canada. In the same study, six different species of parasites caused only 17% of the mortality in the gall-inducers, with an additional 13% mortality by other inquilines. Consequently, one inquiline species had a much more dramatic impact on the gall-inducers than six other parasite species and other inquilines combined. When you add the cumulative effect on a gall-inducer population, the combined loss can reach 80%–90% of a population. These numbers and the suggested impacts vary greatly from one species to another, as well as from one circumstance or environment to another, but their role and importance are staggering.

In another study, researchers found that a wasp, *Tetrastichus cecidobroter*, an inquiline, attacked the galls of the tumor stem-gall midge (*Asphondylia atriplicis*) on the four-wing saltbush (*Atriplex canescens*). In so doing, this inquiline creates its own galls, called ENDOGALLS, within the primary host gall. The developing galls of the inquiline bulge into the larval cavities, crushing the larvae. In this rather unusual case, most of the gall midge larval loss is actually due to the presence of the inquiline (see "Saltbush Galls" in the Gall Species Accounts). "Galls within galls" seems strange, but this is not the only case, as we shall see later with the midge *Rhopalomyia bigeloviae*, which creates galls inside the galls of the bubble-gall tephritid (*Aciurina trixa*) on rabbitbrush (see "Rabbitbrush Galls" and Plate 2).

Plate 2:. Gall of tephritid *Aciurina trixa* with endogall of the gall midge *Rhopalomyia bigeloviae* protruding.

In 2018, researchers in Florida found that a plant called love vine (*Cassytha filiformis*) that normally sends its roots into the tissues of trees and shrubs, draining them of nutrients, was found doing the same thing to some galls on oak trees. The result was that the gall larvae of cynipid wasps (*Belonocnema treatae*, *Andricus quercuslanigera*, *A. quercusfoliatus*, *Disholcaspis quercusvirens*, and *Neuroterus minutissimus*) starved and were mummified.

These strange interactions and relationships paint a picture of the intricacies of survival. Theoretically, even in years of high loss to parasites and inquilines and other environmental factors, enough of the gall-inducers survive and mature to continue their species. The inhabitants of galls, whether they are gall-inducers, inquilines, parasites, or hyperparasites, can serve as focal points, which, in turn, attract many other predatory insects and other animals. The actual number of insects supported by the galls, including the gall-inducers and associated insects, can easily exceed several dozen species. Even if we look only at galls, the ecological web of a chaparral or woodland community is a jumble of interactions, dependencies, and implications that far exceeds our wildest imagination.

Parasite-Inquiline Influence on Gall Shape

Parasites and inquilines can severely impact the normal development of gall tissues. The timing of insertion and attack, general behavior, and, perhaps, added chemistry of parasites and inquilines can either abort gall development or cause galls to develop in a manner that makes them look like they belong to new species of gall-inducers. As you find and collect galls, you will certainly find specimens that do not match the photographs or illustrations in this guide and others, even though they are a species described here. While it may be tempting to assign new species status to such finds, we need to be careful in studying and understanding the exact nature of the complex relationships between gall-makers and their associated parasites and inquilines first. Inquiline-modified galls are more common than one might imagine.

As mentioned earlier, all kinds of insects emerge from galls, not just the gall-inducers, and their exit holes may look similar. Some examples of inquiline-influenced galls are provided later in this guide (see the species accounts for the beaked spindle-gall wasp [*Heteroecus pacificus*] and the stem-gall wasp *Diplolepis nodulosa*).

Gall-Inducer Defense

Seemingly vulnerable larvae may be protected in a number of ways. Some are discussed here and in the next section, "Honeydew and Bees, Yellow Jackets, and Ants."

Normal plant defenses against herbivorous insects (**TERPENES**, **TANNINS**) may be influenced by gall-inducers and used to their own advantage. While tannins, for example, are absent from the nutritive tissues surrounding the larval chambers in cynipid oak galls, tannin levels are usually very high in other gall tissues near the larval chambers, which may discourage deeper penetration to the chambers by inquilines, thereby protecting the larvae.

Gall-inducers use a variety of defenses. Studies have shown that larvae of the sawfly *Neodiprion sertifer* have the ability to sequester terpenes from their hosts in pouches of the foregut. When disturbed, the larvae regurgitate terpene compounds as a borrowed defense against attack. A similar behavior was observed with an Australian sawfly, *Perga affinis*, using eucalyptus oils as an orally discharged defense. Sawflies are known for their ability to eject a pungent, vinegary fluid from their ventral, eversible glands. Sawflies raise and wave their abdomens when disturbed to better expose these "stink glands." Even with such pungent defenses, sawflies often die when their galls are destroyed by gall-tissue-eating inquilines.

A number of mitigating factors influence the degree of success parasites have in locating gall insects and parasitizing them. The thickness and hardness of some galls' epidermis may prevent a parasitic wasp such as an ichneumon from reaching the larvae with its ovipositor. Thick, tightly packed coverings of hair or numerous stiff spines could impede parasite and inquiline success in gaining access to gall tissues and larvae. Also, in **POLYTHALAMOUS** galls (with numerous larvae in separate larval chambers) (Figure 9), the innermost larvae are less vulnerable to parasitic attack than those closer to the gall's surface. In small, **MONOTHALAMOUS** galls (containing one or more larvae in a single, common chamber) (Figure 10), larvae are more vulnerable to attack.

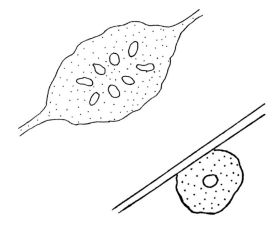

Far left: Figure 9.
Polythalamous gall.

Left: Figure 10.
Monothalamous gall.

One of the characteristics of cecidomyiid galls is that often several larvae occupy a common chamber, which makes them particularly vulnerable to attack because of the ease with which parasites and predators locate victims.

In a study of chalcid parasitoid attacks on cynipid wasp galls (*Acraspis hirta*), researchers found that chalcids concentrated their attacks on host galls while the galls were still fresh, tender, and growing. Softer tissues of developing galls were more conducive to parasite attack than galls that had matured and hardened. Parasite oviposition was significantly inhibited as a result of the hardening of gall walls. Gaining entry under the right conditions for parasites does not always mean immediate death of the gall insect's larvae. In some cases, even though entry and location of the gall insect larvae occurred during early stages of gall development, the gall larvae were allowed to develop normally before actual parasite feeding began.

Furthermore, it was found that there were significant differences in parasite success between galls that were spaced out on the host plant to a density of one gall per leaf versus multiple galls per leaf. Galls widely separated from each other showed less gall larvae mortality due to parasites than galls that were spaced at several galls per leaf. This suggests that parasitic insects conserve energy by concentrating their efforts in small areas rich in opportunities.

In a study of the sawfly *Pontania proxima*, a gall-inducer on willows in Ireland and the eastern United States and now in Washington, researchers found that the natural defenses of larvae against oviposition and attack by parasites, especially the wasp *Pnigalio nemati*, increased with development of the larvae, particularly in the fourth and fifth instars. As the gall-inducer's larvae became more aggressive with age, there was increased failure to complete oviposition once begun by the parasites. When contacted by parasites, sawfly larvae jerk, bite, and strike with their head and the posterior end of their abdomen. As an additional hedge against parasitism, sawfly larvae also continuously clean the interior of the gall, discarding any **FRASS** to the outside, which might be used by parasites as a cue to the presence of larvae.

Of all the *Pontania proxima* galls examined in this study, 23% were empty, with no signs of any *Pontania* eggs or larvae. Since there was no additional evidence to suggest that the galls had been damaged or opened, it was assumed that the galls had always been empty. Since galls of *Pontania* species begin development as a result of chemicals released by the adult and are well developed by the time the eggs hatch, it was concluded that far more galls were induced than the number of eggs laid. Based on this, it has been suggested that these empty galls may act as decoys, distracting parasites from occupied galls, while increasing the time and distance for the parasites to locate actual hosts. Only 2% of the galls of this sawfly were actually parasitized, which may lend credence to this theory.

Finally, other researchers found that parasites had more success in parasitizing the **BISEXUAL**, leaf-galling generation of the cynipid wasp *Callirhytis cornigera* than the **UNISEXUAL (AGAMIC)** generation of stem-gallers. Larvae of the latter generation were more protected by the thickness and density of woody tissues than the bisexual generation larvae covered by soft, thin leaf tissues. Such a high rate of survival among the unisexual generation females allowed the population to build over time, even though 60%–80% of the bisexual generation would be lost to parasitism.

Honeydew and Bees, Yellow Jackets, and Ants

Along with dense covering of long hairs or spines and thick woody walls, which have been shown to reduce mortality resulting from parasites, some gall-inducing insects have evolved "reward-based mutualistic relationships" with ants, bees, and yellow jackets. The presence of **ANTAGONISTIC** insects such as honeybees, yellow jackets, and ants can also prevent inquilines, parasites, and hyperparasites from gaining access to a gall and successfully entering or ovipositing their eggs into the eggs or larvae of the gall-inducers. Five separate studies have shown that ants significantly reduce parasite and inquiline access to galls.

The evolution of this relationship seems to be particularly prevalent among cynipid wasps, which can lay their eggs close together, resulting in clusters of galls, making it easier for ants and yellow jackets to access the galls' honeydew. These relationships are often seen among members of the genus *Disholcaspis*. The key players in this ecological twist include several Pacific States gall-inducing cynipid wasps (flat-topped honeydew-gall wasp [*Disholcaspis eldoradensis*], twig-gall wasp [*D. mellifica*], round honeydew-gall wasp [*D. canescens*], clasping twig-gall wasp [*D. prehensa*], mottled acorn-gall wasp [*Callirhytis carmelensis*], and kidney stem-gall wasp [*Andricus reniformis*]), as well as others in the Southwest. These gall wasps stimulate the production and release of sweet phloem exudates (referred to as honeydew) on the surfaces of their galls during the vulnerable period in the growth of the gall and the development of the larvae. This sweet exudate attracts ants, bees, and yellow jackets, which generally do not tolerate the presence of other competitors or species, making it nearly impossible for parasitic wasps and others to do their work. Honeydew is known as an important food resource especially for yellow jackets in late summer.

One study showed that the yellow jacket *Vespula pensylvanica* was a frequent forager of honeydew produced on coast live oaks by the mottled acorn-gall wasp (*C. carmelensis*). In one instance a queen yellow jacket visited the same gall four times in two hours to collect honeydew. When a different species of wasp showed up, the queen interrupted her feeding to face the intruder, raising her forebody and front legs in an apparent threat posture, causing the incoming wasp to veer away. In another case involving the same species, a queen yellow jacket returned to a gall previously visited, only to find an intruding wasp (of a different species). The queen attacked the intruder, and the two grappling wasps tumbled off the gall to the ground. I have also seen this behavior involving the flat-topped honeydew-gall wasp (*D. eldoradensis*) on valley oaks (*Quercus lobata*). It seems that once queen yellow jackets start harvesting honeydew, they claim a specific gall as their territory and drive off trespassers, as I have witnessed major battles between queens and other intruding yellow jackets.

Plate 3. Galls of wasp *Disholcaspis canescens* with ants feeding on honeydew.

In August and September some oak trees are humming with bees and yellow jackets and columns of ants taking advantage of this late-season source of sweet nutrients (Plate 3). I have also seen galls of the twig-gall wasp (*D. mellifica*) on Oregon oak oozing with honeydew and covered with yellow jackets on one branch, while a nearby branch with the same galls was swarming with ants, suggesting intolerance for each other on the same branch. Standing back from this rather small tree, I saw hundreds of yellow jackets swarming about the tree as if there were a major hive in it. In the San Joaquin Valley of California, honeybees gather an estimated 13 to 18 kg of this sweet honey in a single season, which can actually lead to their early death due to the high mineral content of the exudates.

Insect Predators

Common insect threats to cynipid and tenthredinid gall-inducers include chalcid, torymid, braconid, ichneumon, and pteromalid wasps—all parasites and hyperparasites—and beetles and moths as inquilines (sometimes also as predators). Similarly, cecidomyiid larvae are often attacked by wasps from several families. There are some non-galling cecidomyiid midges that prey on gall midge larvae and take over their "home" rather than induce their own. In a rather rare case, the tephritid *Oxyna palpalis* serves as an inquiline in the gall of the midge *Rhopalomyia florella*, on Great Basin sagebrush (*Artemisia tridentata*), in the West, but becomes a major predator of midge larvae. In another rare case, a syrphid fly was discovered preying on the adelgids (related to aphids) inside a cone gall. Some parasitic mites attack either gall-inducing mites or other gall insects. Also, certain dance flies (Empididae) catch adult gall midges in flight for food and for use in their courtship with females. The empidids that eat the gall midges may, in turn, be captured and eaten by spiders, dragonflies, damselflies, or birds of numerous species.

This seemingly complex interplay of host, inquiline, parasite, hyperparasite, and predator is best seen in the example of the willow-apple-gall sawfly (*Pontania californica*). At least eight different species act as inquilines or parasites in the galls of this sawfly. These include six wasps, a moth, and a weevil. The moth and weevil are inquilines that feed mainly on gall tissue. The moth larvae, however, will kill intruders upon contact, including their own kind. The same is apparently true for the weevil. The adults of parasitic wasps probe with their long ovipositors, which have built-in heat receptors to pick up metabolic heat from the potential hosts they require for their eggs. In some cases, adult parasites sting gall larvae to paralyze them before depositing their eggs. Surviving to complete its life cycle may not be as easy as one might assume for such a tiny insect as the willow-apple-gall sawfly.

Birds and Other Predators

Another large group of predators represents a serious threat to gall insects at some point during their lives. Fallen leaf galls and gall-inducer pupae hidden among leaf litter are good sources of protein for shrews, mice, wood rats, and squirrels. Birds such as California towhees (*Pipilo crissalis*), spotted towhees (*P. maculatus*), and fox sparrows (*Passerella iliaca*) probe leaf litter for seeds and insects. Many galls can be easily mistaken for seeds. While California scrub-jays (*Aphelocoma californica*) and Steller's jays (*Cyanocitta stelleri*) are known to eat small galls, sapsuckers (*Sphyrapicus* spp.) dig into large galls to extract the occupants, as in the case of *Andricus quercuscalifornicus*. During the fall and winter months when these galls are loaded with numerous species of insects, and the tissues are spongy and drier than during the growing season, sapsuckers and maybe other woodpeckers will chip out inch-wide holes in search of the tender morsels inside. Other birds including evening grosbeaks (*Coccothraustes vespertinus*) have been observed opening aphid-induced roll galls and eating the occupants. Cedar waxwings (*Bombycilla cedrorum*) have also been seen picking small galls off the underside of willow leaves. Black-capped chickadees (*Poecile atricapilla*) and downy woodpeckers (*Picoides pubescens*) have been observed digging into goldenrod galls for their larvae. Bushtits (*Psaltriparus minimus*) have been seen pecking into the succulent galls of the stem-gall tephritid *Eutreta diana* on Great Basin sagebrush. Small flocks of these birds have also been observed hunting for the box-thorn stem-gall moth (*Symmetrischema* sp.) during the winter months when the adult moths emerge.

If adult gall insects hatch and attempt to fly up to their host's branches, they become vulnerable to fly-catching birds (phoebes [*Sayornis* spp.] and others) en route, and insect eaters such as vireos (*Vireo* spp.), kinglets (*Regulus* spp.), chickadees (*Poecile* spp.), and nuthatches (*Sitta* spp.), among others, once they land on leaves or branches.

I have found galls of the beaked spindle-gall wasp (*Heteroecus pacificus*) on branches of huckleberry oak (*Quercus vaccinifolia*) close to the ground that have had their tips chewed off by chipmunks (*Eutamias* spp.) and/or golden-mantled ground squirrels (*Spermophilus lateralis*) to get at larvae (Plate 4). Similarly, in the same area of the central Sierra Nevada, California, I found the rather large galls of a sawfly, *Blennogeneris spissipes*, on creeping snowberry (*Symphoricarpos mollis*) plants that were ravaged by chipmunks and/or golden-mantled ground squirrels (Plate 5). Also, the western gray squirrel (*Sciurus griseus*) chews into the integral stem galls of the tapered stem-gall wasp (*Protobalandricus spectabilis*) to expose the larval chambers and larvae. Actually, I think most squirrels throughout the West have discovered sources of protein in gall larvae they find.

Some gall-inducers escape this onslaught of dangers and successfully lay eggs to continue their species. As nature would have it, life is not easy, and each species must face the perils of a world with many other creatures looking for food. This incredible interplay of predator and prey seems to never end as one studies the exchange of energy throughout a food chain and food web starting with gall-inducers. In nature's ever-fascinating way, the apparent victor (for the moment) may well fall victim to yet another predator higher up the food chain. When you consider the vast feeding associations starting with the gall-inducers and the parasites and inquilines that are attracted to the galls and their parasites and hyperparasites; the birds, spiders, and lizards that eat the adults and the parasites they support; combined with the top predators of these animals, including hawks and snakes; cynipid gall-inducers are critical **KEY-STONE SPECIES** that turn a seemingly static oak woodland into a vibrant zoological jungle of complex interrelationships that stretch far beyond what is seen. A single blue oak by itself can be equivalent to any major city we know—teeming with life.

Plate 4. Gall of wasp *Heteroecus pacificus* on huckleberry oak chewed open by a golden-mantled ground squirrel to get larvae.

Plate 5. Galls of sawfly *Blennogeneris spissipes* on creeping snowberry also chewed open by golden-mantled ground squirrel to get larvae.

Gall Food Web

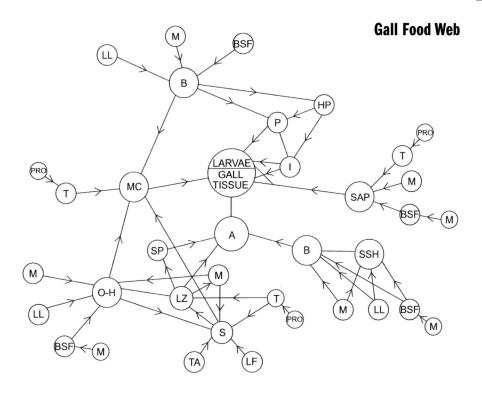

KEY

A = Adult gall-inducers

B = Birds

BSF = Bloodsucking flies

HP = Hyperparasites

I = Inquiline insects

L = Larvae

LF = Liver flukes

LZ = Lizards

LL = Lice

M = Mites

MC = Mice

O-H = Owls and Hawks

P = Parasites

PRO = protozoans and bacteria/disease transmitters

S = Snakes

SP = Spiders

SSH = Sharp-shinned Hawk

SAP = Sapsuckers (birds)

T = Ticks

TA = Tapeworms

This food web model represents the interrelationships centered around a typical cynipid gall, in this case that of the California gall wasp (*Andricus quercuscalifornicus*). The direction of the arrows indicates what each organism feeds on. In the case of sapsuckers (*Sphyrapicus* spp.), these birds regularly dig into the gall tissue of these large oak apples looking for any larvae or adult insects.

The cast of characters in the world of plant galls is quite extensive and global. Plant galls have been found on every continent except Antarctica. Even in the Arctic tundra, there are galls on prostrate willows (*Salix* spp.) and huckleberries (*Vaccinium* spp.), among other plant species. The prominence of any one gall-inducing group varies from continent to continent. While cynipid wasps (Cynipidae) and gall midges (Cecidomyiidae) dominate North America north of Mexico, for example; mites (Eriophyidae) and gall midges are the principal gall-inducers in Asia; scale insects, psyllids, and whiteflies (Sternorrhyncha) in Australia; and midges and mites in India.

In this section, the basic biology of all the groups of major gall-inducers found in the western states is discussed. Individual behaviors and interactions are presented in the gall accounts. The primary gall-inducers described here are: bacteria, rust and sac fungi, mistletoes, eriophyid mites, aphids and adelgids, psyllids, coccids, moths, beetles, leaf-mining flies, tephritid fruit flies, gall midges, tanaostigmatid wasps, sawflies, and cynipid wasps.

Bacteria

A few galls induced by bacteria are worthy of note in this guide. Most are associated with the roots or crowns of trees. One species is associated with eruptions and swellings that occur on the main branches of Douglas-fir (*Pseudotsuga menziesii*), particularly young trees, and the canes of blackberry (*Rubus ursinus*). This crown gall bacterium (*Agrobacterium tumefaciens*) is associated with a variety of trees and shrubs, particularly fruit trees and commercial roses, as discussed in the "Damage to Host Plants" section of the Introduction. Another group of bacteria is associated with the production of root nodules on a number of native plants, particularly those that get started in nutrient-poor soil where nitrogen is generally scarce. Leguminous plants such as lupines (*Lupinus* spp.) and alfalfa (*Medicago sativa*) form nodules around invading bacteria of the genus *Rhizobium*, while several non-leguminous plants benefit from their association with bacteria in the genus *Frankia* (Plate 6). The development of these root nodules varies between the two groups of bacteria, but the end result is that the host plants are able to assimilate atmospheric nitrogen that has been converted by bacterial enzymes into usable

Plate 6. Nitrogen-fixing nodules of a *Frankia* sp. on a Sitka alder (*Alnus sinuata*) seedling.

ammonium ions. Over 100 species of non-leguminous plants in the United States have *Frankia*-induced nitrogen-fixing nodules on their roots. This includes over 30 species of *Ceanothus*. Nodules generally form within the upper 30 cm of soil, with some just under the surface. Nodules begin development when a strain of *Frankia* bacteria invades damaged or deformed root hairs. Growth and activity depend on a variety of environmental conditions, including soil moisture, temperature, season, and oxygen levels.

In general, nitrogen-fixing plants are able to survive in environments such as glacial outwash plains, flood zones, and landslide and avalanche areas that are missing certain plant nutrients, including nitrogen, and are otherwise unsuitable for species of plants that are more dependent on higher levels of organic material in the soil. By getting established with the help of bacteria in such inhospitable places, these pioneer plants not only add available nitrogen to the soil; they also provide shade and moist micro-sites for seedlings of other species, capture seeds blown by wind, and stabilize the soil. Throughout Alaska and other mountainous regions, where the smallest amount of moss begins growing on sheer rock walls, small ledges, in crevices, or on glacial outwash, landslide, and avalanche sites, you often find the seedlings of alder (*Alnus* spp.) and lupine (*Lupinus* spp.) among other pioneers.

Nitrogen fixation may not be the only element that fosters plant succession in barren environments, but the ability of these pioneer plants to establish a foothold in such places helps set the stage for the natural succession of an area into a climax forest over many decades.

Fungi (Families Exobasidiales, Uredinales, and Taphrinales)

Three major groups of fungi act as gall-inducers in the West. These include *Exobasidium* fungi, rust fungi, and sac fungi. In addition, a powdery mildew, *Sphaerotheca lanestris*, causes witches' brooms on coast live oak (*Quercus agrifolia*), as well as several other oaks in California and, perhaps, other western oaks. These are discussed in the gall species accounts. Unlike plants, fungi lack chlorophyll and cannot produce their own food. As a result, fungi act as either parasites (depending on live tissues) or **SAPROPHYTES** (depending on dead tissues) for their nourishment. Reproduction is by means of microscopic spores, which are usually released from infected tissues produced on the host plants. Many fungal spores are transported by winds to new hosts. In the absence of a new host, some of these spores can survive for years, even at high altitudes (13,000 m above sea level). If a viable spore lands on the proper host or substrate, under the right conditions it may germinate, producing fungal threads called **HYPHAE**. The hyphae combine to form larger **MYCELIAL** threads that also act as penetrating strands, drawing nourishment from their hosts. Sometimes, an individual hypha can penetrate host tissues. While most infections are systemic, the presence of these irritating invaders within host plants induces the development of swellings or witches' brooms on trunks and stems, and sometimes swollen leaves or fruit. Generally, these swellings are the sites of spore production. The life cycles of the three major groups of fungi vary greatly from one another, with no one scenario applying to all.

EXOBASIDIUM FUNGI attack false azalea (*Menziesia ferruginea*), manzanitas (*Arctostaphylos* spp.), huckleberries (*Vaccinium* spp.), bog rosemary (*Andromeda polifolia*), crowberry (*Empetrum nigrum*), rhododendrons and azaleas (*Rhododendron* spp.), and Labrador tea (*Ledum groenlandicum*). *Exobasidium* gets its name from its habit of producing its spores on the surface of the plant part it has affected rather than from its own fruiting body, as in mushrooms. Some species of *Exobasidium* produce indoleacetic acid, which is thought to play a role in gall formation. Some of these fungi act systemically, while others attack local organs from the outside, creating swollen leaves or witches' broom.

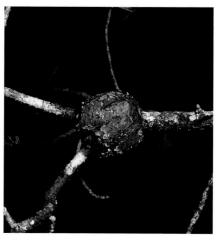

Plate 7. Gall on false azalea caused by fungus *Exobasidium vaccinii*.

Plate 8. Gall on shore pine in Alaska caused by rust fungus *Endocronartium harknessii*.

Swollen, galled leaves of false azalea usually have a white appearance, created by the presence of spores. Once the spores have spread, leaf tissues turn brown and die. *Exobasidium* galls that appear on manzanita and false azalea leaves look like massive, globular swellings on one side, with corresponding pockets or depressions on the opposite side (Plate 7).

RUST FUNGI have complicated life cycles that often involve more than one species of host plant. Rust fungi go through as many as four different spore-producing stages, yielding four functionally different kinds of spores. Some rusts go through all four stages, while others omit one or more stages, producing fruiting spores after just one stage.

Plate 9. Author standing next to a pine log galled by *Endocronartium harknessii* and used as a totem in a yard in Nome, Alaska.

Rust fungi are often not restricted to a species but may attack several species within a genus or use several different alternate seasonal hosts. The western gall-rust fungus (*Endocronartium harknessii*), for example, attacks nearly all western pines, creating large knobby galls on branches and roots (Plate 8). Large galled pine trunks float down the Yukon River into the Bering Sea, where many of them wash up on the beaches of Nome, Alaska. Locals use some of these galled trunks as totems in their yards (Plate 9).

Rusts often initiate integral stem swellings from which orange powdery spores are released. Some rust fungi appear as simple orange, swollen blisters on leaves of service-berries (*Amelanchier* spp.), grasses, and roses (*Rosa* spp.), among others. Still other rust fungi produce long, gelatinous brown or orange fingers or slimy blobs that hang from needles, galls, and branches, as in cedar-apple rust (*Gymnosporangium juniperi-virginianae*) on common juniper (*Juniperus communis*) and incense cedar rust (*G. libocedri*) on incense cedar. Rust fungi also cause witches' brooms, as seen on incense cedars with incense cedar rust. A number of rust fungi initiate globose swellings of stems and trunks and even develop on exposed large, lateral roots. Table 6 lists common plants that host rust-caused galls of the swelling and witches' broom types.

TABLE 6. GALLS INDUCED BY FUNGI AND PRODUCING WITCHES' BROOMS OR SWELLINGS

Host Plant	Fungus	Type of Gall
Picea pungens	*Chrysomyxa arctostaphyli*	Witches' broom
Quercus spp.	*Sphaerotheca lanestris*	Witches' broom, swelling
Callitropsis nootkatensis	*Gymnosporangium nootkatense*	Swelling
Cupressus arizonica	*G. cunninghamianum*	Swelling
	Uredo cupressicola	Swelling
Hesperocyparis pigmaea	*U. cupressicola*	Swelling
Baccharis pilularis	*Puccinia evadens*	Witches' broom, swelling
Abies spp.	*Melampsorella caryophyllacearum*	Witches' broom, swelling, burls
Vaccinium spp.	*Pucciniastrum goeppertianum*	Witches' broom
Calocedrus decurrens	*Gymnosporangium libocedri*	Witches' broom, swelling
Juniperus spp.	*G. juniperi-virginianae*	Swelling (Rockies)
	G. aurantiacum	Swelling
	G. confusum	Swelling
	G. inconspicuum	Swelling (Utah)
	G. nidus-avis	Swelling
	G. speciosum	Swelling (Utah)
	G. tremulloides	Swelling
	G. tubulatum	Swelling (Rockies)
Arctostaphylos spp., *Menziesia ferruginea* (see latter species for complete list of hosts)	*Exobasidium vaccinii*	Swelling
Sorbus spp.	*Cronartium comptoniae*	Swelling
Malus fusca	*C. coleosporioides*	Swelling
Pinus leiophylla	*C. conigenum*	Swelling (cone)
P. jeffreyi	*C. coleosporioides*	Swelling
P. contorta subsp. *murrayana*	*C. coleosporioides*	Swelling
P. ponderosa	*C. coleosporioides*	Swelling
Pinus spp.	*C. comandrae*	Swelling
	C. comptoniae	Swelling
P. jeffreyi, P. contorta subsp. *murrayana* and possibly other species	*Endocronartium harknessii*	Witches' broom, swelling
Wax myrtle (*Morella californica*)	*Cronartium comptoniae*	Swelling

TABLE 7. SAC FUNGI (*TAPHRINA* SPP.) GALLS

Host Plant	*Taphrina* Species	Type of Gall
Alder (*Alnus* spp.)	*T. occidentalis*	Cone tongues (enlarged bracts)
	T. amentorum	Cone tongues (Alaska)
	T. robinsoniana	Cone tongues (East)
Buckeye (*Aesculus* spp.)	*T. aesculi*	Witches' broom
Cottonwood (*Populus* spp.)	*T. populisalicis*	Leaf pockets
Nectarine, Peach (*Prunus* spp.)	*T. deformans*	Leaf curl
Native plums, cherries (*Prunus* spp.)	*T. flectans*	Leaf curl
	T. prunisubcordatae	Bladder plums
	T. confusa	Witches' broom
Service-berry (*Amelanchier* spp.)	*T. amelanchierii*	Witches' broom
Skunk bush (*Rhus aromatica*)	*T. purpurascens*	Leaf curl
Wood fern (*Dryopteris arguta*)	*T. californica*	Leaf swelling

In some rusts, the availability of spores attracts a broad variety of spore-eating insects as well as other insects that explore the fissures of the galls. One blister-gall rust on a lodgepole pine (*Pinus contorta* subsp. *murrayana*) was found to support 137 species of insects.

SAC FUNGI are among the most interesting gall-inducing fungi. Spores of sac fungi are produced in microscopic sacs or envelopes and are forcibly discharged in late spring to midsummer to infect new host tissue. Among the sac fungi, several species of the genus *Taphrina* are widely known for initiating leaf blisters, leaf curls, swollen fruit called BLADDER PLUMS, and witches' brooms (Table 7). The best known of the 100 or so species in the genus is peach leaf-curl fungus (*T. deformans*), a major concern for nursery workers, farmers, and landscapers because it attacks peaches and nectarines. Other species of *Taphrina* attack cottonwood (*Populus* spp.), alder (*Alnus* spp.), service-berry (*Amelanchier* spp.), choke cherry and wild plum (*Prunus* spp.), and wood fern (*Dryopteris arguta*). A related sac fungus, the black knot-gall fungus (*Apiosporina morbosa*), attacks the stems of all members of the genus *Prunus*, initiating large, black knot-galls on the stems (see the black knot-gall fungus species account).

Mistletoes (Family Viscaceae)

Only two genera (*Phoradendron* and *Arceuthobium*) of mistletoes in western states are prominent inducers of stem swellings or witches' brooms (Table 8). Simple, localized stem swellings occur in response to invasion of mistletoe and generally are not considered true galls, but I list here all species that induce witches' brooms or stem swellings. A third genus of mistletoe involves a European species introduced to California, *Viscum album*, which is not treated here.

All mistletoes are parasitic on branches of their hosts. *Arceuthobium* spp. derive water, nutrients, and small quantities of organic compounds from their host trees. *Phoradendron* spp. obtain most of their nutrients through photosynthesis and gain little from their host. *Phoradendron* spp. have male and female flowers on separate plants. Initial infection begins when a single viscous seed lands on a tree branch. Once the plant grows and flowers, multiple infections occur through the seeds produced by the original mistletoe. Stems of mistletoe contain chlorophyll, and this is where most photosynthesis takes place, even though the plant may have small leaves.

TABLE 8. MISTLETOE GALLS (WITCHES' BROOMS AND STEM SWELLINGS)

Host Plant	Mistletoe Species	Type of Gall
Catclaw (*Senegalia greggii*)	*Phoradendron californicum*	Broom, swelling
Cypress (*Cupressus arizonica*)	*P. bolleanum*	Swelling
Douglas-fir (*Pseudotsuga menziesii*)	*Arceuthobium douglasii*	Broom
Fir (*Abies* spp.)	*A. abietinum*	Broom, swelling
Hemlock (*Tsuga* spp.)	*A. tsugense*	Broom, swelling
Incense cedar (*Calocedrus decurrens*)	*Phoradendron juniperinum*	Broom, swelling
Juniper	*P. juniperinum*	Broom, swelling
Larch (*Larix* spp.)	*Arceuthobium laricis*	Broom, swelling
Pine		
Lodgepole (*Pinus contorta* subsp. *murrayana*)	*A. americanum*	Broom, swelling
Pinyon (*P. edulis*)	*A. divaricatum*	Swelling
Ponderosa (*P. ponderosa*)	*A. vaginatum*	Broom
	A. campylopodum	Broom, swelling
Sugar (*P. lambertiana*)	*A. californicum*	Broom, swelling
White (*P. strobiformis*, AZ)	*A. apachecum*	Broom
Western white (*P. monticola*)	*A. cyanocarpum*	Broom, swelling
Bishop (*P. muricata*)	*A. occidentale*	Broom, swelling
Coulter (*P. coulteri*)	*A. occidentale*	Broom, swelling
	A. campylopodum	Broom, swelling
Gray (*P. sabiniana*)	*A. occidentale*	Broom, swelling
Monterey (*P. radiata*)	*A. occidentale*	Broom, swelling
Jeffrey (*P. jeffreyi*)	*A. campylopodum*	Broom, swelling
Knobcone (*P. attenuata*)	*A. campylopodum*	Broom, swelling

Mistletoes in the West are usually associated with pine (*Pinus* spp.; Plate 10), juniper (*Juniperus* spp.), fir (*Abies* spp.), larch (*Larix* spp.), hemlock (*Tsuga* spp.), and desert shrubs such as catclaw (*Senegalia greggii*).

Mites (Family Eriophidae)

Mites are fascinating animals distantly related to spiders and scorpions. For many years they have been recognized as serious pests of livestock, vegetables, and fruit crops. Over the millennia of their evolution, mites have developed ecological niches that would surprise most people—from the fruit of a tree, to the feather of an eagle, to the skin of a pig.

Plate 10. Integral stem swelling on pine caused by the dwarf mistletoe *Arceuthobium americanum*.

TABLE 9. SELECTED LIST OF ERIOPHYID MITE GALLS

Host Plant	Mite Species	Type of Gall
Alder (*Alnus* spp.)	*Acalitus brevitarsus*	Erineum
	Phytoptus laevis	Leaf beads
Alfalfa (*Medicago sativa*)	*Eriophyes medicaginis*	Witches' broom
Ash (*Fraxinus* spp.)	*E. fraxinivorus*	Catkin
Ash, mountain (*Sorbus scopulina*)	*Tetraspinus pyramidicus*	Leaf blister
	Phyllocoptes calisorbi	Erineum
Aspen, cottonwood (*Populus* spp.)	*E. neoessigi*	Catkin
	Phyllocoptes didelphis	Erineum
	Eriophyes parapopuli	Bud
Buttonbush (*Cephalanthus* spp.)	*E. cephalanthi*	Leaf beads
Chamise (*Adenostoma fasciculatum*)	*Phytoptus adenostomae*	Leaf beads
Coyote brush (*Baccharis pilularis*)	*E. baccharipha*	Leaf pits
Douglas-fir (*Pseudotsuga menziesii*)	*Tricetagus pseudotsugae*	Stunted needles
Gooseberry (*Ribes* spp.)	*E. breakeyi*	Leaf beads
Grape (*Vitis* spp.)	*Colomerus vitis*	Erineum
Huckleberry, blueberry (*Vaccinium* spp.)	*Acalitus vaccinii*	Bud, berry
Juniper (*Juniperus* spp.)	*T. quadricetus*	Berry
Meadowsweet (*Spiraea* spp.)	*Phytoptus paraspiraeae*	Flower
Mountain maple (*Acer glabrum*)	*E. calaceris*	Erineum
OAK		
Live oak (*Quercus* spp.)	*E. paramackiei*	Witches' broom
	E. mackiei	Erineum
Canyon live (*Q. chrysolepis*)	*E. mackiei*	Erineum
Blue (*Q. douglasii*)	*E. trichophila*	Erineum
Pine (*Pinus* spp.)	*T. alborum*	Stunted needles
Plum, cherry (*Prunus* spp.)	*Phytoptus emarginatae*	Leaf nails
Poison oak (*Toxicodendron diversilobum*)	*Aculops toxicophagus*	Lead beads
Sagebrush (*Artemisia* spp.)	*Aceria paracalifornica*	Leaf pits
Scale-broom (*Lepidospartum squamatum*)	*E. lepidosparti*	Bud
Seep willow (*Baccharis salicifolia*)	*E. baccharices*	Leaf pits/warts
Skeletonweed (*Chondrilla juncea*)	*E. chondrillae*	Bud
Snowberry (*Symphoricarpos* spp.)	*Phyllocoptes triacis*	Leaf roll
Tobacco brush (*Ceanothus velutinus*)	*E. ceanothi*	Leaf beads
WALNUT		
California black (*Juglans californica*)	*E. caulis*	Petiole
	E. brachytarsus	Leaf beads
	E. neobeevori	Catkin
English (*J. regia*)	*E. erineus*	Erineum
Hind's (*J. hindsii*)	*E. brachytarsus*	Leaf beads
	E. spermaphaga	Catkin
Willow (*Salix* spp.)	*Aculops aenigma*	Bud, catkin
	A. tetanothrix	Leaf beads

Some of these mites, called eriophyids, have developed intimate relationships with plants that result in the creation of galls (Table 9). While their tiny size (less than 0.3 mm) (Figure 11) conceals them from view, the damage that results from their feeding habits is often quite noticeable. The galls that form can look like blisters, globular beads, pouches, clubs, swollen and folded leaf edges, witches' brooms, or the hair-covered depressions called erinea. Erineum galls are common on oaks, alders, crab apples (*Malus* spp.),

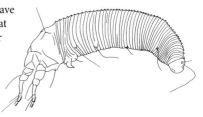

Figure 11. The eriophyid mite *Phytoptus emarginatae* measures 0.3 mm long.

and walnuts (*Juglans* spp.). The bead, pouch, and club galls created by eriophyids are often covered with minute hairs and almost always have openings at the base to allow escape of adults and young. In most cases, eriophyid mites are highly specialized plant-cell feeders that have evolved relationships with specific host plants. In a few cases, eriophyid mites will be found on several species of a genus, such as *Juglans*, *Populus*, and *Salix* (Plate 11). In the western United States, including all of Alaska, there is a vast number of eriophyid bud and leaf galls that are likely new species to science. It might take another lifetime to categorize them all.

Gall formation occurs as a result of the attack on individual plant cells. With their piercing mouthparts, eriophyid mites are able to drain the contents of plant cells. A single egg-laden female can initiate gall formation through piercing and feeding on plant cells while releasing chemicals into the wounds during the process. Females who do not come into contact with the **SPERMATOPHORES** (sacs containing sperm) left by males will produce only males. Females that do contact male spermatophores will produce males and females. In some cases, females retain sperm through winter, producing their young in spring. Offspring remain in the gall with their parent, contributing to further gall development through their feeding activities. Young mites pass through two nymph stages, with adults developing from the second stage. Growth from egg to adult often takes only two weeks.

Adult females often hibernate in fissures in bark or among bud scales during winter. Males generally do not survive winter. Mites travel by drifting in the wind or riding on insects and

Plate 11. Large bead galls on walnut caused by eriophyid mite *Eriophyes brachytarsus*.

birds that come into contact with host plants. This hitchhiking helps dispersion to new host plants. The galls initiated by eriophyid mites are usually much more difficult to discern as mite galls than the more distinct galls caused by other organisms.

Aphids and Adelgids (Families Aphididae and Adelgidae)

Of the two families represented here, aphids induce most of the galls described in this guide. For this reason, the following discussion focuses on aphid biology, noting there are significant differences between the two families.

Aphids belong to the same order of insects as leafhoppers, spittlebugs, mealybugs, and scale insects. In one way or another, aphids have long been considered serious pests by nursery workers and home gardeners. Galling species of aphids represent a small proportion (approximately 10%) of all 4,400 aphid species known. They feed by piercing the epidermis of a leaf or bud with their long, needlelike mouthparts, called **STYLETS**, and sucking juice from **PHLOEM** tissue. Aphids have the ability to convert plant starch into soluble sugars through enzymes in their saliva. Several studies have concluded that aphid saliva contains indole-3-acetic acid and that this **AUXIN** (plant hormone) is the principal gall-stimulating agent in aphid saliva. The shapes of aphid galls are species-specific.

Aphids have complex life cycles, particularly the gall-inducing species. Most, such as *Tamalia* spp., apparently have single hosts. Others, such as *Pemphigus* spp., may have alternate hosts. Many species also engage in an **ALTERNATION OF GENERATIONS**, as do some cynipid wasps (see "Cynipid Wasps" in this section of the guide).

For the most part, gall aphids go through several **PARTHENOGENETIC** (female reproduction without contact with a male) generations, culminating in a sexual generation that lays its fertile eggs on the bark of primary host trees in fall. Here, the eggs overwinter. In spring, an adult aphid called a **FUNDATRIX**, or **STEM MOTHER**, emerges, initiates a gall, and reproduces parthenogenetically. With some species, stem mothers display strong territorial behavior and will engage in intraspecific fights for prime galling sites. The fundatrix and later generations of wingless females are capable of initiating gall formation. One interesting aspect of specialization in galling aphids is the development of sterile morphs, called soldiers, that apparently have a defensive function against potential predators. They react to colony disturbance and will bite or cling to intruders. In some cases, soldiers remove excess honeydew and stand guard at the entrance to the galls. The rest of the stem mother's offspring develop wings around June or July to become **ALATES** (Figure 12). They usually fly to the ground, where they colonize roots of secondary hosts, feeding all summer without producing galls. In fall, alates pass into another stage and fly to the primary host tree or shrub. These individuals produce males and females that overwinter. Stem mothers develop the following spring. Two separate groups of aphid-like insects and their galls are considered here. One group comprises true aphids, belonging to the family Aphididae (*Pemphigus* spp. and *Tamalia* spp.) (Plate 12). The second group has been mistakingly called aphids though their members actually belong to the family Adelgidae (*Adelges* spp.). Galls of *Pemphigus*

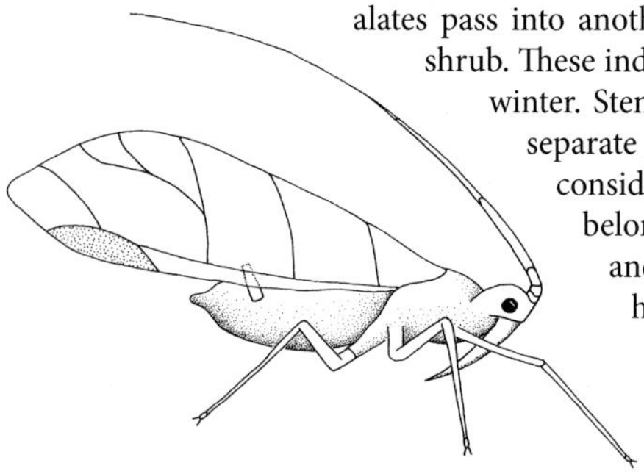

Figure 12. A winged alate of an aphid.

Plate 12. A petiole gall of the aphid *Pemphigus populicaulis*.

spp. typically occur on cottonwood petioles or leaves. The red-pink galls of the fold-gall aphid *Tamalia coweni* occur on the new leaves of nearly all **GLABROUS** manzanitas, and one stage of this aphid also galls manzanita inflorescences.

Fourteen adelgid species are associated with conifers in the United States. Of these, *Adelges cooleyi* and *A. piceae* are among the most prominent. Galls of *A. cooleyi* occur on new terminal twigs of spruce (*Picea* spp.), as do those of *A. piceae* on fir.

More details on these species are presented in the gall accounts.

Psyllids (Family Psyllidae)

Psyllids (Figure 13), or jumping plant lice, are important gall-inducers all over the world, especially in countries such as Australia, but have little role in galls in North America, where only 11 species are known. Of the 350 or more gall-inducing species worldwide, nearly half occur in Asia and Africa. Gall-inducing psyllids usually initiate pit or pouch galls on leaves, although in some areas they induce leaf-roll galls. These galls differ from those of eriophyid mites in that they lack the hairy erineum, in addition to having thicker walls and more regular shapes. The newly hatched nymph of the psyllid is the principal in initiating gall formation. Offspring can occur in the galls of their parents. Like other insects, psyllids suck cellular sap with their piercing mouthparts. The psyllid that galls hackberry (*Celtis* spp.) inserts its stylets into the host leaf and stimulates "cellulosolytic effect," causing dissolution of intercellular walls. Giant multinucleated cells form as a result. Cells begin differentiating beneath these giant cells, which ultimately leads to the formation of galls.

In the West, psyllids gall the ornamental pepper tree (*Schinus molle*; Plate 13), ornamental Australian brush-cherry (*Eugenia myrtifolia*; see Plate 590 in the Ornamental Plants section), and

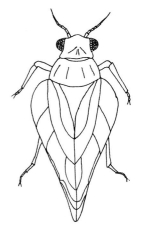

Figure 13. A generalized psyllid.

Plate 13. Pit galls on leaflets of pepper tree caused by the psyllid *Calophya rubra*.

hackberry (*Celtis reticulata*) in the East. Also, a non-galling lerp psyllid occurs on the leaves of blue gum eucalyptus (*Eucalyptus globulus*).

Coccids (Family Kermesidae)

There are over 8,000 species of coccids, or scale insects, worldwide. Most suck juice from plant tissues. Excess fluid drained from plant tissues is often excreted by the coccids as honeydew, which attracts ants that serve as mutualistic partners keeping predators away. Some scale insects hide under shells that can look like domes (on oak branches) or wax covers that look like oyster or mussel shells. Some scale insects reproduce sexually, while others are asexual, reproducing parthenogenetically. Scale insects are widely known as garden pests, creating masses of white, waxy tufts on a variety of plants. These are the insects associated with cochineal, used for red fabric dye and food coloring. While Australia has several species that induce galls on *Eucalyptus* trees, there is only one known coccid species (*Olliffiella cristicola*) in North America associated with gall-inducing. This species occurs on Emory oak (*Quercus emoryi*) in the Southwest.

Moths (Families Gelechiidae, Tortricidae, and Cosmopterigidae)

Several gall-inducing moths are treated in this field guide; numerous others are known to occur in the West (see Table 10 for more species). Worldwide, over 350 gall-inducing lepidopterans are currently known, and new species are described occasionally. The family Gelechiidae has the largest number of gall-inducers, with 47 species in 20 genera. Povolny (2003) described 25 species of *Gnorimoschema* occurring in the West. The moth genera covered here include **Gnorimoschema** (Gelechiidae), found on coyote brush (*Baccharis pilularis*), desert broom (*B. sarothroides*), rabbitbrush (*Chrysothamnus* and *Ericameria* spp.), and gumweed (*Gindelia hirsutula*); **Scrobipalpopsis** (Gelechiidae) on horsebrush (*Tetradymia* spp.); **Sorhagenia** and **Periploca** (Cosmopterigidae) on coffeeberry (*Frangula* spp.) and ceanothus (*Ceanothus* spp.), respectively; and **Eugnosta** (Tortricidae) (Figure 14) on cheesebush (*Ambrosia salsola*). In addition, several species are inquilines in the galls of other insects or pathogens. The inquiline

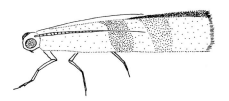

Figure 14. A gall-inducing moth similar to *Eugnosta* spp.

TABLE 10. MOTH GALLS

Moth Family and Species	Host Plant	Plant Part Affected
Argyresthiidae		
Argyresthia pseudotsuga	Douglas-fir (*Pseudotsuga menziesii*)	Terminal twig, swelling
Cosmopterigidae		
Periploca ceanothiella	Ceanothus (*Ceanothus* spp.)	Stem
Sorhagenia nimbosa	Coffeeberry (*Frangula* spp.)	Leaf swelling
Stagmatophora enchrysa	Bluecurls (*Trichostema* sp.)	Stem
S. iridella	Bluecurls (*Trichostema* sp.)	Root
Gelechiidae		
Gnorimoschema baccharisella	Coyote brush (*Baccharis pilularis*)	Stem
G. cf. octomaculellum	Great Basin sagebrush (*Artemisia tridentata*)	Shoot tip
G. octomaculellum	Rubber rabbitbrush (*Ericameria nauseosa*)	Terminal leaf
G. coquillettella	Goldenbush (*Ericameria* spp.)	Stem
G. crypticum	*Isocoma menziesii*	Fleshy stem
G. crypticum	*Hazardia squarrosa*	Fleshy stem
G. ericamariae	Goldenbush (*Ericameria* spp.)	Terminal bud
G. subterraneum	*Aster chilensis*	Stem
G. grindeliae	Gumweed (*Grindelia hirsutula*)	Stem
G. powelli	Desert broom (*Baccharis sarothroides*)	
Gnorimoschema sp.	Desert broom (*B. sarothroides*)	Terminal leaf
Eurysaccoides gallaespinosae	Horsebrush (*Tetradymia* sp.)	Stem
Scrobipalpopsis tetradymiella	Mojave horsebrush (*T. stenolepis*)	Stem
Scrobipalpopsis sp.	Scale broom (*Lepidospartum squamatum*)	Stem
Symmetrischema sp.	Cooper's box-thorn (*Lycium cooperi*)	Stem
Momphidae		
Mompha "unifasciella"	Fireweed (*Chamerion angustifolium*)	Stem
Mompha sp.	California fuchsia (*Epilobium canum*)	Stem
Nepticulidae		
Ectoedemia popullela	Aspen (*Populus tremuloides*)	Petiole
Plutellidae		
Ypsolopha sp.	*Ephedra* sp.	Stem
Tortricidae		
Epiblema rudei	Matchweed (*Gutierrezia* sp.)	Stem
Eugnosta beevorana	White bur-sage (*Ambrosia dumosa*)	
Eugnosta sp.	Cheesebush (*Ambrosia salsola*)	Stem
Unknown	*Vaccinium membranaceum*	Leaf roll

Note: This is a partial list of the moth gall-inducers known in the West.

Plate 14. Integral stem gall on coyote brush caused by the moth *Gnorimoschema baccharisella*.

Batrachedra salicipomonella occurs in *Pontania* (sawfly) galls on willows, and while largely herbivorous, it will prey on any insect encountered within galls. Another example is the inquiline *Dioryctria banksiella*, which feeds on galled tissues of jack pine (*Pinus banksiana*), a southeastern species, but not on the *Endocronartium harknessii* that induces the galls. The ecology of gall-inducing insects and their inquilines and parasites is vastly complicated and ripe for further research.

While each species has significant differences from the others, the basic biology of the stem-gall moth *Gnorimoschema baccharisella* on coyote brush (Plate 14) makes a good sample life history. Eggs of this moth are deposited on peripheral branches in fall, where they overwinter. Newly hatched larvae seek new growing shoots and burrow in sometime after the first of the year. The gall begins growing at the point of entry and surrounds the larvae. These spindle-shaped swellings are evident by February. By June or July, many larvae have been lost to parasites. At maturity, usually June to August, surviving larvae cut holes through the gall walls and drop to the ground on silken threads. Pupation occurs fairly soon after emergence, without any diapause. In other areas and with other species, larvae may form cocoons in leaf litter or sand and spend winter there. With some of these species, the galls they induce are often close to the ground.

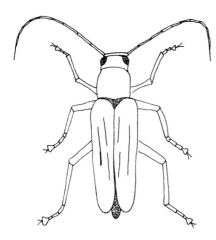

Figure 15. A gall-inducing longhorn wood-boring beetle similar to *Saperda* spp.

Beetles (Family Cerambycidae)

Only one beetle is treated here as a gall-inducing insect: *Saperda populnea*, a round-headed wood borer that occurs on cottonwoods (Figure 15). This beetle creates integral stem galls (Plate 15). Sometime in spring, depending on elevation and weather, adult beetles emerge from old stem galls. Adults chew horseshoe-shaped incisions in the bark of small branches or saplings or near the tips of branches of older trees and place one or two eggs in each incision. These dark brown, half-moon incision scars may remain visible for years. After hatching, larvae feed on phloem tissue, mining their way down through the stem. The host tree reacts by producing callus tissue around the wound, which accumulates,

Plate 15. Gall on black cottonwood caused by beetle *Saperda populnea*.

forming globose galls two or three times the diameter of the stem. The entry wounds created by adults open the tree to invasion of the dangerous pathogenic canker fungus *Hypoxylon mammatum*. Adults complete their life cycle in the galls, emerging in the following spring.

Leaf-Mining Flies (Family Agromyzidae)

Leaf-mining flies (Figure 16) are known worldwide for their activities. Some are major crop pests, while other species are used as biological controls. Most of the 2,500 species known are leaf or plant tissue miners. Larvae typically create erratic trails (mines) that start out small but get wider as the larva grows, leaving brown epidermal tissue at the surface. Some species create SHOT HOLES where the tissue had been mined in circles. For the most part, these mining flies lay their eggs in plant tissue, where larvae either mine channels through leaf tissue or feed inside roots, stems, or seeds. In the West, a few species induce galls, and two species are prominent. One, the twig-gall fly *Hexomyza schineri*, creates large integral stem galls on quaking aspen (*Populus tremuloides*; Plate 16) and some cottonwoods; the other fly, *Ophiomyia atriplicis*, creates

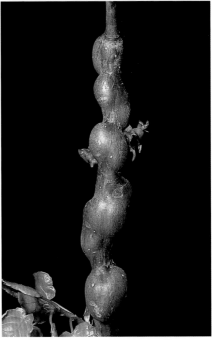

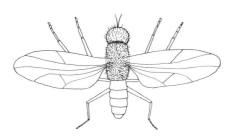

Above: Figure 16. A generalized leaf-mining fly.

Right: Plate 16. Galls of leaf-mining fly *Hexomyza schineri* on aspen sapling.

LEAF-MINING FLIES (FAMILY AGROMYZIDAE) 41

leafy bud galls on saltbush (*Atriplex* spp.). These gall-inducers usually overwinter as larvae and either pupate inside the galls or drop to the ground, where they pupate in the soil.

Tephritid Fruit Flies (Family Tephritidae)

Our knowledge of the role of tephritid fruit flies (Figure 17) as gall-inducing agents has become much clearer over the last 40 years, based largely on the works of Richard Goeden, James Wangberg, and David Headrick, among others. This fly family is one of the largest, and perhaps most famous, with about 4,200 species known worldwide. While many members of the family are **FRUGIVOROUS** (feed on fruit), many others are considered **NON-FRUGIVOROUS**, and it is among these latter flies that we find gall-inducers. With a few exceptions, most gall-inducing tephritids rely on plants in the sunflower family (Table 11). These flies initiate galls on both aerial and subterranean plant tissues. The adults emerge at a time when host plants are suitable for oviposition; most deposit eggs in terminal or axillary buds, though a few species deposit eggs in immature flower heads. They reproduce sexually, and courtship and mating are highly complicated and extremely varied among the species. Adults of most species live for 25 to 30 days and can lay up to 150 eggs in different locations, either singly or in clutches of up to 16. Some species can overwinter as adults, living up to 200 days. It is not unusual for larval stages to last for some time, as the galls they inhabit develop over a long period of time, sometimes from several months to nearly a year. It appears that some species even overwinter in a third-instar larval stage. Some species are freeze-tolerant, producing **CRYOPROTECTANT** compounds such as sorbitol and glycerol to slowly buffer the internal gall environment from freezing temperatures on the outside. This cold-hardiness is especially important for numerous species found on mid- to high-elevation plants such as Great Basin sagebrush (*Artemisia tridentata*) and rabbitbrush (Plate 17), which are subject to heavy snow cover in winter.

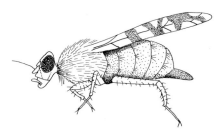

Above left: Figure 17. A generalized tephritid fruit fly.

Left: Plate 17. Bud galls on rabbitbrush caused by the tephritid fruit fly *Procecidochares* sp. A.

TABLE 11. TEPHRITID GALLS

Host Plant	Tephritid Species	Plant Part Affected
White bur-sage (*Ambrosia dumosa*)	*Procecidochares kristineae*	Woolly bud
	P. stonei	Bud
Woolly bur-sage (*Ambrosia eriocentra*)	*Procecidochares lisae*	Woolly bud
Cudweed (*Gnaphalium luteo-album*), pearly everlasting (*Anaphilus margaritacea*), and *Pseudognaphalium luteualbum*	*Trupanea signata*	Woolly terminal bud
Desert broom (*Baccharis sarothroides*)	*Aciurina thoracica*	Integral stem
Goldenbush (*Isocoma acradenia*)	*Procecidochares blanci*	Terminal/lateral buds
Goldenrod (*Solidago californica*)	*P. anthracina*	Terminal/lateral buds
Great Basin sagebrush (*Artemisia tridentata*)	*Oxyna aterrima*	Woolly bud
	Eutreta diana	Integral stem
Groundsel (*Senecio douglasii*)	*Trupanea stigmatica*	Integral stem
Yellow rabbitbrush (*Chrysothamnus viscidiflorus*)	*Aciurina semilucida*	Terminal/lateral buds
Yellow rabbitbrush (*C. viscidiflorus*) and rubber rabbitbrush (*Ericameria nauseosa*)	*A. michaeli*	Bud
E. nauseosa	*A. trixa*	Bud
E. nauseosa	*A. bigeloviae*	Woolly bud
C. viscidiflorus	*A. idahoensis*	Bud
C. viscidiflorus	*A. ferruginea*	Bud rosette
E. nauseosa	*Valentibulla californica*	Integral stem
Chrysothamnus viscidiflorus and *C. humilis*	*Procecidochares* sp. A	Leafy bud
E. nauseosa	*Procecidochares* sp. B	Leafy bud
Seep willow (*Baccharis salicifolia*)	*Tephritis baccharis*	Integral stem
Silver wormwood (*Artemisia ludoviciana*)	*Eutreta simplex*	Bud
Trixis californica	*Trupanea conjuncta*	Integral stem

Note: This list does not include all known species of tephritids.

Gall Midges (Family Cecidomyiidae)

The world has over 5,450 species of cecidomyiids (Figure 18), and new species are described annually, thanks to the monumental work of Raymond J. Gagné and others (Gagné and Jaschhof 2017). Over 1,150 species of cecidomyiids are known from North America. Some cecidomyiids specialize in feeding on fungi or as inquilines in galls of other midges and are not involved in gall-inducing behavior. Of the total known to occur in North America, more than 800 species are associated with galls as inducers. Some genera are particularly well represented as gall-inducers (*Asphondylia, Rabdophaga, Rhopalomyia,* and *Contarinia*). As with the tephritid fruit flies, the biology of cecidomyiids is varied and complex. Eggs hatch within a few days after deposition. Some eggs are laid directly in plant tissue, while other eggs are simply deposited on the host plant. In this latter case, larvae crawl about until they locate the proper plant organ for gall formation. Many die en route. Galls develop in response to larval secretions and behavior. Larvae that live in leaf-roll galls are usually gregarious, with several within the larval chamber. More complex galls tend to have individual larval chambers. Gall development begins after the larvae commence feeding on plant tissues. Unlike cynipid wasp larvae, cecidomyiid larvae, when feeding on nutritive cells lining chamber walls, do not destroy the cells, because they lack the chewing mouthparts that cynipids possess. Instead, a mild necrosis of cells occurs as a result of the cecidomyiids' sucking-feeding behavior. The nutritive cells of cecidomyiid larval chambers have a high metabolic rate, which, like the cells of cynipid galls, is controlled by the larvae.

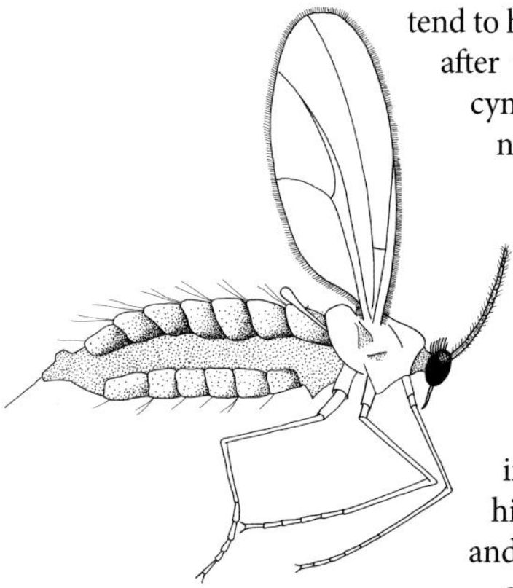

Some cecidomyiids do not initiate their own galls but instead deposit eggs next to those of gall-inducers. The hitchhiking midges stay close to the gall-inducing larvae, and once galls have developed, they act as inquilines and occasional predators.

Upon completion of larval development, some cecidomyiids leave the galls to pupate (typical of roll-gall species), while others pupate within the gall, leaving later as adults. Those that leave as larvae drop to the soil, dig in, and pupate. Those that stay with the galls use one of two exit strategies. In one scenario, full-grown larvae cut tunnels through the gall tissue almost to the outside with a specialized, elongate epidermal structure called a **SPATULA**, leaving a thin skin at the surface of the gall through which the pupae later escape. In the other case, pupae cut through the gall tissues. In both scenarios the mature pupae exit only about two-thirds of the way out, using the pressure of the last part of the passage to hold them firmly in place while transformation into adults is completed. Emergence of adults is generally well timed to the host plant's biology and growth patterns. Most gall midges are restricted to one host species or, in some cases, to related species within a genus. A few generalist gall midges (some *Prodiplosis* spp.) feed on members of several plant families.

One of the most interesting aspects of cecidomyiid biology is the regular occurrence of white fungi in the galls of all *Asphondylia* (Plate 18) and some *Lasioptera, Kiefferia*, and *Schizomyia* species. These galls are called **AMBROSIA GALLS**. Gall midges of the *Asteromyia* genus have also been associated with ambrosia galls. The fungi coat the interior walls of the gall, creating a smooth surface. Ambrosia galls tend not to be lined with nutritive cells. Instead, gall larvae extract nourishment directly from vascular bundles of the interior gall or from fungal mycelia. In many cases it appears that the fungi serve as food for the larvae (*Asphondylia* spp.), while in other cases the fungus is not eaten, yet completely surrounds the larvae (*Asteromyia* spp.). In this latter situation, the fungus eventually turns black and forms a hardened shell around the larvae, which possibly protects the larvae from parasites. In the galls of those species whose larvae feed on the ambrosia fungi, fungus growth appears to be affected, as proposed in the case of the gall midge *Schizomyia galiorum*. After its larvae

Figure 18. A gall midge, *Asphondylia* sp.

Plate 18. An ambrosia bud gall on saltbush induced by the gall midge *Asphondylia floccosa*.

left the galls to pupate in the soil, gall fungi grew, filling the larval chambers. Shorthouse and Rohfritsch (1992) reported, "It appears that the larvae of the four ambrosia gall species take food from fungal mycelium and that they are able to inhibit excessive fungal growth."

The method by which the fungus is introduced along with eggs into plant tissue is not precisely known. It is possible the consumed fungal material passes into the pupae and then the adult. In some cases, infected (spore-laden) feces and other secretions are deposited during egg-laying, which may allow fungal growth in the gall cavity. In other cases, fungal material may be scooped up by a shoveling action of the rear end of the abdomen of emerging females and subsequently deposited with eggs and accessory secretions. Once plant cells begin differentiating to form the gall, fungal spores germinate and rapidly develop mycelia. Nevertheless, the relationship between these symbiotic fungi and their cecidomyiid associates is intriguing and worthy of much greater study.

Finally, cecidologists have thought that galls are unique in appearance, structure, and color to each species of gall-inducer, particularly with cecidomyiids and cynipid wasps. While in general this may still hold true, scientists in Japan discovered that a single species of gall midge in the genus *Rhopalomyia* can produce galls of different shape and size; this is known as **POLYMORPHISM**. This means that for now, at least in the case of *Rhopalomyia* gall midges, species identification can be determined only by DNA sequencing analysis. Recent research has shown a similar situation in cynipid wasps of the species *Dryocosmus juliae* whose sexual generation produces two different-looking galls.

A full list of gall-inducing cecidomyiids is not included here (as I supplied for groups such as eriophyids and tephritids), simply because such a list of hundreds of species far exceeds the capacities of this guide.

Gall Wasps (Families Tanaostigmatidae, Tenthredinidae, and Cynipidae)

Wasps in the families Tanaostigmatidae, Tenthredinidae, and Cynipidae are known to induce galls in North America. Of these several families of gall-inducing wasps, only one family, Cynipidae, is prominent. Only two species of tanaostigmatid gall-inducers are included here. The tenthredinids, or sawflies, are particularly prominent on willows. Cynipid wasps, by far, are the star gall-inducers throughout the United States, especially in the West, where over 30 oak species serve as primary hosts. The 22 species of oaks in California, a high number, support more cynipid gall wasp species (136-plus) than the oaks of any other state.

Tanaostigmatid Wasps (Family Tanaostigmatidae)

The western states have only one named gall-inducing species of tanaostigmatid wasp (Figure 19, Plate 19); a second, unknown species is included here, and possibly more are yet to be described. One of the more notable related species is the symbiotic fig wasp (*Blastophaga psenes*), which is important to the production of figs. Most tanaostigmatid species are small, metallic black, dark brown, or red, and function as parasites or hyperparasites on other insects, especially caterpillars and fly larvae. A few species are gall-inducers. Compared to the larger groups of cecidomyiids and cynipids,

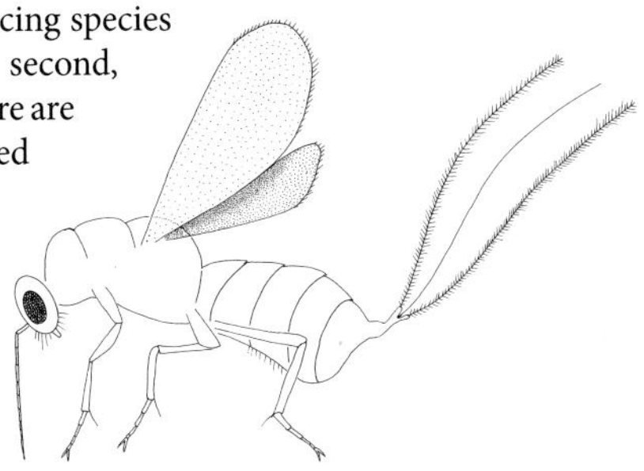

Figure 19. A generalized tanaostigmatid wasp.

the tanaostigmatids play a small role in gall formation in the West. The species included in this guide occur on catclaw (*Senegalia greggii*) in the deserts of the Southwest.

Sawflies (Family Tenthredinidae)

Sawflies (Figure 20) are actually diminutive wasps, less than 8 mm long, that get their strange name from their sawlike ovipositors. Four genera are considered here: on willows (*Salix* spp.) the leaf-galling *Pontania* spp. and *Phyllocolpa* spp. and the stem-galling *Euura* spp.; on snowberry (*Symphoricarpos* spp.) a bud-galling *Blennogeneris* species. Not all sawflies are gall-inducers. The genera

Plate 19. Gall on catclaw caused by the tanaostigmatid wasp *Tanaostigmodes howardii*.

that induce galls on willows have distinctly different habits, which also contrast with those of cynipid wasps. With sawflies, gall formation begins with secretions released by females as they deposit eggs into plant tissue. In some cases (*Euura* spp.), galls are well developed before the eggs hatch, and yet the larvae contribute to further gall development through their feeding and chemical actions. Adult sawflies have biting-chewing mouthparts, which are particularly important to some members of the *Euura lasiolepis* (Plate 20) group that chew their way out of their woody stem galls following pupation inside the galls. In contrast, the last-instar larvae of the *E. exiguae* group cut exit holes and plug them with frass before retreating back into the gall for pupation. Adults push the frass out to emerge. Those members of the *E. lasiolepis* group normally associated specifically with willows subject to flooding in streambeds usually do not cut exit holes before pupation, which may allow them to survive flooding. Following emergence, *Euura* males and females will drink water and feed on willow stamens, pollen, and nectar. *Euura* sawflies produce a single generation each year. These sawflies are not only host specific but also show a preference for specific clones within a species of willow.

Some reports indicate parthenogenetic reproduction among certain sawfly species. The rather small adult females are 4–5 mm long and must be responsible for gall formation, since the galls are fully developed before the eggs hatch. With some species, larvae contribute to gall growth, but the adults are the primary gall-inducers.

Most members of the genus *Pontania* also produce a single generation each year. In some locations, the willow-apple-gall sawfly (*P. californica*) breeds year-round, producing as many as six generations. These larvae press their voided feces into the walls of the larval chamber, maintaining a clean, frass-free feeding area. Ultimately, the pressed frass is incorporated into the gall tissue. Since the larvae have the ability to mine gall tissues right out to the thin epidermal layer, the tunnels are often backfilled with pressed frass to prevent intrusion of organisms. Other species apparently eject frass from time to time through holes, later used by the prepupae to escape the galls. With the willow-apple-gall sawfly, the prepupae exit the gall, drop to the ground by silk threads, and spin cocoons within the leaf litter. These

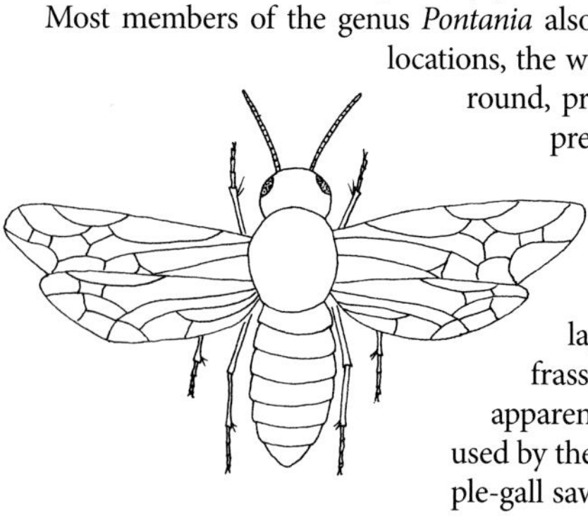

Figure 20. A generalized sawfly.

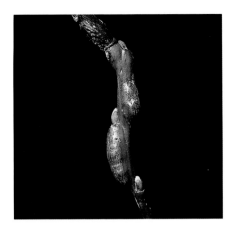

Plate 20. Integral stem galls caused by the sawfly *Euura lasiolepis*.

sawflies overwinter as prepupae. They pupate and emerge in spring in tune with the development of willow leaves. Adults live for 35 to 45 days. Strangely enough, it has been reported that *P. viminalis* galls in Europe (these also occur here) develop adventitious roots from the fleshy interior walls of the gall larval chamber. These roots grow out of the gall through the exit holes after the galls have dropped to the ground with leaf fall. What happens next is not clear.

One of the great surprises in my outdoor explorations was the discovery of a lone, near-prostrate willow covered with bright red *Pontania* galls growing on the vast outwash plain of Baird Glacier, just north of Petersburg, Alaska. This boulder- and gravel-strewn plain was largely barren except for scattered sapling Sitka alders (*Alnus sinuata*), mosses, some lichens, and one willow with no others in sight. And yet, here the willow and its guest sawflies were united in their own isolated microworld, and neither the worse for the chance encounter.

Cynipid Wasps (Family Cynipidae)

Galls of cynipid wasps (Figure 21) were among the first galls recognized for their commercial and medicinal uses by early naturalists, as far back as 460 BC. While uncommon in some parts of the world, cynipid wasps, along with cecidomyiid midges, are the dominant gall-inducers in North America, where over 700 cynipid species are known, most of which occur on oaks (*Quercus* spp.) (Plate 21). Several other cynipids induce galls on members of the rose family, such as *Diplolepis* spp. on wild roses (*Rosa* spp.) and *Diastrophus kincaidii* on thimbleberry (*Rubus parviflorus*). Pacific States cynipids are also found on chinquapin (*Chrysolepis* spp.) and tanoak (*Notholithocarpus densiflorus*), and one species occurs on a common weed, cat's-ear (*Hypochaeris radicata*).

CYNIPID TAXONOMY has been in a state of flux since the days of Alfred Kinsey's work in 1922. Even though improvements were made in cataloging cynipids with Weld's 1957b publication, the use of morphological characters alone has now proven inadequate in assigning species to appropriate genera in many cases. In 2002, Melika and Abrahamson proposed a number of major generic revisions, some of which have stood the test of time. Advances in DNA analysis have led to a greater understanding of the evolutionary history among species but also have proven that we have a long way to go before we fully understand the phylogenetic relationships of cynipid gall wasps. As a result, I am using names provided by Juli Pujade-Villar and by Weld (1957b, 1960) alongside those from subsequent work of researchers such as Lyon, Dailey, Zimmerman, Nicholls, and others to represent

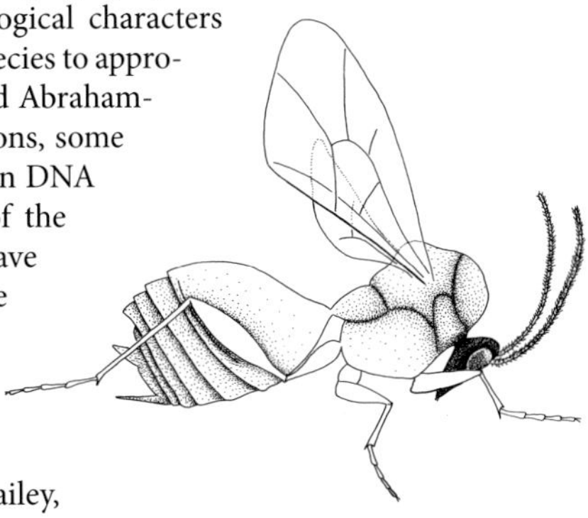

Figure 21. A generalized gall wasp, *Andricus* sp.

Plate 21. Spangle galls of the cynipid wasp *Antron douglasii* on valley oak.

some consistency until such time as the proper changes are sorted out. In addition, I am also inserting the name changes, where applicable, made by Melika and Abrahamson (2002), and others since, beneath the established names in parenthesis and marked by an asterisk. With either name, the species is therefore traceable.

NEW SPECIES: We might not ever be able to finalize the number of cynipid wasps that exist in the West. As evolution is not a static phenomenon and since new species are being discovered and described each year, I would expect the actual number of identified cynipid wasps to grow substantially.

Finally, I was able to confirm the identity of several galls that are obscure or confusing in the most common sources available today by reviewing the original detailed descriptions of early taxonomists as far back as 1881. In two cases, photographs of Kinsey's specimens in the American Museum of Natural History confirmed the identity, of *Amphibolips fusus* and *A. nassa*. The early pioneers scoured the earth looking for cynipid galls, and their papers include many more species names that are either no longer valid, have been changed over time, or have become obscure in modern literature.

CYNIPID DEVELOPMENT: The majority of galls arise on leaves and buds due to the annual high level of metabolic activity of these plant organs. Other galls occur on stems, branches, flowers, fruit, and roots. Cynipid wasps are responsible for the most extreme galls in color and shape. Galls that look like miniature stars, sea urchins, golf balls, cups, saucers, clubs, teardrops, goblets, and bow ties are among the fascinating shapes that stir the imagination. The shape, size, location, and color of cynipid galls are wasp species–specific, which often allows identification of the gall-inducing wasp without ever seeing the insect. Some galls even exude sweet honeydew as an attractant.

In cynipid galls, tannins are absent from the nutritive tissues, even though tannins occur in the outer layers of the galls, where they may serve as a defense against some gall-penetrating enemies. Tannins may also suppress invasion by pathogenic fungi that could kill wasp larvae. Cynipid wasp galls are either monothalamous (single chamber) or polythalamous (multiple chambers). While most cynipid wasps are gall-inducers, some act as inquilines, feeding on gall tissues of another cynipid wasp and sometimes creating their own chambers within the host galls.

Cynipids typically exhibit an **ALTERNATION OF GENERATIONS**, called **HETEROGONY**, with a spring sexual generation emerging from a different gall (often from a different plant organ) than the summer-fall generation of unisexual females (agamic generation). The latter females overwinter in diapause as prepupae (usually in the galls) and then pupate and emerge in spring, timed in harmony with the development of the preferred plant organs. Eggs produced and deposited by these females result in larvae and galls of the spring sexual generation. This alternation of generations is rather rare in the animal kingdom but also known in aphids and rotifers. This interesting alternation of reproductive modes confused early entomologists, as the alternating generations of the same species induced galls with different morphologies. This led researchers to believe the different galls belonged to separate species or even other genera. Research over the past 50 years by multiple scientists, especially with the advent of DNA-based methods, has matched the alternating generations of several cynipid species, clarifying our understanding of the complex life cycles exhibited by this group of wasps as well as identifying new species. Males are now being identified for species previously known to be female only (especially in the genus *Andricus*) and therefore parthenogenetic (Stone et al. 2008). Parthenogenesis as a lifestyle seems rare among cynipids. What can complicate this even further is the recent discovery through DNA sequencing of a cynipid wasp on chinquapin whose sexual generation alone produces multiple different gall morphologies on separate plant organs (Nicholls et al. 2018a). The knowledge of the diversity of galls between and within species now opens a huge door for potential taxonomic reevaluation.

In some species, for example, the California gall wasp (*Andricus quercuscalifornicus*), there are currently no known males in the population, implying the sexual generation has been lost. Females reproduce parthenogenetically, producing clones of the female parent. Someday, males may be identified for this species.

Once eggs hatch, larvae commence feeding by using their strong chewing mouthparts to rupture cell walls within the thin layer of nutritive cells surrounding the larval chamber and then consume the juice or cell sap released by these tissues. The thin layer of nutritive cells is constantly renewed through larval stimulation. The hard larval chamber wall of cynipid galls is usually well defined, smooth, firm, and either round or oval, in contrast to the irregular larval chambers of cecidomyiids and tephritids.

Cynipid larvae have intestines that are closed for most of their larval life; just before pupation, the gut opens and emits liquid wastes, which may be absorbed by gall tissues, since there is no evidence of these products during prepupae or adult stages. Cynipid larvae do not produce solid wastes that would otherwise foul the chambers. Pupation occurs mostly inside galls, the adults chewing their way to just under the epidermal skin of the gall, where sometimes they wait until weather conditions are favorable before pushing through the thin skin to emerge. Cynipid adults are generally small, around 2–3 mm, live only about a week, and do not feed.

In contrast to the tenthredinid sawflies, the larvae of cynipids are the principal gall-inducers, not the adults. Cynipid larvae release auxin-like substances that are believed to be responsible for gall growth very soon after hatching and continue to do so throughout their larval development. They are also able to convert plant starch into soluble sugar through enzymatic action.

Cynipid galls are distinguished by the presence of solid, concentric zones of differentiated cells around the larval cavities. The outermost layer or zone is typical of epidermal tissue. Beneath the epidermis is a zone of parenchyma cells covering the so-called protective zone of sclerenchyma cells. It is on the inner side of this sclerenchyma zone that the nutritive zone of small cells, rich in amino acids and other useful nutrients, forms to create the larval chamber wall. This feature of specialized nutritive cells in the larval chamber is unique to cynipid wasps (see the related discussion in the section on cecidomyiids).

Among cynipids, there are exceptions to this concentric-zones concept. Several paper-thin cynipid galls, called oak apples, exist in which the larval chambers are suspended in the middle of the galls, held in midair and supported by radiating fibers that connect to the epidermis of the gall (*Trichoteras vaccinifoliae, T. coquilletti*, and *Besbicus mirabilis*). The larvae are sustained through nutrients transmitted from the epidermis through the radiating fibers into the nutritive cells of the chamber walls. Certainly, this configuration must nearly eliminate inquilinous insects, since there is no gall flesh to eat, except for the thin skin. Several questions arise over the survival value or benefit to the gall organisms for such an unusual arrangement. Since galls with this design seem to occur either at high elevations (more than 1,500 m) or in areas of extreme summer heat, does the air mass insulate the larvae and pupae from extremes of heat or cold? Does the suspension of the larval chamber make infiltration more difficult for parasites? Someday, we may better understand the complexities of such unique features.

Because galls tend to be specific to the causative organisms in size, shape, and color, detailed descriptions of galls and the biology of their inducers are arranged according to host plant. For example, all the galls occurring on alders are grouped together in one section, with the gall-inducers listed in phylogenetic order. The host plants are arranged alphabetically by common name even if scientific names have changed (e.g., cheesebush and rabbitbrush).

This guide proceeds from trees to shrubs, with a final section on miscellaneous native herbs and ferns, ending with ornamental plants. There are no common names in the literature. The names associated with each gall were created based on location, significant features, or resemblance to items recognized by people. Species that bear only a generic name are likely species new to science or species for which larvae were identified and adults have yet to be reared and classified officially.

In many cases, the location of discovery or study is mentioned. Since there is an absence of data on the full range of gall organism species, it is presumed possible that a gall's range may be related to the range of the host plants, but on a species-by-species basis. There are many cases where a gall organism, such as *Besbicus heldae* or *Andricus bakkeri*, is restricted to a specific geographic area, even though its host is more widespread.

TREE GALLS

There are numerous trees in the West that support gall organisms, and some tree hosts support far more than others. Other trees seem to support only one or two species of gall organisms, while still others seem to be free of any such relationships. For the purposes of clarity, I am defining trees as those woody plants, of various heights, with one central trunk. Table 12 illustrates the biological significance of several tree species or groups.

TABLE 12. MAJOR TREE GALL HOSTS (WITH NUMBERS OF GALL SPECIES IN THIS GUIDE)

Alders	6
Aspens, cottonwood, poplar	24
Juniper	8
Oaks: Pacific States	136
Oaks: Southwest	95
Pines	6
Willow	24

Alder Galls

At least four species of alders occur in the western states: Sitka alder (*Alnus sinuata*), red alder (*A. rubra*), white alder (*A. rhombifolia*), and mountain or thinleaf alder (*A. tenuifolia*). Both Sitka and mountain alder can appear as small trees or shrubs, whereas mature red and white alders tend to be relatively tall. For the most part, none of the six gall organisms described here seem to be restricted to any one species. Gall organisms of alder include a nitrogen-fixing bacterium, a sac fungus, two mites, and two gall midges.

ROOT-GALL BACTERIA   *Frankia* spp.   Pl. 22

These bacteria induce root galls that are rarely noticed unless you make an effort to look for exposed roots near stream banks or pull a small sapling out of the ground. Nitrogen-fixing bacteria create these galls by extracting nitrogen from the atmosphere and fixing this nutrient in a form that can be used by host plants. The 5–30 mm wide, round, tubercled, or knobby galls occur just under the soil surface and completely encircle the trunk or are fixed along the roots of seedlings and saplings. Dozens of these galls can occur on a small seedling no more than 15 cm tall. Technically, these perennial nodules are called ACTINORHIZAE. The nodules may live on alders for three to eight years. The bacteria fix much more nitrogen than can be used in their own growth and maintenance. So, the remainder is translocated to other parts of the host

Plate 22. Nitrogen-fixing nodules induced by a *Frankia* sp. on an alder seedling found on the outwash plain of Baird Glacier in southeast Alaska.

plant. After affected roots die, nitrogen and other nutrients are recycled at the site and become available to other plants' feeder roots. Initial access occurs through root hairs, which begin swelling at the point of entrance. A lateral root also develops at this site and ultimately turns into the nodule. This relationship is critical because it allows pioneer plants to get started and survive in nitrogen-poor soils, which can include avalanche and landslide sites, glacial outwash plains, and flood zones where nutrient-poor materials have been deposited. Strains of *Frankia* are host-specific, and in addition to alders, occur on antelope brush (*Purshia tridentata*), bayberry (*Myrica pensylvanica*), buffalo berry (*Shepherdia argentea*), casuarinas (*Casuarina* spp.), ceanothus (*Ceanothus* spp.), mountain-mahogany (*Cercocarpus* spp.), Russian olive (*Elaeagnus angustifolia*), wax myrtle (*Myrica californica*), and other plants. See Table 5.

CONE-GALL FUNGUS *Taphrina occidentalis*   Pl. 23

This fungus induces broad, flat, twisting cone bract galls during late spring and early summer, depending on elevation. The extended cone bracts expand wildly into tongue-shaped

Plate 23. Swollen female cone bracts of *Taphrina occidentalis* galls on red alder.

enlargements 40 mm long by 5 mm wide. Infected cones rarely have only a few enlarged bracts. The infected cone can be obscured by dozens of these tongue-shaped galls. Sometimes an individual cone will have two or three eruptions of distorted bracts while still showing the shape of the cone. The galls are usually green with red along the margins. Those fully exposed to sunlight may be all red. Old, dark brown infected cones may remain on the trees for years. As cones develop to near their full size, the serpentine enlargements of the infected bracts begin protruding. Cone galls on alders at low elevations develop by late spring, whereas those on alders at high elevations develop later. Usually by August, cone galls in the Sierra Nevada and other mountainous areas, for example, have matured and started to turn brown and wither. The spores of this sac fungus survive winter and reinfect the host trees in spring. This fungus in winter resembles yeast during the asexual part of its life. It occurs throughout the western United States and is common among native alders as well as those varieties used for garden and neighborhood park landscaping. The red tongue-shaped galls of *Taphrina amentorum* on the female cones of red alder in Alaska are much larger than this species.

BEAD-GALL MITE   *Phytoptus laevis*   Pl. 24

This mite induces round, green, yellow, red, and reddish-brown bead galls on both surfaces of leaves. These small, 2 mm wide bead galls reveal a rough surface under close inspection with a hand lens. As with other bead galls induced by mites, these show corresponding hair-lined openings on the opposite side of the leaf. Galls appear singly or in large numbers per leaf. The galls do not develop until after leaves have reached full size. Adult mites that emerge from these summer galls spend winter in the fissures of the host tree's bark. No significant damage is done to the affected leaves. This mite does go through an alternation of generations. It was first described in Europe and is now widespread in western states, including Alaska.

ERINEUM-GALL MITE   *Acalitus brevitarsus*   Pl. 25

This mite creates white to cream-colored erineum pockets on the underside of alder leaves. These 3–5-mm-wide, hair-covered galls are quite different from most erineum pockets, which tend to be

Plate 25. Erineum galls of *Acalitus brevitarsus* on alder.

Plate 24. Bead galls of *Phytoptus laevis* on alder.

smaller and brown. You will notice the hair pockets on the leaf underside, or you will see the corresponding bumps on the upper surface of the leaves. They almost always occur in large numbers per leaf, distorting the affected leaves enough to visually separate them from non-galled leaves.

FOLD-GALL MIDGE   *Dasineura* sp. A   Pl. 26

This midge creates long midrib folds that protrude on the underside of leaves. The swollen galls consume one-half to three-fourths of the length of the leaf. Galled leaves appear pinched along the midrib when you look at the dorsal surface. The gall becomes quite noticeable when seen from the underside because it protrudes down about 10 mm. The gall midge targets young leaves in spring. The larvae spin cocoons within the galls and pupate there. These galls have been recorded on red alder from British Columbia to California.

CATKIN-GALL MIDGE   *Dasineura* sp. B   Pl. 27

This midge induces globular, lumpy polythalamous galls on the male catkins of red alder and probably other alders. The large, swollen, puffy bracts of the gall are much larger than normal catkin bracts. Galls measure 15 mm in diameter by up to 25 mm long. Normal, unaffected catkin tissues usually hang below galled tissues. The surface of the galls appears smooth, with well-defined jointed bracts that fit together snugly. Interior larval chambers are branched and interconnected. Galls collected in September issued adult catkin gall midges two weeks after collection. If females also emerge under natural conditions in September, they may lay their eggs in next year's catkin buds. Other galls collected at the same time of year had been thoroughly parasitized by eulophid wasps.

Above left: Plate 26. Fold gall of *Dasineura* sp. A on alder.

Plate 27. Swollen bracts of male catkin galls of *Dasineura* sp. B on alder.

Plate 28. Erineum galls of
Tetraspinus pyramidicus on
mountain ash.

Ash Galls

There are two distinct groups of trees in the western states with the common name "ash." One, referred to simply as **ASH**, is in the genus *Fraxinus*, family Oleaceae, while the second group, called **MOUNTAIN ASH**, is in the genus *Sorbus*, family Rosaceae. Oregon ash (*F. latifolia*) is known to support an eriophyid mite, *Eriophyes fraxinivorus*, which induces galls on the flowers. While I have not found this in the field, I have found an eriophyid mite galling the leaves of a mountain ash (*S. scopulina*), as described here. The taxonomy of mountain ash mites is complicated. I have not found any other gall-inducing species on mountain ash.

LEAF-GALL MITE   *Tetraspinus pyramidicus*   Pl. 28

This mite produces small, yellow, slightly raised blisters on dorsal surfaces of mountain ash leaflets, with corresponding brownish, hair-lined depressions on the underside. These erineum galls measure 1–5 mm across, with some individual galls coalescing to form larger clusters. Each leaflet can contain dozens of these galls. Both *S. scopulina* and *S. californica* are known to support a different eriophyid mite, *Phytoptus sorbi*, that induces larger, green blisters on the dorsal surfaces of leaflets. In California, *S. scopulina* is often heavily affected by this mite. Its galls project higher than those of *Tetraspinus pyramidicus*. A third eriophyid mite, *Phyllocoptes calisorbi*, causes large white erineum galls on the underside of leaflets of both species of mountain ash.

Aspen, Cottonwood, and Poplar Galls

Aspens, cottonwoods, and poplars (*Populus* spp.) are attacked by a variety of organisms, including two fungi, three eriophyid mites, several aphids, a moth, a beetle, a leaf-mining fly, and at least seven gall midges. Additionally, aspens and cottonwoods host a number of canker fungi that cause weeping, ruptured bark and swollen tissues, but these are not dealt with here. The tree species considered here include black cottonwood (*P. balsamifera* subsp. *trichocarpa*), Fremont cottonwood (*P. fremontii*), narrowleaf cottonwood (*P. angustifolia*), quaking aspen (*P. tremuloides*), and the introduced Lombardy poplar (*P. nigra-italica*).

Aphids are by far the most common gall-inducers found on cottonwoods in the West. They usually occur on stems, petioles, leaf bases, or the leaves themselves. Their taxonomy and genetic relationships are complicated and in need of clarification. Based on genetic analysis, there appear to be western "races" of eastern species, for example, that make species identification difficult and confusing. Some of the species names used here may change with continued research.

CORKY-BARK FUNGUS *Diplodia tumefaciens*   PI. 29

This **ASCOMYCETE** fungus gall is easily seen on trunks and often branches of older aspens or those of low vigor. These large, dark brown to black eruptions of outer bark tissue can be 35 cm in diameter and occur one after the other in a vertical row up the trunk. This fungus occurs on numerous hosts in the West and was found to be commonly infecting other aspens in the immediate area of the one shown in the photo. Fissures of these galls open the host tree to secondary invaders, including other fungi and beetles.

Plate 29. Trunk galls of *Diplodia tumefaciens* on aspen. Photo by Ron Russo Jr.

LEAF-BLISTER-GALL FUNGUS *Taphrina populisalicis*   Pls. 30 & 31

This fungus causes erineum-like yellow depressions or pockets between the veins on either surface of leaves of black cottonwood and Fremont cottonwood. Convex, light green bumps correspond to yellow depressions on the opposite side of the leaf. When galls are developing, depressions are pale beige. The yellow pigment develops as the galls mature and begin to sporulate. The pigment is actually in oil

Plate 30. Leaf-blister-gall pockets induced by *Taphrina populisalicis* on cottonwood.

Plate 31. Dorsal surface of leaf-blister-gall pockets of *T. populisalicis*.

droplets of the asci (spore-producing sacs) where the spores are produced. Depressions and corresponding bumps measure 5–15 mm long by 4–10 mm wide and are round to irregular in shape. Sometimes the depressions or bumps coalesce, creating a long chain running parallel to the midrib. The galls cause little damage to the leaves and host trees. These galls can be confused easily with those of eriophyid mites or certain rust fungi. This fungus actually is globally distributed, occurring on a variety of poplars as well as red willow (*Salix laevigata*). Galls have been collected from multiple locations in the West including Alaska. A related species, *T. caerulescens*, induces similar large convex/concave pocket galls on eastern red oaks planted as ornamentals in the Pacific States.

BUD-GALL MITE   *Eriophyes parapopuli*   Pl. 32

This mite induces nodular, rough, minutely hairy bud galls on quaking aspen, black cottonwood, and Fremont cottonwood in western states. The galls usually form on axillary and terminal buds and often involve large sections of stems. Galls may be quite abundant on the affected tree. This mite also produces large, singular bud galls on branches of black cottonwoods, which are usually round and bright red. Galls measure up to 40 mm long by 25 mm across and may last on host trees for several years. Fresh galls are pale green with pink to reddish tints but ultimately become dark brown with age. Heavy infestations can cause noticeable deformations of petioles and branches, with some stunting occurring. In places where the growing season is short, the activities of large numbers of this mite can seriously impact the growth habits of stems, leaves, and flowers. It is not uncommon to find heavily galled trees growing right next to trees completely free of galls.

Plate 32. Large knobby bud galls of *Eriophyes parapopuli* on aspen.

CAULIFLOWER-GALL MITE   *Eriophyes* sp.   Pl. 33

The cauliflower-like galls of this mite occur on branches and trunks of aspens and black cottonwoods and are quite large, with some reaching 10 cm across. When fresh in late spring or early summer, galls can be bright red and appear with numerous eruptions and fissures across the surface, but they turn dark brown with age. New shoots or leaves do not emerge from these growths. The galls induced by this mite are quite distinct from all other known species at this time.

Plate 33. Cauliflower gall of *Eriophyes* sp. on trunk of aspen.

ERINEUM-GALL MITE *Phyllocoptes didelphis* PI. 34

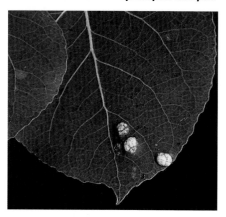

Plate 34. Dorsal lumps caused by *Phyllocoptes didelphis* on aspen leaves.

This mite induces yellow-green or pink-flushed, veiny lumps on either surface of leaves of quaking aspen in spring and early summer. The corresponding hair-lined depressions (erinea) on the opposite side of the leaves are yellow reddish when fresh and brown when old. Some galls have hairs that are hardened lobes and not the typical hairs found in other erineum galls. The galls measure 5–15 mm in diameter and rise above the surface by 2 mm. Exaggerated veins of the leaves show on the convex surface of the galls. Frequently, leaf tissue near the galls blackens as a result of the redirection of nutrients into gall tissue. Galling activity is more frequent on the lower, shaded branches of trees. Galls occur singly or in large numbers per leaf. Mites live within the hair-lined depressions and remain motionless when disturbed. Adults overwinter around the buds. This gall mite is extremely common and abundant in some areas and absent in others. Another mite, *Aculus dormitor*, is an inquiline in the gall.

VAGABOND-GALL APHID *Mordwilkoja vagabunda* PI. 35

This aphid induces the largest aphid galls in the West. These convoluted, bladderlike leaf galls occur on nearly all cottonwoods. Fully developed masses usually exceed 30 mm wide and are composed of the crumpled leaves of terminal buds. In spring, eggs hatch and young nymphs (fundatrices) move to developing buds and begin sucking plant juices. This feeding causes normal leaf tissues to transform into irregular masses of swollen leaf tissue. The feeding fundatrices are literally trapped within the galls during early stages of development. Aphids appear able to continue stimulating gall growth during their feeding. As galls mature and the season progresses, the ends of small projections on the galls dry and split open, allowing escape. The alternate host(s) are not known, but by late summer the winged generation returns to cottonwood hosts and inhabits old galls, where it lays eggs. These aphids overwinter as eggs in old galls or bark crevices and have multiple generations each year. Old galls may last on the trees through the next season. This gall and its aphids occur throughout much of the United States and especially from the Rocky Mountains to the West Coast.

Plate 35. Convoluted leaf gall of *Mordwilkoja vagabunda* on aspen.

PETIOLE-GALL APHID   *Pemphigus populitransversus*   Pl. 36

This aphid induces fleshy, spherical, singular green galls with transverse slits on petioles at the base of leaves on Fremont, black, and narrowleaf cottonwoods and aspen. Prominent, angular or transverse slits often protrude slightly, taking on the appearance of lips. A tiny opening develops in the center of each slit. Galls measure up to 14 mm in diameter. The galls are smooth, green to red (depending on sun exposure), and usually located on one side of the petiole. Rapid growth of the petiole often causes a bend at the site of the gall. The swelling gall begins its development around the stem mother as she feeds, which provides the stimulus for gall development. Eventually, the gall completely encompasses the stem mother. This female lays numerous eggs, filling the gall with hungry offspring.

Plate 36. Petiole gall of *Pemphigus populitransversus* on Fremont cottonwood.

The white, waxy secretions of the young often conceal them. As galls become overcrowded, the young exit and crawl about on the leaves and stems, sometimes moving into other galls. One study has shown that these aphids abandon their "home gall" when a heavily galled host tree begins to prematurely drop galled leaves (as a defense) or when predators show up. Often aphids seek other galls and crawl in to finish their development. Aphids are usually present in the galls all summer long. In fall, as the leaves change color, wither, and drop to the ground, petiole galls remain green and succulent for up to two weeks. Once galls begin to dry, the transverse slits open, allowing escape of the aphids.

Along rivers, galls of this aphid develop at varying times depending on the height of winter flooding. Those sections of trees above the high-water mark produce galls earlier than lower sections subject to winter flooding. Flooding may destroy the overwintering aphids from the previous season's galls. Usually, galls on lower sections of host trees do not develop until aphids have moved down from already formed galls. Cottonwoods in the warm interior valleys develop galls earlier than do trees of cooler coastal valleys or high mountain areas. Green lacewing (*Chrysopa carnea*) insect larvae and several birds are predators of this aphid. A greater threat to these aphids is a fungus that develops within galls, causing a high mortality among early nymph stages. The alternate "root hosts" of this aphid include a number of cruciferous plants such as turnips (*Brassica rapa*) and cabbage (*B. oleracea-capitata*).

GOUTY-PETIOLE-GALL APHID   *Pemphigus populicaulis*   Pl. 37

This aphid induces globular, rough-surfaced galls on petioles at the base of leaves of aspen and several cottonwoods, especially black cottonwood. This gall, unlike the preceding species, has a spiral slit along which a series of small holes develop later in the season, through which aphids squeeze out. These bulging galls occur singly or paired on each side of the petiole. A slight twist to the petiole often develops at the point of juncture with the leaf. Shapes vary slightly from round to ovular, and there are often small bumps across the surface. Galls measure 10–15 mm long by 8–10 mm across. Ants have been observed chewing through walls of the galls.

Plate 37. Petiole galls of *Pemphigus populicaulis* on black cottonwood. (See also Pl. 12.)

Plate 38. Stem gall of *Pemphigus populiramulorum* on Fremont cottonwood.

On several occasions in late summer in the Sierra Nevada mountains at about 1,500 m, I have found ants within empty galls. Did aphids leave upon arrival of ants? Did ants consume the aphids and their sweet exudate? It has been shown that water parsley (*Oenanthe sarmentosa*) is the alternate host for this aphid.

STEM-GALL APHID *Pemphigus populiramulorum*   Pl. 38

This aphid induces integral stem galls on new growth of Fremont cottonwood and black cottonwood, usually just below a leaf-bearing petiole. The vertical slit, which distinguishes this species' galls, sometimes has slightly protruding lips. The slit measures about 7 mm long, while the entire gall measures 10 mm in diameter. A few specimens have reached 25 mm in diameter. The fundatrix leaves the gall between July and September for an unknown secondary host. This species has been recorded in several locations in western North America, notably Colorado, Utah, South Dakota, and California, and may have several races or subspecies in these areas.

LEAF-GALL APHID *Pemphigus populivenae*   Pl. 39

This aphid, also known as the sugar beet root aphid, induces elliptical, wrinkled fold galls on leaves of cottonwoods. Often, the galls are located in rows along the midrib or along the edges of leaves. The aphids actually feed on the underside, causing leaf tissue to fold around them, creating corresponding bumps on the dorsal surface of leaves. The pale green to yellow-red galls measure 10 mm long by 3–5 mm wide. Linear slits form on the underside of the galls, allowing escape of the aphids later. Individual leaves with numerous galls can be severely distorted. There is some evidence that some clones of cottonwoods may be resistant to attack, while others are more vulnerable. This species has been recorded from Colorado to California and uses sugar beet (*Beta vulgaris*) roots, lamb's-quarter (*Chenopodium album*), and pigweed (*Amaranthus* spp.) as alternate hosts.

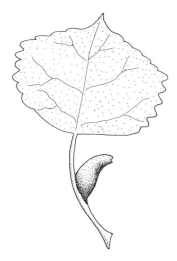

Plate 39. Fold galls of *Pemphigus populivenae* on black cottonwood.

Figure 22. Petiole gall of *Pemphigus bursarius*

FLASK-GALL APHID *Pemphigus bursarius* Fig. 22

This aphid induces tubular, flask-shaped, mid-petiole galls on Lombardy poplar. One to four galls may be found on a single petiole. Galls measure 10–15 mm long. Within the galls, stem mothers can produce over 300 of their winged offspring, which later fly to secondary hosts including lettuce (*Lactuca sativa*), lamb's-quarter (*Chenopodium album*), and carrot (*Daucus carrota*), infesting their roots. While on these secondary hosts, the aphids go through additional generations, ultimately producing the reproductive stage. Pregnant females of this generation return to the primary host, Lombardy poplar, to lay eggs that overwinter. This introduced aphid from Europe is widespread across North America.

PETIOLE-GALL APHID *Pemphigus spirothecae* Pls. 40 & 41

This aphid induces galls in spring on the petioles of Lombardy poplar but may also occur on black cottonwood. Feeding activity of the stem mother causes the petiole to twist, forming

Plate 40. Petiole galls of *Pemphigus spirothecae* just starting.

Plate 41. Fully mature gall of *Pemphigus spirothecae* in late August.

an ever-tightening spiral, as seen in Plate 40. Spiraling of the petiole continues until the stem mother is completely surrounded by gall tissue. A noticeable slit that develops on the exterior opens later, allowing escape of the aphid progeny. Two to three generations may occur per season. Galls measure 10–12 mm in diameter and mature by late August (Plate 41) in most locations and open by leaf fall in autumn.

PETIOLE-GALL APHID   *Pemphigus* sp. A   Pl. 42

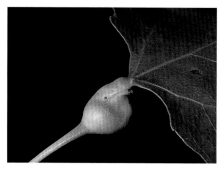

Plate 42. Petiole gall of *Pemphigus* sp. A.

This aphid induces twisted petiole galls near the base of leaves of Fremont cottonwood. Until recently, in most publications, these galls were usually associated with *Pemphigus nortoni*. Advances in DNA analysis of the adults and alates have shown that insects from these galls are closely related to the stem-gall aphid (*P. populiramulorum*) group, which may have several western "races" or subspecies. The galls look superficially like those of the gouty-peti-ole-gall aphid (*P. populicaulis*), except that the exit hole of these galls is a spiral slit near the base of the leaf, and the galls are smooth. Galls measure 14 mm long by 10 mm across. Stem mothers can produce 700–1,000 or more offspring in each gall. Fungal infections that start in early June are the principal cause of in-gall mortality for this aphid. As with other aphid galls, lacewing larvae and select birds are predators of these aphids. Continued research may clarify the relationships of several undescribed relatives in the stem-gall aphid group in the West.

MIDRIB-GALL APHID   *Pemphigus* sp. B   Pls. 43 & 44

This aphid induces large, globular galls that protrude from the ventral midrib of Fremont cottonwood leaves. The dorsal surface of the galled leaves reveals a slight, discolored swelling

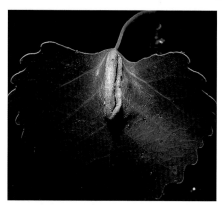

Plate 43. Dorsal view of an unusual midrib gall of *Pemphigus* sp. B on Fremont cottonwood.

Plate 44. Ventral view of the midrib gall of *Pemphigus* sp. B.

highlighted by a linear slit that runs down the midrib for the length of the gall. Tissues around the slit are usually yellow in May. The knobby, somewhat spiraled swellings forming the galls underneath measure 20–25 mm long by 12 mm across. Galls disrupt the flow of nutrients enough to cause yellowing and death of outer tissues of the leaves. In May, galls are full of winged offspring along with the fat stem mother. DNA analysis has shown that aphids removed from these galls appear to be a western "race" of the gouty-petiole-gall aphid (*P. populicaulis*), even though the galls of these two insects are quite distinct. While there may be variability in the form of the galls as well as site selection, there may also be several undescribed relatives of the gouty-petiole-gall aphid in the West.

PETIOLE-GALL MOTH   *Ectoedemia popullela*   Pl. 45

This moth attacks quaking aspen in the upper section of the petiole at its junction with the leaf. These round to ovoid, pea-size swellings measure 5 mm high by 3 mm in diameter by late July. Galls are brown, with furrows or shallow cracks over the surface. Interior flesh of the gall is green. The larval chamber has a chocolate-colored packet of dried frass in the middle, placed there in liquid form by the caterpillar. There is one light green caterpillar per gall. Full-grown caterpillars have been found in early August. After feeding ceases, caterpillars exit the galls and drop to the ground, burrow in, and overwinter. Adults emerge in late spring or timed with development of buds and leaves, depending on elevation.

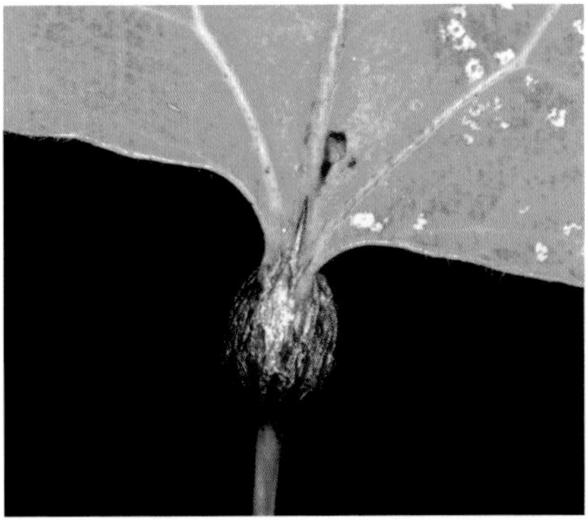

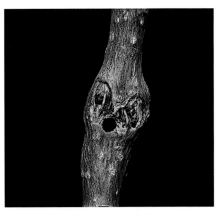

Plate 45. Petiole gall of *Ectoedemia popullela* on aspen.

TWIG-GALL BEETLE   *Saperda populnea*   Pls. 46 & 47

This beetle, a round-headed wood borer, produces integral stem swellings on cottonwoods and willows (*Salix* spp.), particularly saplings. Galls of this beetle are recognized by the hemispherical cuts (scars) made by adult beetles into which eggs are inserted between the phloem and xylem tissues. Each gall measures 12–20 mm across and is generally ovoid, tapered gently, and not an abrupt swelling. Galls usually contain a single beetle larva (although two are occasionally found) that mines the interior wood, disrupting the flow of nutrients to outer areas of the branch. As a result, twigs beyond the galls weaken and are subject to breakage. Mature legless larvae measure about 25 mm long. Galls collected from Fremont cottonwood on the first of May

Plate 46. Old gall of *Saperda populnea* on cottonwood branch showing exit hole.

Plate 47. Adult beetle *Saperda populnea* on cottonwood branch.

Plate 48. Gall of *Hexomyza schineri* on aspen.

issued adult beetles 14 days later. Adults are 20 mm long including antennae. The dusty-black adults, although capable of flying, tend to walk all over the branches of the host trees, constantly testing the air with their antennae.

TWIG-GALL FLY   *Hexomyza schineri*   Pl. 48

This leaf-mining agromyzid fly induces large, abrupt, integral stem swellings on cottonwoods, poplars, and especially aspen. Saplings and young trees are particularly vulnerable to attack. Galls range from 20 mm to over 40 mm across and are characteristically abrupt swellings. These flies overwinter within gall tissues as full-grown, yellow-green larvae. Larvae develop into pupae within the galls, but the pupae work their way out of the galls and drop to the ground in winter or early spring. The 4-mm-long adults emerge later, timed with new growth of their host. During the day, flies rest and sun themselves. Impregnated females seek new growth and insert their eggs. Once the eggs hatch and the larvae begin feeding, the characteristic galls develop. Young branches can support dozens of these galls, sometimes in chains with one gall after another (see Plate 16). Individual galls usually contain two or three larvae, which become obvious by late summer and fall. This fly is particularly vulnerable to the parasitic chalcid wasp *Eurytoma contractura*, which normally accounts for 20%–30% loss, but can kill up 80% of the larvae in some years. Chickadees (*Poecile* spp.) are major predators of pupae. A Cytospora canker fungus often gains entrance to the gall through the exit wound of the fly. I have found a field of aspen saplings with nearly every sapling and every branch on the saplings supporting multiple galls. Once thought to be limited to the Rocky Mountains, these flies and galls are now found in the Sierra Nevada and likely elsewhere.

BIG-BUD-GALL MIDGE   *Dasineura* sp.   Pls. 49 & 50

The big-bud-gall midge induces galls on black cottonwood. The galls are composed of greatly enlarged bud scales covered by orange, sticky liquid. Galls measure 15–25 mm high by 10–15

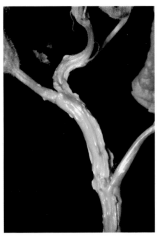

Plate 49. Big-bud gall of *Dasineura* sp. (left) beside normal bud (right).

Plate 50. Twisted gall of *Contarinia* sp. on aspen.

mm across. When fresh in May and June, galls are leaf green but turn brown by fall or earlier if temperatures are abnormally hot. Larvae are red, orange, or white and are found between bracts, bathed in viscous fluid. Cocoons are formed in fall between bud scales, and larvae are in diapause until they pupate in spring. Old galls are flared open and may remain on trees for more than a year.

STEM-GALL MIDGE   *Contarinia* sp.   PI. 50

This gall midge induces integral polythalamous stem galls that are either straight or bent and twisted on spring terminal shoots of quaking aspen. Each larva occupies its own larval chamber just under the surface, with several larvae per stem gall. Aspen stem galls measure 10–15 mm in diameter by up to 50 mm long. Curious liplike protrusions appear on the outside of the stem along the length of the gall, which mark future exit locations for the larvae. Larvae leave the galls by mid- to late June, before gall tissues turn woody, to overwinter in the soil until spring. This new species was found in Washington.

ROLL-GALL MIDGE   *Prodiplosis morrisi*   PI. 51

This gall midge induces rose-pink to yellow-green roll galls along the leaf margins of aspens. Galls often form along the entire edge of both sides of leaves, creating a rippled, curled appearance. The roll forms inwardly toward the leaf's dorsal surface. By mid- to late summer, these roll galls usually have a contrasting yellow-green and adjoining dark brown discoloration. They are no

Plate 51. Roll gall of *Prodiplosis morrisi* on aspen.

more than 5 mm wide. Eggs are laid in newly developing leaf buds. Several larvae share the same space within the leaf rolls and drop to the ground to pupate. Galled leaves usually turn brown at the end of the larval cycle. Severe stunting can occur on affected terminal branches. This gall midge was previously recorded on aspens and some poplars from the East Coast to Kansas and Texas. Specimens shown here were collected from the central Sierra Nevada in California.

LEAF-GALL MIDGE *Harmandia* sp. A Pl. 52

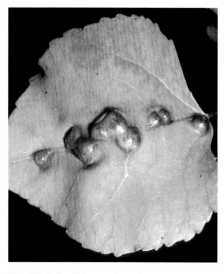

Plate 52. Galls of *Harmandia* sp. A on aspen.

This gall midge induces globular, fleshy, integral galls that protrude from both surfaces of aspen leaves. Galls occur along the midrib and occasionally lateral veins of leaves in early summer. Galls are green to reddish and smooth, with a sparse arrangement of short white hairs. Galls measure 4–6 mm in diameter, but some coalesce into larger masses. One or more irregular-shaped larval chambers develop in the upper half of each gall, with one larva per chamber. By mid-June, round apical openings develop on the dorsal surface of the leaf, which ultimately connect to one or more larval chambers. From mid-June to mid-August, depending on area temperatures, larvae emerge from the galls and drop to the ground, burrow in, and overwinter. Since galls of this midge do not fit any existing keys, it might turn out to be a new species, or it could be related to an eastern species, *H. helena*.

BEAD-GALL MIDGE *Harmandia* sp. B Pl. 53

The bead galls of this midge on aspen leaves are easily distinguished from galls of *Harmandia* sp. C by having openings at the top of each gall, even if they are temporarily plugged with fibrous strands, as seen here. These round, monothalamous, glabrous, smooth galls measure 2 mm by 2 mm. Galls develop on the midrib and lateral veins. Larvae leave the galls by mid-August to overwinter until spring. Old galls are often used by aphids.

BEAD-GALL MIDGE *Harmandia* sp. C Pl. 54

This gall midge induces bead galls on aspen leaves that are slightly different from those of the preceding, *Harmandia* sp. B. The surface of these galls looks glabrous; when viewed under a hand lens, the surface shows a few scraggly, long hairs. Also, the surface has micro-depressions and lateral bumps, unlike the smooth apple-like surface of sp. B. These galls protrude on either side of leaves and show a hairy slit on the ventral side. The top of the galls lacks the clear openings of sp. A, and the larvae instead leave through the slit on the bottom of the galls. Galls are round and measure 3 mm high by 2 mm in diameter. Like sp. B, these midge larvae emerge by mid-August in Washington, where they were first found.

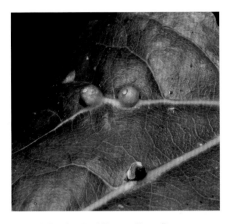

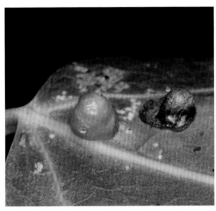

Plate 53. Bead galls of *Harmandia* sp. B on aspen.   Plate 54. Bead galls of *Harmandia* sp. C on aspen.

PETIOLE-GALL MIDGE   Unknown   Pls. 55 & 56

This unknown gall midge induces one to several galls along the length of aspen petioles in early summer. Galls of this species occur only on the petiole at the base of the leaf or scattered along the length of the petiole. Mature galls develop open lips that allow escape of the larvae, but also the entrance of guests or pests like aphids. These galls bear a similarity in basic appearance to the preceding species' gall. Galls are monothalamous and can be 2–5 mm long and laterally compressed. Immature galls can be recognized by this abnormal flattening of the petiole and an apical bump that eventually becomes the lip or exit hole. By mid-August in Washington where these galls were first discovered, most gall-inducers have emerged, dropped to the soil to remain in diapause until the following spring.

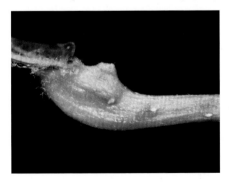

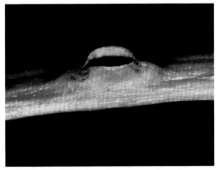

Plate 55. Gall of new species of petiole-gall midge,   Plate 56. Close up of liplike exit of petiole-gall,
Unknown, on aspen.   **Unknown**.

Red Cedar Galls

CONE-GALL MIDGE *Cupressatia thujae* PI. 57

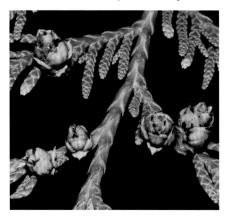

Plate 57. Galls of *Cupressatia thujae* on western red cedar.

The cone galls of this midge are found on western red cedar (*Thuja plicata*) long after normal cones have dropped and are most prominent in fall. Galls are composed of slightly enlarged cone scales and measure 7 mm high by 5 mm in diameter. Galled cones are usually smaller than normal cones. Larvae initially feed around the periphery at the base of cone scales, and numerous larvae are found around the outer edges. In fall, galls are beige-green, often with black tips on each cone bract. Adults emerge in spring and lay eggs. Larvae feed through summer and spin cocoons in the cones in early fall. While this species has been found in British Columbia, Washington, and Oregon, it could extend into Alaska as well.

Cypress Galls

Three known stem galls on cypresses are swellings induced by rust fungi (see Table 6). Three bud galls induced by gall midges also occur on cypresses in the West. One causes noticeable swelling of branchlet tips, while the second induces small branch-tip galls. A third species induces large, swollen, four-sided bud galls. The cypress species considered here include: pygmy cypress (*Hesperocyparis pygmaea*), Sargent cypress (*H. sargentii*), Monterey cypress (*H. macrocarpa*), and Nootka cypress (*Callitropsis nootkatensis*).

GALL MIDGE *Walshomyia cupressi*   PI. 58

Plate 58. Bud galls of *Walshomyia cupressi* on cypress.

This gall midge induces large, monothalamous, four-sided galls in summer on at least two cypress species. These galls form at the tips of branches of pygmy cypress within the stunted, bonsai-like forests in Mendocino County, California, and the lofty Sargent cypress of Sonoma County. They appear as massive replicas of the terminal buds and often occur in clusters of three or four individual galls. Galls are 30 mm long by 10 mm wide. Each gall starts out as a swollen, beige, globular bud. But as development proceeds, the overlapping scales separate from each other near their tips. At this stage, the four-sided pattern is seen when you look down the axis of the galls. Galls at different stages of development can be found from spring through fall. Abandoned old galls do not remain on the host plant for long. Adult gall midges emerge through the side near the top after nearly two years in the larval stage within the galls. Adults live for only a few days in spring while they reproduce and lay eggs. Vigorously growing cypress trees seem to host more galls than stunted specimens nearby.

TIP-GALL MIDGE   *Chamaediplosis nootkatensis*   Fig. 23 & Pl. 59

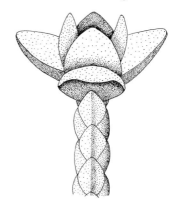

This gall midge induces slight swelling of the branchlet tips of Nootka cypress and pygmy cypress and possibly other cypress species. These monothalamous galls develop in spring and are light beige-yellow when fresh. Galls measure 3 mm high and wide and consist of swollen and distended leaf scales. The swollen scales flare away from the main stem, creating an open rosette or flowerlike pattern. Galls are often found in clustered groupings with several adjoining branch tips affected. Larvae pupate in the galls later in spring and adults emerge soon thereafter. There may be two generations per year, as fresh galls can be found in summer and fall. This gall midge has been recorded in all Pacific states as well as British Columbia.

Above right: Figure 23. Gall of *C. nootkatensis* on Nootka cypress branchlet

Plate 59. Bud galls of *Chamaediplosis nootkatensis* on cypress.

GALL MIDGE   *Chamaediplosis sp.*   Fig. 24 & Pl. 60

This midge induces tiny, barely noticeable bud galls at the branch tips and occasionally along the sides of branches on Monterey cypress and pygmy cypress. Galls measure 1 mm high and wide and are the same diameter as the normal branches below, except the leaf scales forming

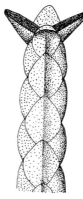

the tip flare out, turn yellow or reddish brown, and reveal a central depression. These galls are detectable because normal terminal buds are rounded, while galled tips appear as tiny cups. Hundreds of these galls can occur on a single small tree. This species is currently known only from California but is likely to be found elsewhere.

Above: Figure 24. Gall of *Chamaediplosis* sp.
Left: Plate 60. Bud galls of *Chamaediplosis* sp. on cypress.

Douglas-Fir Galls

STEM-GALL BACTERIUM *Agrobacterium tumefaciens*   Pl. 61

This is a globular, abruptly swollen gall that can exceed 30 cm across, but most are under 10 cm. Galls appear on twigs, branches, and trunks of young trees. The swellings cause eruption of the normal bark, which can open the tree to secondary invaders including fungi and beetles. Galls tend to appear in crowded stands on moist mountainsides. This bacterium can suppress growth in young plants, resulting in dieback. These galls have been recorded from British Columbia to Utah and Arizona.

Plate 61. Knobby stem gall of *Agrobacterium tumefaciens* on Douglas-fir.

DWARF MISTLETOE *Arceuthobium douglasii*

This mistletoe induces tapered swellings of branches and massive witches' brooms that easily exceed 1 m across, even though the mistletoe itself is rather small and inconspicuous. The brooms are quite noticeable from a distance and, like other brooms, are composed of numerous tightly packed branches. Douglas-fir trees are severely damaged by this mistletoe. Heavily "broomed" trees are weakened, deformed, and often die. This is the only mistletoe found on Douglas-fir. These brooms have been found in Washington, Oregon, California, and Utah, but could be elsewhere. On occasion, this mistletoe occurs on true firs (*Abies* spp.) and spruces (*Picea* spp.) growing in close association with infected Douglas-firs.

See Plate 66 for a similar broom.

DOUGLAS-FIR-NEEDLE MIDGE *Contarinia pseudotsugae*   Pl. 62 & Figs. 25 & 26

This gall midge induces distinctive galls, usually at the base of needles on Douglas-firs. On the dorsal surfaces, galls appear as smooth, yellowish, succulent swellings, while on the underside the needle tissues swell around the larva with ridges of tissue growth. These galls are only slightly swollen. Galls measure 5–10 mm long by 3 mm wide. While two other gall midges occur in Douglas-fir needles, this species is by far the most abundant. It has been recorded from California to British Columbia, Idaho, and Montana, but may occur elsewhere in the full range of its host. This midge produces one generation annually, emerging from the soil in May to lay its eggs on the new needles. The yellowish larvae feed on the needles, inducing swelling to occur around the larvae. There may be several larvae per needle, with two or more galls occurring away from the usual location at the base of the needle. Full-grown larvae drop to the ground in late fall and early winter and then pupate in spring. Heavy infestations cause the needles to drop and twigs to die. This is a serious pest of trees grown on farms. The other two gall midges on needles of this host are *C. constricta* and *C. cuniculator*. Both occur from British Columbia to Montana. *C. constricta* has been found in California.

Plate 62. Needle galls of *Contarinia pseudotsugae* on Douglas-fir.

Figures 25 and 26. Comparative view of needle galls of *C. pseudotsugae* (left) and *C. constricta* (right).

Fir Galls

Seven true firs are considered here: white fir (*Abies concolor*), grand fir (A. grandis), noble fir (*A. procera*), red fir (*A. magnifica*), balsam fir (*A. balsamea*), subalpine fir (*A. lasiocarpa*) and Fraser's fir (*A. fraseri*). A number of gall-inducers are known, including rusts, mistletoes, adelgids (*Adelges* spp.), and gall midges. Of the gall midges, most are associated with cone scales or seeds and are difficult, at best, to locate. I have chosen to focus only on a mistletoe, an adelgid, and a gall midge, which produce galls that are common and recognizable by the casual observer.

DWARF MISTLETOE *Arceuthobium abietinum* subsp. *concoloris* Pl. 63

This mistletoe produces tapered-elliptical stem swellings at the point of mistletoe growth on white fir and grand fir. It occurs rarely on sugar pine (*Pinus lambertiana*) and on Brewer spruce (*Picea breweriana*). Galls caused by this mistletoe are typically 16–25 cm long. Older trees may show brooming as well as large cankers caused by a secondary invasion of Cytospora fungus. This mistletoe is common throughout the range of its hosts, from Washington through the Sierra Nevada to the coastal mountains of southern California and along the coast into Mendocino County. A separate subspecies has been found on red fir.

Plate 63. Swollen stem gall and mistletoe of *Arceuthobium abietinum* subsp. *concoloris* on white fir.

BALSAM WOOLLY ADELGID *Adelges piceae* Pl. 64

This adelgid induces stem swellings, usually near the tips of new growing shoots on fir trees. Sometimes several galls occur on a single branch at previous years' terminal nodes. Galls occur on several fir species in the West, and the degree of damage varies greatly from species to species. Introduced from Europe or Asia around the turn of the 20th century, this adelgid has spread throughout North America and is responsible for stunting and killing thousands of fir trees. It has been found in most western states and is a common pest of tree farms in the West. These aphid relatives are about 1 mm long and purplish to black. Only females are known in the United States. Eggs hatch into CRAWLERS that are so small they are easily blown about by the wind. Usually, they crawl around until they find a suitable place to settle and begin feeding.

Those blown away by the wind have a significantly reduced chance of locating a proper host and location for feeding. Once settled, the crawlers insert their long, sucking mouthparts into plant tissue and begin taking juice from the tree's tissues. White, wax ribbons are secreted from the sides and back of these feeding crawlers, ultimately covering them with a white woolly material. Swellings or galls develop from secretions inserted into plant tissues by these feeding adelgids and are often 20 mm or more in diameter and near the tips of branches. While minimal damage usually occurs with noble fir, heavy infestations of this galling organism can kill subalpine fir, even before the galls reach full size. You might first see these galls on fir trees sold in Christmas tree lots, although there is a growing trend to cut off infected tips prior to sale. Several predaceous syrphid fly larvae, as well as introduced lady beetles and aphid flies from Europe, are important biological controls of this adelgid.

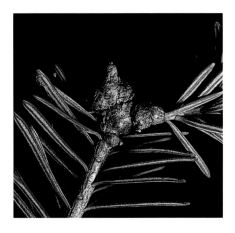

Plate 64. Bud gall of *Adelges piceae* on subalpine fir.

NEEDLE-GALL MIDGE   *Paradiplosis tumifex*   Pl. 65

This midge induces swollen, elliptical, green-beige galls near the base of needles of white fir, balsam fir, and Fraser's fir. There can be more than one gall per needle. While most form near the base of the needles, some appear midway along the needle. Galls measure 6 mm long by 3 mm in diameter. They are usually green through at least midsummer but turn beige in fall. Females lay their eggs in spring when needles are growing. Larvae crawl to spots near the base of needles and begin to feed. With stimulation from the larva, the needle swells around each larva. There is only one larva per gall. Larvae usually leave the galls in late summer or early fall and drop to the ground, where they enter diapause. They pupate in the following spring. Galled

Plate 65. Needle galls of
Paradiplosis tumifex on white fir.

needles usually die and drop off after the larvae leave. This midge may occur elsewhere along the Pacific Coast throughout the range of its hosts.

The life history of this gall midge has an interesting twist. The inquiline cecidomyiid *Dasineura balsamicola* lays its eggs shortly after the gall midge has laid its eggs and before the galls have formed. One or more larvae of *D. balsamicola* hang around a gall midge larva until completely enclosed within the gall. Once within the gall, the inquiline larva feeds on the gall, growing faster than the gall midge larva, which eventually dies as a result of the inquiline. The larvae of the inquiline along with their "borrowed" home needles usually drop later than needles occupied by just the gall midge larvae. Pupation of the inquiline also takes place the following spring.

Hemlock Galls

DWARF MISTLETOE   *Arceuthobium tsugense* subsp. *mertensianae*

This mistletoe induces witches' brooms on mountain hemlock that are similar to those of western hemlock (*Tsuga heterophylla*) dwarf mistletoe (*A. tsugense* subsp. *tsugense*). Mountain hemlock (*T. mertensiana*) dwarf mistletoe occurs in the higher elevations of the Cascade Range, Sierra Nevada, Rocky Mountains, and northern Idaho. At high elevations, where branching can be sparse due to strong winds, numerous compact brooms stand out. Severe witches' broom formation and host mortality are characteristic of this mistletoe. Strangely enough, even though this mistletoe does not appear on western hemlock (*T. heterophylla*), it does grow on noble fir (*A. procera*), subalpine fir (*A. lasiocarpa*), and white bark pine (*Pinus albicaulis*).

See Plate 66 for a similar broom.

DWARF MISTLETOE   *Arceuthobium tsugense* subsp. *tsugense*   PI. 66

This mistletoe initiates massive witches' brooms that often exceed 1 m across on western hemlock (*Tsuga heterophylla*). Sometimes, entire forests of hemlock are infected with this mistletoe, leaving nearly every tree with multiple brooms. Also accompanying the brooms are spindle-shaped swellings and fasciations of the branches, but the brooms are the dominant feature. "Broomed" branches and trunks often split open, allowing invasion of secondary pests and fungi. Heavily-broomed trees suffer limb loss, stunting, deformation, and in young trees, death. While this mistletoe is rarely found on mountain hemlock (*T. mertensiana*), it does occur on noble fir (*A. procera*) and shore pine (*Pinus contorta* subsp. *contorta*, on Orcas Island,

Plate 66. Witches' broom caused by *Arceuthobium tsugense* subsp. *tsugense* on western hemlock.

Washington). I have seen an entire forest of western hemlock severely impacted by this mistletoe in southeast Alaska. This mistletoe occurs from Alaska to northern California.

Incense Cedar Galls

Incense cedar (*Calocedrus decurrens*) is found in the mountainous areas of California and western Oregon. Over 35 species of arthropods are known to be associated with incense cedar, but only four species (plus a rust fungus) are recognized here as gall-inducing agents: four gall midges that may be new to science. These four gall midges are tentatively placed in the genus *Walshomyia*, based on larvae, until further classification studies involving adult comparisons are complete. A mistletoe, *Phoradendron juniperinum*, induces stem swellings on incense cedar, but no brooms.

INCENSE CEDAR RUST *Gymnosporangium libocedri*   Pls. 67 & 68

This is one of the most common rust fungi on conifers in the West. It alternates between incense cedar and shrubs in the rose family, such as service-berry (*Amelanchier* spp.). This fungus is occasionally found on apple (*Malus* spp.), pear (*Pyrus* spp.), quince (*Cydonia oblonga*), and mountain ash (*Sorbus* spp.). On incense cedar, it causes small to moderate-size, erect witches' brooms generally less than 30 cm across. Even young seedlings of incense cedar can develop brooms. The fungus may weaken the host tree or kill branches beyond the broom but rarely kills the tree, unlike some mistletoes. This fungus has an orange, gelatinous, TELIAL STAGE that lasts for a few days in spring immediately following rains in May in northern California. A heavily infected tree can be found practically dripping with blobs of orange, jellylike slime 40–70 mm long. Later, the SPORIDIAL STAGE is blown to a rose family host. There, cup-shaped fruiting bodies produce the AECIOSPORES that infect new incense cedar hosts.

Plate 67. Witches' broom gall caused by *Gymnosporangium libocedri* on incense cedar.

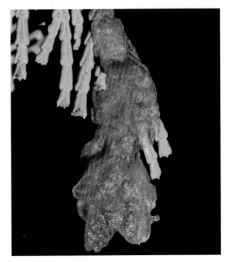

Plate 68. Telial stage of the rust fungus G. *libocedri* after spring rains.

BUD-GALL MIDGE *Walshomyia* sp. A

Pl. 69 & Fig. 27

This midge induces noticeable green, four-sided, terminal-bud galls with flared, leafy bracts on incense cedar. Galls measure 10–15 mm long by 8–10 mm across. Each bract is about 4 mm at the base and 9 mm long. A top-down view reveals the four-sided appearance. Larval chambers are located at the base of each leafy bract. Damage to the host tree is negligible. It is presently known only from northern California.

Plate 69. Bud galls of *Walshomyia* sp. A on incense cedar.

Figure 27. Bract of bud gall *Walshomyia* sp. A.

HEART-GALL MIDGE *Walshomyia* sp. B

Pl. 70

This midge induces heart-shaped bud galls, either singly or in clusters of opposing pairs on each side of new growth of incense cedar. These monothalamous, swollen buds have vertical furrows running parallel to the branches. The tip of each gall bears a pointed bract with a vertical slit that opens at the apex with age, allowing escape of the adults after pupation at the bottom of the chamber. Galls measure 6 mm long by 3 mm wide. Galls are relatively fresh, containing small orange larvae, in February in northern California. Adults have been reared in spring, with most emerging by May. This new species appears to be rather common in the Mount Shasta area and the Siskiyou Mountains of northern California. It may also occur elsewhere.

Plate 70. Galls of *Walshomyia* sp. B on incense cedar.

TIP-GALL MIDGE   *Walshomyia* sp. C.

Pl. 71

Galls of this midge occur at the tips of branches of incense cedar and initially look like normal buds or developing fruiting bodies in spring. The round, monothalamous bud galls with overlapping bud scales are light beige to yellow. Ultimately, galls reach 5 mm in diameter and occur in close proximity to each other, with some branches showing large clusters of dozens of branchtip galls. During early development of the larvae, the larval chambers are vertical, beginning at the base of the galls. Sometime after larvae stop feeding and begin transformation into pupae, the gall chambers lengthen until they reach the apex of the galls, where the bud scales separate, creating an opening to the outside. The chambers remain open, exposing the developing pupae inside to predation from one to several days prior to actual pupation and emergence of adults. Most adults appear to emerge by mid- to late April, leaving the pupal exuviae at the bottom of the chambers. As with the preceding species, this midge was found in northern California.

POINTED-BRACT-GALL MIDGE   *Walshomyia* sp. D

Pl. 72

Galls of this midge are distinct from the three previous species in that they are swollen terminal buds made of pointed bracts with elongated shoots or tips protruding from the main gall body on incense cedar. Galls are polythalamous, bright green, with long, pointed bracts, and measure 15–20 mm long by 7 mm wide. Each bract measures 4 mm wide at the base by 6–7 mm long. Larval chambers are inside a fleshy covering at the base of each bract. Larvae of this species and those of *Walshomyia* spp. A, B, and C are indistinguishable at present. Comparison of adults will be required to clarify whether these are indeed different species within the genus *Walshomyia*.

Plate 72. Two pointed-bract galls of *Walshomyia* sp. D on incense cedar.

Plate 71. Galls of *Walshomyia* sp. C on incense cedar.

Juniper Galls

Several species of shrub and tree junipers (*Juniperus* spp.) occur in the western states, including California juniper (*J. californica*), western juniper (*J. occidentalis*), Utah juniper (*J. osteosperma*), and common juniper (*J. communis*). Researchers in 2014 found 37 species of insects and one mite associated just with the berries of western juniper—a great statement on the biodiversity and importance of a single tree species.

With minor exceptions, there seem to be no host species–specific restrictions among the several gall-inducing agents, which include rust fungi, mistletoe, and gall midges. The juniper mistletoe (*Phoradendron juniperinum*) is common on western juniper and causes noticeable stem swellings. Unfortunately, the gall midges involved with juniper belong to the genus *Walshomyia*, which currently is another gall insect group with taxonomy that needs clarification. Several species of rust fungi attack junipers and are listed in Table 6. Eight midge galls are described here.

TIP-GALL MIDGE   *Oligotrophus betheli*   Pl. 73

This gall midge induces galls on branchlet tips of western juniper. Galls are barely discernible, as there is no overt swelling or obvious abnormality. Normal shoot tips are rounded and generally yellow to beige (left in photo). Galled tips are open and concave, with flared bract scales (right). Galls measure 1–2 mm wide. One monothalamous gall occurs per tip, though several may occur in close proximity. Multiple generations per year can occur, with the last overwintering in the gall and pupating in spring. The galled tip dies and turns brown after the adult emerges. This midge is widespread on several different species of juniper from New Jersey to British Columbia.

BURR-GALL MIDGE   *Oligotrophus juniperi*   Pl. 74

This midge induces rounded galls with an open apex and flaring bracts, spreading in all directions, on the whorled leaves of Utah and California junipers. Galls measure up to 20 mm wide and occur singly or in clusters. The bracts flare out from the sides of the galls without recurving downward, creating a burr-like appearance.

Plate 73. Gall of *Oligotrophus betheli* on juniper branch tip (right) beside normal bud (left).

Plate 74. Burr galls of *Oligotrophus juniperi* on juniper.

URN-GALL MIDGE   *Walshomyia juniperina*   Pl. 75

This midge induces pea-size, urn-shaped galls on buds of California and western junipers. Galls measure 7 mm wide by 10 mm long and have three to four clasping lobes or bracts around the base, each 2–3 mm wide at its base and 2–3 mm long. These monothalamous galls often blend in with the normal cones of juniper. When fresh, the galls are usually greenish-gray to yellow-brown, smooth, glossy, and closed at the apex. With age, they generally develop a silver-gray bloom, and the tips of the galls split open into three to five lobes, which recurve and flare out, allowing escape of the gall midges. Old galls are rusty brown, sometimes with a silver-gray bloom, and wrinkled. Galls found in desert areas are fresh in March and April, while those on high mountain junipers are fresh in May and June.

Plate 75. Urn gall of *Walshomyia juniperina* on California juniper.

In July and August in the central Sierra Nevada galls contain larvae in their last-instar stage. After this period, any open galls rarely have gall midge larvae, hosting instead the larvae of other insects. Hundreds of these galls can be found on a single juniper. As with other members of this genus, there is a single generation per year.

GALL MIDGE   *Walshomyia* sp. A   Pl. 76

This species induces cone-like, monothalamous galls with open, reflexed or recurved bracts on buds of Utah juniper. The apex of the galls is almost always colored with a silver-gray bloom, while the lower bracts are olive green. Galls measure 14 mm high by 17 mm wide; the recurved bracts are 2–3 mm wide at their base. Galls occur singly or in clusters of up to eight. An entire cluster may measure 30–35 mm across. A single generation per year occurs with galls maturing in late fall and winter.

Plate 76. Bud galls of *Walshomyia* sp A on Utah juniper.

CONE-GALL MIDGE   *Walshomyia* sp. B

PI. 77

This midge induces robust, olive-size, cone-like galls on buds of western, Utah, and California junipers. Galls, each measuring up to 20 mm across, often occur in clusters of 3–18. Clustered galls are usually smaller. Galls are broad-based but narrow toward the tips and composed of overlapping scales or bracts that are pressed together. Bracts do not have an open or recurved form but remain closed, except at the tip. When fresh, the galls are olive green and often sticky but turn brown with age. Sometimes they have a silvery bloom.

Plate 77. Bud galls of *Walshomyia* sp. B on Utah juniper.

TUBE-GALL MIDGE   *Walshomyia* sp. C

PI. 78

This midge induces elongate, tubular, monothalamous galls on buds along the sides of scaly leaves of Utah juniper. Galls occur singly and are brown or light yellow with brown tips. These galls have been erroneously identified as deformed fruit. Galls measure 6 mm long by 3 mm wide. Occasional large specimens measure 8 mm high by 4 mm wide. Some have a slightly flared base. At maturity, the galls split open at the apex into three or four lobes with a central exit hole. Those galls that are parasitized do not split open at the apex; the parasite emerges through an exit hole on the side near the top of the gall.

Plate 78. Bud gall of *Walshomyia* sp. C on juniper.

BUD-GALL MIDGE *Walshomyia* sp. D

Pl. 79

Galls of this midge appear on western juniper in spring throughout the Sierra Nevada and Siskiyou Mountains of California. These soft, fleshy, monothalamous galls are normally smaller than nearby blue-gray berries. Galls measure 4–5 mm in diameter and are smooth, glabrous, and fawn- to beige-colored. They often have reflexed lobes or bracts at the basal attachment point. Some galls in late April show either a slight dimple or nipple at the apex. These galls are not elongated with flaring tips as in *W. juniperina*. The walls of the larval chamber are smooth and slightly glossy and are thick, measuring more than 1 mm.

Plate 79. Bud gall of *Walshomyia* sp. D (left) next to a juniper berry (right).

ARTICHOKE-GALL MIDGE *Walshomyia* sp. E

Pl. 80

Galls of this midge on western juniper look like miniature artichokes, with slightly appressed bud scales and closed tips. Galls are green-brown when fresh and measure 5 mm high by 3 mm wide. The bud scales that make up the exterior of the galls do not flare out or recurve. Generally, there is only one gall per shoot, but occasionally two may be found side by side. These monothalamous galls are noticeably larger than the shoots below and are easily distinguished from normal flower buds by their size, color, and sharply pointed bud scales. Normal flower buds have rounded bud scales and are yellow-beige. This species superficially resembles *Chamaediplosis nootkatensis*, which occurs on cypresses. While these galls have been found in northern California, they may also occur on Great Basin region junipers.

Plate 80. Bud gall of *Walshomyia* sp. E (right) on western juniper.

Maple Galls

ERINEUM MITE *Eriophyes calaceris*

Pl. 81

This mite induces pink to purplish-red erineum galls on leaves of mountain maple (*Acer glabrum*) from the Rocky Mountains to the West Coast and north into southeast Alaska. Galls appear on the upper surfaces of leaves, mostly along the edges (although the erinea may cover entire leaves in some cases). Erineum growth consists of brightly colored papillae. Each papilla

Plate 81. Erineum galls of
Eriophyes calaceris on
mountain maple.

is rounded at the tip and filled with a magenta-colored fluid. The rounded papillae can be seen without magnification. Mites feed between the papillae; other erineum galls usually have pointed hairs covering the feeding mites. The underside of leaves may be distorted, but not as severely as with other erineum galls. Sometimes nearly all the leaves of an individual tree may be covered with this noticeable erineum. This mite undergoes an alternation of generations. Mites continue to colonize the erineum galls until early fall, then migrate to bark crevices where they overwinter. In spring they move to developing buds. The eriophyid mite *Aculops glabri* is an inquiline found in the erineum of this gall-inducing mite.

OAK TREE GALLS

There are over 30 species of native oak trees in the western United States, plus many hybrids and varieties that make identification difficult. Additionally, there are a few imported oaks from the East and a few from Europe used in landscaping. Found among the native oaks is a vast assemblage of gall-inducing organisms, some of which have yet to be discovered, reared, and classified. A 2018 estimate listed 1,364 species of known cynipid wasps worldwide. This guide presents 231 gall-inducing species found on oaks of the Pacific States (136) and the Southwest (95); 63 of these species are currently Unknown (Pacific States, 33; Southwest, 30). Some of these are new to science and may remain **UNKNOWN** until adults are reared and described. The 63 species of **UNKNOWN** galls/wasps on oaks are numbered consecutively for reader reference.

Oaks are usually divided into three subgroups: black (also called red in some areas), white, and intermediate oaks (Table 13).

While one eriophyid mite is found on both coast live oak (a black oak) and canyon live and huckleberry oaks (intermediate oaks), cynipid gall wasps do not use oak hosts from more than one subgeneric group. Gall wasps that use black oaks as hosts, for example, are not found on either white or intermediate oaks. In some cases, entire genera (*Heteroecus* spp.) of cynipid wasps are restricted to a specific group of oaks.

In the context of all the native species of trees and shrubs in the West, the oaks by far support more gall-inducing organisms than any other single group of plants. Lewis Weld (1957b) listed

TABLE 13. OAKS (*QUERCUS* SPP.) OF THE PACIFIC STATES AND THE SOUTHWEST DIVIDED INTO SUBGROUPS

PACIFIC STATES BLACK OAKS	SOUTHWEST BLACK OAKS
Black oak (*Quercus kelloggii*)	Emory oak (*Quercus emoryi*)
Coast live oak (*Q. agrifolia*)	Silverleaf oak (*Q. hypoleucoides*)
Interior live oak (*Q. wislizenii*)	

PACIFIC STATES WHITE OAKS	SOUTHWEST WHITE OAKS
Blue oak (*Q. douglasii*)	Arizona white oak (*Q. arizonica*)
Deer oak (*Q. sadleriana*)	Netleaf oak (*Q. reticulata*)
Engelmann oak (*Q. engelmannii*)	Gambel oak (*Q. gambelii*)
Leather oak (*Q. durata*)	Toumey oak (*Q. toumeyi*)
Muller's oak (*Q. cornelius-mulleri*)	Mexican blue oak (*Q. oblongifolia*)
Nuttall's scrub oak (*Q. dumosa*)	Shrub live oak (*Q. turbinella*)
Oregon oak (*Q. garryana*)	Shinnery oak (*Q. havardii*)
Scrub oak (*Q. berberidifolia*)	Gray oak (*Q. grisea*)
Tucker's oak (*Q. john-tuckeri*)	Sandpaper oak (*Q. pungens*)
Valley oak (*Q. lobata*)	

PACIFIC INTERMEDIATE LIVE OAKS	SOUTHWEST INTERMEDIATE LIVE OAKS
Canyon live oak (*Q. chrysolepis*)	Canyon live oak (*Q. chrysolepis*)
Huckleberry oak (*Q. vacciniifolia*)	
Island oak (*Q. tomentella*)	
Palmer's oak (*Q. palmeri*)	

Note: This is a list of the major western oak species, but not all species. Note that *Quercus turbinella* also appears in five isolated pockets in southern California desert areas, though its main range is in the Southwest.

over 111 species of cynipid gall wasps on Pacific States oaks and an additional 114 species on oaks in the Southwest (Weld 1960). In both cases, Weld left nearly as many unnamed. It is noteworthy that nearly a dozen cynipids found on canyon live oak in the Pacific States region also occur on the same host in the Southwest. Also, several gall species originally described in and known only from Mexico occur in southern Arizona.

For the ease of readers, the treatment of gall insects on oaks is divided into two sections: first comes OAK GALLS OF THE PACIFIC STATES (California, Oregon, and Washington), then OAK GALLS OF THE SOUTHWEST (Arizona, New Mexico, Nevada, and Utah). Shrub live oak (*Q. turbinella*) is treated in the Southwest section, even though it is also known to occur in five isolated patches in southern California.

As mentioned earlier, cynipid taxonomy is in a state of flux, with many name changes being proposed by various authors (see cynipid taxonomy in discussion of these wasps in "The Gall-Inducers"). In fact, there are questions about the existence of the genus *Callirhytis* in the West (of which there are several species included here). These species may ultimately be moved into other genera.

WOOLLY OAK GALLS HAIR CHARTS: In this guide, I am introducing a new mechanism for distinguishing woolly-oak-gall species from one another: Hair Charts, for both the Pacific States (see p. 132) and Southwest (see p. 190) species. During the work leading up to this guide, I discovered that woolly galls on oaks possess SIGNATURE HAIRS that appear to be species-specific. When the hairs of any woolly-oak-gall species are gently scraped off, there is either a collection of similar hairs or a mix of simple hairs and signature hairs of a unique design. Some signature hairs are forked, branched, twisted into inseparable groups, coiled, or covered with stellate clusters along the main hair stem.

UNKNOWN SPECIES NUMBERING: Some of the galls in this book were discovered during the years before and after the publication of Russo (2006). Their galls are included here to document their existence and for the future convenience of the user. Because of the volume of UNKNOWN oak gall species covered, I have introduced a numbering system so that each unknown species can be separated from others when referring to them or when names become available.

COMMONNESS: Finally, I am including an assessment on the commonness of each gall-inducing agent for oaks based on the frequency of encounter, as reflected in detailed notes kept for every field trip I've conducted over the past 50 years. Unfortunately, this record suggests that in a few cases, a single tree supports a species that I have not found elsewhere, which, thus, could vanish with the loss of the host tree. I hope this assessment will help the reader better understand the nature and fragility of those species encountered. The definitions of "commonness" are as follows:

WIDESPREAD ABUNDANT: Numerous specimens on many trees throughout range of hosts, sometimes with hundreds or thousands of individuals per tree.

COMMON ABUNDANT: Specimens regularly occur in a variety of locations, but never in high numbers per tree.

LOCALLY COMMON: Numerous specimens occur on many trees in certain areas, but not widespread over the range of the hosts.

COMMON: Specimens occur regularly in low numbers, over the range of the hosts.

UNCOMMON: A few specimens occur occasionally, but never widespread or abundant.

RARE: Fewer than 10 specimens found in only one place or on a single host tree.

Oak Galls of the Pacific States
Black (Red) Oak Galls

The bulk of the galls described here from the Pacific States are typically found on coast live oak (*Quercus agrifolia*) and interior live oak (*Q. wislizenii*). Fewer galls are found on black oak (*Q. kelloggii*) in the field, even though this oak is listed as a potential host for many by Weld (1957b). The bulk of the gall-inducers on the black oak group are cynipid wasps. An unknown gall midge creates leaf-fold galls, while an eriophyid mite develops erineum galls on leaves. The following galls are listed by the plant organ affected.

TRUNK-GALL WASP   *Callirhytis apicalis*   Pls. 82–4
(*Andricus apicalis*)*

Galls of this wasp occur at ground level on the trunk and roots of coast live oak, interior live oak, and black oak. Trunk galls are either bright yellow or brick red and measure 12–18 mm in diameter when fresh. These polythalamous galls are round to ovoid, smooth, glabrous, and spongy. With age, galls turn bark gray-brown and become much less noticeable. During late spring, the soft flesh surrounding the larval chamber consists of lenticular air pockets that radiate outward. Adults have been found in galls from December to April. Normal emergence appears to be in late spring, with fresh galls appearing soon thereafter. Uncommon.

Plates 82 and 83. Yellow and red versions of the galls of *Callirhytis apicalis* on coast live oak, each with an old gall above it. Photos by Joyce Gross.

Plate 84. Adult female from gall of *C. apicalis*. Photo by Joyce Gross.

SAUSAGE-FLOWER-GALL WASP   *Callirhytis congregata*   Fig. 28
(Andricus congregata) *

Figure 28. Catkin gall of *Callirhytis congregata* on coast live oak.

This cynipid wasp induces large, elongate, fleshy polythalamous catkin galls, especially on coast live oak. When fresh in early spring, the red and green sausage-shaped galls stand out from normal male catkins. Sometimes, when all the catkins in a group are galled, these galls occur in swollen clusters. Generally, the entire catkin is involved in gall development. Under these conditions, only the anthers protrude from the gall mass. Galls measure 40 mm long by 10 mm in diameter. Young growing galls often release a sweet phloem exudate, which attracts ants and bees. At the peak of the population cycle for this wasp, as many as 90% of the catkins on an individual tree can be galled. Adults have been reared from the galls in November. Locally common.

KERNEL-FLOWER-GALL WASP   *Callirhytis serricornis*   Pl. 85 & Fig. 29
(Andricus serricornis) *

This cynipid wasp induces clusters of hard, tiny, kernel-like, monothalamous galls of the bisexual generation on the male flowers of coast live oak and interior live oak. The individual

Above: Plate 85. Summer–fall unisexual-generation gall of *Callirhytis serricornis*. Photo by Joyce Gross.

Left: Figure 29. Spring bisexual-generation galls of *C. serricornis* on coast live oak.

galls normally occur in grapelike clusters at the upper end of the catkins. The entire mass may measure up to 20 mm in diameter. The individual, chocolate-brown, glossy galls measure only 2–3 mm long. The obtusely pointed galls develop from the pollen sacs at the base of the flowers. Exit holes are conspicuous in spring, as males and females of this generation hatch out to reproduce and deposit eggs for the unisexual summer–fall generation. Females oviposit into the veins on the underside of the leaves. By July, the galls of this agamic generation are quite noticeable. These green and red galls, about 1 mm across, are round, with a cap or collar on top of each rounded base. During the following spring, unisexual females lay their eggs in the unopened buds of staminate flowers, and the cycle begins again. Locally common.

TWO-HORNED-GALL WASP *Dryocosmus dubiosus* Pls. 86 & 87

This cynipid wasp induces glossy, dark brown, club-shaped, monothalamous galls on the catkins and new leaves of coast live oak and interior live oak. These bisexual-generation galls are 2 mm wide by 4–5 mm long. Occasionally, two or more galls coalesce, creating what appears to be one large gall. Generally, however, they appear singly or grouped together on a catkin or along the edges of new leaves. Galls on leaves generally cause indentations and, in some cases, can produce considerable malformation, making the leaves unrecognizable. Adults emerge in late April and live for about seven days. Females oviposit in the midrib and lateral veins on the underside of the leaves. After the eggs hatch, laterally compressed galls, looking like little pouches or purses, develop with a horn or point at each end. Fresh galls of this unisexual generation are green and measure 3 mm long. Dozens of these galls can occur on a single leaf. As they develop on the veins, they appear to reroute nutrients into the galls, depriving the leaf tissues beyond the galls of essential elements. This process results in the edges of the leaves turning brown. By September, when this wasp is at its peak population, entire trees can appear as if they are burned or dying. Galls of the unisexual generation can be found on leaves well into fall and, often, through winter. Larvae overwinter in diapause and pupate the following spring when flower buds are developing. See "Environmental Factors" in the Introduction regarding this species and the California Oak Worm (*Phryganidia californica*). Common abundant.

Plate 86. Single unisexual-generation gall of *Dryocosmus dubiosus* on ventral vein of coast live oak leaf.

Plate 87. Single bisexual-generation gall of *D. dubiosus* on edge of coast live oak leaf.

Acorn Galls

MOTTLED-ACORN-GALL WASP *Callirhytis carmelensis* Pl. 88
(Andricus carmelensis) *

This cynipid wasp induces glossy, mottled galls at the base of acorns of coast live and interior live oaks. I have not found them on California black oaks, even though they are recorded as occurring on this species. Galls measure 6 mm high by 4 mm wide. They are maroon or green with light-colored mottling, and each has a small nipple at the apex. These detachable galls are monothalamous, laterally compressed, and usually protrude from one side of the affected acorn, which is often severely stunted. The larval chamber has a white nutritive layer and is 2 mm across. Galls produce honeydew that attracts ants, bees, and yellow jackets. Uncommon.

Plate 88. Acorn gall of *Callirhytis carmelensis* on coast live oak.

ACORN-GALL WASP *Callirhytis eldoradensis* Pls. 89 & 90
(Andricus eldoradensis) *

Galls induced by this wasp in the acorns of coast live oak can easily escape the untrained eye. Unlike galls of other cynipid wasps, which can be brightly colored or greatly deform plant tissue, these monothalamous galls look like normal acorns except that they may reveal exit holes and can stay on the branches long after non-galled acorns have dropped to the ground. This species is unusual in that the bisexual adults emerge in September and October from acorns formed in spring and summer. The unisexual generation adults emerge in spring from spherical bud galls, 4 mm in diameter, with white-haired basal bud scales. Since these wasps are cynipids whose larvae occupy a specific chamber with nutritive walls, as with all other cynipid

Plates 89 and 90. Acorns of coast live oak galled by *Callirhytis eldoradensis*, whole and cut in half. Photos by Joyce Gross.

gall-inducers, they are included here, even though the galls are not obvious distortions of tissue, to broaden the reader's awareness of the complexity and diversity of galls and gall organisms, especially on oaks. Locally common.

ACORN-CUP-GALL WASP   Unknown #1   Fig. 30 & Pl. 91

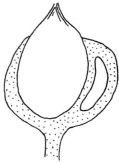

This cynipid wasp induces galls that cause acorn cups on black oak to bulge out into distinct, rounded segments, each a monothalamous gall. Galled acorns stand out readily from non-galled acorns. Galled segments of the cup usually measure 5 mm wide by 10 mm high. The larval chamber is 4 mm long and either centered in the gall or set toward the base. Oaks examined in mid-July in Mount Shasta, California, were thoroughly affected by this gall insect, yet it has not been seen elsewhere. Uncommon.

Above right: Figure 30. Cross section of acorn-cup gall with larval chamber **Unknown #1**.

Plate 91. Gall of acorn-cup-gall wasp, **Unknown #1**, on black oak.

Stem Galls

WITCHES'-BROOM FUNGUS   *Sphaerotheca lanestris*   Pl. 92

This fungus is a powdery mildew that initiates white witches' brooms on new shoots, which are commonly produced only in spring and early summer. The fungus is inactive in winter, so any new shoots produced then are not infected. This mildew fungus infects several species of oaks, including coast and interior live oaks, canyon live oak, valley oak, and tanoak (*Notholithocarpus densiflorus*, not a true oak), and is especially common in coastal areas. Infection starts with buds but usually results in a proliferation of shoots with dwarfed, whitish leaves and stems. These noticeable brooms can severely restrict spring growth in heavily infected trees. Infected trees often produce new shoots below the brooms, but these can also become infected. Brooms

Plate 92. Witches' broom of *Sphaerotheca lanestris* on coast live oak.

normally measure 20 cm or more across. In southern areas, spores survive winter on the surfaces of leaves, while in northern areas, spores reside amid buds. Unlike fungi that require wet conditions, this fungus can do well even in low humidity and without condensed moisture and can move systemically in young twigs. This mildew can penetrate leaf tissues with its hyphae. Many other mildews are superficial only, feeding on the epidermal cells of leaves and stems and sometimes flowers and fruit. A study of a different powdery mildew, *Erysiphe alphitoides*, in Iran found that trees with the heaviest infections had the lowest numbers of gall-inducing cynipid wasps. Whether this situation is also the case with *S. lanestris* is unknown at this time. Locally common.

RUPTURED-TWIG-GALL WASP   *Callirhytis perdens*   Pl. 93
(Andricus perdens)*

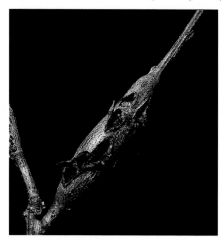

Plate 93. Stem galls of *Callirhytis perdens* on oak.

This cynipid wasp induces polythalamous, tapered, integral stem galls that rupture at maturity, expelling the kernel-like larval chambers, on all three Pacific States black oak species. The galls measure up to 70 mm long by 25 mm in diameter. While the gradually tapered galls are bark-colored, the linear black fissures that develop easily distinguish them from other stem galls. The fissures begin developing as the larvae mature. A dozen or more glossy, laterally flattened, beige larval capsules are forced to the surface and then drop to the ground. This exiting process usually takes place while the stems are still somewhat green and soft, usually after the first fall rains and before the stems harden in fall. Once on the ground, the larval capsules nearly disappear amidst leaf matter and other debris. Even though the diapausing larvae in the chambers are somewhat protected by the shell of the capsules, birds and mice routinely eat the gall capsules and larvae. Sometimes larval capsules are carried off by ants, which also occurs with the two-horned-gall wasp (*Dryocosmus dubiosus*). An interesting advantage to this rupturing process is that the adult gall wasp need only chew its way out through the thin capsule or chamber wall and not the thicker, hard tissue of the entire gall. On the other hand, the gall wasp becomes more vulnerable to predation when exposed to life on the ground. As with other integral stem galls, damage does occur to the branches beyond the galls. Common abundant.

BUD-GALL WASP *Callirhytis quercusagrifoliae* Fig. 31 & Pl. 94
(*Andricus quercusagrifoliae*)*

This cynipid wasp induces bright green, purple, beige, or white, mottled, round, monothalamous bud galls. These minutely pubescent unisexual galls measure 6–9 mm in diameter. Larger specimens seem to occur on coast live oak than on interior live oak. Development begins in early summer. In October and November, the now brown galls drop to the ground, sometimes by the hundreds. Many are taken by squirrels, mice, and wood rats. In February, parthenogenetic females emerge to oviposit in leaf buds. As the leaves unfold, tiny, 2-mm-long, one-celled blister galls develop on leaves, in aborted buds, and on petioles. These galls develop rapidly, and bisexual males and females emerge in April, seven to eight weeks after egg deposition. While the blister galls of the bisexual generation are difficult to see, the round galls of the unisexual (agamic) generation are easier to find. Locally abundant.

Above: Figure 31. Spring bisexual-generation gall of *C. quercusagrifoliae*.

Right: Plate 94. Unisexual-generation bud gall of *Callirhytis quercusagrifoliae*.

APPLE-GALL WASP *Callirhytis quercuspomiformis* Pls. 95–7
(*Amphibolips quercuspomiformis*)*

This cynipid wasp induces two distinct galls belonging to separate generations of this species on coast and interior live oaks. Parthenogenetic females emerge from the previous summer's polythalamous galls from January to March and oviposit in unopened leaf buds. As the leaves unfold, the alternate, bisexual-generation galls begin developing on the underside of leaves. These galls appear singly or in groups of two or three. They are 5–7 mm wide and high. When fresh, they resemble goblets or mushrooms, with light green, yellow, red, and pink tones. With age they turn beige. These monothalamous galls develop rapidly, usually within two weeks after oviposition. Males and females emerge from mid-May to early June. The females oviposit in stem buds, resulting in the development of the summer, unisexual-generation galls, which are large (up to 30 mm across), round, and covered with numerous, short (about 2 mm long), prickly spines or projections. Specimens of these galls on coast live oak are often smoother than those on interior live oak. Fresh galls are succulent and green to red. With age, galls fade to beige, and some develop black sooty molds on the surface. These polythalamous, pulpy galls have central larval chambers. Parthenogenetic females emerge the following spring. Robert Lyon (1959), the researcher who discovered the unique relationship between alternating generations for this species, found evidence that suggested some of the parthenogenetic females laid eggs that produced only sexual females, while others laid eggs that produced only males. Lyon estimated that more than 75% of the bisexual, spring galls were parasitized. Common.

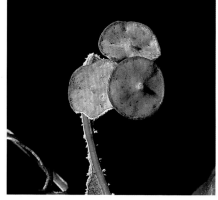

Above left: Plate 95. Unisexual-generation gall of *Callirhytis quercuspomiformis* on coast live oak.

Above right: Plate 96. Three bisexual-generation galls of *C. quercuspomiformis* showing the disc-shaped tops.

Left: Plate 97. Bisexual-generation galls of *C. quercuspomiformis*.

STEM-GALL WASP   *Callirhytis quercussuttoni*   Figs. 32 & 33
(Andricus quercussuttoni) *

This cynipid wasp induces round to globular, potato-shaped, woody stem galls on coast and interior live oaks. These integral polythalamous galls are stem-colored, abrupt swellings that reach up to 100 mm long by 40 mm wide but are usually smaller. Older galls are often riddled with exit holes of the gall wasps, their inquilines, and parasites. These unisexual-generation monothalamous galls begin their development in summer and continue to grow until the following spring. Larval development terminates in late spring, with pupation taking place in fall of the second year. Adults emerge from midwinter through March, nearly two years after the beginning of gall formation. Females of this unisexual generation oviposit in leaf buds. As the leaves unfold in spring, small, 3-mm-long, green blisters develop on the petioles and leaf veins.

From these monothalamous bisexual-generation galls emerge males and females. Mated females normally oviposit in green twigs 3–5 mm in diameter of the previous year's growth. In summer, the integral stem galls of the unisexual generation begin development. Development of the unisexual-generation galls usually causes the death of branches beyond the galls. In an oak woodland with many natural controls (predators and parasites), this gall wasp rarely causes any serious harm to the overall vigor and health of the host tree. Without natural controls in landscape situations, serious damage can occur. Common abundant.

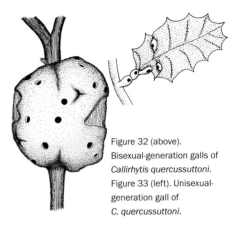

Figure 32 (above). Bisexual-generation galls of *Callirhytis quercussuttoni.*
Figure 33 (left). Unisexual-generation gall of *C. quercussuttoni.*

Leaf Galls

Four common leaf galls occur on members of the black oak group in addition to the bisexual-generation galls mentioned under the gall wasp (*Callirhytis quercuspomiformis*) and gall wasp (*C. quercusagrifoliae*). As a group, the black oaks of the West Coast clearly do not support the diversity of leaf galls found on members of the white oak group or the intermediate oaks.

ERINEUM MITE   *Eriophyes mackiei*   Pl. 98

This erineum mite induces fuzzy, concave depressions on the underside of leaves of all live oaks in the black oak and intermediate oak groups. This crossover from one group of oaks to another is unique among oak gall-inducers. The erineum pockets on the underside of leaves are normally rusty brown but can also be beige, pink, or rosy. These pockets are matched by corresponding convex bumps on dorsal surfaces. Some leaves are so thoroughly infested with this mite that the entire undersurface of the leaves is covered with the expanded hairs, and the upper surface is considerably distorted. Normally, you can find small erineum pockets that are only 1–2 mm in diameter. Mites generally overwinter in the erineum pockets or among bud scales. New leaves are infested in spring and early summer. Expanded hairs of the erineum pockets are merely extensions of normal plant hairs. Common abundant.

Plate 98. Erineum galls of *Eriophyes mackiei* on coast live oak.

PUMPKIN-GALL WASP *Dryocosmus minusculus*

PI. 99 & Fig. 34

This cynipid wasp induces tiny, 1 mm wide, pumpkin-shaped galls on the upper surface of leaves of all species in the black oak group. When fresh in late spring and summer, these monothalamous galls are light yellow with dark red or purple centers. As galls mature and lose their color, they resemble Lilliputian-size pumpkins, with several lines or furrows radiating toward the depressed centers. Most galls drop to the ground in autumn, where they blend in with leaf litter. Birds and mice eat some of these galls as they forage through fallen leaves. Fresh and active galls can be found just about any time of year as you go from one region to another. Adults emerge the following April, and the cycle starts again. Locally abundant.

Above: Plate 99. Gall of *Dryocosmus minusculus* on oak.

Above right: Figure 34. Enlarged version of gall of *D. minusculus*.

PETIOLE-GALL WASP *Melikaiella flora*

Figs. 35 & 36

This cynipid wasp induces large, hard, smooth-surfaced, irregularly shaped galls that usually engulf the entire petiole and sometimes part or all of the midrib of leaves of live oaks in spring. These integral, polythalamous galls of the bisexual generation measure 40 mm long by 10 mm across. Galls show more on the underside of the petioles and leaves than on the upper side, which can be distorted by gall development. When fresh, the petiole galls are green, but they soon turn glossy brown with age. From these galls, males and females emerge in May and June. Impregnated females deposit their eggs in young acorns. In fall, the aborted, galled acorns drop to the ground, where the unisexual generation larvae remain in a pre-pupal stage for about a year and a half. Some of the females of this generation emerge from the galled acorns to oviposit in petioles in February and March. Others delay emergence until the fourth or sixth year, a few coinciding with the maturation of acorns. Squirrels and deer eat many of the galled acorns and their occupants once they are on the ground, while Steller's jays (*Cyanocitta stelleri*) harvest any acorns for planting elsewhere as late winter food. Locally common.

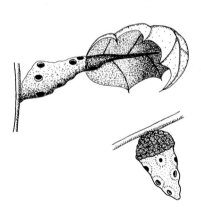

Above: Figure 35. Bisexual-generation petiole gall of *Melikaiella flora*.

Below: Figure 36. Unisexual-generation gall of *M. flora*.

LEAF-BALL-GALL WASP *Callirhytis pervoveata*

Fig. 37

(Andricus pervoveata) *

This cynipid wasp induces round, monothal-amous, integral leaf galls in spring on all species in the black oak group. Galls resemble balls surrounded by leaf tissue that protrude on both sides of the leaf equally. When fresh, the galls are succulent and green, and with age they turn brown and become hard. These smooth, glossy galls are usually about 10 mm in diameter. In cross section, there may be empty cavities next to the central larval chamber. Adult males and females emerge in April and May. Thus far, any alternate unisexual generation that might be expected to follow a spring cycle such as this has not been identified. Locally common.

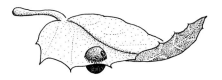

Figure 37. Integral leaf gall of *Callirhytis pervoveata*.

White Oak Galls

White oaks compose the largest group of oaks in the western states, including a number of oaks in the Southwest (covered later). As mentioned previously, the oaks in this complex group support the greatest number of cynipid wasps and the most extravagant galls in color and shape. The principal white oaks from the Pacific States considered here are blue (*Quercus douglasii*), Muller's (*Q. cornelius-mulleri*), valley (*Q. lobata*), scrub (*Q. berberidifolia*), Nuttall's scrub (*Q. dumosa*), leather (*Q. durata*), Engelmann (*Q. engelmannii*), and Oregon (*Q. garryana*) oaks. See Table 13 for a partial breakdown of oak species. The majority of galls on oaks of this group occur on the stems and leaves, including buds. Many more species and/or their alternate generations remain unknown. While a few flower galls and a couple of acorn galls are known, they have been difficult to find.

Stem Galls

IRREGULAR-SPINDLE-GALL WASP *Andricus chrysolepidicola*

Fig. 38 & Pl. 100

This cynipid wasp induces integral, polythalamous, spindle-shaped stem galls on blue, valley, scrub, and leather oaks. Galls of this unisexual generation measure up to 70 mm long by 25 mm in diameter. The abruptly swollen galls are the same color as normal branches. Some-what soft when they form in late spring–early summer, the galls are sometimes knobby and extremely hard by late summer and fall. Galls appear to cause little damage to branches and leaves beyond their location on the stem. Adult females chew their way out of the galls the following April or May and lay their eggs in buds. The bisexual generation galls, as described by Burdick (1967), develop rapidly. These ovoid, 2-mm-long bud galls are covered with fine hairs. Males and females emerge, with females ovipositing into new stem

Figure 38. Bisexual-generation gall of *Andricus chrysolepidicola*.

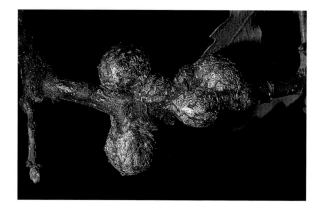

Plate 100. Unisexual-generation galls of *Andricus chrysolepidicola* on blue oak.

growth. It is not uncommon for cynipids to have a short bisexual generation season coupled with a rather long unisexual generation, as in this case. Common.

CLUB-GALL WASP *Andricus coortus* Pl. 101
(Callirhytis coortus)*

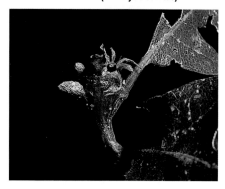

Plate 101. Terminal-bud gall of *Andricus coortus* on Oregon oak.

This cynipid wasp induces integral, polythalamous, round to globular, club-like galls on the tips of new stems of Oregon, blue, and scrub oaks. These galls form in spring and measure 13 mm high by 8 mm wide. Galls often have other normal and viable buds, and sometimes stunted leaves, protruding from their sides. During the season after initial gall formation, buds that had protruded from galls can elongate and become new stems. Two or three generations of galls may occur on the same branch. New galls are stem green with some red tones where they are exposed to direct sun. Unisexual adults emerge the following spring. Locally common.

CALIFORNIA GALL WASP *Andricus quercuscalifornicus* Pls. 102–5

This cynipid wasp induces the largest of the insect galls in the western states. Like many cynipids, this species is known only from parthenogenetic females. Neither males nor an alternate generation have been found. The honey- or golden-brown females are among the largest of cynipid wasps, measuring 5 mm long. While some females emerge from August to November, others may not pupate and emerge for a year or more after gall formation. Within the range of this species in the West, there seems to be some plasticity in the timing of emergence, oviposition, and new gall growth. Females deposit a dozen or more eggs per site in late fall directly into stem tissue, yet the galls do not begin development until the following spring. Generally, between March and May, stems rupture, revealing rapidly growing galls. Sometimes a second

Plate 102. Early spring galls of *Andricus quercuscalifornicus*.

Plate 103. Summer form of galls of *A. quercuscalifornicus*.

Plate 104. Cross section of gall of *A. quercuscalifornicus* showing an adult female prior to emergence.

Plate 105. Adult female of *A. quercuscalifornicus* on gall.

brood of galls begins development in July, although the eggs were laid at the same time as those of the spring galls. The reason for the delay and the development of two separate broods is not clear. Strangely, females from both broods appear to emerge at the same time, even though one group had a head start. These polythalamous galls can measure 120 mm long by 80 mm across. Larvae are clustered centrally in separate chambers, each surrounded by a thick layer of pulpy tissue.

New galls are succulent, green or red, smooth, and glossy. By late summer, these lightweight, solid galls turn creamy white and occasionally have a few short knobs or wart-like protruberances. By fall, galls are beige. As the galls age, they are often covered with black sooty mold. Galls may stay on the host trees for three or more years. Galls occur singly or in clustered groups of a dozen or more. The general shape looks much like a potato, but under clustered conditions, the galls assume a pear shape.

Old galls yield a variety of chalcid, braconid, and ichneumon wasps, as well as several other inquilines, parasites, and hyperparasites, over a three- to four-year period. Sapsuckers (*Sphyrapicus* spp.) may dig into the galls searching for larvae, leaving behind large holes. Southern California native peoples made an eyewash from the galls. These wasps and their galls are common from southern Washington and Oregon through California into northern Mexico. This species occurs on nearly every species of white oak in the Pacific States listed in Table 13. Widespread abundant.

ROUND-HONEYDEW-GALL WASP   *Disholcaspis canescens*   Pl. 106

Plate 106. Honeydew-exuding galls of *Disholcaspis canescens* with ants.

This cynipid wasp induces densely hairy, monothalamous, detachable, round, silvery, slightly mottled bud galls on blue and scrub oaks. The silvery-gray bloom that covers the galls rubs off easily. The globular galls measure about 20 mm in diameter. Scattered tubercles are found on the surfaces of most galls. Unisexual females emerge in February and March. Fresh, growing galls are often found covered with ants, as these galls produce droplets of a sweet phloem exudate (honeydew) on the exterior. As mentioned earlier, several studies have shown a significant drop in parasitism rates along with a corresponding increase in gall wasp larval survival. Abandoned galls may remain on host trees for some time after insects have emerged. Common.

WITCHES'-HAT-GALL WASP   *Disholcaspis conalis*   Pl. 107

Plate 107. Galls of *Disholcaspis conalis* on Oregon oak.

This cynipid wasp induces pointed, conical, glabrous, monothalamous stem galls on Oregon oak. These detachable galls develop in summer and occur singly or in groups, separated along the length of a branch. Galls measure 15 mm high by 9 mm wide at the base. Galls have smooth sides, which flare out at the base, wrapping over the stem in an undulating manner. This gall belongs to a unisexual generation. Females are known to emerge in early fall. Neither an alternate generation nor males are known for this species. This wasp has been found in the central Sierra Nevada mountains but is expected to occur elsewhere in the range of its host tree. Galls of this species resemble those of *Disholcaspis* sp. B in the Southwest Oak section. Uncommon.

CORAL-GALL WASP *Disholcaspis corallina*   Pl. 108

This cynipid wasp induces round, monothalamous, orange, yellow, and reddish, detachable stem galls in summer on blue oaks. The key feature of these 10-mm-wide galls is the presence of blunt, club-like, 2-mm-long projections. The surface is minutely hairy. These features create a resemblance to a South Seas coral head. With age, galls lose their colors, turn black with a sooty mold, and harden. They occur singly or in tight clusters of three or four on the stem, at the base of leaf petioles. Unisexual females emerge in fall. This species induces one of the more attractive cynipid galls. Common abundant.

Plate 108. Gall of *Disholcaspis corallina* on blue oak.

FLAT-TOPPED-HONEYDEW-GALL WASP *Disholcaspis eldoradensis*   Pl. 109 & Fig. 39

This cynipid wasp induces round to elliptical, monothalamous, detachable stem galls on valley, scrub, leather, and Oregon oaks in summer. These are the galls of the agamic, or unisexual, generation. Galls are generally elliptical, with a flat or slightly convex top. The sides of the galls are glossy, sometimes wrinkled, and yellowish light brown. Tops of the galls are dull, nonglossy, pitted or fissured, rough, and dark brown. Galls have nippled attachments at the bases that fit into the stems. When they are pulled off, prominent holes in the stems indicate where the galls were attached. Galls usually reach their maximum size of about 8 mm by September. While the larvae are actively feeding and growing, the galls release a sweet

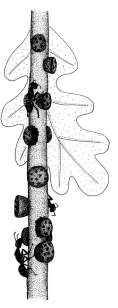

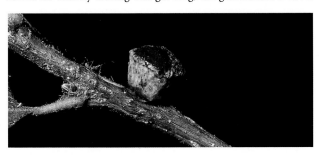

Above: Plate 109. Gall of *D. eldoradensis* showing the honeydew.

Right: Figure 39. Arrangement of galls of *Disholcaspis eldoradensis*, with ants harvesting honeydew.

phloem exudate that attracts large numbers of ants and especially yellow jackets. During late summer, these galls provide honeydew to yellow jackets at a time when other sources are scarce. Galls may remain on the trees for several years, as evidenced by the presence of lichens on many specimens. Gall development occurs in rows, tight clusters, or singly. Adults emerge through holes in the sides of the galls in January and February. Evans (1972) described the bisexual generation as developing inside small, aborted, nondescript bud galls in spring. Common.

BULLET-GALL WASP   *Disholcaspis mamillana*   Pl. 110

This cynipid wasp induces round, monothalamous, finely hairy bud galls on blue and scrub oaks. The light beige galls may have a rose flush near the base. They measure about 10 mm in diameter, with a short (1–3 mm), rounded nipple at the tip. The larval chamber is 3 mm long and connected to adjoining tissue. It does not float freely in a larger cavity, as it does in the galls of the dried-peach-gall wasp (*D. simulata*). Uncommon.

Plate 110. Galls of *Disholcaspis mamillana* on oak.

TWIG-GALL WASP   *Disholcaspis mellifica*   Pls. 111 & 112

This cynipid wasp induces elliptical, flat-topped galls that appear to burst out of cracks in stems of scrub, leather, and Oregon oaks. The monothalamous galls usually appear in rows and often

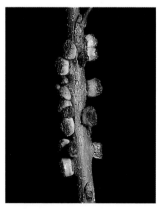

Left: Plate 111. Galls of *Disholcaspis mellifica* on oak.
Above: Plate 112. Galls of *Disholcaspis mellifica* showing drops of honeydew.

on several sides of affected stems. Sides are beige to red, and the tops are pitted, rough, and darker brown or brick red. Galls measure 5 mm long by 2 mm wide and 3 mm high and are laterally flattened when viewed from the top. When developing in summer, these galls exude copious quantities of honeydew, which attracts ants, yellow jackets, and bees. One tree I found near Weed, California, supported hundreds of these galls and the accompanying hordes of yellow jackets and, on separate branches, ants. This gall may be confused with that of the flat-topped honeydew-gall wasp (*D. eldoradensis*). Because the galls appear in summer and fall, with adults emerging the following spring, it suggests there may be an alternate generation. Locally common.

BEAKED-TWIG-GALL WASP *Disholcaspis plumbella* Pls. 113 & 114

This cynipid wasp induces one of the more spectacular stem galls in the West. The galls appear in two color forms: one is greenish overall with round yellow spots or lumps, and the other is deep wine red with bright yellow spots or lumps. These dramatic color patterns separate this species from all other look-alike bud galls, including those of the bullet-gall wasp (*D. mamillana*). Additionally, the often long, curved, pointed beak at the apex is a distinctive feature, although a form of this gall species that occurs on Muller's oak in the Mojave Desert has either a short, beak-like projection or one that is barely noticeable. The round, monothalamous galls of the beaked twig-gall wasp occur on blue, scrub, scrub live, and leather oaks in late spring and early summer. The main body of the gall measures up to 15 mm in diameter. The otherwise solid gall has a central larval chamber. Gall development begins in May, in some areas, and galls reach full growth by August. On scrub oaks, these galls remain for several years, ultimately turning black with sooty mold. Adults emerge in November and December through exit holes in the sides of galls. They are comparatively large, measuring 3–4 mm long. This gall wasp appears to be extremely common throughout the range of its host trees. Common.

Plate 113. Red and yellow form of gall of *Disholcaspis plumbella* on oak.

Plate 114. Green and yellow form of gall of *D. plumbella*.

CLASPING-TWIG-GALL WASP *Disholcaspis prehensa* Pl. 115

This cynipid wasp induces monothalamous, mushroom-shaped stem galls on scrub and leather oaks. The flaring sides of these galls are smooth and glossy, while the tops are rough, pitted, and nonglossy. The broadly clasping bases of the galls wrap around the stem, covering the points of attachment and concealing the stems. The sides rise to a narrow, constricted neck, upon which

Plate 115. Galls of *Disholcaspis prehensa* with honeydew on the surface.

sets the pitted cap. Galls usually measure about 10 mm wide at the base; caps are about 5 mm wide. Altogether, the galls are 7–10 mm high. The sides of the galls facing the sun are often red, while the shaded sides and galls that are completely shaded are yellow, light green, or beige. These galls can occur singly or in tight rows and clusters on opposing sides of stems. Another form of this gall occurs in the Mount Diablo, California, area that is more phallic in shape, with conical, pitted caps, little or no neck constriction, and the usual flaring, clasping base. Galls of this latter form are often taller than the mushroom-shaped versions, ranging from 12 to 14 mm high. Both forms begin development in spring and reach maturity by early summer. Fresh, developing galls exude copious quantities of sweet phloem sap, which attracts ants. When removed from the stems, the galls leave deep pits where they were attached. The elliptical larval chambers are located at the base of the otherwise solid galls. Adults emerge through holes in the sides in late winter and early spring. Smaller inquilinous insects pupate in and emerge from the caps at another time. Common.

DRIED-PEACH-GALL WASP   *Disholcaspis simulata*   Pls. 116 & 117

This cynipid wasp induces monothalamous, round, densely hairy stem galls on scrub, leather, blue, Oregon, and Engelmann oaks. These pointed or nippled galls look like small peaches. Galls often grow next to each other or singly. Galls measure 20 mm long (with nipple) by 17 mm wide. Color varies, with an undertone of green blushed with brick red and darker mottling. Hairs do not rub off easily. Upon completion of larval growth, chambers appear to separate from the slightly larger cavity wall, allowing the chamber to float freely. This unusual feature is uncommon among cynipid wasp galls but does occur occasionally. What significance this separation has for the pupa or the later emerging adult is not known. Larval cells measure 3–4 mm

Above: Plate 116. Galls of *Disholcaspis simulata* on scrub oak.
Right: Plate 117. Adult female *D. simulata* with the gall from which it emerged. Photo by Joyce Gross.

in diameter inside a 5 mm cavity. Adults appear to emerge in winter. Galls of this species can be confused with those of the bullet-gall wasp (*D. mamillana*), except for the latter's absence of a free-floating larval cell. Uncommon.

ROUND-GALL WASP *Disholcaspis washingtonensis* Pl. 118

This cynipid wasp induces detachable, monothalamous, solid stem galls on blue and valley oaks that are sometimes confused with the galls of the fuzzy-gall wasp (*Besbicus conspicuus*). The outer surface of the 8–10-mm-wide gall is usually covered with short, beige to rusty-brown hairs. Longer, whitish hairs may be sparsely interspersed with the short hairs. Inner gall tissue is usually a rich chocolate brown. Single specimens of these galls are usually perfectly round. They possess a short neck at the point of attachment. Galls occur singly or in clusters that can grow squeezed together, forcing the sides to flatten and taper toward the bases. Galls are fully grown by August. With age, galls become pitted and fade to a gray-brown, bark-like color. Adults emerge in late winter and early spring. Locally common.

FUZZY-GALL WASP *Besbicus conspicuus* Pl. 119
(*Cynips conspicuus*)*

This cynipid wasp induces round, fuzzy, detachable, monothalamous stem galls on almost all white oaks in the Pacific States. The 8-mm-wide galls have a mealy-granular texture, usually have small knobs or bumps over the surface, and often have a furrowed neck at the point of attachment. Color ranges from beige to dirty gray. These galls occur singly or in groups. The larval chamber is centrally located in the otherwise solid gall. Adults emerge in November. With age, the brown galls develop a shallow, wrinkled surface texture. Old galls can remain on the trees for a year or so after emergence of the adults. Beetles feed on old gall tissue, often hollowing out the interior to the point where the skin is only a skeletal reminder of the once solid gall. Galls of this wasp are sometimes confused with those of *Disholcaspis washingtonensis*. Locally common.

Plate 118. Galls of *Disholcaspis washingtonensis* on valley oak.

Plate 119. Galls of *Besbicus conspicuus* on valley oak.

THORNY-GALL WASP   *Besbicus heldae*   Pl. 120
                                   (Cynips heldae)*

This cynipid wasp induces hard, spiny, detachable, monothalamous bud galls on Oregon and valley oaks. The spines covering the globular galls are flattened laterally, platelike, and often bent over and twisted rather than erect. Sometimes they appear randomly scattered across the galls' surface. When these unisexual galls are fresh in summer and early fall, they are rose pink, with a mealy-granular surface, and measure 6–16 mm in diameter. Galls turn brown by winter, after the larvae have stopped feeding. Galls occur singly or in clusters. Coalesced clusters can exceed 20 mm across and may remain on the tree for several months. Uncommon.

Plate 120. Fresh bud galls of *Besbicus heldae* on Oregon oak.

Leaf Galls

The most spectacular colors and shapes among oak galls in the West occur on white oak leaves. These leaf galls reflect the ultimate variety in design and color within the gall-inducing insect world. Weld (1957b) listed 47 species of cynipid wasps inducing leaf galls on white oaks in the Pacific States. In the intervening years a few additional species have been described, as well as new species I have found, but certainly many other undiscovered species are out there.

ERINEUM MITE   *Eriophyes trichophila*   Pl. 121

This eriophyid mite induces large, globular erineum galls on the underside of blue oak leaves. The concave depressions are covered with whitish hairs, among which the mites feed. There are corresponding convex bumps on the upper leaf surface. The bumps and corresponding depressions measure up to 15 mm across. These erineum galls are most noticeable during late summer and fall. This mite is also found on Gambel oaks (*Q. gambelii*) in the Southwest. Uncommon.

Plate 121. Erineum galls of *Eriophyes trichophila* on blue oak.

BRISTLE-GALL WASP *Andricus albicomus* Pl. 122

This cynipid wasp induces monothalamous, round, bristly galls, mostly on the underside, and sometimes on the dorsal surface, of Oregon oak leaves. These white-beige galls are covered with short, stellate hairs. Galls occur singly or in scattered groups along the edges of the leaves or near the midrib and measure 4 mm high and wide. By October a small hole is usually apparent at the apex. Unisexual females emerge in April, depositing their eggs in new leaves. This appears to be a northern California species. Uncommon.

Plate 122. Galls of *Andricus albicomus* on Oregon oak.

STRIPED-VOLCANO-GALL WASP *Andricus atrimentus* Pls. 123 & 124

This cynpid wasp induces two unique monothalamous galls on blue oak leaves: one a hollow ball, the other a striped cone. Bisexual generation galls are bulbous and hollow, with a thin, felty and web-like, transparent skin. Inside, a dark blue-black central larval chamber is supported by dark fibers connected to the outer skin. When fresh in early March, these galls are light green to pink, but they ultimately turn beige with age. Galls measure 3–4 mm in diameter. Females of this generation emerge within a two-week period in April and oviposit on the underside of leaves near the margin. Within 90 days after oviposition, galls of the unisexual generation begin development. These volcano-shaped, cream-colored galls with red stripes are flat-bottomed and flared at the base and measure 4 mm high and 4 mm wide. Parthenogenetic females emerge during late October through November and oviposit in leaf buds. After new leaves open in spring, galls of the bisexual generation develop and are well formed by March. Widespread abundant.

Plate 123. Summer unisexual-generation gall of *Andricus atrimentus* on blue oak.

Plate 124. Spring bisexual-generation gall of *A. atrimentus* on blue oak.

PINCHED-LEAF-GALL WASP *Andricus bakkeri*

Pl. 125

Plate 125. Galls of *Andricus bakkeri* on oak.

This cynipid wasp induces beige-pink, monothalamous galls on the underside of leaves of Oregon and scrub oaks. These detachable galls usually occur in large numbers per leaf and appear as though they are pinched inward, like pursed lips. The pinched edges are often dark. Galls measure 3 mm long by 2 mm wide. Galls are scattered across the undersurface of the leaf between veins and sometimes on veins. Larval chambers are located at the base beneath the pinch. Galls appear in early summer months and grow quickly until maturity in August. Pupation occurs in fall, with unisexual adults emerging in February and March. I have found these galls only near Cave Junction, Oregon, although they were described from a site in southern California. Uncommon.

CLUSTERED-GALL WASP *Andricus brunneus*

Pl. 126

Plate 126. Galls of *Andricus brunneus* on oak.

This cynipid wasp induces round, monothalamous, hairy galls on the ventral midrib of leaves of most white oaks along the Pacific Coast. Galls usually occur in clusters, although single specimens can be found. They are dull lavender, pink, or brick red to tan and are covered with short, cream-colored, matted hairs. Galls measure up to 6 mm in diameter. The outer wall of the gall is thick and hard. The larval chamber is centrally located and surrounded by lavender-colored cell tissue. Unisexual females emerge in fall. No alternate generation is known. These easily detached galls cause little or no damage to the leaves. Common.

CONVOLUTED-GALL WASP *Andricus confertus*

Pl. 127

This cynipid wasp induces convoluted, brain-like midrib clusters of detachable, monothalamous galls with fine hairs on the underside of leaves of valley oak. The pink-rose gall mass is composed of individual, triangular galls measuring 3–5 mm in height and clustered on the midrib. The individual galls develop in such close proximity to each other, they look like one large mass measuring up to 14 mm in length. The lines creating the convoluted appearance actually separate each individual gall. There is usually only one gall mass per leaf. Gall development begins in early summer. Unisexual females generally emerge the following spring, but some do not emerge until a year or more after gall development. Common.

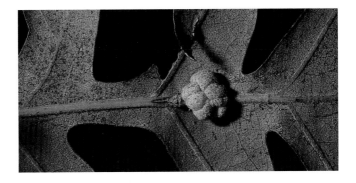

Plate 127. Cluster of galls of *Andricus confertus* on valley oak.

CRYSTALLINE-GALL WASP   *Andricus crystallinus*   Pls. 128–30 & Fig. 40

This cynipid wasp induces caterpillar-like masses of bristly haired galls on the ventral side of leaves of blue, scrub, leather, and Oregon oaks in late spring and early summer. Brittle-haired gall masses are actually composed of small, individual, elliptical-spherical, monothalamous galls arising from separate points of attachment. Individual galls measure 12–14 mm high by nearly 7 mm across (including the hairs). Several galls growing in close proximity can reach 35 mm long by 25 mm wide and completely encompass the entire underside of the affected leaf (see Plate 128).

Each individual gall usually has a slightly curved beak at the apex and a sparse coating of crystalline hairs. While the gall body may be a solid bright red, hairs may be white, rose pink, red, or brown. Hairs are branched and brittle chipping off easily (see Hair Chart, page 132). Beaks often protrude through the hairy mass. These are the galls of the unisexual generation. In late winter, females emerge from galls through exit holes near the tips of the beaks. They reproduce and lay eggs in leaf buds. About 17 to 20 days after oviposition, noticeable green, conical, slightly curved, monothalamous galls with cottony fibers develop on the upper surfaces of leaves. These galls of the bisexual generation superficially resemble individual galls of the

Plate 128. A large number of *Andricus crystallinus* galls on blue oak. Photo by Joyce Gross.

Above: Plate 129. Cluster of unisexual-generation galls of *Andricus crystallinus* on blue oak.
Right: Plate 130. Individual unisexual-generation gall of *A. crystallinus*.
Below: Figure 40. Bisexual-generation galls of *A. crystallinus*.

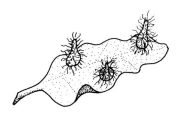

unisexual generation. The fibers are generally 2–3 mm long and project laterally from the galls, which are 3 mm high and 1 mm wide. These are the galls of the bisexual generation. Males and females emerge in March, and the females oviposit into the tissues of the underside of leaves. Little damage seems to occur to the host's leaves, even though summer–fall galls may completely cover leaves. Widespread abundant.

DISC-GALL WASP *Andricus discularis*

Pl. 131

The striking unisexual galls of this wasp have been found on the ventral surface of leaves of Oregon oak in October. These flat, disc-shaped galls measure 4–6 mm across and are dull pink to rose. They occur on veins, with one or more galls per leaf. These monothalamous galls have a central larval chamber. Female adults have been found in galls in November, which suggests they emerge in time to produce a spring bisexual generation, which has yet to be identified. A Southwest version of this gall occurs on shrub live oak (*Q. turbinella*). Uncommon.

Plate 131. Gall of *Andricus discularis* on oak. Photo by Joyce Gross.

YELLOW-WIG-GALL WASP   *Andricus fullawayi*   Pl. 132

This cynipid wasp induces small, oval galls covered with a dense mat of long, straw yellow to fawn-colored hairs in spring and early summer. These monothalamous, detachable, fluffy-haired galls measure 5–8 mm in diameter. Galls occur singly on the ventral midrib of leaves of most white oaks. Long, soft hairs distinguish this gall from all other hairy leaf galls on white oaks. Unisexual females emerge the following spring in March and April. It is not clear whether there is an alternate generation. This species will be included in a future version of the Hair Chart. Common.

Plate 132. Gall of *Andricus fullawayi* on blue oak.

SAUCER-GALL WASP   *Andricus gigas*   Pl. 133 & Fig. 41

Plate 133. Unisexual-generation galls of *Andricus gigas* on oak.

This cynipid wasp induces small, 3–4-mm-wide, slightly concave, monothalamous summer galls on the upper leaf surface of blue, scrub, and Engelmann oaks. The saucerlike unisexual-generation galls are narrowly attached at the base and have thin, flaring edges that are either smooth or toothed (crenate). The larval chamber is a central bump in the otherwise concave gall. The surface of the gall is usually nonglossy. Color varies from shades of pink to red, purple, or brown. Under magnification, the galls are seen to be covered with short, matted hairs. Galls occur singly or in large groups, with as many as 25 to 30 per leaf. Adult females emerge between December and February. By April, bisexual-generation galls develop on the staminate flowers and leaves. These galls are conical, tan, and about 3 mm high.

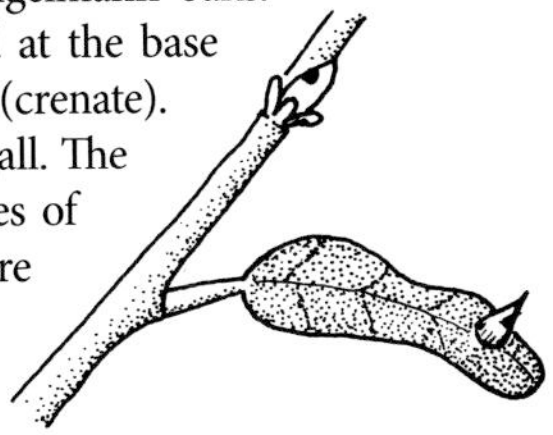

Figure 41. Bisexual-generation gall of *A. gigas.*

Males and females emerge from these galls (also monothalamous) in late spring to start the summer–fall unisexual generation. The unisexual-generation galls may be confused with those of the disc-gall wasp *A. parmula* if not carefully examined. Common abundant.

RED-CONE-GALL WASP *Andricus kingi* Pls. 134 & 135

This cynipid wasp induces one of the more striking galls on white oaks. The red, monothalamous, detachable, cone-shaped galls occur on both sides of the leaves of blue, valley, and Oregon oaks. The cone of these summer, unisexual-generation galls rises from a rounded, flared base that is narrowly attached to the leaf. The apex of the gall, although pointed, is blunt-tipped. Galls measure 5 mm high by 3–5 mm wide at the base. Under magnification, you can see fine hairs covering the entire surface of the galls. The larval chamber is large, occupying most of the base of the gall by early fall, when the galls drop to the ground. Parthenogenetic females emerge through exit holes at the tips of the galls in February. Galls occur singly or by the dozens on each leaf. I have found trees with thousands of these galls attached to nearly all of the leaves. Widespread abundant.

Above: Plate 134. Unisexual-generation galls of *Andricus kingi* on oak.

Right: Plate 135. Single unisexual-generation gall of *A. kingi*.

FIMBRIATE-GALL WASP *Andricus opertus* Pl. 136

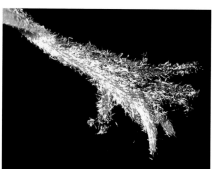

This cynipid wasp induces small, monothalamous galls on the tips of new spring leaves of scrub, leather, blue, and valley oaks. These are the galls of the bisexual generation formerly known as *A. fimbrialis*, corrected by Evans (1972). Galls have a shredded appearance, with long, fiber-like projections emanating from the gall body. In some cases, galls are extensions of the midrib. In

Plate 136. Spring gall of *Andricus opertus* on Oregon oak.

other cases, the galls consume entire buds, completely disrupting leaves. Upon close examination, the veins of the host leaf can be seen as prominent ridges throughout the form of the gall. Galls can be 23 mm long (with its projections) by 6 mm in diameter at the widest point. When fresh, galls are leaf green with reddish hues, but they turn brown with age. Galls usually persist until fall, when they drop with the host's leaves. Adults emerge in late spring. Like so many small spring galls, those of this species can easily be overlooked as just a leaf deformity. The agamic or unisexual summer–fall generation develops in nondescript, aborted bud galls. Uncommon.

DISC-GALL WASP   *Andricus parmula*   Pl. 137

This cynipid wasp induces monothalamous, flat, disc-shaped, glossy, detachable galls on both sides of the leaves of most white oak species. Galls measure up to 3 mm in diameter and have a narrow base of attachment and a smooth edge. The surface is often streaked with red and brown tones against a faint yellow. The upper surface of the otherwise flat gall is marked by a slight knob or umbo over the centrally located larval chamber. Galls occur singly or in small clusters but are not confined to main veins. Unisexual females emerge in April. Common.

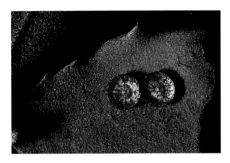

Plate 137. Summer galls of *Andricus parmula* on blue oak.

PLATE-GALL WASP   *Andricus pattersonae*   Pls. 138 & 139

This cynipid wasp induces thin, flat, detachable, monothalamous galls on the underside of leaves of most white oaks. These summer galls of the unisexual generation are usually light greenish yellow and measure 7–9 mm in diameter and 1 mm thick. Galls have smooth or

Above: Plate 138. Bisexual-generation gall of *Andricus pattersonae*.

Left: Plate 139. Unisexual-generation galls of *A. pattersonae* on blue oak.

crenate edges and are narrowly attached under the central larval chamber. The upper surface of the galls is usually smooth, with a central depression marking the larval chamber. Several galls may occur on the same leaf, with the edges of some overlapping others. Gall development is usually well under way by midsummer. Adults emerge the following spring. The 2–3-mm-long spring bisexual-generation galls are pear-shaped, reddish or black with age, and form at leaf margins. Males and females emerge in May. Locally common.

HAIR-STALK-GALL WASP *Andricus pedicellatum* Pl. 140

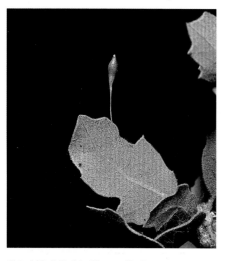

Plate 140. Gall of *Andricus pedicellatum* on oak.

This cynipid wasp induces thin, horse-hair-like, stalked, monothalamous, pointed galls along the margins of leaves on blue, valley, scrub, and Oregon oaks. A pointed bulge at the tip, which is the larval chamber, characterizes this early spring gall. These galls are extensions of leaf veins and measure up to 20 mm high and 2 mm wide at the bulge. The stalk supporting the larval chamber is thin, less than 1 mm in diameter. Spring galls are yellow to orange, glossy, and hairless, but by summer, galls are beige. These smooth galls are fully developed by April, with males and females emerging between April and June. Galls remain on host leaves until fall, even though the occupants have left. This would appear to be the bisexual generation of an as yet undescribed unisexual, summer–fall generation with its own distinct gall. Common.

SUNBURST-GALL WASP *Andricus stellaris* Pl. 141

Plate 141. Galls of *Andricus stellaris* on blue oak.

This cynipid wasp induces convex, round, monothalamous galls with radiating crystalline projections on the underside of leaves of blue and Oregon oaks. These unique galls measure 4 mm across by 2 mm high and are white, pink, and red. The central larval chamber is usually dark red. The crystalline projections are not hemispherical but radiate out laterally. When viewed from the side, the projections emanating from the larval chamber are separate and shorter than those that come from the base. Basal projections sometimes appear club-tipped. Galls occur between the lateral veins, often along the margins of the leaves, either singly or in groups. Females emerge in spring. An alternate generation has not been found. Common.

STELLAR-GALL WASP *Andricus stellulus*   Pl. 142

This cynipid wasp induces stalked, cuplike,
monothalamous galls on leaves of Nuttall's
scrub oak and shrub live oak, but for the latter
host, only in the southwestern Mojave Desert
near Twentynine Palms, California. Galls
occur singly, in pairs, or rarely in clusters of
four or more. Leaf tissue beyond the point
of attachment for these galls usually dies,
turning brown. The most noticeable feature of
the galls is the terminal cups, with four to six
toothlike lateral projections, atop prominent,
hairlike stalks connected to midrib or lateral
veins, mostly on the dorsal surface of leaves.
There is a tiny collar around the stalk at its
point of attachment. The top measures 3 mm
in diameter; the thin stalk is 6–7 mm long.
Stalks are usually brick red to brown, while
the cup may be greenish, yellow, or mottled
with red. Old galls are usually brown. While
some galls are perpendicular to the leaf, most

Plate 142. Fresh gall of *Andricus stellulus* on oak.

appear phototactic and systematically bend upward, toward the sun. The larval chambers take
up most of the space in the cups. There may be some delay with the onset of gall formation
to avoid the extremes of summer, or simply two cycles for this wasp: one pulse of gall growth
in spring and a second in fall, as both old and fresh galls have been seen in November in
the southern Mojave Desert, California. Adults have been recorded emerging in February
and March, with larvae and pupae present later in spring. This wasp appears to be a southern species occurring on scrub oaks in the Mojave Desert and other parts of San Bernardino
County, California. Common.

ROSETTE-GALL WASP *Andricus wiltzae*   Pl. 143

This cynipid wasp induces leafy, terminal,
polythalamous bud galls on valley oak. Large
galls almost always appear on terminal buds
of new stem growth and are recognized by the
massive, compacted collection of distorted
leaves. In spring, galls are the same green
as normal leaves, but later they turn brown.
Galls measure up to 40 mm across. Unisexual females emerge in spring and oviposit in
developing leaf buds at the tips of branches.
This species may have an alternating generation. Uncommon.

Plate 143. Gall of *Andricus wiltzae* on valley oak.

WOOLLY-BEAR-GALL WASP *Sphaeroteras trimaculosum* Pl. 144
*(Atrusca trimaculosa)**

Plate 144. Galls of *Sphaeroteras trimaculosum* on oak. Photo by Joyce Gross.

This cynipid wasp induces round-ovoid, monothalamous, solid, bristly galls on the ventral midrib and lateral veins of valley, scrub, blue, and Oregon oak leaves. These detachable, rusty-brown galls are characterized by the short, stiff, crystalline, erect hairs that uniformly cover the entire surface. Galls measure 3–4 mm across and occur singly or in groups on leaves. When several of these galls develop in close proximity to each other, the mass takes on the appearance of a woolly-bear caterpillar. Only parthenogenetic females are known to emerge from these summer galls. Emergence has been recorded at various times of the year, but most exit during late winter and early spring. Locally common.

LOBED-GALL WASP *Andricus* sp. Pl. 145

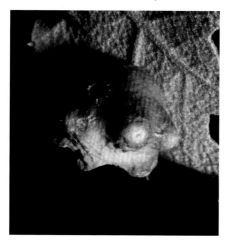

Plate 145. Gall of *Andricus* sp. on oak.

Galls of this wasp tend to be convex to flat-topped, with two to six robust lateral lobes or projections. These monothalamous galls occur in large numbers on the underside of leaves of Muller's oak. Fresh galls are usually smooth, rose-brick red fading to a light yellow at the lobed tips. Several galls may occur on a single leaf. Galls measure 7–10 mm wide and high. This interesting species has prepupae that are capable of staying dormant inside the gall for up to four years after gall formation. The larval chamber is narrowly attached to the inside of the gall wall by short fibers. These fibers break off after the larvae stop feeding, leaving the chamber detached and free-floating. This species seems quite abundant only in the Santa Rosa Mountains area of southern California. It was reported as the udder-gall wasp in Russo (2006, plate 131) but has since been identified as *Andricus* sp. The gall bears a resemblance to Kinsey's (1929) *Cynips dumosae* or *C. schulthessae*, but the taxonomy of these species needs to be reevaluated. Locally common.

SUCCULENT-GALL WASP *Neuroterus fragilis* Pl. 146

This cynipid wasp induces integral, polythalamous swellings of the petioles and midrib of leather, scrub, and blue oak leaves. New galls are succulent and green as early as March but turn

Plate 146. Succulent spring gall of *Neuroterus fragilis* on blue oak.

brown by midsummer. Galls measure 10–30 mm long and are most showy on the upper section of the petioles and the lower side of the midrib. The swellings severely distort both the petiole and midrib, often pinching the base or sides of the leaf together. Males and females emerge from late spring to early summer, implying there may be a unisexual generation in summer. Uncommon.

JUMPING-GALL WASP   *Neuroterus saltatorius*   Pls. 147 & 148

This cynipid wasp induces tiny (1 mm in diameter), round, monothalamous, detachable brown galls on the underside of leaves of valley, blue, scrub, and Oregon oak. Late spring unisexual generation galls occur singly but often in large numbers per leaf. The smooth, glossy, beige-brown galls make their first appearance in May and can be found through September. During early autumn, galls begin dropping to the ground by the thousands. They get their name from the actions of the larvae once the galls have dropped to the ground. The periodic rapid movements of the larvae cause the tiny galls to flip or jump just enough (about 10 mm) to help work the galls deeper into leaf material covering the woodland floor. Galls collected in September were still hopping in early November after being refrigerated to simulate natural conditions. As a result of this action, the galls and larvae may benefit, receiving increased shelter protecting them from extreme temperature changes, predation, and other factors that can cause loss. Nonetheless, an extremely high number of galls are parasitized. Galls that escape their enemies usually have pupae in October and November. Females generally emerge within a 20-day span between March and April. Bisexual-generation galls develop on leaves shortly thereafter. These integral leaf galls measure 2 mm long by 1 mm wide and are green when fresh, turning brown with age. This bisexual generation was previously

Plate 147. Unisexual-generation galls of *Neuroterus saltatorius* on oak.

Plate 148. Bisexual-generation galls of *Neuroterus saltatorius*.

described as a separate species, *N. decipiens*. Rosenthal and Koehler (1971a) found that more than half of the adults of the unisexual generation emerge between 4:45 a.m. and 6:30 a.m., with the remainder exiting throughout the morning. All females seem to leave by 1:30 p.m. None of the adults lived more than 24 hours after emergence. The pteromalid wasp *Guolina psenophaga* is a prime parasite of the summer, unisexual-generation gall larvae of this species. A smaller variety of this species (*N. saltatorius* var. *decrescens*) occurs on white oaks in Arizona. Common abundant.

MIDRIB-GALL WASP   *Neuroterus washingtonensis*   Pl. 149

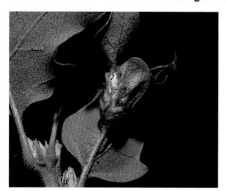

This cynipid wasp induces integral, polythalamous galls on the midrib and lateral leaf veins of Oregon oak. These spring, green, abrupt swellings are most noticeable on the underside of leaves. Galls measure 10–30 mm long by 10–20 mm wide and turn brown by summer. Most males and females have emerged by August. Uncommon.

Plate 149. Gall of *Neuroterus washingtonensis* on oak.

FLAT-TOPPED-GALL WASP   *Neuroterus sp.*   Pl. 150

This gall wasp deposits its eggs in clusters amid spring terminal leaf buds of only Muller's oak. As these bud scales separate into new leaves, the developing galls become clustered together at the tips of branches. Only the toothed edges of the new leaves remain protruding along the front, upper edge of these flat-topped galls. The polythalamous, smooth, fleshy, somewhat succulent galls measure 14 mm in diameter. The bulk of gall development occurs on the underside

Plate 150. Cluster of galls of
Neuroterus sp. on oak.

of leaves. Most galls are rounded, glabrous, and green flushed with red or maroon. Larval chambers are arranged concentrically. This new species was discovered in the southwestern Mojave Desert, California, in early April, with adult males emerging soon thereafter. Presumably, this is a spring bisexual generation of a known species or a yet-to-be determined unisexual generation. Uncommon to rare.

CRYSTALLINE-TUBE-GALL WASP   *Trichoteras tubifaciens*   Pls. 151 & Fig. 42
                                     *(Andricus tubifaciens)**

This cynipid wasp induces unique, tubular galls with short, crystalline bristles on the underside of leaves of Oregon oak. These midrib, monothalamous galls usually occur in tight clusters of up to 35 individual galls. They rarely occur in small groups of a few galls. Normal clusters measure 20 mm long by 10 mm wide and 10 mm high, but some can cover the entire underside of the leaf. Individual tubes are 8–10 mm tall by 2 mm wide. The bristly hairs are 1 mm long. The

Plate 151. Galls of *Trichoteras*
tubifaciens on oak.

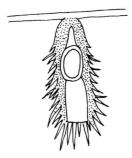

galls vary from a solid cream to yellow with crimson-red bristles, to wine red overall. Each gall has a 1.5-mm-wide opening at the apex that leads to the top of the thin-walled larval chamber. This feature may facilitate escape of the adults. Unisexual females have been found in galls in November, with emergence presumed to occur in winter. Uncommon.

Figure 42. Cross section of gall of *Trichoteras tubifaciens* (after Weld 1957b).

SPINED-TURBAN-GALL WASP   *Antron douglasii*   Pls. 152–4
                                     (Cynips douglasii) *

This cynipid wasp induces monothalamous, detachable, spiny, unisexual-generation galls on the underside of leaves of blue, valley, and scrub oaks. While often flat-topped with a stalk or neck, the galls of this wasp can also be round with short spines or stalkless with spines emerging all over the surface of the gall. The color varies from white with purple-tipped spines to bright pink, rose, or light purple. Some galls have a smoky-gray bloom on the surface that rubs off. Galls can measure 15 mm high by 10 mm wide and are narrowly attached at the base, detaching easily. Larval chambers are located near the top of the galls, with an empty chamber below the larva near the base. The function of this cavity is unknown. Females emerge in January and February to oviposit in the buds of the host tree. In spring, much less conspicuous, bisexual-generation, monothalamous, round bud galls develop. Galls of this generation reach a diameter of 7 mm. Like the galls of the urchin-gall wasp (*A. quercusechinus*), the bisexual bud galls of this species are succulent and green, but with tubercles scattered over the surface. Males and females emerge in May, and females oviposit in new leaves. By late June, unisexual crown galls are well developed. The pteromalid wasp *Quercanus viridigaster* is a parasite of the unisexual-generation larvae. Widespread abundant.

Plate 152. Unisexual-generation galls of *Antron douglasii* on valley oak.

Plate 153. Unisexual-generation galls of *A. douglasii* obscuring oak leaf.

Plate 154. Bisexual-generation gall of *A. douglasii*.

URCHIN-GALL WASP *Antron quercusechinus* Fig. 43 & Pls. 155 & 156
(*Cynips quercusechinus*)*

This cynipid wasp induces one of the most spectacular unisexual-generation galls in the western states on blue and scrub oaks. These brilliant, monothalamous galls are either red-purple or pink with white tips. They usually occur in groups of several individuals on the underside of leaves. The thick, hard spines measure 3–4 mm long and often terminate in a point, but some are club-tipped or bifurcated. Spines radiate outward across the entire surface of the galls. These summer-fall galls are rather hard, measure to 10 mm across, and resemble sea urchins. Galls either drop attached to leaves in late fall or break off with the wind and drop to the ground. Adults are found in galls in November and emerge soon thereafter. These parthenogenetic females oviposit in leaf buds. The monothalamous, bisexual-generation galls that develop as a result are difficult to find, as they are swollen buds that are succulent,

Above right: Figure 43. Bisexual-generation gall of *Antron quercusechinus*.

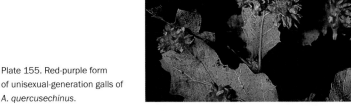

Plate 155. Red-purple form of unisexual-generation galls of *A. quercusechinus*.

thin-walled, hollow, green, and ovoid-globular in shape. From these 6-mm-long bud galls, males and females emerge in late spring. By midsummer, the purple urchin-like galls of the unisexual generation are easily noticed. The pteromalid wasp *Quercanus viridigaster* is a parasite of the unisexual larvae of this species. (The urchin gall was responsible for the beginning of my work in this field). Widespread abundant.

CLUB-GALL WASP   *Xanthoteras clavuloides*   Pl. 157
(*Atrusca clavuloides*)*

Plate 157. Gall of *Xanthoteras clavuloides* on valley oak

This cynipid wasp induces detachable, monothalamous, hairy, club-shaped leaf galls on valley oak. These summer galls normally occur singly on veins of the underside of leaves, stand erect, and measure to 8 mm high by 2 mm in diameter. Sometimes the galls are bent over. The cylindrical galls are characterized by a bulb about three-fourths of the way toward the narrow-pointed tips. The bulge indicates the location of the larval chamber. Most galls have a basal collar at the point of attachment. When fresh and exposed to sun, galls are green with rose or wine-red tones. A single gall disrupts the flow of nutrients enough to starve the outer leaf tissues, resulting in browning and death of sections of the leaves. Females emerge in spring. No alternate generation is currently known. Locally common.

BALL-TIPPED-GALL WASP   *Xanthoteras teres*   Pl. 158
(*Trigonapsis teres*)*

This cynipid wasp induces monothalamous, stalked galls on the underside, near the margins of the leaves of Oregon and leather oak. These short-haired, light green, straw-yellow, or rose-red galls are characterized by a round ball sitting atop a distinctly narrower stalk. With age the galls often turn beige or rusty brown. Galls almost always stand erect. There are several per leaf attached to lateral veins. Galls measure 4 mm in diameter at the bulb by 5 mm high. They are

Plate 158. Galls of *Xanthoteras teres* on Oregon oak.

usually full grown by July. Unisexual females are present in the galls in November. Emergence and oviposition occur sometime later. Locally common.

BROWN-EYE-GALL WASP   *Dryocosmus* sp.   Pl. 159

This species was listed as undescribed in Russo (2006) but since has been identified to genus. Galls are in small clusters on the ventral leaf midrib of a hybrid white oak in spring. Individual chocolate-brown monothalamous galls protrude from the tightly bound mass of white hairs, creating the little brown-eye illusion. The apex of each gall is smooth, round, and glabrous. Clusters of galls measure 6 mm wide, with each gall at 1 mm in diameter. This species has been found only in the Santa Rosa Mountains of the western Mojave Desert above Palm Desert, California. Rare.

Plate 159. Cluster of galls of *Dryocosmus* sp. on oak.

PEAR-GALL WASP   *Besbicus maculosus*   Pl. 160
(*Cynips maculosus*)*

This cynipid wasp induces monothalamous, pear-shaped galls attached to the ventral midrib of leaves of leather and scrub oaks. When fresh, galls are green, sometimes mottled, and with a slightly fuzzy surface. The narrowest point of the gall is attached to the midrib. At full size, galls measure 9 mm high by 6 mm in diameter at their widest point. With age, a thin layer of skin separates from the gall body. Adults emerge in late fall. Fresh galls have been found as late as September, which suggests a long life cycle, different emergence periods, or an alternate generation. Uncommon.

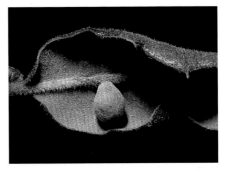

Plate 160. Gall of *Besbicus maculosus* on leather oak.

SPECKLED-GALL WASP *Besbicus mirabilis*
(*Cynips mirabilis*)*

This cynipid wasp induces large, round, hollow, monothalamous oak-apple galls on the midrib on the underside of leaves of Oregon oak. Galls are rarely found on the dorsal surface. Unisexual-generation galls are yellow with red spots when fresh in mid- to late summer, but they eventually turn beige or rusty brown with darker spots. These galls have a velvetlike covering of short, sparse hairs. Galls measure 25–30 mm in diameter and are sometimes called "pop balls" (for the sound they make when stepped on). As with all oak-apple galls, these have a thin skin, a central larval chamber, and radiating fibers that support and connect the larval chamber to the outer skin in the otherwise hollow galls. Galls may occur singly or in groups of up to three. When multiple galls are present on the same leaf, they often compress each other, creating flat sides at the points of contact. Galls are fairly resilient, remaining on the leaves during high winds and even after the leaves have fallen. When developing, the skin of these galls is fairly soft and fleshy, but as the galls mature and the larvae complete their growth, the skin becomes thin and brittle. Parthenogenetic females emerge December through February and lay eggs in leaf buds. Evans (1967) discovered that the larvae from these eggs form the inconspicuous monothalamous bud galls of the bisexual generation. Males and females emerge from April to June. Following mating, females oviposit their eggs into the midrib, completing the cycle. It has been estimated that only about 4% of the larvae of the unisexual-generation galls survive to become adults, as a result of parasitism. The caterpillar of an inquilinous moth, *Melissopus latiferreanus*, feeds on all the tissue inside the galls, including the fibers that support the larval chamber, which likely kills the wasp larvae. Similarly, I have found earwigs (*Forficula auricularia*) feeding on the succulent-fleshy fibers inside fresh galls, after having chewed their way through the outer skin in late August. These wasps and their galls are common from northern California through western Oregon and Washington. Locally common.

Plate 161. Gall of *Besbicus mirabilis* on Oregon oak.

Plate 162. Cross section of gall of *B. mirabilis* showing radial fibers that support the central larval chamber.

GRAY-MIDRIB-GALL WASP   *Besbicus multipunctatus*   Pl. 163
(Cynips multipunctatus) *

This cynipid wasp induces round, hairy, monothalamous galls on the ventral midrib of leaves of blue oak. The light-gray coating is actually composed of scattered clusters of stellate hairs on top of a darker-gray gall surface. Galls measure 8 mm in diameter and are solid and detachable. Galls usually occur singly, but on rare occasions, two are attached to the same midrib. Larval chambers are large, reaching nearly 3 mm in diameter. Adults have been found in December. Locally common.

Plate 163. Gall of *Besbicus multipunctatus* on blue oak.

BANDED-URN-GALL WASP   *Phylloteras cupella*

This cynipid wasp induces urn-shaped, monothalamous galls on the underside of leaves of scrub, leather, blue, and Engelmann oaks. They can occur singly, but in some cases a dozen or more can be found standing erect near the margins of leaves. Locally common. See this species (Plate 325) in the Southwest oaks section for full discussion.

PINK-BOW-TIE-GALL WASP   Unknown #2   Pls. 164 & 165

This cynipid wasp induces detachable, monothalamous galls on the underside of leaves of blue, scrub, and leather oaks. These summer galls develop initially as flat, round discs with a pink center and outer margin and speckled white between. As galls mature, they pinch in from opposing sides, creating the bow tie appearance seen in Plate 165. Galls usually occur on lateral veins and singly or in scattered groups of two or three per leaf.

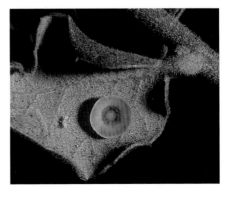

Plate 164. Disc form of gall of pink-bow-tie-gall wasp, **Unknown #2**, on blue oak.

Plate 165. Pinched or bow-tie form of gall of **Unknown #2**.

They measure 4 mm in diameter in the disc phase and 7 mm long in the bow-tie form, when pinched in from the sides, suggesting some growth after the pinching process. These wasps and their galls are common throughout the range of the host trees. Common.

DISC-GALL WASP Unknown #3   Pl. 166

This cynipid wasp induces flat, beige-yellow, monothalamous galls on the underside of leaves of Oregon oak. Galls are distinguished by having randomly occurring, toothlike projections along the outer margins of the galls and occur singly or rarely more than two per leaf. They measure 4 mm wide and are nearly paper-thin. This gall was pictured in Weld's book (1957b, fig. 174). Uncommon to rare.

PINK-CONE-GALL WASP Unknown #4   Pl. 167

This cynipid wasp induces shiny, smooth, pink galls with a dark nipple at the apex on the underside of Muller's oak leaves. These monothalamous galls measure 7 mm high by 5 mm in

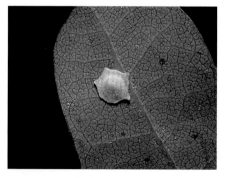

Plate 166. Gall of disc-gall wasp, **Unknown #3**, on Oregon oak.

Plate 167. Gall of pink-cone-gall wasp, **Unknown #4**, on Muller's oak.

diameter and are ovoid-cone-shaped and detachable. Galls usually occur one to two per leaf on lateral veins. While the base of the gall is flat-bottomed, the sides rise in an ovoid shape to a point. This species is found in the Santa Rosa Mountains near Palm Springs, California. Locally common.

MINI-LEAF-GALL WASP   Unknown #5   Pl. 168

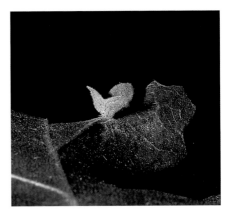

This cynipid wasp induces monothalamous green, leafy extensions of veins on the upper surface of leaves of valley oak in spring. These mini-leaf galls tend to project vertically from the surface, mostly along the margins of leaves, and are either tubular or crown-like. While most galls occur on lateral and marginal veins, some occasionally appear on the midrib. Galls measure 5 mm high by 3–4 mm wide. Individual galls have a dark green upper surface and a lighter lower surface. These spring galls are most likely those of a yet-to-be determined bisexual generation of perhaps a known unisexual gall-maker. Adults have been reared from these galls but have not yet been identified or linked to another generation of a known species. Common.

Plate 168. Gall of mini-leaf-gall wasp, **Unknown #5**, on valley oak.

BASKET-GALL WASP   Unknown #6   Pl. 169

Galls of this wasp occur on the dorsal surface on veins and at the outer margins of leaves of blue oak. Galls are monothalamous, generally rounded, somewhat basket-shaped, and measure 3 mm high and wide. The distinctive feature of these galls is the way the thin sides rise up from the basal larval chamber and turn inward at the apex, terminating in a crenate, or toothed, edge. The sides are either pale yellow with red stripes or deep red, depending on exposure to the sun. The surface is glabrous to slightly mealy-granular. The central bulb over the separate

Plate 169. Galls of basket-gall wasp, **Unknown #6**, on blue oak.

larval chamber creates a space between the larval chamber and the air. Galls appear to be the summer–fall unisexual generation of either a previously known or unknown spring species yet to have its unisexual counterpart identified. Live prepupae have been found two to four years after collection, suggesting disparate emergence periods for adults. This gall has been seen only in the Redding, California, area. Rare.

FLANGE-GALL WASP   Unknown #7   Pl. 170

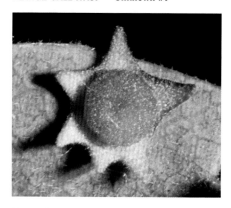

Plate 170. Gall of flange-gall wasp, **Unknown #7**, on blue oak.

This wasp induces a gall with a central, round, ball-like larval chamber surrounded by flanges that flare outwardly in a stellate pattern. This monothalamous gall occurs on the underside of leaves of blue oak. The pale pink to yellow larval chamber (bulb) measures 2 mm in diameter, while the entire gall measures 4–5 mm across from tip to tip. Flanges may have red or maroon along the outer edges. The surface of the gall has a mealy-granular texture composed of extremely short, compact hairs. This summer–fall unisexual-generation gall is quite distinct from that of the disc-gall wasp pictured in Plate 166. While a single specimen of this species was found in Redding, California, it has not been seen since. Rare.

PLATE-GALL WASP   Unknown #8   Pl. 171

The round, convex, platelike, monothalamous leaf galls of this wasp occur on Oregon oak and valley oak. These summer, unisexual-generation galls develop on ventral veins of leaves, with sometimes a dozen or more galls per leaf. Galls of this wasp are distinct from other species in appearance: thick, plump, non-glossy, smooth-edged, and brick red when fresh and beige-brown later with a small, central dark spot. The larval chamber is quite large, taking up most of the gall in cross section. Galls measure 3–4 mm in diameter by 1 mm thick. Galls have been

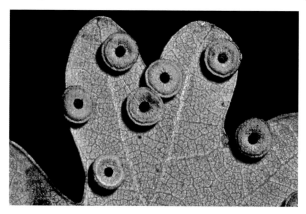

Plate 171. Galls of plate-gall wasp, **Unknown #8**, on oak.

found in several locations and appear to be locally abundant in northern Central Valley, California. Live prepupae have been found inside the galls up to three years after gall formation, with adults emerging sometime later. Galls of this species differ from those of *Andricus gigas* (Plate 133), which are thin and reddish with crenate margins; while the galls of *A. parmula* (Plate 137) are glossy, red-purple, and often striped. Locally common.

ORANGE-CAP-GALL WASP   Unknown #9 PI. 172

Galls of this wasp occur along the margins of the ventral leaf surfaces of Oregon oak. Galls are monothalamous, round, disc-like, and sparsely hairy. The central larval chamber is surrounded by a depression. Galls appear somewhat appressed to the leaf surface. When fresh in August and September, these galls are bright red-orange and measure 3 mm in diameter. Galls occur singly or in small numbers per leaf. The subtle characters of this species' gall as described here distinguish it from the galls of *Andricus gigas* (Plate 133), *A. parmula* (Plate 137), and *A. discalis* (Plate 296) in the Southwest section, as well as the preceding species. This species has been found in only one location, near Whiskeytown Reservoir, west of Redding, California. Rare.

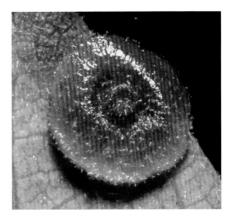

Plate 172. Gall of orange-cap-gall wasp, **Unknown #9**, on Oregon oak.

MELON-GALL WASP   Unknown #10 PI. 173

This wasp induces round, monothalamous bud galls on Muller's oak in the southern Mojave Desert, California. These spring galls are smooth, glabrous, and dark green, often with faint dark stripes, resembling the skin of a watermelon. Occasionally these galls have small, barely noticeable tubercles. Galls measure 7–8 mm in diameter and have a satin sheen. They are narrowly attached at the base and are easily dislodged. Gall walls are 1–2 mm thick, with a large larval chamber, which has a black fungus lining. Galls collected in mid-April yielded adults a few days after collection, suggesting this is the gall of a spring bisexual generation for either a known summer–fall unisexual generation or a yet-to-be determined unisexual counterpart of

Plate 173. Gall of melon-gall wasp, **Unknown #10**, on Muller's oak.

a new species. Unfortunately, males are apparently more difficult to identify, and no generic determination was possible at the time of discovery. These galls have been found only near Twentynine Palms, California, on a single host tree. Rare.

PEACH-GALL WASP   Unknown #11

Pl. 174

Plate 174. Gall of peach-gall wasp, **Unknown #11**, on Muller's oak.

This wasp induces small, round, monothalamous galls on the underside of leaves of Muller's oak. Galls occur singly and are narrowly attached to lateral veins and easily removed. While appearing generally smooth to the naked eye, the surface of the galls is covered with short, pile-like hairs (visible under magnification). Galls are straw yellow and measure 4–6 mm in diameter. These spring galls likely belong to the bisexual generation of either a new species or a known unisexual species whose counterpart has yet to be identified. This species was also discovered in the Twentynine Palms area of California. Rare.

PIP-GALL WASP   Unknown #12

Pl. 175

Plate 175. Gall of pip-gall wasp, **Unknown #12**, on Muller's oak.

Galls of this wasp, referred to by Weld (1957b) as "pip" galls, occur next to developing acorns of Muller's oak, and reportedly on scrub oak, in spring. When fresh, the galls are green. A gall collected in April was already beige and exhibited a single exit hole along the side. These monothalamous galls are covered with a fine, dense coating of hairs and measure 8 mm across by 4 mm high. The flat or concave top is marked by a slightly darker spot at center. Galls easily detach, as shown by the attachment scar to the right of the gall in Plate 175. This species does not appear to be common or abundant, as I have seen it only once in 50 years. It was found on a single Muller's oak in the southern Mojave Desert, California. Rare.

BOWL-GALL WASP   Unknown #13

Pl. 176

This cynipid wasp induces pink, bowl-shaped monothalamous summer galls on the underside of leaves of Oregon oak. Galls occur between lateral veins and measure 4 mm wide by 2–3 mm high. The central larval chamber is located at the base. Adults have been removed from their chambers in late October. Galls from this wasp have been collected in the Calistoga and Sugar

Plate 176. Galls of bowl-gall wasp, **Unknown #13**, on Oregon oak.

Loaf Mountain areas of northern California. These galls bear a slight resemblance to those of *Phylloteras poculum*, an eastern species. No name can be assigned until the adults are examined. Uncommon.

Intermediate Oak Galls

Galls associated with the intermediate group of oaks, including the Pacific States species canyon live oak (*Quercus chrysolepis*), huckleberry oak (*Q. vacciniifolia*), Palmer's oak (*Q. palmeri*), and island oak (*Q. tomentella*), are distinct from those of the white oak and black oak groups. In some cases, specific cynipid genera, such as *Heteroecus*, are limited to these trees. Strangely, several of the galls that occur on the canyon live oaks of the Pacific States also show up on canyon live oaks in the Southwest (Table 14). It is interesting that Palmer's oak supports several cynipid wasps not yet found on other members of the intermediate oak group.

TABLE 14. CYNIPID GALLS OCCURRING ON CANYON LIVE OAK IN TWO REGIONS

Hairy-gall wasp (*Andricus lasius*)

Round-gall wasp (*A. truckeensis*)

Tapered-stem-gall wasp (*Protobalandricus spectabilis*)

Split-twig-gall wasp (*Dryocosmus asymmetricus*)

Golden-gall wasp (*Heteroecus melanoderma*)

Disc-gall wasp (*Paracraspis guadaloupensis*)

Little-oak-apple-gall wasp (*Trichoteras coquilletti*)

Leafy-bud-gall wasp (*T. frondeum*)

Little-urn-gall wasp (*T. rotundula*)

Funnel-gall wasp **Unknown #21**

Note: These cynipid wasp species occur in distinct populations of related oaks in the Southwest and Pacific States regions. These species were originally listed as occurring on canyon live oak (*Q. chrysolepis*) in the Pacific States and on *Q. wilcoxii* in the Southwest; that latter taxon is now considered a junior synonym of *Q. chrysolepis*.

1. *Andricus crystallinus*
Hairs 3.5 mm

2. *Heteroecus melanoderma*
Hairs 3 mm

3. *Heteroecus dasydactyli*
Hairs 5 mm

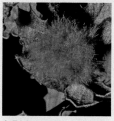

4. *Trichoteras burnetti*
Hairs 4 mm

5. Unknown #14
Hairs 2 mm

6. Unknown #19
Hairs 8–10 mm

1. *Andricus crystallinus* (Plate 129): Hairs branched, arboreal, and brittle, chipping off easily.

2. *Heteroecus melanoderma* (Plate 185): Hairs in tufts or in groups with individuals difficult to separate.

3. *Heteroecus dasydactyli* (Plate 181): Hairs matted, puffy, cotton-like, much thinner than those of *H. melanoderma* and highly intertwined.

4. *Trichoteras burnetti* (Plate 220): Hairs bent and twisted, with tiny knobs at bend joints, in a puffy, cotton-like mass like those of *H. dasydactyli*.

5. Unknown #14 (Plate 177): Hairs short, very sticky, and difficult to separate, with multiple bends and seemingly jointed, held close to galled ovary.

6. Unknown #19 (Plate 206): Hairs long, extremely thin, relatively straight, in soft, cotton-like dense cluster. Difficult to separate due to intertwined mass, like hairs of *H. dasydactyli*.

FLOWER-GALL WASP   Unknown #14   Pl. 177

The monothalamous galls of this wasp occur in clusters on the staminate flowers of huckleberry oak and canyon live oak in late spring and early summer. On huckleberry oak, galls occur in localized situations, where most flowers of oaks in one area are covered with these galls, while nearby shrubs of this species are unaffected. Galls measure 5–10 mm in diameter and are densely hairy with short, bent, sticky, white-green hairs that are difficult to separate (see Hair Chart, opposite). Rearing attempts have thus far failed to yield adults. Locally common.

Plate 177. Galls of flower-gall wasp, **Unknown #14**, on huckleberry oak.

CHERRY-GALL WASP   Unknown #15   Pl. 178

Galls of this wasp generally occur singly or in small numbers on staminate flowers of canyon live oak. These monothalamous, bright pink, round galls are glabrous, smooth, and measure 2–3 mm in diameter. Galls are fleshy and succulent. Flower galls of this species bear a close resemblance to those of *Andricus palustris* (Felt 1965) on black oaks. Uncommon.

Plate 178. Gall of cherry-gall wasp, **Unknown #15**, on canyon live oak.

Acorn Galls

ACORN-GALL WASP   *Andricus chrysobalani*   Pl. 179
                       (Callirhytis chrysobalani) *

The monothalamous, early summer, acorn galls of this wasp occur on canyon live oak. The larval actions of this wasp stop the development of the acorn at a young stage, leaving it lopsided, undersize, and barely protruding beyond the cup. Galled acorns measure 8 mm wide by 6 mm high. Galls turn beige-brown by midsummer and last on the host tree for a year or

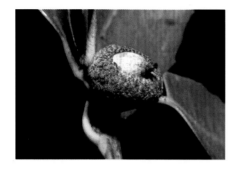

so. Last season's galls collected in late April contained live prepupae. Some adults emerge in late May, while others don't emerge until August. It is unclear what happens next, but emergence so early in May suggests an alternate generation. Common.

Plate 179. Acorn gall of *Andricus chrysobalani* on canyon live oak.

Stem Galls

SPLIT-TWIG-GALL WASP   *Dryocosmus asymmetricus*   Pl. 180

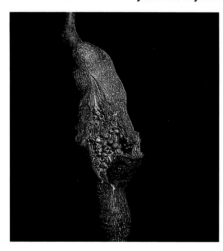

Plate 180. Integral stem gall of *Dryocosmus asymmetricus* showing exposed larval chambers on canyon live oak.

This wasp induces integral, polythalamous stem galls that rupture and split, exposing a nest-like cluster of larval chambers resembling a clutch of brown, elliptical eggs. Larval chambers are bunched together and not separated by a thick mass of cell tissue as with other polythalamous galls. When fresh, galls appear as normal stem swellings and measure 50 mm long by 20 mm in diameter. As galls mature during summer months, outer walls on one side of the galls rupture widely, creating large openings into the galls' interior, exposing the 2-mm-long larval chambers. This process converts the once symmetrical gall into an asymmetrical structure without disrupting the flow of nutrients in the stem. The exposure of the larval chambers at the right time might seem an advantage to the emerging adult wasps, because they only have to chew through thin walls of the larval chambers, not thicker, hardened, woody tissue of the gall proper. It might also be a disadvantage, due to the exposure of the pupae and adults (prior to emergence) to parasites and predators. Adults appear to emerge before fall. As with some others, this species also occurs on canyon live oak in the Southwest. Common.

GOLDEN-WOOLLY-GALL WASP   *Heteroecus dasydactyli*   Pl. 181 & Fig. 44

This wasp induces detachable, globular, monothalamous, woolly, unisexual-generation bud galls on canyon live oaks. These summer galls are covered with a yellow-beige, dense, soft, woolly mass of thin, puffy, cotton-like hairs that are intertwined (see Hair Chart, page 132). The long hairs rub off easily in mats to expose the hard, solid, glossy, spindle-shaped gall beneath.

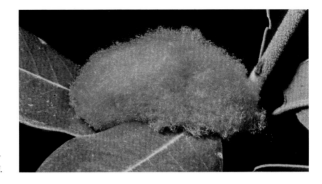

Plate 181. Bud gall of *Heteroecus dasydactyli* on canyon live oak.

Below right: Figure 44. Bisexual-generation gall of *H. dasydactyli*.

Sometimes a heavy rain is enough to dislodge hairs. Galls measures 25 mm long by 10 mm in diameter and can occur singly or in tightly clustered groups. Naked galls bear a ring or collar around the base. The tips of the galls are often slightly recurved, though some are straight. Galls are normally light green to straw yellow but ultimately turn beige with age. There may be scattered tubercles and furrows near the base and apex. Adult females emerge near the base of the galls in spring and deposit eggs in leaf buds. The bisexual-generation galls are monothalamous, integral blister galls that appear in new leaves. Males and females emerge from these galls in late spring to early summer to start the cycle once again. Common abundant.

LEMON-GALL WASP   *Heteroecus fragilis*   Pl. 182

This wasp induces monothalamous, light yellow bud galls at the base of petioles of Palmer's oak in summer and fall. Galls have a slightly roughened exterior texture, and some have a slight nipple at the apex suggesting the shape of a lemon. The central larval chamber is surrounded by soft and spongy tissue. Galls measure 5–8 mm in diameter and usually occur singly. Adults emerge sometime in early spring. This species has been found in several locations in San Luis Obispo and Riverside Counties, California; Mojave County, Arizona; and northern Baja California, Mexico. The gall pictured here was found in the Santa Rosa Mountains near Palm Desert, California. Locally common.

Plate 182. Gall of *Heteroecus fragilis* on Palmer's oak.

LYON'S GALL WASP   *Heteroecus lyoni*   Pl. 183

Plate 183. Galls of *Heteroecus lyoni* on Palmer's oak.

This cynipid wasp induces nearly flat-topped, monothalamous, unisexual, bud galls with flaring sides known only from Palmer's oaks. The top of each gall can be slightly convex or concave. Specimens from Mexico have ribbed sides and depressed tops. This detachable gall measures about 11 mm high and wide. The sides narrow below the flared top, and the base wraps partially around the stem at the attachment point. The larval chamber is central in the otherwise solid gall. Galls collected in fall produced adults in late winter and early spring. No alternate generation is known. This species has been found in select locations on its limited-range host in Riverside, San Benito, and San Luis Obispo Counties of California as well as in northern Mexico. This species was named in honor of Robert J. Lyon, who contributed so much to cynipid taxonomy and biology. Locally common.

BULLET-GALL WASP   *Heteroecus malus*   Pl. 184

This wasp induces round, monothalamous spring galls in grapelike clusters on branches of canyon live oak. Galls are glabrous and relatively smooth, with a slight nipple at the apex, and measure 15 mm in diameter. Color ranges from rose-brown in sun exposure to green in the shade. Galls are solid, with a dense spongy flesh surrounding the central larval chamber. Male and female adults emerge in April, suggesting this is the spring bisexual generation of a summer–fall unisexual generation, which has yet to be identified. Locally common.

Plate 184. Cluster of galls of *Heteroecus malus* on canyon live oak.

GOLDEN-GALL WASP *Heteroecus melanoderma* Pls. 185 & 186

This cynipid wasp induces tubular, detachable, monothalamous, woolly bud galls on canyon live and huckleberry oaks in summer. Short, golden-yellow-beige hairs covering galls occur in tufts or groups and rub off only with persistent effort; these hairs tend to be in tight clusters and are difficult to separate individually (see Hair Chart, page 132). The hardened gall beneath has a mealy-granular, nonglossy appearance. Galls do not have a collar at the base but instead rise straight upward, flaring out to form the club shape typical of this species. Galls measure 20 mm in length by 6 mm in diameter. They have a centrally located larval chamber. Unisexual females emerge in spring through holes in the neck near the base of galls. This species also occurs on canyon live oak in the Southwest. Common.

Above: Plate 185. Summer gall of *Heteroecus melanoderma* on oak.
Right: Plate 186. Gall of *H. melanoderma* with outer hairs rubbed off.

BEAKED-SPINDLE-GALL WASP *Heteroecus pacificus* Pls. 187 & 188

This wasp induces long, spindle-shaped, monothalamous, glabrous stem or bud galls on canyon live and huckleberry oaks. These summer, unisexual-generation galls are often elongate, with a slightly curved beak, and measure 30 mm long by 8 mm in diameter. Shapes of these unisexual-generation galls can be severely altered by inquilines. Lyon (1963) found inquilinous insects normally associated with squat and robust forms of this gall, rather than with the typical tall, slender form. When fresh in July and August, the galls

Plate 187. Normal unisexual-generation gall of *Heteroecus pacificus* on huckleberry oak.

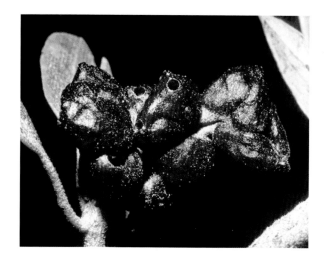

Plate 188. Cluster of spring bisexual-generation galls of *Heteroecus pacificus*.

are normally solid and mottled green and red or various shades of green and purple, pure green, or beige, with a slight waxy bloom. Fresh galls are usually smooth and glossy, while older galls have wrinkled or cracked surfaces. The elliptical larval chamber is centrally located in a solid mass of tissue. Galls occur singly or in tight groups around the nodes of stems or terminal buds.

Parthenogenetic females emerge through holes situated near the base of galls in April and May and oviposit on the underside of new leaves. Resulting bisexual-generation galls are conical, thorn-shaped, red-wine-colored, monothalamous, and often in clusters. These galls measure 6 mm long by 3 mm in diameter and are not easily removed without damaging leaves. Males and females emerge from these galls in June. Lyon discovered that only males emerged out of certain gall clusters, while other clusters released only females. This suggests that individual unisexual-generation females lay eggs that produce either females or males but not both. Oviposition takes place soon thereafter, producing the summer unisexual-generation galls. This species is common throughout the range of host trees. Common.

MUSHROOM-GALL WASP   *Heteroecus sanctaeclarae*   Pl. 189

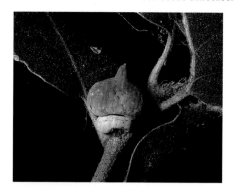

Plate 189. Gall of *Heteroecus sanctaeclarae* on oak.

This wasp induces monothalamous, detachable bud galls that resemble mushrooms or Russian church steeples on canyon live and huckleberry oaks. A round basal section capped with a pyramidal, nippled, detachable top characterizes the two-story gall. The top half of the gall is non-glossy and smooth or faintly tubercled or furrowed near the slightly recurved apex. The larval chamber is located within the lower unit of the gall where it attaches to the upper half. Galls measure 15 mm high and wide. Generally, the two sections of the gall are equal in size, but on occasion the upper segment is much larger.

Adults emerge from the base in April and May. Gall development reaches its peak in July in most areas. No alternate generation is known. Common.

KERNEL-GALL WASP   *Heteroecus sp.*

Pl. 190

Plate 190. Kernel gall of *Heteroecus* sp. on Palmer's oak.

This new wasp induces oval or kernel-shaped, monothalamous bud galls amid clusters of normal terminal buds only on Palmer's oak. Old galls appear slightly wrinkled, smooth, and beige, and usually have exit holes near the base. Three or four galls may appear in a single cluster of buds. Fresh, green galls have been found in January covered with sparse, short beige hairs. Some galls are laterally compressed and have blunt, rounded tips. Galls measure 4–5 mm high by 2–3 mm in diameter. Although superficially similar to the galls of the spindle-gall wasp Unknown #17, these galls are distinguished by the consistent shape and the habit of clustering amid terminal buds, whereas the spindle gall develops from new branches. This species was originally discovered in Short Canyon in Owen's Peak Wilderness along the eastern slopes of the southern Sierra Nevada. I subsequently found it among Palmer's oaks in the Santa Rosa Mountains southwest of Palm Desert, California. Uncommon.

MUFFIN-GALL WASP   *Disholcaspis chrysolepidis*

Pl. 191

Plate 191. Gall of *Disholcaspis chrysolepidis* on canyon live oak.

This cynipid wasp induces hard, detachable, humped, polythalamous galls that burst out of the stems in clustered rows on canyon live oak, huckleberry oak, and Palmer's oak. When viewed from the side or end, these galls bear a close resemblance to muffins, with their overlapping, dark, pitted caps. Fresh specimens have a dark rusty-brown top and light brown sides. Young galls may be greenish-tan on the sides. The convex top has a cracked, bread-crust texture with a linear ridge, while sides are relatively smooth. A single gall can measure 15 mm wide by 20 mm long. Clusters can exceed 60 mm in length. The top of a gall flares down from the cockscomb-like ridge, overhanging the base. Below the cap, the sides taper down toward the point of attachment. Each gall can support one or two larvae in separate chambers. When fresh and developing, these galls secrete a sweet phloem exudate from the base. Parthenogenetic females emerge through the sides in midwinter. No alternate generation has been determined. Common.

POTATO-STEM-GALL WASP   *Disholcaspis sp. A*   Pl. 192

The large, polythalamous, potato-shaped detachable stem galls of this wasp occur on canyon live oak. The exterior texture is smooth and does not crack with age, as does that of *Andricus truckeensis* (Plate 197). When fresh in summer, galls are light green; they turn beige-brown by fall. These unisexual-generation galls measure 37 mm long by 22 mm wide and issue adults in early April. Whether there is an alternate, bisexual generation or not has yet to be determined. A single specimen of this species was found on a lone tree in the Mount Shasta area of northern California. Rare.

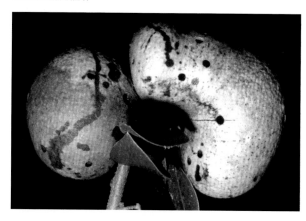

Plate 192. The potato-stem gall of *Disholcaspis* sp. A on canyon live oak.

LENS-GALL WASP   *Disholcaspis sp. B*   Pl. 193

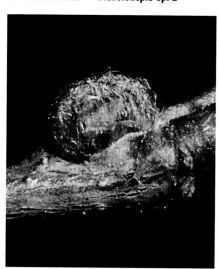

Plate 193. Lens gall of *Disholcaspis* sp. B on huckleberry oak.

This new species of wasp induces lens-shaped, laterally flattened, monothalamous stem galls exclusively on huckleberry oak. Galls occur singly and develop in early summer, with the long axis of the gall parallel with the stem. They measure 4–5 mm long by 2 mm thick. Each gall has a pronounced ridge or crest running along the upper edge. A noticeable swelling below identifies the larval chamber. When fresh, galls are often maroon and have white, sparsely arranged scraggly hairs, but by late summer, hairs fall off and galls become smooth, beige, and hard. Galls collected in late October issued adults the following June. Given the elevation and heavy snow cover of their home range, and the timing of adult emergence, this appears to be a species with one summer–fall unisexual generation per year. It has been found in the central Sierra Nevada near Sierra Buttes and in the Siskiyou Mountains of northern California. Common.

ABRUPT-STEM-GALL WASP　*Neuroterus* sp.

Pl. 194

The integral stem galls of this new species of wasp are polythalamous, abruptly swollen, and symmetrical, and have been found so far only on huckleberry oak. Galls measure 12–15 mm in diameter and are usually noticeably cracked on the outer surface by later summer or early fall. Galls are strikingly different from those of *Dryocosmus asymmetricus* (Plate 180) or *Protobalandricus spectabilis* (Plate 198), both of which occur on canyon live oak, in that these *Neuroterus* sp. galls are consistently abruptly swollen and lack the exposed larval chambers seen in the other species. This new species has been found only in the Siskiyou Mountains of northern California at about 2,134 m elevation. Rare.

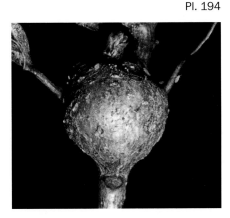

Plate 194. Abrupt-stem gall of *Neuroterus* sp. on huckleberry oak.

TORPEDO-GALL WASP　*Andricus projectus*

Pl. 195

This cynipid wasp induces bullet-shaped, monothalamous bud galls in the axil of leaves or on catkins in late spring on canyon live oak. When fresh, these solid, elliptical galls are either red with a light yellow tip or solid brick red. Galls measure 10 mm long by 4 mm in diameter. Bud scales surround their base. The elongate larval chamber is in the lower half of the gall. The apex of these hard galls is either obtuse or slightly nippled. Adult females emerge in April, either the following spring or as much as three years after gall formation. No alternate generation is known. Uncommon.

Plate 195. Bud galls of *Andricus projectus* on canyon live oak.

KIDNEY-STEM-GALL WASP　*Andricus reniformis*
(*Callirhytis reniformis*)*

Pl. 196

This wasp induces detachable, polythalamous, kidney-shaped summer galls on canyon live, huckleberry, and Palmer's oaks. When fresh, galls are mottled red, yellow, and green, and exude copious quantities of honeydew, attracting ants. With age, they turn tan-beige. These solid galls measure up to 30 mm long

Plate 196. Gall of *Andricus reniformis* on oak.

by 15 mm in diameter. The larval chambers are arranged radially around a central core that runs the length of galls. Parthenogenetic females do not emerge until two or three years after gall formation. Specimens collected in 1973 still contained prepupae in the spring of 1976, with adults emerging a few weeks later. This gall is frequently found in the central Sierra Nevada of California, particularly on huckleberry oaks. Common.

ROUND-GALL WASP   *Andricus truckeensis*   Pl. 197

Plate 197. A cluster of galls of *Andricus truckeensis* on canyon live oak.

This cynipid wasp induces solid, polythalamous, smooth galls on stems of canyon live, huckleberry, and Palmer's oaks. At maturity the tan-colored, slightly glossy galls measure up to 60 mm long by 30 mm in diameter. These round to ovoid galls are characterized by thin skin that cracks and peels along the edges, sometimes exposing the pulpy inner tissue. Normally, no more than a few galls occur on any one branch. Little damage results from the activities of this gall wasp. Parthenogenetic females emerge in January and February in some areas. This wasp is also found galling canyon live oak in the Southwest. Common.

TAPERED-STEM-GALL WASP   *Protobalandricus spectabilis*   Pls. 198 & 199
(*Disholcaspis spectabilis*)*

This cynipid wasp induces integral, abruptly swollen, polythalamous, large stem galls on canyon live oak. The bark-colored swellings measure up to 60 mm long by 30 mm in diameter.

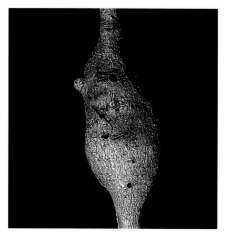

Plate 198. Integral stem gall of *Protobalandricus spectabilis* on canyon live oak.

Plate 199. Gall of *P. spectabilis* with gray squirrel chew marks.

The general texture is much like that of normal bark—rough with faint cracks. Damage to branches and leaves beyond the galls is uncommon. Gall development begins in late spring and reaches full size by midsummer. Western gray squirrels (*Sciurus griseus*) chew into these galls, exposing the larval chambers to get at the nutritious larvae and pupae. Larvae that survive and pupate emerge during the following spring. This species was moved from *Andricus* to *Protobalandricus* by Nicholls et al. (2018c). This wasp also occurs on canyon live oak in the Southwest. Common.

LEAFY-BUD-GALL WASP *Trichoteras frondeum* Pl. 200
(*Andricus frondeum*)*

The cylindrical, monothalamous bud galls of this wasp are covered with thin, narrow bracts and occur only on canyon live oak. Galls develop along axillary buds well back from shoot tips. They measure 10 mm wide by 18 mm high. Those collected in late April were already vacant and brown. Adults have been found in galls in January, suggesting an early spring emergence. This wasp has been found occasionally in several areas of California from Mount Shasta to Idyllwild, as well as in Arizona. Uncommon.

Plate 200. Old gall of *Trichoteras frondeum* on canyon live oak.

OAK-APPLE-GALL WASP *Trichoteras vaccinifoliae* Pl. 201 & Fig. 45
(*Andricus vaccinifoliae*)*

This cynipid wasp induces round, paper-thin, hollow, monothalamous oak-apple galls on the stems of canyon live oaks and huckleberry oaks. These summer galls are characterized by being thin-walled, lightweight, and yellow-green with red mottling or spots. Some galls have noticeable bumps or umbos across the surface. By September they become dry, light brown, paper-thin, and brittle. Galls measure up to 30 mm in diameter. Inside the hollow gall is a centrally suspended larval chamber supported by numerous radiating fibers connecting to the outer wall. Galls usually occur singly or in small groups on older branches, not new spring or summer growth. Under the canopy of leaves they are somewhat protected from direct sun. Fresh specimens examined in August usually

Plate 201. Galls of *Trichoteras vaccinifoliae* on huckleberry oak.

Figure 45. Gall of *Trichoteras vaccinifoliae* with umbos (left), and in cross section (right) showing the larval chamber held by radiating fibers.

contain last-instar larvae. Old, dried galls examined at the same time contained prepupae. Specimens with prepupae were placed in refrigeration to simulate winter and removed the following April. Adults emerged within three weeks at ambient temperatures. Adult emergence in the field is probably timed with snowmelt and warming temperatures. An alternate generation has yet to be identified. Common.

STEM-GALL WASP   *Loxaulus boharti*   Pl. 202

Plate 202. Stem galls of *Loxaulus boharti* on Palmer's oak.

This cynipid wasp, which induces integral, slightly swollen, polythalamous galls, is known to occur only on Palmer's oaks. Galls are barely recognizable until adults emerge and leave pinhead-size exit holes. Larval chambers are arranged just under the surface of bark and measure 2 mm long. Exit holes are about 0.5 mm across, with several per linear 25 mm. Usually there is slight swelling around the exit holes, indicating locations of galled tissue. Unisexual-generation adults emerge in March and April from two-year-old twigs and from lower portions of one-year-old twigs. Adults are small, less than 2 mm in length. Eggs are possibly deposited in buds, where the bisexual generation develops. Adults from these bud galls oviposit in twigs in late spring and early summer. This species is restricted to "island patches" of this host in Contra Costa and Riverside Counties, California, and northern Mexico. Uncommon.

BENT-STEM-GALL WASP   **Unknown #16**   Pl. 203

The polythalamous stem galls of this species occur on new growth near tips of branches of canyon live oak in early summer. Each gall may have one or more protruding leaves. Galls are smooth, glabrous, and often bent or twisted, with a few ridges, and measure 12 mm wide by 20 mm long. Some adults had already emerged from a gall collected in early October in Mount Shasta, California. Areas immediately around emergence holes wither and turn brown, while other areas of the gall, presumably where larvae are still active, remain green. A single specimen of this gall has been seen once on a lone host tree. Rare.

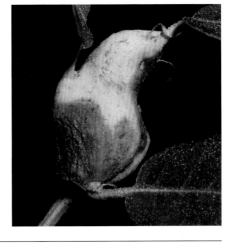

Plate 203. Gall of bent-stem-gall wasp, **Unknown #16**, on canyon live oak.

SPINDLE-GALL WASP   Unknown #17

Pl. 204

This wasp induces single, monothalamous, axillary bud galls on Palmer's oak stems. Galls are smooth or slightly mealy-granular and green when fresh. Later, galls turn beige with subtle white spots. Galls are generally slender and spindle-shaped with a rounded point. Fresh galls have been collected in January usually near branch tips even though older galls may remain on lower branches for some time. Galls measure 6–7 mm long by 2 mm in diameter. A squat form of this gall measures 6 mm long by 4 mm in diameter. When adults emerge is not quite clear although the appearance of fresh galls in January suggests a spring generation. Emergence holes occur at the base of galls. This new species was originally found in Short Canyon in Owen's Peak Wilderness along the eastern side of the southern Sierra Nevada Mountains, California and subsequently found in the northern Santa Rosa Mountains above Palm Desert, California over 483 km away. Uncommon.

Plate 204. Gall of spindle-gall wasp, **Unknown #17**, on Palmer's oak.

SQUASH-NECK-GALL WASP   Unknown #18

Pl. 205

Plate 205. Gall of squash-neck-gall wasp, **Unknown #18**, on Palmer's oak.

Galls of this species are difficult to find, as they are well hidden among branches of only Palmer's oak. They occur singly or in alternate pairs, protruding from branches or the base of petioles. When fresh, these monothalamous, cylindrical or spindle-shaped galls have a sparse granular coating and are slightly mottled green and brown with an obvious long neck at the apex. The pinched tip or neck, which looks like the withered stalk from a squash or pumpkin, is orange to beige. With age, galls turn a uniform beige color. Galls measure 2 mm in diameter and are 4 mm long plus the 1–2-mm-long constricted tip/neck. This species has been seen on Palmer's oaks in two widely separate locations, in the Santa Rosa Mountains and Owen's Peak Wilderness. Uncommon.

COTTON-CANDY-GALL WASP   Unknown #19

Fig. 46 & Pl. 206

The cotton-candy-like galls of this new species of wasp are among the strangest I have seen to date. These monothalamous galls form in the axillary buds of canyon live oak in June. The galls stand out amid the glossy, dark green foliage with their covering of densely packed and intertwined, long, bright pink, extremely thin, cotton-like mass of slightly sticky hairs (see Hair Chart, page 132). Galls measure 10–20 mm across. What makes these galls so interesting to me is that the central round gall

Above left: Figure 46. Cross section of the gall of **Unknown #19** showing fluid-filled capsules.

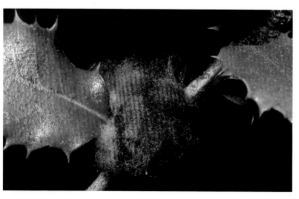

Plate 206. Gall of cotton-candy-gall wasp, **Unknown #19**, on canyon live oak.

body is covered with blunt-tipped, ovoid, thin-skinned, fluid-filled capsules, from which the long, pink, cotton-like hairs arise. These features distinguish this species from all other woolly galls, especially *Heteroecus melanoderma* and *H. dasydactyli*. Galls collected in mid-June in the central Sierra Nevada above Auburn, California, possessed full-grown larvae in the central larval chambers. Adults have yet to be reared. Uncommon.

Leaf Galls

ERINEUM MITE   *Eriophyes mackiei*   PI. 207

This mite has the unique distinction of inducing erineum galls on the underside of leaves
of oaks in both intermediate oaks and black
oaks (see Plate 98). The erineum pockets
created on huckleberry and canyon live oaks
are often very deep, with corresponding large
bumps on the dorsal surface that are more
pronounced than with the other oaks. The
erineum hairs may be white, pink, rose red, or
rusty brown. The pockets are often 2–4 mm
across on huckleberry oak but can be larger
on canyon live oak. Common abundant.

Plate 207. Erineum galls of *Eriophyes mackiei* on
huckleberry oak.

FOLD-GALL MIDGE   *"Dasineura" silvestrii*   Pls. 208 & 209

This midge induces polythalamous folded, thickened lobes or pouch galls along the edges of leaves of canyon live and huckleberry oaks. It has also been reported on Oregon oak, but I have yet to find it. These galls look more like purses or pouches than a simple fold. Galls show more prominently on the lower surface of leaves because as they develop, the galls are folded down

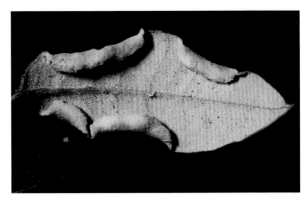

Plate 208. Galls of *"Dasineura"*
silvestrii that have joined
together on canyon live oak.

toward the underside midrib, without significantly distorting the edge of the leaf, as do other typical fold galls. Galls often appear continuously all along the leaf margin, from the apex to the petiole on both sides, or are joined to appear as one long gall. Individual roll galls measure 3 mm long by 3–4 mm wide. When individual galls occur next to each other, the margin of the leaf has a wrinkled appearance. Fresh galls are lime green and hairy. The genus name here is provisional until adults can be fully examined. This species occurs in California and Oregon. Common.

Plate 209. Two galls of *"Dasineura" silvestrii.*

PURSE-GALL MIDGE   *"Dasineura"* sp.   Pl. 210

This midge induces rounded, succulent, swollen, monothalamous–polythalamous, smooth-edged fold galls on the underside and along margins of leaves of canyon live and huckleberry oaks. The puffy nature of these galls gives them the appearance of a pouch or purse. They often occur singly or coalesced and grouped next to or across from each other. I have seen five on one leaf. The wall of the gall of this species, unlike that of the preceding species, is significantly thicker than the normal leaf. Galls are light green to beige and measure 4–5 mm in diameter. Galls of this species are abundant in the central Sierra Nevada on huckleberry oak. Adults pupate in galls and emerge through a slit at the leaf edge. Adults have been reared to tentatively confirm this genus identification. Common.

ROLL-GALL MIDGE   *Contarinia* sp.   Pl. 211

This midge induces narrow polythalamous roll galls on the underside of leaves of both canyon live and huckleberry oaks. Galls form by rolling the edge of the leaf downward and in toward the ventral midrib. The galls are leaf green and measure 12–14 mm long by 1–2 mm in diameter.

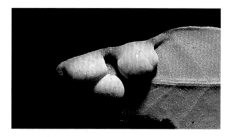

Above: Plate 210. Three galls of *"Dasineura"* sp. on huckleberry oak.

Right: Plate 211. Gall of *Contarinia* sp. on canyon live oak.

There is usually only one roll gall per leaf, although an occasional leaf has opposing edges rolled. Larvae leave galls in late summer, although some are found in galls as late as October. Old galls without gall midge larvae are brown and usually have exit holes. Gall midges pupate in leaf litter, and adults emerge in spring. Common.

BLISTER-GALL WASP   *Heteroecus devorus*   Pl. 212

The small, monothalamous, integral, spring galls of this wasp protrude from both sides of leaves of canyon live oak. Galls can occur in dense clusters of 12–15 galls per leaf. Most galls are round with a flat or convex top, glabrous, and smooth. Galls measure 2–3 mm in diameter and are glossy light brown when mature. These are the galls of a bisexual generation whose summer–fall unisexual-generation counterpart has yet to be identified. Adults have been reared in mid-April in Mount Shasta, California. Lyon's (1984) description did not mention a cluster habit. Uncommon.

Plate 212. Leaf galls of *Heteroecus devorus* on canyon live oak.

ROUND-LEAF-GALL WASP   *Heteroecus flavens*   Pl. 213

This cynipid wasp induces round, integral, monothalamous galls on leaves of huckleberry oak. Galls occur singly in the middle or along the margin of leaves, or in groups that can consume the entire host leaf. As many as 10 galls can occur on a single leaf. Galls protrude equally on both sides of leaves. Galls measure 6 mm in diameter and are either glabrous or have short, sparse hairs. In summer, when the galls are fresh, they are green with red mottling on top and light green to yellow on the lower half. Ultimately, by fall, galls turn a light brown. The larval chamber is central in a solid mass of tissue. Locally common.

Plate 213. Leaf gall of *Heteroecus flavens* on huckleberry oak.

HAIR-CAPSULE-GALL WASP   *Heteroecus* sp. A

Pl. 214

This cynipid wasp induces smooth, pointed, monothalamous leaf galls on huckleberry oak. The pointed larval capsules sit atop a hair-thin stalk that emerges out of a ventral lateral vein. Galls occur singly and measure 12 mm long. The larval capsule at the tip of the gall measures 1 mm in diameter. Galls are green when fresh but turn beige with age. Uncommon.

Plate 214. Gall of *Heteroecus* sp. A on huckleberry oak.

VASE-GALL WASP   *Heteroecus* sp. B

Pl. 215

This wasp induces rose-pink, monothalamous, leaf galls on canyon live oak. Galls of this wasp occur on the dorsal surface on the midrib, with only one per leaf. Galls have a mealy-granular coating composed of short appressed hairs. The tip is truncated. Galls measure 3.5 mm in diameter by 6 mm high. Adults emerged in late July, suggesting there may an alternate generation yet to be discovered. Unexpectedly, this wasp and its galls appeared on a specific tree (in my garden) that I had been monitoring for five years. The first occurrence of these galls on this tree raises many questions about this gall species' relationship to other described or undescribed species on the same tree and its origin (previous host tree). Although fairly isolated, none of the other nine canyon live oaks on the property, in Mount Shasta, California, had previously supported this species. Rare.

Plate 215. Vase gall of *Heteroecus* sp. B on canyon live oak.

ROSY-TEAR-GALL WASP *Heteroecus* sp. C

Pl. 216

The rose-pink, monothalamous galls of this wasp occur on the ventral midrib of canyon live oaks. Fresh galls in late spring are sparsely covered with stubby golden hairs, particularly on the upper half, revealing the color of the smooth gall skin. Unlike the vase gall of *Heteroecus* sp. B, this gall has a rounded tip. Galls measure 6 mm high by 3 mm in diameter. As with the preceding vase-gall wasp, this species suddenly appeared on the same tree that had been under routine surveillance for five years, raising questions about where it came from, since cynipids are weak flyers. I did not find any similar galls in the general area. This species induced a few galls for three years on the same tree and then disappeared, not to be seen in subsequent years, there or anywhere else. It has been collected only in Mount Shasta, California. Rare.

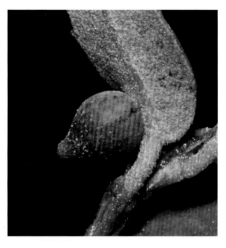

Plate 216. Rosy-tear gall of *Heteroecus* sp. C on canyon live oak.

CLUB-VEIN-GALL WASP *Heteroecus* sp. D

Pl. 217

This wasp induces monothalamous, baseball-bat-shaped galls that are actually extensions of leaf veins, of both canyon live and huckleberry oaks, throughout their range. Galls are usually brick red, brown, or blackish, and measure 7–14 mm long by 2 mm in diameter at the widest point, where the larval chamber is located. Sometimes the sides of the galls are furrowed. Galls often form at the edges of leaves, revealing the source of the vein that has been extended, or directly from a lateral vein. The identity of this wasp eluded scientists for over 50 years, largely due to its extremely small size—it is nearly invisible to the naked eye. Adults are now being studied. These wasps are extremely abundant on both hosts throughout their range. Common abundant.

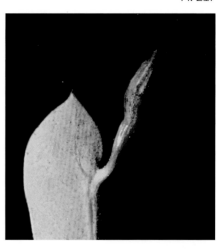

Plate 217. Club gall of *Heteroecus* sp. D on oak.

HAIRY-GALL WASP   *Andricus lasius*
(Disholcaspis lasius) *
                                          Fig. 47

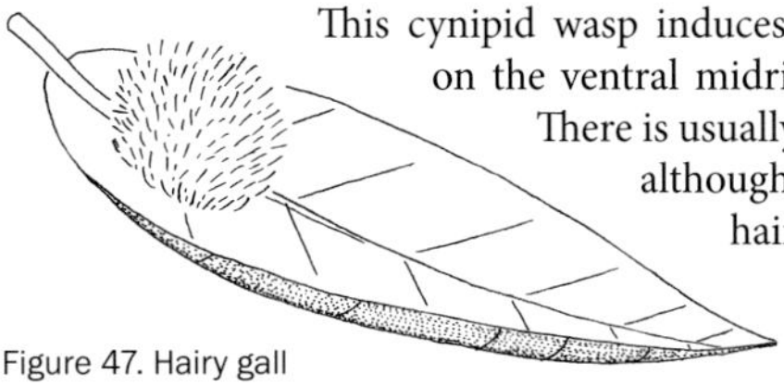

This cynipid wasp induces round, hairy, polythalamous, detachable galls on the ventral midrib or lateral veins of leaves of canyon live oak. There is usually one gall per leaf. Galls often appear dirty beige, although when fresh some have golden-yellow to brown hairs. Hairs are 3–4 mm long; they will be included in a future edition of the Hair Chart but for now can be compared with the hairs in the chart (page 132). The entire gall mass measures up to 10 mm in diameter. Up to six larval cham-

Figure 47. Hairy gall of *Andricus lasius*.

bers are radially arranged near the point of attachment. Females emerge from January to early March. This species also occurs on canyon live oak in the Southwest. Common.

DISC-GALL WASP   *Paracraspis guadaloupensis*
(Acraspis guadaloupensis) *
                                          Pl. 218

This cynipid wasp induces convex to flat, disc-shaped, monothalamous galls on ventral lateral veins of leaves of canyon live oak. Beige, spring galls occur singly or up to three per leaf, not touching each other. Galls measure up to 6 mm in diameter and are easily damaged and dislodged. Gall development begins by May on last year's leaves. Adults emerge from late winter to early spring. Exit holes are usually off-center. While wide-ranging, and also occurring on canyon live oak in the Southwest, this species is not abundant in any one area explored to date. Uncommon.

Plate 218. Gall of *Paracraspis guadaloupensis* on canyon live oak.

CAP-GALL WASP   *Paracraspis insolens*
(Acraspis insolens) *
                                          Pl. 219

Monothalamous galls of this wasp occur on the ventral leaf surfaces of canyon live oak. Galls appear like little hats or caps with an oblong, rolled-over shape when viewed top-down. Galls measure 3 mm wide by 5 mm high and are light green to beige with red-wine edges in May but become light brown with age. Galls of this species have been found in the southern Sierra Nevada. Uncommon.

Plate 219. Two galls of *Paracraspis insolens* on canyon live oak. Photo by Joyce Gross.

BOWL-GALL WASP *Paracraspis patelloides*   Fig. 48
                     (Acraspis patelloides) *

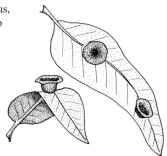

This cynipid wasp induces detachable, monothalamous, usually concave galls with flared rims on ventral midrib or lateral veins of last year's leaves of canyon live oak. In late April in the central Sierra Nevada the young, fleshy galls are rather flat to slightly concave, but as they mature, the sides grow higher, creating a deep central depression and forming the bowl shape. Some galls remain flat-topped. At maturity, galls measure 12 mm in diameter by 5 mm high. When fresh, the galls are a faint pea green or ivory with pink-red margins. By fall, the galls turn beige, retaining hints of the pink-red colors along the margins. Small dark spots appear on some specimens. Sides of the galls are ridged and non-glossy. The larval chamber is centrally located at the gall's base. Adults are found in galls in November and December. Emergence takes place sometime thereafter through holes in the galls' center. Some emerge as late as May. Uncommon.

Figure 48. Galls of *Paracraspis patelloides.*

WOOLLY-GALL WASP *Trichoteras burnetti*   Pl. 220
                    (Andricus burnetti) *

Galls of this species are quite distinct, nearly the size of a golf ball and covered with dense golden-brown, bent, twisted, cotton-like mass of hairs like those of *H. dasydactyli* (see Hair Chart, page 132). Galls measure up to 30 mm or more across and usually occur at the base of petioles. These monothalamous–polythalamous galls are the only woolly galls found on Palmer's oak thus far. Adults emerge in December and January and oviposit in buds. Fresh galls (about 7 mm in diameter) can be found in April, along with fully mature galls left over from the previous season. This species has been found in Riverside County, California, and northern Baja California. I have found these galls only in the northern Santa Rosa Mountains above Palm Desert, California. Uncommon.

Plate 220. Gall of *Trichoteras burnetti* on Palmer's oak.

LITTLE-OAK-APPLE-GALL WASP   *Trichoteras coquilletti*   Pl. 221
(Andricus coquilletti) *

Plate 221. Leaf gall of *Trichoteras coquilletti* on huckleberry oak.

This cynipid wasp induces small, round, thin-skinned, monothalamous oak-apple galls on the ventral side of leaves of huckleberry and canyon live oaks. These rather small galls are usually cream-yellow with bright red spots and turn brown with age. Galls measure 5–7 mm in diameter and usually occur singly, but on occasion up to three galls are attached near each other along a vein. Like the larger gall of its relative the oak-apple wasp (*T. vaccinifoliae*; Figure 45), this gall is hollow, with a centrally located and suspended larval chamber supported by radiating fibers that connect to the outer wall. Galls develop from late spring through midsummer. At higher elevations (greater than 1,500 m) on huckleberry oak, galls are fresh in July and August. At these elevations, adults probably emerge in late spring and early summer. At low elevations (less than 850 m) adults emerge during January and February. This species also occurs on canyon live oak in the Southwest. Common.

LITTLE-URN-GALL WASP   *Trichoteras rotundula*   Pl. 222
(Andricus rotundula) *

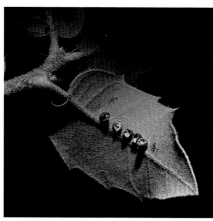

Plate 222. Galls of *Trichoteras rotundula* on oak.

This cynipid wasp induces small, urn-shaped, monothalamous galls along the ventral midrib of leaves of canyon live and Palmer's oaks. Galls usually occur on both sides of the midrib in single rows or clusters of only a few per leaf. When fresh, the galls are green with fine hairs that ultimately rub off. With age, they turn brown and smooth. Galls measure up to 2.7 mm in diameter and exhibit a small hole at the apex. The central larval chamber is supported by radiating fibers connected to the outer wall. Females emerge sometime in fall or winter. An alternate generation of these unisexual-generation galls/wasps has yet to be discovered, if such exists. This species also occurs on canyon live oak in the Southwest. Uncommon.

OAK-APPLE-GALL WASP *Trichoteras* sp. A
(*Andricus* sp.)*

Pl. 223

The monothalamous oak-apple galls of this wasp occur singly or in pairs on the ventral midrib of leaves of Palmer's oak. While the outer skin looks somewhat smooth, a gritty-lumpy surface is revealed under magnification. Galls measure 10–12 mm in diameter and are thin-skinned. A central larval chamber is supported by radiating fibers connected to the outer shell. All galls found in April were brick brown and had exit holes. With adults reported to exit in October and November, this appears to be the summer–fall unisexual generation of this wasp. Uncommon.

Plate 223. Single gall of *Trichoteras* sp. A on Palmer's oak.

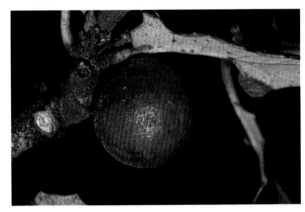

OAK-APPLE-GALL WASP *Trichoteras* sp. B
(*Andricus* sp.)*

Pl. 224

This cynipid wasp induces round, thin-walled, hollow, monothalamous galls on the ventral midrib of leaves of canyon live oak. As do other oak apples, the spring galls induced by this wasp have a centrally located, suspended larval chamber with radiating fibers connected to the outer wall. These spring galls measure 18–20 mm in diameter. Galls occur singly or, uncommonly, in pairs. Fresh spring galls are yellow, apple green, lime green, or reddish, with wine-red spots scattered across the surface. Galls collected in late July at 1,370 m in the central Sierra Nevada contained prepupae and were already brown and paper-thin. Females reared from these galls are quite similar to those of *T. coquilletti*,

Plate 224. Gall of *Trichoteras* sp. B on canyon live oak.

but the galls pictured here have never been found on or near hosts that support the normally smaller gall of *T. coquilletti* (Plate 221). This spring-generation gall could be another example of variability within a species, as seen with *Dryocosmus juliae* on chinquapin. For now, until DNA sequencing analysis is completed, the identity to species level remains unclear. Uncommon.

STARBURST-GALL WASP   Unknown #20

Pl. 225

This cynipid wasp induces small, monothalamous galls along the ventral midrib of leaves of canyon live oak in the central Sierra Nevada and likely elsewhere. Thick projections radiate outward from the central larval chamber, which is covered with bristly, white hairs. When examined under magnification, these hairs appear to be in disarray. Radiating projections can be obtuse, slightly pointed, or joined together, revealing only a toothed edge to the flared base. Galls occur usually in groups of two or three, but as many as nine, lined up along the midrib. Galls are dull pink to ruby red with a lighter-colored larval chamber when fresh. Galls measure 2.5 mm in diameter and about 1 mm high. Development of galls usually starts in early summer, but some galls do not begin growing until early September. Adults need to be reared and studied. Uncommon.

Plate 225. Three galls of starburst-gall wasp, **Unknown #20**, on canyon live oak.

FUNNEL-GALL WASP   Unknown #21

Pl. 226

Plate 226. Gall of funnel-gall wasp, **Unknown #21**, on canyon live oak.

This cynipid wasp induces funnel-shaped, monothalamous spangle galls on the dorsal surface of leaves of canyon live oak. Galls occur singly, with several nearby leaves bearing one gall each. The galls flare out and upward from the point of attachment. They are deep purple or chocolate-colored, with lines or striations that run from the ragged edge to the central larval chamber. Galls measure 4 mm wide by 2 mm high with a 2-mm-wide larval chamber. Weld (1960, fig. 90) pictured a similar gall but reported it occurring on a white oak. Discovery of these galls in California on canyon live oak suggests possible misidentification of Weld's Southwest host oak. Because it is highly unlikely that two species of gall-inducers with such strikingly similar galls would occur on two different groups of oaks, I am treating this as one species on Southwest and Pacific States canyon live oaks. Uncommon to rare.

Galls of this wasp are small, round to pear-shaped, and monothalamous, and occur on the ventral midrib of leaves of canyon live oak. These early spring galls usually occur in pairs, but occasionally three or more occur together. Fresh galls are minutely hairy, yellow-green and red, and measure 2 mm in diameter. With age, these galls become smooth and glossy brown. This species is possibly the previously unknown bisexual generation of either a known unisexual generation or the counterpart of a new species yet to be identified. Uncommon.

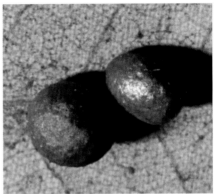

Plate 227. Fresh galls of vein-gall wasp, **Unknown #22**, on canyon live oak.

Plate 228. Older galls of **Unknown #22**.

The small, monothalamous galls of this new species of wasp occur singly along the ventral margins of leaves of canyon live oak. Galls are covered with short, stiff bristles. Galls are rounded at the base but rise to a fine point, somewhat mimicking a pear or teardrop. The dorsal surface of the leaf is marked with a slight dimple or a discolored area that looks like the work of a leaf miner. Galls measure 2–3 mm high by 1.5 mm at the base. Specimens collected in January were still occupied but failed to issue adults. This species has been found only in the Siskiyou Mountains of northern California. Rare.

Plate 229. Gall of bristly-pear-gall wasp, **Unknown #23**, on canyon live oak.

CLUSTERED-BLISTER-GALL WASP   Unknown #24

Pl. 230

The small, integral, monothalamous, blister leaf galls of this new species show on both sides of leaves of canyon live oak. Galls barely protrude above the surface in spring and measure 1.5–2 mm in diameter, which makes them difficult to see. Twenty to 30 galls can occur on a single leaf. Fresh galls collected in early May issued *Synergus* sp. parasites by the first of June. As with some preceding species, these galls and the associated wasp-inducer have been found only in the Mount Shasta area of the Siskiyou Mountains of northern California. Uncommon to rare.

Plate 230. Galls of clustered-blister-gall wasp, **Unknown #24**, on canyon live oak.

FLUTED-GALL WASP   Unknown #25

Pl. 231

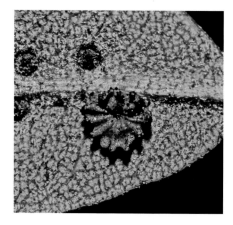

Galls of this new species found on canyon live oak leaves are characterized by fluted ridges radiating out from the center of the galls and terminating in smooth, toothed projections along the edge. From the side, these monothalamous galls look like miniature crowns. Galls measure 1–1.5 mm in diameter by slightly less than 1 mm high. Galls collected in May had already been vacated, suggesting this might be a spring bisexual-generation wasp. This gall has been collected in Siskiyou and Amador Counties, California. Uncommon.

Plate 231. Gall of fluted-gall wasp, **Unknown #25**, on canyon live oak.

BALL-GALL WASP   Unknown #26

Pl. 232

The round, monothalamous galls of this wasp species occur mostly on the dorsal leaf surfaces of canyon live oak. These spring galls cannot be detached without tearing the leaf, as a small amount of gall tissue protrudes on the ventral side. Host leaves tend to bend at

Plate 232. Gall of ball-gall wasp, **Unknown #26**, on canyon live oak.

the point of gall development. Galls measure 4–5 mm in diameter and are solid, with the larval chamber centered near the gall's base. Most galls in June appear rose-brown with slightly darker blotches all over the glabrous surface. This species has been seen only in Siskiyou County, California. Rare.

HAIRY-MUSHROOM-GALL WASP   Unknown #27

Pl. 233

The monothalamous galls of this wasp are unique in that they look like miniature hairy mushrooms on the ventral side of leaves of canyon live oak. Exit holes for the adults are on the dorsal side of the gall attachment. Galls measure 6–7 mm in diameter by 2.5 mm high. Development occurs in late spring and early summer, with galls turning dingy gray with age. Galls of this unknown species were first reported in Weld (1957b, fig. 167) but were not described. They have been collected in Santa Clara and Riverside Counties, California. Uncommon.

Plate 233. Gall of hairy-mushroom-gall wasp, **Unknown #27**, on canyon live oak. Photo by Joyce Gross.

LITTLE-CUP-GALL WASP   Unknown #28

Pl. 234

This cynipid wasp induces small, smooth, concave, monothalamous galls along the ventral midrib of leaves of huckleberry oak. The galls are shaped overall like tiny, round cups. Sides of the galls are smooth, glabrous, and sometimes furrowed vertically. The upper edges are crinkled or undulating and brown or maroon. The tops are concave and glossy. Galls measure 1–2 mm in diameter by 1 mm high and usually occur in groups of two to four per leaf. Adults emerge through exit holes in the sides of galls in fall. This species has been found throughout the Sierra Nevada and Siskiyou Mountains of California. Common.

Plate 234. Two galls of little-cup-gall wasp, **Unknown #28**, on huckleberry oak.

LITTLE-GREEN-APPLE-GALL WASP Unknown #29

Pl. 235

Plate 235. Gall of little-green-apple gall wasp, **Unknown #29**, on huckleberry oak.

Galls of this wasp are monothalamous and occur on the ventral midrib of huckleberry oak leaves. Galls are relatively smooth, although slight tubercles can be seen under magnification. These glabrous galls are bright lime green and measure 3–4 mm in diameter. In contrast, the galls of *Trichoteras coquilletti* on the same host are smooth, glabrous, without tubercles, and are yellow with red spots. This new species was discovered at Kangaroo Lake in the Siskiyou Mountains of northern California. These galls have not been seen elsewhere or on canyon live oak. Rare.

PETIOLE-GALL WASP Unknown #30

Pl. 236

This wasp induces round to ovoid galls on the lower petioles of huckleberry oak leaves. Galls measure 5–7 mm in diameter and are densely covered with scraggly short hairs. Petioles may support one to three galls. Galls are usually light green, with rosy tones where exposed to the sun. There are two separate larval chambers, which are quite large, at 2–3 mm across, with walls that are usually less than 1 mm thick. Larvae are still actively feeding in late October. Adults emerge in late spring and early summer when new leaves are forming. Galls have been found in several locations in the Sierra Nevada. Common.

Plate 236. Galls of petiole-gall wasp, **Unknown #30**, on huckleberry oak.

LUMPY-GALL WASP Unknown #31

Pl. 237

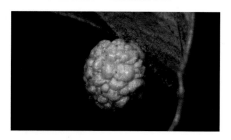

This species induces round, bright lime green, lumpy, single galls on the ventral midrib or lateral veins of Palmer's oak leaves. In April, these monothalamous galls are 3 mm in diameter. Females lay eggs early in the season when leaves are small and close together,

Plate 237. Gall of lumpy-gall wasp, **Unknown #31**, on Palmer's oak.

resulting in clusters of galled leaves. This appears to be the spring bisexual generation of either a new species or a known or unknown summer–fall generation wasp. This species has been collected in the Santa Rosa Mountains near Palm Desert, California. It has not been seen elsewhere on this host or any other intermediate oak. Rare.

PUMPKIN-GALL WASP   Unknown #32   Pl. 238

This wasp induces round, pumpkin-shaped, polythalamous galls on the dorsal midrib of Palmer's oak leaves. Old galls are beige, smooth, and measure 3 mm in diameter. Galls were originally found on a tree in an isolated group of three Palmer's oaks in Short Canyon in Owen's Peak Wilderness near Death Valley, California. Subsequently, they were also found in the Santa Rosa Mountains above Palm Desert, California. Galls of this and the preceding species, found in widely separated populations with no chance of intermingling, reinforce the notion that the climate once supported a more contiguous spread of Palmer's oak across what is now the Mojave Desert, California. Rare.

BULB-GALL WASP   Unknown #33   Pl. 238

Galls of this wasp are distinct in that they come to a point and almost always distort the host leaf at the spot of attachment on Palmer's oak. These monothalamous galls occur on the leaf's dorsal midrib. As galls develop, sides of the leaves nearest the galls are pulled inward toward each gall. Galls found in late April were already brown, suggesting they belong to a spring bisexual generation. Galls measure 4 mm high by 2 mm in diameter. To date, they have been found only in the northern Santa Rosa Mountains above Palm Desert, California. Rare.

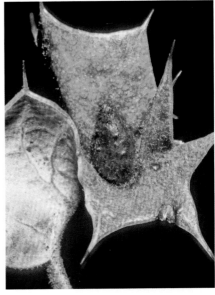

Plate 238. Gall of pumpkin-gall wasp, **Unknown #32**, on Palmer's oak.

Plate 239. Gall of bulb-gall wasp, **Unknown #33**, on Palmer's oak.

Oak Galls of the Southwest

Cynipid wasp galls on Southwest oaks (Nevada, Arizona, New Mexico, Utah) represent a universe unto themselves. The shapes, colors, and diversity are simply staggering. While Lewis Weld (1960) made a serious attempt at cataloging the diversity of galls found on Southwest oaks, listing about 114 identified species, he left almost as many without names. Kinsey (1920, 1922, 1929, 1937a, b, c) also described a number of gall wasps from both Mexico and the Southwest. A number of so-called "Mexican species" are found in southern Arizona on related host trees in the mountains near Nogales and Tucson, but since the study of Southwest galls is still in its infancy, there is little information on exact distribution for any species, Mexican or those in this guide. Add to this inventory the new ones discussed here, plus those that have yet to be discovered and described, and we have an exciting frontier of opportunity and discovery. Research by James Zimmerman has resulted in a fine collection at the University of Arizona's entomology collection in Tucson. Other researchers, including Juli Pujade-Villar and George Melika, have named cynipid species from Mexico, some of which also occur in southern Arizona and appear here. What follows in this section, with 63 species named and described plus 30 species left as **UNKNOWN**, is only an **INTRODUCTION** to these wasps, their galls, and host plants. That I was unable to identify so many is a poignant statement about the diversity of Southwest gall insects and the need for more research.

While galls of Southwest cynipid wasps rival those of the Pacific States and in some cases exceed them in shape and beauty, there can be no mistake that such species deserve far more attention than I can bring in these pages. As it is, my brain burns with the wonder of what is out there that we have yet to discover.

Plate 240. A granitic spire among shrub live oak and Mexican blue oak in the Santa Catalina Mountains, northeast of Tucson, Arizona. Photo by Sheri Russo.

In this section and in concert with the Pacific States' woolly oak galls, I am introducing a means of distinguishing woolly galls based on the characters of individual hairs, depicted here in a chart of seven gall wasp species. During the research for this guide, I discovered that woolly oak galls possess "signature hairs" that appear to be species-specific. When the hairs of any woolly species are gently scraped off, there is either a collection of similar hairs or a mix of simple hairs and signature hairs of a specific design. Some are forked, branched, twisted into inseparable bundles, coiled, or covered with stellate clusters along the main hair stem. See the Hair Chart for Southwest species, page 190.

Some oak woodlands in the southern half of Arizona near Tucson survive on what are called the **SKY ISLANDS** (Plate 240). These incredible, biologically diverse mountains, such as the Santa Catalina, Rincon, and Galiuro ranges, for example, rise out of the lower desert floor, where it is hotter. Oaks on these islands, from Tucson to Nogales and Safford, do quite well at elevations from

1,220 m to 2,439 m, where temperatures are cooler than on the desert floor. In northern Arizona, oaks and associated galls occur in the Coconino and Pinto National Forests and the flat country leading to the Grand Canyon.

The major Southwest oak species are listed in Table 13. Other oak species may also be encountered in this region, as well as a number of varieties and hybrids. Being able to distinguish all the species and varieties is a challenge for the novice (see Rose 2012, Tekiela 2008), as it is in the Pacific States. Finally, there are several galls found in the Southwest that also occur in California, primarily on canyon live oak. See Table 14 for details.

Plate 241. Emory oak with large galls of *Amphibolips trizonata* (see page 175). Photo by Joyce Gross

Flower Galls

WOOLLY-FLOWER-GALL WASP   *Neuroterus floricomus*   Pl. 242

This wasp induces dense, woolly, pale-beige galls, sometimes with floral parts showing, on the staminate flowers of Arizona white, Mexican blue, Toumey, and netleaf oaks. These polythalamous galls measure up to 20 mm long by 8–10 mm across. The staminate axis is covered by tightly woven hairs that completely mask the stem and most floral parts. Common.

CLUSTERED-FLOWER-GALL WASP   Unknown #34   Pl. 243

This wasp species lays its eggs in staminate flowers of Emory oak. The individual monothalamous galls that develop are smooth, mostly glabrous, and protrude from among anthers still

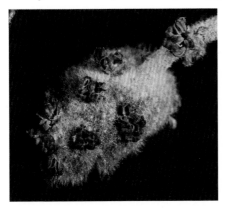

Plate 242. Gall of *Neuroterus floricomus* on oak. Photo by Joyce Gross.

Plate 243. Galls of clustered-flower-gall wasp, **Unknown #34**, on Emory oak.

showing. Clusters of these galls measure 15 mm long by 7 mm wide, with individual cells appearing laterally compressed. Each gall is about 2 mm long. With age, galls are beige-fawn brown. Adults emerge prior to mid-October. Uncommon.

LEAFY-FLOWER-GALL WASP   Unknown #35   Pl. 244

This wasp induces galls near the terminus of branches where flowers form on Mexican blue oak. The initial appearance of these galls is a collection of aborted leaves in disarray with notice-able anthers among the leafy bracts. Galls measure about 10–20 mm across. By October, galls are brown and vacant. Whether this is a spring bisexual-generation gall or not is unknown. Uncommon.

Plate 244. Gall of leafy-flower-gall wasp, **Unknown #35**, on Mexican blue oak.

Acorn Galls

ACORN-CUP-GALL WASP   *Andricus balanella*   Pl. 245

Galls of this wasp protrude either from the outer or inner edge of the acorn cup of Emory oak. These mottled green and dark brown monothalamous galls are glabrous, smooth, glossy, and often covered with honeydew that attracts ants and yellow jackets when fresh. Galls measure 3–5 mm long. Common.

Plate 245. Gall of *Andricus balanella* on Emory oak. Photo by Joyce Gross.

ACORN-CUP-GALL WASP   *Andricus prescotti*   Pl. 246

Galls of this wasp species can be easily overlooked. If acorns are examined carefully, one might notice small, glossy, beige or chestnut-brown chambers emerging from the sides of acorn cups, or large holes if they have dropped out. Several galls or holes can show around the periphery of an acorn cup. These monothalamous galls measure 2 mm by 2 mm. These larval chambers start inside the cup flesh but emerge as they develop and larvae mature. Ultimately, larval chambers drop to the ground, where the prepupae overwinter until adults emerge next spring. This species has been found on shrub live, Arizona white, Mexican blue, netleaf, and Gambel oaks. Found often in some areas, such as the Santa Catalina Mountains, Arizona. Common.

Plate 246. Acorn galls of
Andricus prescotti on oak.

PEAR-GALL WASP   *Andricus* sp.   Pl. 247

This wasp induces pear-shaped galls that usually occur in clusters of two to four at the terminal acorn buds of new branches on Gambel oak in late spring. Galls measure 5–8 mm long by 3–4 mm in diameter and are covered with tightly appressed hairs except where the gall has been contacted and the hairs have rubbed off. Fresh galls are yellow-green to brick brown. This species looks like *A. cistella*, which has been recorded only on Emory and silverleaf oaks. Common.

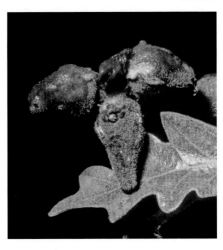

Plate 247. Galls of *Andricus* sp. on Gambel oak.

SPIRE-TOPPED-GALL WASP *Disholcaspis pedunculoides* Pl. 248

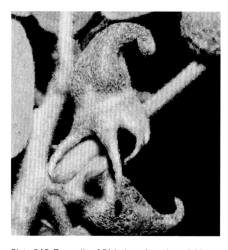

Plate 248. Two galls of *Disholcaspis pedunculoides* on oak.

This cynipid wasp induces one of the most unusual-looking galls on acorn buds in the Southwest on shrub live oak, Arizona white and Mexican blue oaks. These spire-topped galls have long twisted projections surrounding the base. When fresh, galls are rosy red, pink, dark maroon, or green and are covered with short white hairs. With age, they become dark brown. The whole monothalamous gall can measure up to 15 mm long from top to base, with the top spire reaching up to 11 mm long by itself. Some spires rise straight up, while others bend. The larval chamber is located in the broad base above the flanged projections. These galls are encountered frequently throughout the Southwest, especially on shrub live oaks from southwestern Nevada to New Mexico. Common abundant.

Stem and Bud Galls

ERUPTING-STEM-GALL WASP *Antron daileyi* Pl. 249

Plate 249. Clusters of galls of *Antron daileyi* on oak.

This wasp induces clusters of galls on stems of shrub live, Arizona white, Mexican blue, Toumey, and netleaf oaks that stand out from normal branch tissues. Exposed larval cells are 2–3 mm long, while clusters exceed 12 mm long and may rise above the stem surface by 2 mm or more. Individual gall shapes change a bit as each develops, one pushing against the other. Galls are fawn- to chestnut-brown, glabrous, and slightly pitted. Galls were found once in Payson, Arizona. Lyon (1996) described the species and named it in honor of D. Charles Dailey, a cynipid biologist from California. Uncommon to rare.

RINGED-CAP-BUD-GALL WASP *Antron pileus* Pl. 250

This tiny cynipid wasp induces round, monothalamous, convex galls on terminal buds of shrub live oak. The distinctive feature of these galls is the smooth, mostly glabrous main gall body ringed with short gray-brown hairs along the bottom edge. In October, galls are beige and measure 6 mm in diameter and are somewhat dome-shaped from the side view. Adult exit

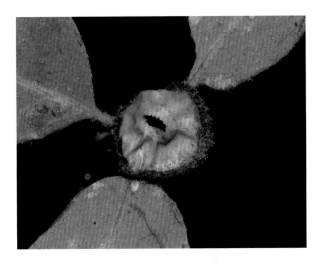

Plate 250. Gall of *Antron pileus* on shrub live oak.

through apical holes that are often jagged rather than perfectly round, suggesting the exit is created by the gall itself and not the insect. Adults emerge prior to October in the Payson area of Arizona. Uncommon.

ELLIPTICAL-STEM-GALL WASP   *Andricus frequens*   Pl. 251
                                   (Callirhytis frequens)*

The elliptical, integral, polythalamous stem galls of this wasp occur on Gambel and shinnery oak. Galls measure 40 mm or more long by 20–30 mm in diameter. The exterior is marked by what appear to be forthcoming splits in the bark. Generally, these galls are tapered at each end, but some can be abrupt at one end. Only females are known for this species. Uncommon.

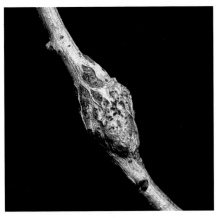

Plate 251. Stem gall of *Andricus frequens* on oak.

ABRUPT-STEM-GALL WASP   *Andricus rhizoxenus*   Pl. 252
                               (Amphibolips rhizoxenus)*

Galls of this wasp are distinguished from most other integral stem galls in being extremely abruptly swollen and small, at 15 mm in diameter. Small branches grow out of the mostly symmetrical, polythalamous, woody and hard terminal galls. Galls may remain on the trees long after adult emergence, ultimately turning sooty black with mold. Weld (1960) reported this

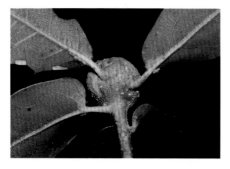

species as *Andricus rhizoxenus* on netleaf oak (*Quercus reticulata*), but given the repeated finding of this gall on Emory oak (*Q. emoryi*) in the Santa Catalina Mountains on separate trips, I believe the netleaf host was misidentified or this is a new species. Uncommon.

Plate 252. Gall of *Andricus rhizoxenus* on Emory oak.

BROWN-FIG-GALL WASP   *Andricus spicatus*   Pls. 253 & 254

The fig-like, individual galls of this wasp occur in tight clusters of a dozen or more on stems of Arizona white, Mexican blue, and Toumey oaks. The surface of the galls is striated with small fissures and micro-bumps. The monothalamous galls are deep wine or purple-brown, and glabrous. Each gall can measure 3–4 mm in diameter; clusters are up to 20 mm across. Galls generally have a pointed apex, but individuals within a cluster can have a rounded apex, while galls in some clusters have a collapsed or flat apex. At this time, there is no clear explanation for these differences in shape except that they might be two separate phases of the species. These galls do not appear to be common or abundant, as they were found only in one area of the Santa Catalina Mountains, Arizona. The species is known to occur on other Sky Islands in Arizona and New Mexico. Uncommon.

Left: Plate 253. Galls of *Andricus spicatus* on Mexican blue oak.
Above: Plate 254. Galls with collapsed centers of *A. spicatus*.

FLARED-DISC-GALL WASP   *Andricus tubalis*   Pls. 255 & 256

The monothalamous, flared galls of this wasp occur on small twigs of last year's growth on Arizona white and Mexican blue oaks. Galls develop from weak buds. The flared top tapers into a sessile or slightly clasping base. Weld's (1960) picture shows a well-formed neck under the cap. The outer edge of the gall top is often broadly toothed and undulating. The top's underside is covered with white, appressed hairs, while the shallow bowl appears glabrous dorsally. When fresh, galls are pale yellow-white, but with age they change to cryptic, camouflaged bark-gray

Plate 255. Top view of gall of *Andricus tubalis*. Photo by Joyce Gross.

Plate 256. Side view showing attachment of gall of *A. tubalis*. Photo by Joyce Gross.

as seen in these photos. Galls measure 6–8 mm in diameter by about 4 mm high. This wasp appears to be a spring, unisexual species, since fresh galls collected in June produced only females. This gall can easily be overlooked. Uncommon to rare.

RUPTURED-STEM-GALL WASP *Andricus tubularius* Pl. 257

This wasp induces one of the most intriguing stem galls in the Southwest, on shrub live oak. In October, stems rupture, exposing rows of yellow, egg-like larval capsules. These integral, polythalamous stem galls can easily exceed 15 mm in length and 6 mm in diameter. Exposed individual larval chambers are about 1–2 mm in diameter. They can resemble the rows of kernels on an ear of corn. These chambers may drop out of the gall to mix in with the leaf litter under the host tree or remain in the gall for a period. With the larval cells exposed in October, the adults need only chew through the thin chamber wall, rather than the woody stem gall, assuming they survive the dangers of such exposure to parasites, mice, squirrels, birds, and the extremes of temperatures. Uncommon.

Plate 257. Gall of *Andricus tubularius* (right) on shrub live oak, with a galled acorn (left).

KNOBBY-STEM-GALL WASP   *Andricus wheeleri*   Pl. 258
(Amphibolips wheeleri) *

Plate 258. Gall of *Andricus wheeleri* on oak.

This integral, polythalamous stem gall is recognized by the broad lobes or umbos scattered across the surface of the gall. This species occurs on Arizona white, Mexican blue, Toumey, and shrub live oaks. Galls are hard, woody, and bark-gray, and measure 26 mm or more in diameter. Branches beyond the galls appear to survive, even though the gall disrupts some flow of water and nutrients. While there are many other species that induce integral stem galls, the lobes of this one are distinctive. A related wasp, *Andricus lebaue*, induces a similar gall along the southern border areas of Arizona and Mexico (Pujade-Villar et al. 2013). Common.

WOOLLY-STEM-GALL WASP   *Andricus* sp. A   Pl. 259

This wasp induces some of the most eye-catching galls in the Southwest, occurring on stems of Arizona white and Mexican blue oaks. Bright crimson or pure white, long hairs conceal the individual galls that make up the polythalamous cluster. Gall clusters measure 30 mm or more long by 10–20 mm wide and either wrap around the branch partially or cover it. Individual galls within a cluster measure 7 mm high by 5 mm wide. This species appears to be infrequent in the areas of Payson, Arizona, and the Santa Catalina Mountains but could occur elsewhere on hosts, along with the woolly galls of *A. furnessulus*, *A. tenuicornis*, and *A. tecturnarum*, which are not included here as I did not find them. Uncommon.

Plate 259. Cluster of galls of *Andricus* sp. A on oak. Photo by Joyce Gross.

CRESTED-STEM-GALL WASP   *Andricus* sp. B   Pl. 260

The polythalamous terminal stem galls of this wasp occur on Emory oaks. Galls measure 20–30 mm in diameter and may remain on trees long after insects emerge. When fresh, galls are rounded, with scattered meringue-like crests gently rising from the surface. No other stem gall has similar crests except *A. toumeyi* (Weld 1960). Galls can cause stems to bend. Fresh galls in October are green with hints of purple or lavender. Gall flesh is solid and pulpy. As galls mature and occupants (inducers, parasites, and inquilines) leave, galls turn bark-brown. The young gall photographed here issued numerous parasites, which may modify the gall's normal development. Uncommon.

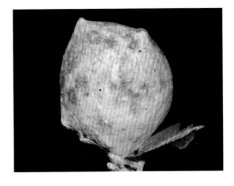

Plate 260. Gall of *Andricus* sp. B on oak.

CLUSTERED-GALL WASP *Disholcaspis edura* Pl. 261

Galls of this cynipid wasp occur in large clusters on stems of Arizona white and Mexican blue oaks. These monothalamous–polythalamous galls are generally rounded and occur in tight compact clusters that can exceed 40 mm in length. The larval chamber is attached to the bottom of the gall with a thick, extremely hard, seemingly impenetrable wall. A cavernous space usually exists above the chamber, which often has an inquilinous moth caterpillar. Normally only three or four galls reach full growth, due to pressure from nearby galls. Each gall measures 12–15 mm in diameter. The surface is rough, with micro-hairs, pits, and dark brown spots. With age, galls become tan-brown and moldy. This species is found from the northern Coconino forest area south to the Sky Islands of southern Arizona. Common.

Plate 261. Galls of *Disholcaspis edura* on oak.

CLUSTERED-GALL WASP *Disholcaspis lacuna* Pl. 262

The large galls of this wasp appear on small stems of only Gambel oak. In the rather tight clusters, usually just three or four globular galls reach full growth, due to the pressure from others that are distorted. Fresh galls measure 12–20 mm in diameter and appear fleshy, yellow at the base, and red-flushed near

Plate 262. Cluster of galls of *Disholcaspis lacuna* on Gambel oak.

the top. The rounded galls have a rough surface that is relatively free of hairs and a central larval chamber. With age, galls wither and turn brown. Galls have been collected at Strawberry Point near Duck Creek Village, Utah, and the Coconino Forest, Arizona. Uncommon.

ROUND-GALL WASP   *Disholcaspis perniciosa*   Pl. 263

Galls of this wasp erupt out of stems of Gambel oak. Initially, galls appear ovoid but ultimately become round and dark brown. Galls measure about 5 mm in diameter and are covered with small, broken patches of bark tissue, but otherwise are glabrous and relatively smooth. Galls can occur on opposite sides of a stem or spaced along the side of a stem. These monothalamous galls have been found in northern Arizona and southern Utah. Uncommon.

Plate 263. Two galls of *Disholcaspis perniciosa* on Gambel oak.

BULLET-GALL WASP   *Disholcaspis rubens*   Pl. 264

The monothalamous, round galls of this wasp occur singly on branches of Arizona white, Mexican blue, and shrub live oaks. Galls measure 10–15 mm in diameter and have either a smooth or slightly rough surface covered with sparse, crusty, tiny patches of three-forked hairs. As with other members of this genus, galls exude sweet honeydew when fresh, which attracts ants and yellow jackets. Galls can be straw yellow or wine red when fresh but turn

Plate 264. Gall of *Disholcaspis rubens* covered with ants. Photo by Joyce Gross.

beige with age. Normally, galls partially wrap over the stem at the point of attachment, making detachment difficult. Common.

HONEYDEW-GALL WASP   *Disholcaspis spissa*   Pl. 265

Galls of this wasp are hairy, round to ovoid, and often occur in long chains all around the stems of Mexican blue, Arizona white, and shrub live oaks. These monothalamous galls are ecologically important in that they produce copious amounts of honeydew while the larvae are actively feeding and growing, attracting hordes of ants and yellow jackets. Galls appear mealy-granular and measure 7–9 mm high and wide. While galls are largely beige-brown, their tops are often black where honeydew accumulates and a sooty mold develops. Each larval chamber sits above the bottom of the gall and is surrounded by pulpy flesh with age. Adults have been reared midwinter, which implies an unknown spring bisexual generation. Galls of this wasp are quite like those of *D. eldoradensis* in California. Common abundant.

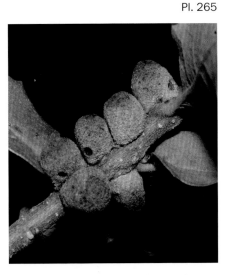

Plate 265. Galls of *Disholcaspis spissa* on oak.

ROUND-TOP-GALL WASP   *Disholcaspis* sp. A   Pl. 266

This unusual species has been found only on shrub live oak in southwestern Nevada. The base of the gall looks somewhat like that of *D. pedunculoides* (Plate 248), with long, fingerlike projections. The upper half of the gall containing the larval chamber is slightly columnar, with a convex top and shallow ridges that continue down to the basal projections. Galls measure up to 10 mm high and wide. These glabrous galls exude honeydew during the early phases of larval growth, which attract ants and yellow jackets. Once larval growth stops, the residues of honeydew attract a black sooty mold. Uncommon.

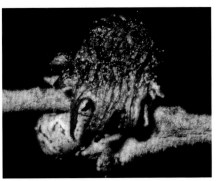

Plate 266. Gall of *Disholcaspis* sp. A on shrub live oak.

THORN-GALL WASP   *Disholcaspis* sp. B   Pls. 267 & 268

This cynipid wasp species induces thorn-shaped, monothalamous, glabrous, galls on shrub live oak. Initially, in October, galls are light yellow-green and smooth, with an undulated, clasping, and expanding base. Galls measure 5 mm wide at the base by 11 mm high. In maturity, galls turn beige-brown with black-pepper-like speckles, and the base often completely encompasses

Plate 267. Old gall of *Disholcaspis* sp. B on shrub live oak.

Plate 268. Fresh gall of *Disholcaspis* sp. B.

the branch. This gall bears a slight resemblance to *D. conalis* from California. These interesting galls were found on only a few trees near Payson, Arizona. Rare.

THORN-GALL WASP   *Disholcaspis* sp. C   Pl. 269

The monothalamous galls of this wasp occur on stems of shrub live oak, often in clusters. The top is thin and long, and the broad base is fan-shaped, with short, pointed tips—and, by comparison, not broken up into long fingerlike projections as on *D. pedunculoides* (Plate 248), which it superficially resembles. Individual galls measure 8 mm high by 6 mm wide at the base, and clusters exceed 30 mm in length. The color of fresh, active galls is not known, as the galls were found after adults had emerged. With age, galls remain covered by a mealy-granular material composed of compressed hairs. Kinsey (1930) originally described *D. insulana* from tightly clustered galls, as seen here, from San Luis, Potosi, Mexico. Uncommon.

SPINDLE-GALL WASP   *Amphibolips fusus*   Pl. 270

The long, monothalamous stem galls of this wasp are spindle-shaped, glabrous, and quite large, with some exceeding 35 mm in length and 10 mm in width. They occur on buds of Emory and

Plate 269. Galls of *Disholcaspis* sp. C on shrub live oak.

Plate 270. Gall of *Amphibolips fusus* on oak.

silverleaf oaks in Arizona. While fresh in late winter and early spring, green galls are slightly mottled with white dots and look much like the galls of *Heteroecus pacificus* (Plate 187). Occasionally, mice and squirrels climb trees to chew into the fresh galls to get at the larvae. With age, galls turn beige and are often marked with scattered tiny, black-pepper-like bumps. The interior flesh is hardened woody tissue, with a larval chamber located in the lower end of the widest part of the gall. This species was described by Kinsey (1937b). Uncommon.

NIPPLED-GALL WASP *Amphibolips nassa* Pl. 271

Galls of this wasp are as long as those of the preceding species, although much broader, and they have a prominent nipple at the apex but retain a slight spindle shape, narrowing toward the attachment point. This species occurs on Emory and silverleaf oaks in Arizona, and likely elsewhere, including on the black oak group in Mexico. When fresh in late winter and early spring, the monothalamous galls, with a central larval chamber, are green, but they turn beige, and the flesh turns pulpy with age. Galls are glabrous, with tiny black-pepper-like bumps across the surface with age, and measure 35 mm long by 20 mm in diameter. Only female wasps are known. Moths are known inquilines of this species' gall, easily detectable by the pre-excavated holes found on the surfaces of older galls, which are temporarily closed with silk prior to the moth's emergence. Common.

Plate 271. Gall of *Amphibolips nassa* on oak.

BALL-GALL WASP *Amphibolips trizonata* Pl. 272

The large, golf-ball-size, monothalamous, bisexual-generation bud galls of this wasp will certainly grab your attention (see Plate 241). Galls occur on Emory and silverleaf oaks, with growth beginning in winter and early spring. They are round, glabrous, and smooth, with a central point of attachment to the host stem and a central larval chamber. Adult males and females emerge in May. While there is an expected unisexual generation, it remains unknown. Galls are beige, lightweight, and measure up to 40 mm in diameter in October (as pictured), with the inner flesh around the larval chamber at this time dry and pulpy.

Plate 272. Gall of *Amphibolips trizonata* on oak.

Even though this thick flesh might insulate larvae from the extremes of temperature, it does not protect them from parasites, inquilines, and other visitors. Common abundant.

STEM-GALL WASP *Dryocosmus coxii*

Pl. 273

The large, integral galls of this wasp encircle stems of Emory and silverleaf oaks. Galls are bark-gray, woody, and hard. They measure up to 40 mm in length by 18 mm across and are irregularly shaped, with numerous knobs or umbos, and distinct rings around exit holes. The polythalamous galls issue female adults in fall and early winter, which implies an unknown spring bisexual generation. The growth of the branch beyond the gall is not affected by the gall's development. Found in Payson, Arizona. Locally common.

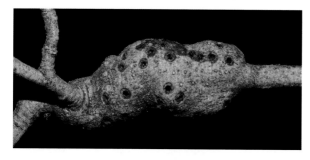

Plate 273. Gall of *Dryocosmus coxii* showing rings around exit holes.

HAIRY-THORN-GALL WASP *"Heteroecus" pygmaeus*

Pl. 274

Plate 274. Galls of *"Heteroecus" pygmaeus* on shrub live oak.

Galls of this wasp occur only on stems of shrub live oak in southwestern Nevada, 19 km west of Las Vegas. These monothalamous galls are densely covered with appressed short, white hairs and usually occur in tight clusters of four to six per branch. They measure 10 mm high by 5 mm in diameter. Adults from these galls have been identified as *"H. dasydactyli* var. *pygmaeus,"* which Kinsey (1922) described from a site in the San Bernardino Mountains, California, without mention of the host or specific location. Since members of the genus *Heteroecus* are known to occur exclusively on intermediate oaks, not white oaks, and since the galls of this species are strikingly different than those of *H. dasydactyli*, I am treating the genus provisionally and retaining the wasp as a separate species until such time as its taxonomic relationship is clarified. While I have collected these galls numerous times at the site mentioned, I have never seen them in California or anywhere other than the Nevada site on shrub live oak. Uncommon.

BROWN-MELON-GALL WASP *Xanthoteras eburneum* *(Biorhiza eburnea)* *

PI. 275

The little chestnut-brown, melon-like galls
of this wasp are known to occur on stems of
Gambel, netleaf, and shrub live oaks. These
glossy, glabrous, monothalamous galls occur
in rows all around the stems of the host tree.
Galls measure 4–5 mm in diameter and are
round to ovoid. Often a rough-appearing
dimple occurs at the apex. Only female adults
are known to date. I have seen this species
only on Gambel oak. Bassett (1881) recorded
this species on leaves while Weld (1960)
shows the galls on stems. Uncommon.

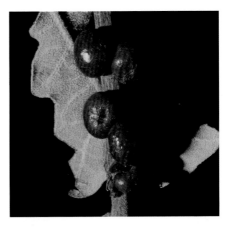

Plate 275. Galls of *Xanthoteras eburneum* on oak.

BALL-GALL WASP Unknown #36

PI. 276

This cynipid wasp induces round, green,
fuzzy monothalamous galls on buds of
Mexican blue oak. Galls occur in leaf axils,
possess a mealy-granular coating of white
hairs, and measure 10 mm in diameter. The
surface, roughened by numerous tiny bumps
and depressions, looks much like the surface
of an orange rind. Galls shrivel following collection, possibly due to the inner white flesh,
which is soft and pulpy. Uncommon.

Plate 276. Gall of ball-gall wasp, **Unknown #36**, on
Mexican blue oak.

THISTLE-HEAD-BUD-GALL WASP Unknown #37

PI. 277

The bud galls of this wasp occur on shrub
live oak and Mexican blue oak. In October,
when fresh, these monothalamous galls are
quite attractive, because of dozens of thin,
hairy, green bracts that emanate from the
central base. Each bract is 12–14 mm long by
less than 1 mm wide. Fresh galls are bright
green, but with age they flare open and turn

Plate 277. Gall of thistle-head-bud-gall wasp,
Unknown #37, on shrub live oak.

beige-brown. Short white hairs are retained throughout growth of the gall. While Weld did not list this species in either his Pacific (1957b) or Southwest (1960) publications, he did list a similar species, *Andricus foliatus*, in his eastern cynipids (1959). Uncommon.

EGG-GALL WASP   Unknown #38   Pl. 278

The monothalamous, smooth, glabrous, egg-like galls of this wasp erupt from stems of Mexican blue oaks. Individual galls, 3 mm long and wide, usually occur in rows up to 10 mm long. Galls are ovoid but can be laterally compressed by others to assume different shapes. Adults emerge prior to October, as they have in the photo. This species was found near Payson, Arizona. Rare.

Plate 278. Galls of egg-gall wasp, **Unknown #38**, on Mexican blue oak.

NECKED-GALL WASP   Unknown #39   Pls. 279 & 280

One of the most unusual galls is induced by this wasp species on branches of Mexican blue oak. Mature galls measure 12 mm in diameter and are attached to the stems by a pronounced 2-mm-long neck. New galls, which form in October, are round and glabrous. These monothalamous galls can be reddish pink, pale yellow with red spots, or dark purple-black. Surfaces of both new and old galls have a slight powdery bloom that rubs off. The outer wall is thick (>1 mm), and the central larval chamber is supported by a dense mesh of intermingling fibers, unlike the 20 to 30 separate strands in most oak apples. Plate 279 depicts a new gall just starting next to a mature gall. Uncommon.

Plate 279. Fresh mature gall and new gall of necked-gall wasp, **Unknown #39**, on Mexican blue oak. Photo by Joyce Gross.

Plate 280. Dark version of mature gall of **Unknown #39**.

STEM-GALL WASP   Unknown #40

Pl. 281

Galls of this wasp occur on branches of gray oak and are round to ovoid, with a slight clasping base where connected to the host branch. While appearing fresh in October, one specimen had two exit holes, not necessarily belonging to the gall-inducer. These galls are covered with fine, short, white hairs and measure 18 mm wide by 14 mm high. Only one specimen of this gall was found over a wide range of potential host trees, which could mean it is a different, known species, or possibly inquiline-modified. Rare.

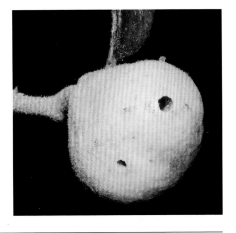

Plate 281. Gall of stem-gall wasp, **Unknown #40**, on gray oak.

NECKED-PUZZLE-GALL WASP   Unknown #41

Pls. 282 & 283

Like Unknown #39, the gall of this species is held away from the stem by a thin 2-mm-long neck on branches of Mexican blue oak. The surface of this species' gall appears to be broken into disjunct plates. This looks as if a collapse of subdermal tissue caused the surface to buckle, creating the illusion of separate plates. This subdermal tissue or inner flesh (Plate 283) is composed of dense, weblike strands. These polythalamous galls are round, beige and pink, and measure 10–14 mm in diameter. While this specimen is treated separately here, further research may prove that the galls of this and #39 are from two separate species, the same species, or are inquiline/parasite-modified. Uncommon.

Above: Plate 282. Gall of necked-puzzle-gall wasp, **Unknown #41**, on Mexican blue oak. Photo by Joyce Gross.
Right: Plate 283. Cross section of gall of **Unknown #41** showing multiple chambers with larvae. Photo by Joyce Gross.

HAIRY-STEM-GALL WASP   Unknown #42

Pl. 284

The galls of this wasp occur on shrub live oak and appear to clasp the stem at the attachment point. The apex of the gall ends in a rounded nipple. These monothalamous galls are densely covered in appressed hairs, measure 7–8 mm in diameter, occur singly, and do not detach easily. This species has been found in only one location in the southwestern portion of Nevada, 19 km west of Las Vegas. Uncommon.

Plate 284. Gall of hairy-stem-gall wasp, **Unknown #42**, on shrub live oak.

PETIOLE-GALL WASP   Unknown #43

Pl. 285

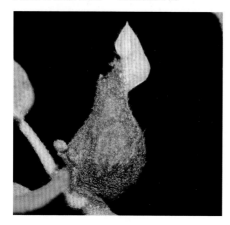

The pear-shaped, monothalamous galls of this wasp consume the entire petioles of Mexican blue oak leaves. While some leaves are aborted and only slightly emerge from the top of the galls, others develop at least partway before stopping. Full-growth normal leaves do not appear to develop. Galls are covered with sparse golden-yellow hairs revealing the chestnut brown of the gall beneath. Galls measure 10 mm long by 5 mm in diameter. These galls were found several times, but only in the Payson, Arizona, area. Uncommon.

Plate 285. Gall of petiole-gall wasp, **Unknown #43**, on Mexican blue oak.

BUDDING-STEM-GALL WASP   Unknown #44

Pl. 286

The integral, polythalamous stem galls of this wasp species, found on Gambel and shrub live oaks, usually have several active buds developing on the gall surface in October, when they are fresh. These buds apparently do not progress much more than is shown in the photo. Galls are bark-gray, often with a green flush near the top, where most buds occur. Galls measure 22 mm long by 11 mm wide. Several specimens were found in an area of the Santa Catalina Mountains, Arizona. Uncommon.

Plate 286. Gall of budding-stem-gall wasp, **Unknown #44**, on oak.

BULLET-GALL WASP   Unknown #45

Pl. 287

The round, monothalamous bullet-shaped galls of this wasp occur on branches of shrub live oak. Galls are dark reddish brown, generally mottled with dark blotches, and glossy, with a short, broad nipple at the apex. The surface of the gall is a bit rough or bumpy. The pictured gall has some mold on it. Galls measure 8–14 mm in diameter. Most occur singly or in opposing pairs but not clustered, as with *Disholcaspis spissa* (Plate 265). The larval chamber is central and surrounded by pulpy flesh. Found only at the southwest Nevada site near Las Vegas. Uncommon.

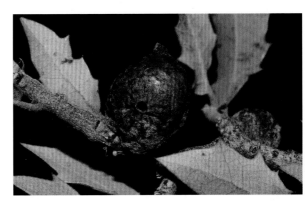

Plate 287. Gall of bullet-gall wasp, **Unknown #45**, on shrub live oak.

ERUPTED-GALL WASP   Unknown #46

Pl. 288

This wasp species induces one of the most unusual integral polythalamous stem galls in the Southwest, on Mexican blue and shrub live oaks. These galls generally appear as if they had erupted from the stem, expanding into various ill-defined shapes, which change based on the angle of view. The galls' surface is rough, pitted, furrowed, and broken into small irregularly shaped plates or lobes. While the galls are bark-gray when fresh, they turn black with age. Fresh galls in October measure 20 mm wide and thick. No damage occurs to leaves and branches beyond galls. Uncommon.

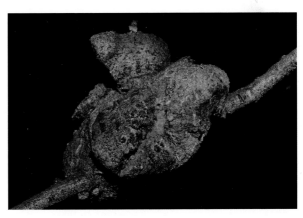

Plate 288. Gall of erupted-gall wasp, **Unknown #46** on oak.

LOPSIDED-STEM-GALL WASP Unknown #47 Pl. 289

The polythalamous galls of this wasp species do not uniformly encircle the stem but develop on only one side, creating a lopsided appearance. Unlike the stem galls of *Dryocosmus coxii* (Plate 273), this species' galls occur only on shrub live oaks, and they are much smaller, measuring up to 25 mm long by 12 mm in diameter. While fresh, galls are bark-gray and slightly knobby, but they turn black with age. Adults emerge in February and March, suggesting there is a spring bisexual generation. Uncommon.

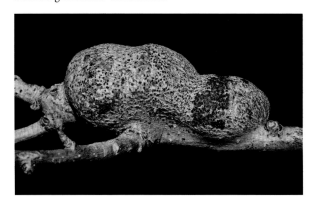

Plate 289. Gall of lopsided-stem-gall wasp, **Unknown #47**, on shrub live oak.

Leaf Galls

ERINEUM MITE *Eriophyes trichophila* Pl. 290

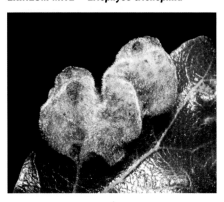

The large, lumpy erineum galls of this mite are quite common on Gambel oak leaves. Galls bulge out on the leaves' dorsal surface, with a corresponding hair-lined depression on the underside. Galls can be 10–20 mm wide and often engulf entire lobes of leaves. This mite is also found on blue oak in California. Uncommon.

Plate 290. Erineum galls of *Eriophyes trichophila* on Gambel oak.

ERINEUM MITE *Eriophyes* sp. Pl. 291

Another eriophyid mite occurs in Utah and Arizona, but on Emory and silverleaf oaks. This mite creates small 2–4-mm bumps on the dorsal surface of leaves that are matched by fawn brown or light brown, hairy, depressions on the underside. This species was discovered in the Payson, Arizona, area. Locally common.

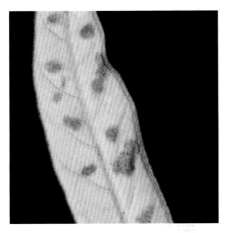

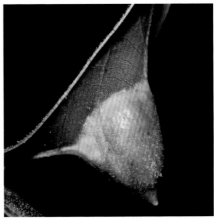

Plate 291. Galls of *Eriophyes* sp. on silverleaf oak.

Plate 292. Integral leaf gall of *Olliffiella cristicola* on Emory oak.

THORN-GALL COCCID   *Olliffiella cristicola*   Pl. 292

The integral, monothalamous leaf gall induced by this coccid insect looks like a green thorn emerging from the underside of leaves of Emory oak in Arizona and possibly sandpaper oak in New Mexico. While the bulk of the gall protrudes from the leaf's underside, there is a slit opening on the dorsal surface. The orange-colored coccid feeds just under the surface of this opening. Galls measure 10–15 mm high by 8–10 mm in diameter and are covered with sparse hairs. These galls generally come to a point at the bottom, creating the image of a thorn. There is usually one gall per leaf, but occasionally two galls coalesce into one. This is the only known coccid in North America to induce a gall. A thrips (*Torvothrips kosztarabi*) is known to co-inhabit these galls, as is an unidentified moth larva that is suspected of preying on the coccid. Found initially in the Santa Catalina Mountains, Arizona. Locally common.

RUSTY-URN-GALL WASP   *Andricus amphorus*   Pl. 293

The striking little, monothalamous galls of this wasp generally occur along the ventral margins of leaves in clusters on shrub live, Mexican blue, and Arizona white oaks in the fall. Galls measure 4–5 mm high by 3–4 mm in diameter and are distinguished from other urn-like galls in that the outer walls form an amphora shape, widest in the middle and narrowed at the base and apex, which has a small opening. The walls of other urn-like galls are straight or gently rounded and have openings

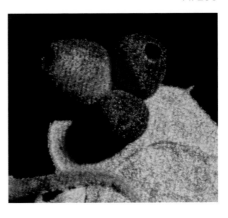

Plate 293. Three galls of *Andricus amphorus*, one with the opening closed.

nearly as wide as the sides; or are covered with a noticeable crystal coating; or lack the rusty hairs. Only female wasps are known so far, which opens the possibility of a spring bisexual generation yet to be discovered. This species occurs from Nevada throughout Arizona and New Mexico. Common.

BRISTLE-VASE-GALL WASP   *Andricus caepula*   Pls. 294 & 295

The bristle-coated, vase-shaped little galls of this wasp occur on leaves of Mexican blue and shrub live oaks throughout Arizona and likely the range of its hosts. These monothalamous galls occur on the leaves' underside and often in large numbers. They can be pink with a yellow base, fawn brown, or white, measure 2–3 mm high and wide, and have a wide opening at the apex. The stiff, crystalline, erect hairs distinguish this species' galls from most other galls, which have crumbled hairs that look like sugar crystals. Common.

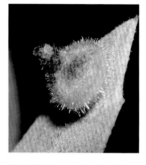

Plate 294. Fresh gall of *Andricus caepula* in the fall on Mexican blue oak.

Plate 295. Two older galls of *A. caepula* showing apical opening on same host.

LITTLE-DISC-GALL WASP   *Andricus discalis*   Pl. 296

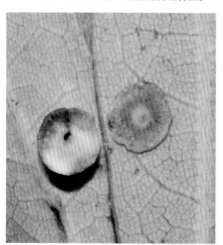

Galls from this wasp occur on ventral lateral veins of Mexican blue oak. These monothalamous galls are flat discs with a slight point in the center and are often tightly appressed to the leaf. Discs usually have a yellow outer ring and a bright pink center marked by a dark spot indicating the location of the larval chamber. Galls measure 2 mm in diameter by less than 1 mm thick. Adults emerged in winter, suggesting there might be an alternate generation that has yet to be identified. Uncommon.

Plate 296. The galls of *Andricus discalis* on Mexican blue oak.

PINCHED-EDGE-GALL WASP *Andricus pilularis*

Pl. 297

The monothalamous, hairy, integral galls of this wasp occur along the margins of leaves of Arizona white, Mexican blue, Toumey, Gambel, netleaf, and shrub live oaks. Usually, there is only one gall per leaf. Galls measure 4 mm in diameter and occur at the end of a lateral vein, which causes the leaf edge to indent noticeably. Most of the gall occurs on the dorsal surface, with a little protruding on the underside. Adults emerge sometime before late October. A similar gall induced by *A. pilula* occurs only on Gambel oak. Common.

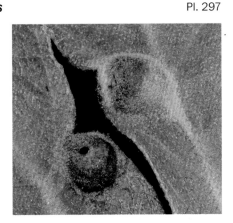

Plate 297. Galls of *Andricus pilularis* on two oak leaves.

OLIVE-LEAF-GALL WASP *Andricus reticulatus*

Pl. 298

The glossy, olive to brown, monothalamous galls of this wasp are integral near the base of leaves of Arizona white, Mexican blue, Toumey, netleaf, Gambel, and shrub live oaks. Galls measure 6–8 mm in diameter and are glabrous or have a few scattered hairs. Galls are generally round and protrude about equally on both surfaces of the leaf. Some specimens have broadly rounded points on top. Unlike those of *Neuroterus lamellae* (plate 324), the galls of this species occur away from the leaf edge and are not covered in a dense mat of yellowish hairs. Common.

Plate 298. Gall of *Andricus reticulatus* on oak.

LITTLE-RED-CUP-GALL WASP *Andricus scutella*

Pl. 299

These red, cup-shaped, monothalamous leaf galls occur on Mexican blue and shrub live oaks. Normally, they occur one to several per leaf along the margins. Galls are hairy, rose pink to red-brown, and measure 2 mm high and wide. Fresh galls were found in late October. Only females of this wasp species are known. Uncommon.

Plate 299. Galls of *Andricus scutella* on oak. Photo by Joyce Gross.

CUP-GALL WASP　*Andricus sessilus*　　　　Pl. 300

The squat, chalice-shaped galls of this wasp occur on the underside of leaves of Arizona white and Mexican blue oaks. Galls occur on lateral veins, with only one or two per leaf. Galls are glossy, smooth, and glabrous, have a slightly bumpy surface, and measure 4 mm wide and 3 mm high. When fresh in October, galls are shades of pink and yellow, but turn red-brown with age. Galls look like cups sitting on top of broad stalks that usually have flared bases at the point of attachment, which can be lacking in some specimens. The larval chamber is just below the surface of the open cup. Common.

Plate 300. Two galls of *Andricus sessilus* on oak.

SPIKED-TUBE-GALL WASP　*Andricus splendens*　　　　Pl. 301

Galls of this wasp occur on the ventral side of leaves of only shrub live oak. These striking monothalamous galls are tubular, with scattered, stiff projections or spikes protruding from their sides, including the top edge. Galls measure 5–6 mm high by 2–3 mm wide and occur in clusters. When fresh, galls are deep rose and pale yellow, which fades with age. Only female wasps are known. Locally common.

Plate 301. Galls of *Andricus splendens* on shrub live oak.

CRYSTAL-TUBE-GALL WASP   *Andricus sulfureus*   Pl. 302

The eye-catching monothalamous galls of this wasp occur on the underside of leaves of Arizona white and Mexican blue oaks. Sulfur-yellow and red bristles stand erect from the galls' sides. Normally, the sides exposed to direct sunlight are red, while the shaded sides are yellow. These densely hairy, bristly galls measure 10 mm high and wide. Galls occur on the midrib and lateral veins, often in groups of six or more. Only female wasps are known. Locally common.

Plate 302. Galls of *Andricus sulfureus* on oak. Photo by Joyce Gross.

FUZZY-DISC-GALL WASP   *Andricus viscidus*   Pl. 303

The disc-shaped, monothalamous galls of this wasp occur on the underside of leaves of shrub live oak. While there is a superficial resemblance to the galls of *Andricus gigas* (Plate 133) and *A. parmula* (Plate 137) from the Pacific States, and *A. discalis* (Plate 296) from the Southwest, the disc galls of *A. viscidus* differ in that the edges are rounded up, with stiff, light yellow bristles below the edge, and are not tightly appressed to the leaf surface. Galls measure 3 mm in diameter by 1.5 mm high. The chocolate-brown dorsal surface of the gall has a sparse arrangement of hairs but much less than the bottom half. The center of the gall rises like a miniature volcano, which becomes the exit for the adult. Uncommon.

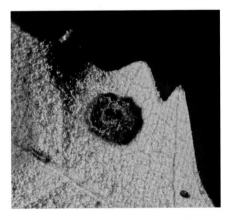

Plate 303. Gall of *Andricus viscidus* on shrub live oak.

WOOLLY-RUSSET-GALL WASP   *Andricus* sp. A   Pl. 304

The polythalamous galls of this wasp species occur on the ventral midrib of Arizona white and Mexican blue oaks. Several leaves in close proximity can support these galls, but only one per leaf. Galls are normally 10 mm long by 5 mm wide and about 3 mm high. Individual larval cells occur beneath the long, light brown, pinkish hairs, which appear scraggly and disarrayed.

Each hair has occasional starburst clusters of clear smaller hairs (see Hair Chart, page 190), not matted as they are in *Antron quercusnubila* (Plate 314). These hairs may offer some protection from certain parasites. Adults emerge in early winter, suggesting the possibility of a spring bisexual generation yet to be discovered. This species is related to *Andricus tecturnarum*. There are several variously colored woolly galls that occur on these host plants, including the larger *Andricus* sp. B, but none like this one. Common.

Plate 304. Gall of *Andricus* sp. A on oak.

WOOLLY-LEAF-GALL WASP   *Andricus* sp. B   Pl. 305

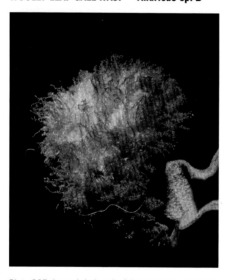

The polythalamous galls of this wasp fit the description of what Kinsey (1920) described as *Andricus incomptus* from an unknown oak in San Luis, Potosi, Mexico. Galls in Arizona occur on shrub live, Toumey, and Arizona white oaks. Galls are densely covered with hairs that are white at the base and golden brown to rusty at the edges. The scraggly, wavy hairs with numerous microscopic starburst clusters along the main stem appear brushy at first and are distinct from the hairs of all other woolly galls (see Hair Chart, page 190). Galls measure 20 mm or more across and often cover the entire underside of the host leaf. Adults have emerged in early winter, which suggests the possibility of a spring bisexual generation yet to be discovered. These galls have occasionally been misidentified as galls of *A. tecturnarum*, which has tightly pressed hairs, not scraggly and in disarray. Uncommon.

Plate 305. Large bristly gall of *Andricus* sp. B on oak.

MASKED-WOOLLY-TUBE-GALL WASP   *Andricus* sp. C   Pls. 306 & 307

Galls of this wasp occur on the underside of leaves of Mexican blue and shrub live oaks. These galls are challenging, in that it took me several observations on several host trees to figure out the sequence of gall development. Initially, the rosy-red to brick-brown tube-shaped galls start out hidden beneath a mass of highly sticky, whitish, short, woolly hairs (see Hair Chart, page 190), which may prevent parasites and inquilines from gaining access to the tender new galls and vulnerable larvae. It is difficult to near impossible to separate individual hairs from a detached small mass. A hint of pink or rose can be seen beneath the hairs of what initially look like typical woolly galls. What seems to separate this species from all other white, woolly

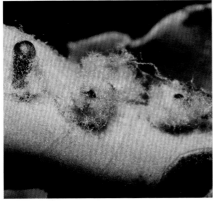

Plate 306. Galls showing full sequence of emergence for *Andricus* sp. C.

Plate 307. Three mature galls of *Andricus* sp. C.

leaf galls is that the hair cover is only temporary. As the small monothalamous galls develop and possibly harden, their brown columns rise above the basal hair to show their round, often glabrous heads, leaving most of the fibers behind. Mature galls are 4 mm high by 1.5–2 mm wide; the entire hairy gall mass reaches 5–8 mm long or wide. There can be one to three masses per leaf. Galls occur singly or in sets of two or three together rising from the same woolly mass. Adults emerged in midwinter from fresh galls collected in October, suggesting the possibility of a spring bisexual generation connected to this new species. This species is quite similar to one found by James Zimmerman in Nayarit, Mexico. I found it in both the Santa Catalina Mountains and Payson area, Arizona. Common.

WOOLLY-BEAR-GALL WASP *Andricus* sp. D   Pl. 308

Galls of this cynipid wasp occur on Mexican blue and shrub live oaks. Unlike all other woolly galls, they are tricolor or banded, usually with crimson red at both ends and a band of white hairs in the middle. Galls measure 4–5 mm long by 3 mm wide. The hairs of this species have occasional bright, wine-red, tight curls (see Hair Chart, page 190), while the hairs of similar *Andricus* sp. E (Plate 309) have numerous such curls, which may mean these two species are related, and one is inquiline-modified, to account for the banding. Individual galls were found in several locations, yet not frequently. Adults emerge in midwinter, which suggests a possible spring bisexual generation. Adults are similar to *Neuroterus* spp. but are related to *Andricus tecturnarum*. Locally common.

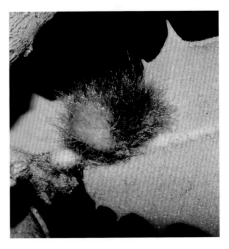

Plate 308. Gall of *Andricus* sp. D on oak.

7. *Andricus* sp. D
Hairs 2 mm

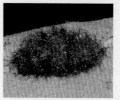

8. *Andricus* sp. E
Hairs 2 mm

9. *Antron quercusnubila*
Hairs 5 mm

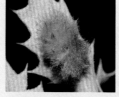

10. *Andricus* sp. A
Hairs 2.5 mm

11. *Andricus* sp. B
Hairs 2.5–3 mm

12. *Andricus* sp. C
Hairs 1.5 mm

13. Unknown #48
Hairs 2.5–3 mm

7. *Andricus* sp. D (Plate 308): Hairs with occasional coils midway.

8. *Andricus* sp. E (Plate 309): Hairs with frequent coils near base.

9. *Antron quercusnubila* (Plate 314): Hairs branched at apex with flared base.

10. *Andricus* sp. A (Plate 304): Hairs with occasional starburst clusters of clear hairs along main stem.

11. *Andricus* sp. B (Plate 305): Hairs with numerous starburst clusters of clear hairs along main stem.

12. *Andricus* sp. C (Plate 306): Hairs matted, sticky, short, difficult to separate.

13. Unknown #48 (Plate 328): Hairs with single, smaller hairs projecting from side of main stem.

RUSSET-MIDRIB-GALL WASP   *Andricus* sp. E   Pl. 309

This wasp species induces single galls on the lower half of the ventral midrib of Mexican blue and shrub live oaks. Galls measure 6–8 mm long by 4–5 mm wide. When fresh, the woolly hairs covering the individual galls are deep rose or brick red, which fades to dark brown with age. Under a microscope, numerous tiny, dark purple-red, tightly coiled, "pigtail" signature hairs are revealed. These coils usually occur on the lower half of the hair, with a long straight section emerging from the coil (see Hair Chart, page 190). One small shrub live oak can host hundreds of these galls.

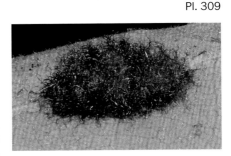

Plate 309. Gall of russet-midrib-gall wasp, *Andricus* sp. E on oak.

Adults emerge in February, which suggests there might be an alternate generation. Adults are also similar to *Neuroterus* spp, but are related to *Andricus tecturnarum*. Common.

SUCCULENT-GALL WASP   *Andricus* sp. F   Pl. 310

The green, hairy, fleshy-succulent galls of this wasp are found only on new leaf growth of shrub live oak. These monothalamous, delicate galls measure 6 mm in diameter and completely distort the shape of a new leaf. White hairs covering galls are spaced apart. In October, fresh galls quickly wither if collected. Adults emerged in early winter, suggesting that there is an alternate spring–summer

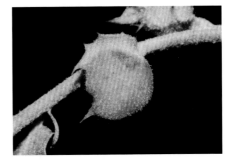

Plate 310. Galls of *Andricus* sp. F on shrub live oak.

generation, perhaps a gall included in this guide or another species. Adults are also similar to *Neuroterus* spp. This species was found only on a few shrub live oaks in the Santa Catalina Mountains, Arizona. Common.

PORCUPINE-GALL WASP *Antron acraspiformis* Pl. 311
(Cynips acraspiformis) *

The monothalamous, chestnut-brown galls of this wasp occur on the underside of leaves of Toumey and shrub live oaks. Galls occur one per leaf on the midrib and measure 5–10 mm in diameter. Rigid spines are rounded and inflated at the base, but rise to fine, thin points that may thwart some parasites and inquilines. Adults emerge prior to March. Common.

Plate 311. Gall of *Antron acraspiformis* on oak.

BUMPY-APPLE-GALL WASP *Antron madera* Pl. 312
(Cynips madera) *

Galls of this wasp occur on the underside of leaves of shrub live and Arizona white oaks. These monothalamous galls are typically red (sunny side) and yellow (shade) and measure 3–4 mm in diameter. Galls are distinguished by having sparse hairs along with white or pale yellow micro-bumps across the surface. The interior is spongy in older galls. Uncommon.

Plate 312. Galls of *Antron madera* on oak.

PRUNE-GALL WASP *Antron magdalenae* Pl. 313
(Cynips magdalenae) *

This wasp induces small, monothalamous galls on the underside of leaves of shrub live oak. The gray-brown galls are round to globular, measure 3–5 mm in diameter, and occur one gall per leaf. The surface is usually heavily wrinkled, with pronounced ridges as on a prune, and has a mealy-granular coating. Only female wasps are known from this species. Found once in Payson, Arizona. Rare.

Plate 313. Gall of *Antron magdalenae* on shrub live oak.

WOOLLY-GALL WASP · *Antron quercusnubila* · Pl. 314
(Cynips quercusnubila)*

The woolly galls of this wasp occur on the ventral midrib of leaves of Arizona white, Mexican blue, Toumey, and shrub live oaks. Each of the individual monothalamous galls covered by the hairs measures 3–6 mm in diameter, while the whole mass measures 20 mm in diameter by 10 mm high. Hair color can vary from pink to bright crimson red; often, the hairs' outer tips are whitish. Unlike those of other woolly galls, the hairs on the galls of this species are appressed or matted (see Hair Chart, page 190). Only female wasps are known for this species. Locally common.

Plate 314. Gall of *Antron quercusnubila* on oak.

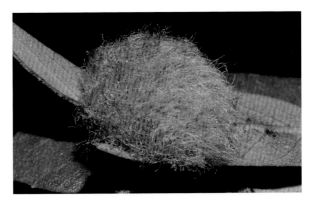

OAK-APPLE-GALL WASP · *Atrusca bella* · Pl. 315

The large, smooth, round, monothalamous galls of this species occur on the underside of leaves of Arizona white, Mexican blue, netleaf, Toumey, and shrub live oaks. While some occur at the margins of leaves, most seem attached to the midrib. Galls measure 20–25 mm in diameter; parasitized galls are smaller. Galls can be beige, pink, or yellow-green in the shade, but always have a smooth skin with a dusty bloom across the otherwise glabrous surface. The outer wall of the gall is thin, less than 1 mm thick. From its interior extend radiating fibers that support and provide nourishment to the central larval chamber, which is about 3 mm in diameter. Some fibers do not attach to the larval chamber but extend only from one section of the wall to another. These galls are sometimes difficult to separate from those of the following species, *A. brevipennata*, which is less common, smaller, and darker-colored. Common.

Plate 315. Gall of *Atrusca bella* on oak.

LITTLE-OAK-APPLE-GALL WASP *Atrusca brevipennata*   Pl. 316

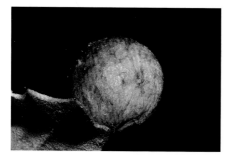

Plate 316. Gall of *Atrusca brevipennata* on oak.

This small oak-apple gall occurs on the underside of leaves of shrub live and Gambel oaks. On shrub live oak, galls occur only near a marginal spine. Galls measure 10–15 mm in diameter, are not perfectly round, and occur only one per leaf. The surface of these monothalamous galls is slightly rough or veiny, irregular, and somewhat pink-beige to rusty brown, blotchy, dull, and non-glossy. Under magnification, occasional tiny hairs or granular material appear on the surface. Galls are hollow, with a thin skin and a central larval chamber supported by radiating fibers. These fibers branch at their connecting point with the skin. Some adults had already emerged from galls found in early December. As mentioned, this species is often confused with the previous species, *A. bella*. Kinsey (1922) originally found these galls in Colorado. I have seen this gall only on shrub live oaks west of Las Vegas, Nevada. Locally common.

STRIPED-OAK-APPLE-GALL WASP *Atrusca capronae*   Pl. 317

Plate 317. Gall of *Atrusca capronae* on shrub live oak.

This wasp induces easily noticed galls that occur on the underside of leaves of shrub live oak throughout its range. These monothalamous oak-apple galls, with their centrally located larval chambers supported by radial fibers, measure 15–20 mm in diameter. Galls usually have a white, gray, or rarely bluish background color with irregular, bold red, maroon, or purple stripes that proceed from the point of attachment to the apex. The boldness of stripes may vary from northern to southern specimens. As with humans and their fingerprints, no two galls appear to have the same stripe pattern. No other species can be confused with this one north of the Mexican border. Only females are known for this species, even though it is possible there is an alternate generation yet to be discovered. Common.

RUSTY-OAK-APPLE-GALL WASP *Atrusca sp.*   Pl. 318

Galls of this wasp species tend to get your attention, as they are large, bright rusty red, and uniformly covered with fine, short, white hairs. Galls occur on the underside of leaves of shrub live oaks and are so large that one gall dominates its leaf. These monothalamous

Plate 318. Galls of *Atrusca sp.* on shrub live oak.

round galls measure up to 20 mm in diameter and are fresh in southwest Nevada in October. Some have confused this gall with that of *A. bella* (Plate 315). Common.

HEDGEHOG-GALL WASP *Acraspis* sp.   Pl. 319

The monothalamous galls of this wasp occur on the ventral midrib of leaves of Gambel oak. These galls measure 4–5 mm in diameter and are usually found one per leaf. Galls are distinguished by the short, stiff, sharp-pointed green projections that cover the gall body when fresh, giving it the resemblance to a small hedgehog. With age, the points turn brown and begin falling off. Galls have been found in several locations, including Arizona, and Utah. A similar-looking gall of a separate species was described from *Quercus macrocarpa* in Colorado and named *A. macrocarpae*. Common.

Plate 319. Gall of *Acraspis* sp. on Gambel oak.

CHESTNUT-BALL-GALL WASP *Cynips arida*   Pl. 320

The round, monothalamous galls of this wasp occur one per leaf on the ventral midrib of Arizona white and Mexican blue oaks. Galls are chestnut brown with a slight bloom that rubs off easily. The crater-like, nearly polygonal depressions across the surface, separated by rounded ridges, are the key feature distinguishing this species' gall from all other round leaf galls. Galls measure 8–11 mm in diameter. They are fresh in October in the Santa Catalina Mountains, Arizona. Only female wasps are known for this species, originally described by Kinsey from Mexico. Uncommon.

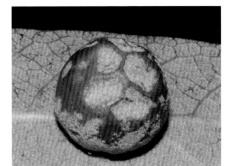

Plate 320. Gall of *Cynips arida* on oak.

PEACH-GALL WASP *Cynips plumbeum*   Pl. 321

The single, monothalamous round galls of this wasp occur on the ventral midrib of leaves of Mexican blue oak. The dense but thin covering of short hairs does not rub off easily. One side of the gall is almost always a light green, while the other is subtle rosy red

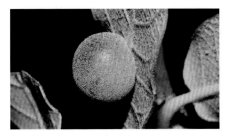

Plate 321. Gall of peach-gall wasp, *Cynips plumbeum*, on Mexican blue oak.

to dull brick brown. Galls measure 8 mm in diameter. This species was found in several locations in Arizona. Common.

MIDRIB-GALL WASP *Melikaiella lupana* Pl. 322
*(Callirhytis lupana)**

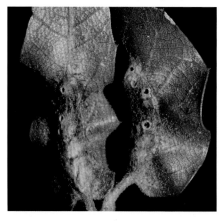

Galls of this wasp occur on the midrib of leaves of Emory and silverleaf oaks. While showing a bit on the dorsal surface, the bulk of these integral, polythalamous galls shows on the ventral side. They are green when fresh but turn brown with age. As the galls occupy half or more of the midrib, they often cause the leaf to bend. Galls measure 12 mm long by 3 mm across. In October, galls exhibit many exit holes. The genus for this species was changed from *Callirhytis* (Pujade-Villar et al. 2014). Uncommon.

Plate 322. Galls of *Melikaiella lupana* on oak.

STARBURST-GALL WASP *Neuroterus argentatus* Pl. 323

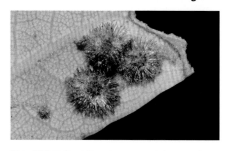

Plate 323. Galls of *Neuroterus argentatus* on oak.

These rather small, monothalamous galls are sometimes difficult to see on the underside of leaves of Mexican blue, shrub live, or Gambel oaks. Galls measure 2 mm in diameter and are brownish pink. They are distinguished by stiff, mostly lateral spines or bristles that radiate from the larval chamber, which is also covered with micro-hairs. Several of these galls can occur per leaf. Fresh galls have been found in October. Only female wasps are known. Uncommon.

BULGING-LEAF-GALL WASP *Neuroterus lamellae* Pl. 324

The round to ovoid, monothalamous, integral leaf galls of this wasp bulge out equally on both surfaces at the margin of leaves of shrub live oak. Galls usually occur one per leaf and are uniformly covered with short yellow hairs, which are slightly longer on top. The surface color varies from light green to brown. Galls

Plate 324. Bulging-leaf gall of *Neuroterus lamellae* on shrub live oak.

measure 10 mm in diameter and are often found by the dozens on a single, small tree. Only females are known. Uncommon.

BANDED-URN-GALL WASP *Phylloteras cupella*

Pl. 325

This cynipid wasp induces urn-shaped, monothalamous galls on the underside of leaves of several Southwest oaks. Galls occur singly or in groups of up to a dozen or more and stand erect near the margins of leaves. Galls have an in-rolled lip or edge at the apex but straight sides. When fresh, galls have bands of color in various shades of yellow, red, and purple. As galls mature, the color changes, with the lower half of the gall becoming dark purple while the top edge becomes rose-pink. Old galls turn brown. Galls measure 2 mm high by 1.5 mm in diameter, with a central opening forming the urn. These galls appear covered with minute crystals that are actually small hairs, with sides that have a slightly pitted surface. Adult females emerge in spring. An alternate generation has not been found. This species was originally reported in Arizona and New Mexico but is also found on several white oaks in California. Common.

Plate 325. Galls of *Phylloteras cupella* on oak.

BALL-GALL WASP *Xanthoteras pulchripenne*
(*Atrusca pulchripenne*)*

Pl. 326

The round, monothalamous, shiny galls of this wasp occur along both sides of the ventral midrib of Arizona white, Mexican blue, shrub live, Toumey, and netleaf oaks. Galls measure 3–4 mm in diameter, occur singly—not in clusters—but may be in distinct rows on either side of the midrib, with space between each gall and the next. Galls are usually fawn brown, some

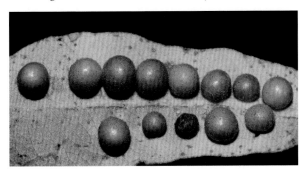

Plate 326. Galls of *Xanthoteras pulchripenne* on oak.

with small spots. While they appear glabrous at first glance, close examination reveals a sparse arrangement of short hairs. Only female wasps are known for this species. Common.

CRYSTALLINE-TUBE-GALL WASP *Xanthoteras* sp.   Pl. 327

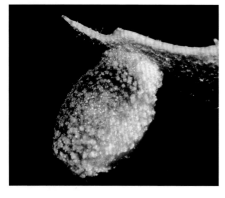

Plate 327. Gall of *Xanthoteras* sp. on oak.

The beautiful, tubelike, monothalamous galls of this wasp occur on ventral lateral veins on leaves of Mexican blue, sandpaper, and shrub live oaks. One to several galls occur per leaf and measure 5 mm high by 2.5 mm in diameter. The surface is coated with crystalline granules, which appear to be crusted hairs. The larval chamber is basal, supported by radial fibers attached to the outer wall. The gall apex is rounded, without a hole, at least when fresh in October. Lyon's (1996) *X. pungens* is much like this species except it occurs on the dorsal surface. This species appears on host trees in the Payson and Santa Catalina Mountains areas of Arizona. Common.

FUZZY-LEAF-GALL WASP Unknown #48   Pl. 328

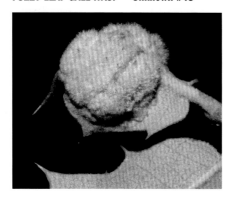

Galls of this wasp occur on the underside of leaves of shrub live oak. These polythalamous galls are covered with short, appressed, off-white woolly hairs. The hairs are simple: multiple lateral short hairs emerge from the main stem (see Hair Chart, page 190). Galls often cover the entire leaf surface and can reach 12–15 mm in diameter. This species occurs on this host in southwestern Nevada as well as occasionally in Arizona. Uncommon.

Plate 328. Gall of fuzzy-leaf-gall wasp, **Unknown #48**, on shrub live oak.

SMALL-URN-GALL WASP Unknown #49   Pl. 329

These tiny, thin-walled urn galls appear on the underside of leaves of only shrub live oak. Galls are smooth, glabrous, monothalamous, and beige-pink when fresh in spring. Galls measure 1–2 mm high by 1 mm in diameter. The larval chamber is at the base, beneath the

Plate 329. Galls of small-urn-gall wasp, **Unknown #49**, on shrub live oak.

open cup above. I have never found these galls on any other oak nor in any location except the western Nevada site, 19 km west of Las Vegas. Rare.

CLUSTERED-TUBE-GALL WASP   Unknown #50   Pl. 330

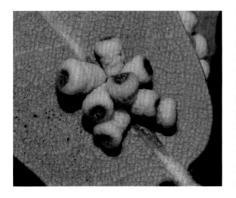

This wasp lays all its eggs close together on the ventral midrib of Gambel, Mexican blue, and shrub live oaks, and the resulting galls appear in single clusters of 12 or more galls. Individual galls measure 4 mm long by 1.5–2 mm in diameter. Each glabrous, monothalamous, light yellow gall has a brown or rosy, concave apex along with little bumps on the sides. Galls have been found in the Santa Catalina Mountains, Arizona. Common.

Plate 330. Galls of clustered-tube-gall wasp, **Unknown #50**, on oak.

ROSY-TUBE-GALL WASP   Unknown #51   Pls. 331 & 332

The rosy to red-purple leaf galls of this wasp occur on the ventral midrib on Arizona white and Mexican blue oaks. These monothalamous galls are 4 mm high by 3 mm in diameter. Like the galls of Unknown #50, these glabrous galls have numerous small bumps on the sides and a concave apex. Unlike Unknown #50, this gall occurs not in large clusters but in mostly small groups of two to four specimens. There seem to be three similar galls: the preceding, this one, and a light pink, ring-topped version (pictured). Ultimately, they may prove to be separate species or varieties of one. Locally common.

Plate 331. Galls of rosy-tube-gall wasp, **Unknown #51**, on oak.

Plate 332. Pink, ring-topped galls similar to those of **Unknown #51**

PINK-THORN-GALL WASP   Unknown #52

Pl. 333

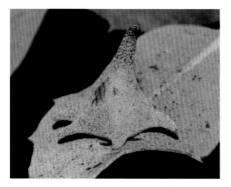

Plate 333. Gall of pink-thorn-gall wasp, **Unknown #52**, on shrub live oak.

This wasp's gall was one of the most exciting discoveries on a collecting trip to Payson, Arizona. These fascinating monothalamous galls occur one per leaf on the dorsal midrib of shrub live oak. The top half of the gall rises into a distinctive, thornlike point, while the base flares outwardly into a star shape. Shapes sometimes vary, but the thornlike top (which sometimes bends over) and the star base are consistent. Galls are pink, with a white bloom that rubs off. These striking galls measure 10 mm high and wide at the base. Weld (1960, fig. 163) pictured this but did not name it. I found and photographed three galls of this species only once, on a single tree. Rare.

MIDRIB-GALL WASP   Unknown #53

Pl. 334

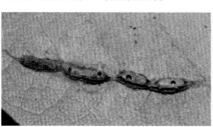

Plate 334. Galls of midrib-gall wasp, **Unknown #53**, on Mexican blue oak.

Close examination is required to detect the swelling of the ventral midrib and the associated polythalamous galls of this wasp on the leaves of Mexican blue oak. Galled midribs are only slightly larger than normal until the larval cells are exposed. Chains of larval cells reach 15 mm long, with each gall (cell) measuring 2 mm long by 1 mm wide. By October, adults have emerged. There does not appear to be much damage to the leaf except for slight discoloration. Uncommon.

RED-TOPPED-CUP-GALL WASP   Unknown #54

Pl. 335

Plate 335. Gall of red-topped-cup-gall wasp, **Unknown #54**, on Mexican blue oak.

This rather unusual monothalamous gall has some characters similar to the galls of Unknown #50 and #51. Galls of this species or variety occur just off the ventral midrib on Mexican blue oak leaves. This gall has a yellow base column that is covered with small white bumps. As the column rises, it flares out into a round, dark red bowl. Galls measure less than 3 mm high and 1 mm wide. This single gall or variety, which may be related to *Andricus sessilus* (Plate 300), was found only once and may be inquiline- or parasite-modified. Rare.

RED-APPLE-GALL WASP   Unknown #55

Pl. 336

The red to brick red integral galls of this wasp protrude equally on both dorsal and ventral sides of leaves of silverleaf oak. These round to ovoid, monothalamous, galls measure up to 5 mm in diameter, with some coalescing to form larger, odd shapes. Galls start out smooth but then wrinkle with age, showing pronounced ridges. Individual galls occur on either side of the midrib, with several per leaf, which causes some damage to the tissues beyond the galls. They superficially resemble the galls of the willow-apple-gall sawfly (*Pontania californica*, Plate 374). This new species was found in Payson, Arizona. Uncommon.

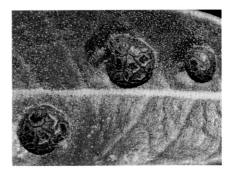

Plate 336. Galls of red-apple-gall wasp, **Unknown #55**, on silverleaf oak.

HAIRY-FOLD-GALL WASP   Unknown #56

Pl. 337

Galls of this wasp are unmistakable in that they distort the shape of leaves of Mexican blue oak by folding the edges inwardly. The bulk of the gall shows on the ventral side. These integral polythalamous galls are completely covered by short, white hairs and measure 10 mm long by 8 mm wide. Galls in October were fresh, with active larvae feeding within. This species was found in only one group of trees near Payson, Arizona. Uncommon.

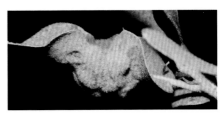

Plate 337. Gall of hairy-fold-gall wasp, **Unknown #56**, on Mexican blue oak.

BURR-GALL WASP   Unknown #57

Pl. 338

This wasp induces distinctive little monothalamous galls on the ventral side of the leaves of Arizona white and Mexican blue oaks. Galls occur one per lateral vein, but several can be scattered on one leaf. Galls are covered with short, swollen, maroon-tipped spines. The base color is a vibrant green, but it is the maroon tips that make these galls stand out. Galls measure 2 mm in diameter and are fresh in October. Weld (1957b, fig. 161) illustrated this gall but never reared adults. This species was found in one location in the Santa Catalina Mountains, Arizona. Uncommon.

Plate 338. Gall of burr-gall wasp, **Unknown #57**, on oak. Photo by Joyce Gross

LITTLE-TEARDROP-GALL WASP   Unknown #58 Pls. 339 & 340

This tiny wasp induces equally small monothalamous galls on Mexican blue oaks that are most difficult to find as they occur only one per leaf and can be easily missed. Galls measure 1–2 mm high and usually occur at the margins of leaves. Galls in October were fawn brown and had a swollen base that contains the larval chamber. From the base, the gall rises into a fine, long point. The basal hairs, which look like golden-yellow cobweb strands, sometimes persist up the sides toward the point. Adults had emerged before late October. Found only in the Santa Catalina Mountains near Tucson, Arizona. Rare.

Plate 339. Gall of little-teardrop-gall wasp, **Unknown #58**, with adult exit hole, on Mexican blue oak.

Plate 340. Gall of **Unknown #58**, still occupied.

CRYSTAL-GALL WASP   Unknown #59 Pl. 341

Galls of this wasp species occur on the underside of leaves of Mexican blue oak. Two or more galls can occur per leaf, each measuring 3–4 mm in diameter. These monothalamous galls look like they are covered with crystalline granules that appear to be made of white hairs. As with some other species, the sides exposed to direct sunlight are red, while the sides mostly shaded are yellow. Uncommon.

Plate 341. Gall of crystal-gall wasp, **Unknown #59**, on Mexican blue oak.

ROUND-MIDRIB-GALL WASP   Unknown #60

Pl. 342

This wasp's galls occur on the ventral midrib of gray oak. They are easily separated from all other round, ball-type galls by the white powderlike substance that covers them and easily rubs off, showing the green body marked with random red or maroon splotches. Galls are hard and measure 10 mm in diameter. They are monothalamous, with a central larval chamber surrounded by white flesh. Larvae were active in October. This species was found on only one tree in the Santa Catalina Mountains, Arizona. Uncommon.

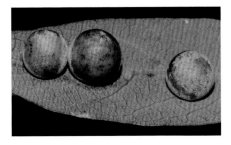

Plate 342. Galls of round-midrib-gall wasp, **Unknown #60**, on gray oak.

COLUMNAR-GALL WASP   Unknown #61

Pl. 343

The monothalamous galls of this wasp occur on ventral lateral veins of leaves of gray oak. These tubular or column-like galls stand alone, with one to four galls per leaf, and measure 6 mm high by 2 mm in diameter. The straw-yellow body of the gall shows through the uniform covering of short white hairs. Fresh galls found in October were fully developed, with intact larvae. Common.

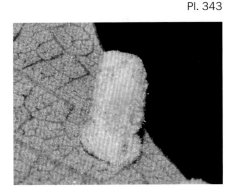

Plate 343. Galls of columnar-gall wasp, **Unknown #61**, on gray oak.

GREEN-URCHIN-GALL WASP   Unknown #62

Fig. 49 & Pl. 344

The monothalamous galls of this wasp occur on the underside of leaves at the juncture of leaf and petiole of shrub live oaks. Galls occur one per leaf. The lime-green main body of the gall is covered with soft, long, brown-tipped bristles that swell toward the base, making it look like a sea urchin. Sometimes the tips are brittle and break. Galls measure 5 mm in

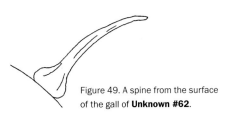

Figure 49. A spine from the surface of the gall of **Unknown #62**.

Plate 344. Gall of green-urchin-gall wasp, **Unknown #62**, on shrub live oak.

diameter. This species is likely in the genus *Acraspis*; the shape of its spines does not match any of Kinsey's (1929) illustrations of spiny *Acraspis* galls, including *A. russa, A. expositor, A. prinoides*, and *A. erinacei*, nor of *Antron acraspiformis*. This gall was found in the mountains near Payson and in the Santa Catalina Mountains, Arizona. Uncommon.

HAIRY-CUP-GALL WASP   Unknown #63

Pl. 345

The monothalamous galls of this wasp occur on lateral veins on the underside of leaves of shrub live oak. Galls measure 3 mm in diameter and occur one per leaf. Galls are a fawn brown, somewhat flat, rounded cup, with short, stiff, white crystalline hairs around the lower portion. The interior edge of the cup turns inward and is markedly uneven and ragged. The point of attachment is a thin stalk, apparent when viewed from the side. Adults had not emerged yet when this gall was found in December. Only one gall was found among dozens of host trees at a southwest Nevada site west of Las Vegas; this species was found nowhere else. Rare.

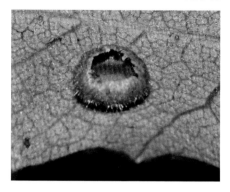

Plate 345. Gall of hairy-cup-gall wasp, **Unknown #63**, on shrub live oak.

Pine Galls

At least 18 species of pine trees are native to western states. The principal pines considered here are Coulter pine (*Pinus coulteri*), Jeffrey pine (*P. jeffreyi*), ponderosa pine (*P. ponderosa*), gray pine (*P. sabiniana*), Monterey pine (*P. radiata*), lodgepole pine (*P. contorta* subsp. *murrayana*), knobcone pine (*P. attenuata*), singleleaf pinyon pine (*P. monophylla*), and Colorado pinyon pine (*P. edulis*). Most galls associated with pines are best seen on small trees, except for massive witches' brooms that are obvious from a distance. Several rust fungi attack and gall pine trees (see Table 6). Only one species is described here, along with two species of mistletoe that cause witches' brooms. Additional species are listed in Table 8. Also included in this section are a few of the gall midges that form needle galls.

WESTERN GALL-RUST FUNGUS   *Endocronartium harknessii*

Pls. 346 & 347

This fungus induces globose to pear-shaped, woody stem galls on Coulter, Jeffrey, ponderosa, gray, and Monterey pines in the West, as well as the ornamental Aleppo pine (*P. halepensis*). This fungus may also appear on other species, including other ornamental pines. Galls occur on stems and exposed roots and continue growing year after year. These galls can exceed 60 cm in diameter (see Plate 9). As the galls increase in size, so does the damage to branches and needles beyond the galls, ultimately killing the branches. During late spring and early summer months, bright orange-yellow aeciospores form in ruptures in the surfaces of the galls and are dispersed each morning for a period of two to three weeks. Heavily infected trees often produce witches' brooms in response to the presence of this rust. Because germination of the spores requires specific humidity and weather conditions, there appear to be waves of infection that coincide with

Plate 346. Witches'-broom gall of *Endocronartium harknessii*.

Plate 347. Gall of *E. harknessii* showing spores on ponderosa pine.

banner years of highly conducive weather. Unlike other rusts, this one goes from pine to pine without an intermediate host. These galls even occur on the stunted shore pines (*P. contorta* subsp. *contorta*) scattered in the muskeg of Alaska. Some strains of this fungus also pass from pines to paintbrushes (*Castilleja* spp.).

Secondary fungi and insects that invade galled tissues occasionally kill this rust gall. The hyperparasitic fungus *Scytalidium uredinicola* appears to exert some control over the production of the spores of *Endocronartium harknessii*. The pyralid moth *Dioryctria banksiella* is known to feed on galled tissue (not the fungus) of some pine hosts. This rust fungus has been reported to be limited to North America. Trunks and limbs from galled trees are often used as totems and ornate timber for buildings, railings, and fences along the West Coast.

DWARF MISTLETOES *Arceuthobium campylopodum* and *A. americanum*   Pl. 348

These mistletoes induce elliptical, integral stem swellings and witches' brooms on Jeffrey, lodgepole, ponderosa, knobcone, and Coulter pines. Galls measure up to 150 mm long by 80 mm in diameter. The stem swellings are noticeable beneath a burst of succulent, short, bright yellow-orange, nearly leafless but jointed mistletoe stems. Sometimes the elliptical galls are hidden beneath numerous shoots of the mistletoe or the witches' brooms generated by these mistletoes. As the sticky mistletoe seeds, which are forcibly ejected from their fruits, spread and infection occurs on new branches of the host or other trees, dispersal of the mistletoe initiates new galls

Plate 348. Swollen branch gall of *Arceuthobium americanum* on lodgepole pine.

and brooms. *Arceuthobium campylopodum* is a serious pathogen on Jeffrey pine, while *A. americanum* is common on lodgepole pine.

PINE-NEEDLE-GALL MIDGE *Cembrotia coloradensis* Fig. 50

This midge induces needle galls on Colorado pinyon pine. Galls form at the base of needles and are often covered by a thin, brown sheath (the fascicle). Galls measure 12 mm long by 4 mm in diameter. Galled needles grow only about one-third their normal length. Gall color varies from green to purple-red and yellow. Galls examined in May harbor several 1-mm-long, orange midge larvae in each gall. Larval chambers are enclosed and removable. Larvae do not complete their growth during summer but do so the following spring. Adult emergence occurs in late spring, with egg deposition occurring on new needles in May and June. There is only one generation per year. Needles usually turn brown and drop after the adults leave.

Figure 50. Needle gall of *Cembrotia coloradensis*.

NEEDLE-LIP-GALL MIDGE *Cembrotia* sp. Pl. 349

Plate 349. Needle galls of *Cembrotia* sp. on pinyon pine.

This midge induces short or stunted, bifurcated needle galls on Colorado pinyon pine from Colorado westward, with limited distribution in California in the eastern Mojave Desert. These unique 10-mm-long midge galls usually contain two larvae, each in its own depression or chamber. Another gall midge, *Contarinia cockerelli*, has been found in these galls but is not considered the gall-maker. The needles do not grow beyond the swelling of the galls. The apex of each gall is characteristically split into two parts looking like lips. Galls occur side by side near the tips of new growing shoots. Adults emerge through the hole at the apex. The biology of this species is considered to be similar to that of *C. coloradensis*.

NEEDLE-GALL MIDGE *Pinyonia edulicola* Pl. 350

This midge induces spindle-shaped galls at the base of needles of Colorado pinyon pine from Colorado westward and singleleaf pinyon pine in the New York Mountains of the eastern Mojave Desert, California. Eggs are laid on new needles, and the larvae crawl down to the base of the host needles, where their feeding induces the swollen needle galls. Galls are often light green, or sometimes rose red, and measure 8–15 mm long by 4 mm in diameter. Galls contain up to 40 larvae, which grow during summer and the following spring. Pupation occurs within the gall, and adults emerge early in the second summer. Later, abandoned needles drop off prematurely, before their normal six- to eight-year life span.

Plate 350. Needle galls of *Pinyonia edulicola* on pinyon pine.

Plate 351. Needle galls of *Thecodiplosis piniradiatae* on Monterey pine.

MONTEREY PINE–GALL MIDGE *Thecodiplosis piniradiatae* Pl. 351

This gall midge induces elliptical, spindle-shaped galls at the base of Monterey pine needles. It has also been reported on Coulter and gray pines. Galled needles are usually stunted, about 35 mm long, and do not reach normal size (greater than 110 mm). Actual galls measure 10 mm long by 4 mm in diameter. Normally all three needles within the bundle (fascicle) are swollen. Galls occur among new needles at tips of shoots in spring. Although the galls bulge out, they are flat at point of contact with other needles in the fascicle. Eggs are laid on growing buds usually in January. As with other gall midges on pines, newly hatched larvae crawl to the base of the needles, where they begin feeding, initiating development of the swollen galls. Galls are fully grown by February. Pupation occurs sometime in late fall or early winter. Galled needles die in fall.

Redwood False Galls

The tannic acid load in redwoods normally makes them quite resistant to insects. While some fungi attack redwoods under certain conditions, there are no clearly identified gall organisms, though the following trunk and branch anomalies have been called galls by some authors. The following descriptions apply to coast redwood (*Sequoia sempervirens*). Giant sequoia (*Sequoiadendron giganteum*) may have similar protrusions.

Burls

Coast redwoods are famous for large burls around the base of their trunks, as well as monstrously large (greater than 1 m) trunk eruptions quite high off the ground on one side of host trees. These lopsided eruptions are most likely burls, since no virus, fungus, bacterium, or insect has been associated with their growth (see the discussion of burls in the Introduction). Burl wood is prized for its intriguing grain by furniture makers and other woodworkers.

In rare cases, individual trees in the middle of coast redwood groves are covered with branch tumors ranging in size from 50 to 120 mm in diameter. One such tree exists on the University of California campus in Berkeley. Since no other trees nearby show this malady and no organisms have been associated with their growth, these tumorlike growths are considered genetic anomalies.

Cones
Pl. 353

Another strange discovery revealed young coast redwood cones with scattered, cream-beige, triangular bracts protruding sporadically from between cone scales. These bract-like projections measure 3–4 mm long. Attempts have been made to isolate a causative agent but to no avail. Further research may reveal a gall organism, possibly a *Taphrina* fungus, associated with coast redwoods someday, but for now, there appears to be none.

Plate 353. Cone-bract abnormalities of coast redwood.

Plate 352. Branch tumors on coast redwood.

Spruce Galls

COOLEY-SPRUCE-GALL ADELGID   *Adelges cooleyi*
Pl. 354

The contiguous western states have four native spruces: Sitka (*Picea sitchensis*), weeping (*P. breweriana*), Engelmann (*P. engelmannii*), and Colorado blue (*P. pungens*); Alaska also has black (*P. mariana*), and white (*P. glauca*). This adelgid induces integral, elongate, needled stem galls near the tips of new branches in spring on the native western spruces. It also galls the ornamental oriental spruce (*P. orientalis*). Galls measure 40 mm long by 20 mm in diameter, with some reaching greater size on occasion. When fresh, galls are green, fleshy, and covered with normal-size needles. By midsummer, liplike slits develop above the swollen, expanded needle bases. The adelgids escape these basal chambers through open slits and migrate to the tips of needles, where they turn into winged adult females. These females then migrate to either Douglas-fir (*Pseudotsuga menziesii*) or to another spruce. Eggs laid on needles of Douglas-fir produce only woolly adelgids, not galls. By fall, galls on spruce look like pineapple-shaped cones, turn brown, and lose the needles. Immature females overwinter on spruce host trees or their alternate host. They mature in spring as adult stem mothers and start laying hundreds of eggs on new terminal shoots of spruce trees. This insect is common throughout the West, including Alaska, wherever its host trees are found.

Plate 354. Shoot-tip gall of *Adelges cooleyi* on spruce.

Tanoak Galls

TANOAK-PIP-GALL WASP *Andricus notholithocarpi* Fig. 51

Galls of this new species of cynipid wasp are found on tanoak (*Notholithocarpus densiflorus*—not a true oak). They are quite unusual in that they occur on four different plant organs: axillary buds, catkins, leaf margins, and petiole or midrib of leaves. The small, monothalamous, cone-shaped galls basically look the same, regardless of the location of occurrence. Galls measure 3–5 mm long, are relatively smooth and glabrous, and are marked by longitudinal ridges on the gall surface terminating in a rounded point. When fresh in late spring, galls are light green; they age to light brown by winter. Larvae overwinter inside galls. Adults emerge the following spring in time for new leaf and flower development. Until recently, only root galls were known on this host.

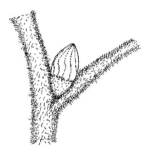

Figure 51. Axillary bud gall of *Andricus notholithocarpi*.

TANOAK-FLOWER-GALL MIDGE *"Dasineura"* sp. Pl. 355 & Fig. 52

This new species induces polythalamous, round-globular, hairy galls on the staminate flowers of both varieties of tanoak (*Notholithocarpus densiflorus* var. *densiflorus*; *N. densiflorus* var. *echinoides*) during spring and early summer. Several galls can occur in clusters along the length of the flower stalk.

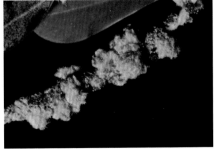

Plate 355. Several flower galls of *"Dasineura"* sp. on tanoak.

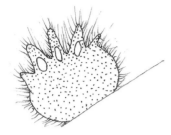

Galls are covered with dense golden-beige hairs and measure up to 5 mm in diameter. The green galls are globular in form but in cross section larval chambers are found beneath fleshy projections covered with the golden hairs. While the larvae appear to belong to *Dasineura* sp., adults will be required to confirm this identification.

Figure 52. Cross section of "*Dasineura*" sp. flower gall showing larval chambers.

Walnut Galls

POUCH-GALL MITE *Eriophyes brachytarsus*   Pl. 356

This mite induces rough-surfaced, veiny, green-red pouch galls on the upper leaflet surfaces of California black walnut (*Juglans californica*). Galls occur singly or in coalesced clumps and when abundant can distort the leaves. Galls measure 3–8 mm in diameter and stand 3–5 mm above the surface of the leaf on a short pedicel. The underside of leaves is marked by corresponding depressions with openings leading up into the galls. These mites overwinter under bud scales.

BLISTER MITE *Eriophyes erineus*   Pl. 357

This mite induces large, feltlike masses of pale yellow hairs on the underside of leaflets of English walnut (*Juglans regia*). Single hair-lined depressions (erinea) often measure up to 17 mm in diameter, but occasionally individual erineum galls coalesce to cover much larger sections of the leaflet. There are corresponding lumps that look like blisters on the dorsal surface of the leaflets. Mites overwinter under bud scales and become active when buds begin to open. This mite is widespread wherever English walnuts grow.

Plate 356. Galls of *Eriophyes brachytarsus* on California black walnut leaflet.

Plate 357. Erineum galls of *Eriophyes erineus* on dorsal surface of English walnut leaflet.

Willow Galls

The western states have over 40 species of willow (*Salix* spp.). As with identification of willows, the gall complex associated with them represents a monumental taxonomic challenge. A colleague quipped, "We would need two more lifetimes to sort out all of the gall insects on willows." Of those we do know about, there are several sawflies, several gall midges, and several species of eriophyid mites, as well as a rust fungus, not described here, that induce galls on willows.

Stem Galls

Several species of sawflies in the genus *Euura* induce integral stem galls on willows in the West, including Alaska. In contrast to other gall organisms, the larvae of which initiate gall formation, the adults of this genus, as well as *Pontania* (leaf-gall sawflies), are responsible for gall development. Colleterial fluids injected into meristematic plant tissues by adults apparently program willows to produce galls. The galls of most *Euura* species reach full development before the eggs hatch. Some species of sawflies clean house by ejecting frass from larval chambers to the outside. During their short, two-week life, adults of both *Euura* and *Pontania* species drink water, eat pollen and nectar, and browse the hairs on leaves. In addition to the stem galls induced by these sawflies, willow stem galls are induced by gall midges of the genus *Rabdophaga*. Keep in mind that the galls described here may occur on willow species other than those mentioned, and anyone examining willows is likely to find galls not described here.

BEAKED-TWIG-GALL MIDGE   *Rabdophaga rigidae*   Pl. 358

Galls of this midge are quite easily found in winter on leafless branches of several species of willows. They are large, measuring 30 mm long by 10 mm in diameter, and distinguished from all other willow-stem galls by the prominent beak that forms at the apex of each gall. These monothalamous galls begin development in spring. A new shoot often protrudes from the upper side of each gall. Although most branches have only one gall, some branches may have two galls within a few centimeters of each other. Adults emerge in spring in time for new shoot elongation. This is one of the most widespread stem-gall midges in the country, reportedly occurring from New England to the West Coast, as well as Asia, including Japan.

Plate 358. Twig gall of *Rabdophaga rigidae* on willow.

TUBER-GALL MIDGE *Rabdophaga salicisbatatus*  Fig. 53

This midge induces large, integral, polythalamous, tuber-like stem galls on several species of willow in the West. The galls are usually abrupt swellings, glabrous, and yellow-green when fresh. Occasionally, there are minor blemishes on the galls' otherwise smooth surface. Galls measure up to 40 mm long by 20 mm in diameter. These galls usually form in spring on new shoots, though the timing depends on elevation. Some galls distort the alignment of the affected stems, causing them to bend. These galls can also damage branches and leaves beyond the galls. By fall, galls are brown and hard. Adult midges pupate at the surface of the galls in spring. Oviposition follows shortly thereafter. One generation per year.

Figure 53. Integral stem gall of *Rabdophaga salicisbatatus.*

ROSETTE-GALL MIDGE *Rabdophaga salicisbrassicoides* Fig. 54 & Pl. 359

This midge induces open or closed rosette, polythalamous bud galls on several species of willow. These detachable galls with leafy bracts often appear at every axillary joint along the length of the galled stem. They look like old cones when dried and brown in winter. When fresh, however, they look more like leaf lettuce, with varying arrangements of leafy bracts. Galls measure up to 20 mm high by 20 mm wide at the base; individual bracts measure 8 mm long by 9 mm wide at the base. The bracts often extend away from the main body of the galls and sometimes are recurved. In spring, these pliable galls are green, often with a red blush at the base of the bracts. In winter, galls are brittle and often lose most of their leafy bracts. Larval chambers are located at the base of the galls. Adults emerge in spring and lay eggs in lateral buds. There is only one generation per year. The predaceous midge *Lestodiplosis septemmaculata* has been reared from these galls. There are also several parasitic pteromalid wasps associated with this gall midge.

Figure 54. Gall of *Rabdophaga salicisbrassicoides* showing thinness of leafy bracts.

Plate 359. Leafy galls of *R. salicisbrassicoides* on arroyo willow.

CONE-GALL MIDGE *Rabdophaga strobiloides*   Fig. 55

This midge induces pinecone-like, monothalamous galls on lateral and terminal buds of several species of willow throughout western states. Leafy bracts usually are appressed, not flaring away from the main gall body. When fresh, galls are green, but they turn brown with age in fall. Galls usually measure 10–15 mm in length by 10–12 mm in diameter. Old galls may remain on host trees for two or three years. The larval chamber is central, near the base. Adults emerge at varying times in spring, depending on elevation. There is one generation per year.

Figure 55. Galls of *Rabdophaga strobiloides*.

BUD-GALL MIDGE *Rabdophaga* sp.   Pl. 360

This midge induces cone-shaped, monothalamous bud galls on members of the arroyo willow (*Salix lasiolepis*) group. While superficially similar in appearance to galls of the rosette-gall midge (*R. salicisbrassicoides*; plate 359), the galls of this species have thick, succulent, strongly recurved, somewhat inflexible leafy bracts that are appressed to the gall body. Between the leafy green bracts, the base of the bracts and the body of the gall are flushed with red-purple. Galls measure to 15 mm long by 10 mm in diameter and develop in summer, at elevations above 1,500 m. Adults emerge the following late spring or early summer, for one generation per year.

Plate 360. Gall of *Rabdophaga* sp. showing thick leafy bracts on arroyo willow.

Below: Figure 56. Galls of *Euura breweriae* on Brewer's willow.

BREWER'S-STEM-GALL SAWFLY *Euura breweriae*   Fig. 56

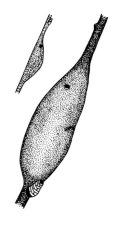

This sawfly induces linear, lopsided, integral, polythalamous stem galls on Brewer's willow (*Salix breweri*). These glossy, smooth, thin-walled galls develop mostly on one side of the stem. When fresh, these galls are slightly fuzzy and are usually bright yellow-green, blushed with a bit of red. Galls measure 20–40 mm long by 15 mm in diameter. Each gall can contain up to three larvae. The larvae of this species do not cut exit holes prior to pupation. As with nearly all gall-inducing *Euura*, there is only one generation per year. Adults emerge in April and May.

STEM SAWFLY *Euura exiguae*   Fig. 57

This sawfly induces linear, gradually tapering, integral stem galls on narrowleaf willow (*Salix exigua*) and dusky willow (*S. melanopsis*) and possibly other related species. These smooth-surfaced galls may be hairless or have minute hairs. At first, galls are green, but they turn brown later, as the sawflies mature and stop feeding. Galls measure 20–70 mm long by 5–15 mm in diameter. Galls are usually lopsided, with most of the development occurring on one side of the stem. Galls of this species resemble those of the stem-gall sawfly (*E. lasiolepis*). Two or more galls may combine in their development because of close oviposition and create what appears as one giant gall. Each gall may contain one or more larvae. When larvae have completed their development, they crawl to the top of the gall and cut an exit hole, which they plug with frass just prior to pupation. Pupation occurs in the gall. Emergence of males and females occurs in spring as new shoots begin to grow. There is one generation per year.

Figure 57. Gall of *Euura exiguae*.

GEYER'S STEM-GALL SAWFLY *Euura geyerianae*   Fig. 58

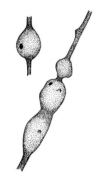

This sawfly induces bulbous, abruptly swollen, integral stem galls on Geyer's willow (*Salix geyerianae*). Fresh galls are often covered with powdery white material. Mature galls are thick-walled and glossy green to mottled red-brown. These polythalamous galls measure up to 20 mm long by 15 mm in diameter. Larvae make an exit hole prior to pupation. Males and females emerge in late spring. Adults of this species have been observed feeding on nectar, pollen, and stamens of host willows. This species is abundant in scattered locations from Oregon through the high-elevation conifer forests and stream canyons along the eastern Sierra Nevada.

Figure 58. Gall of *Euura geyerianae*.

STEM-GALL SAWFLY *Euura lasiolepis*   Fig. 59

This sawfly induces thick-walled, lopsided, integral stem galls on arroyo willow (*Salix lasiolepis*). These glossy, glabrous galls occur singly on one side of the branch, while some galls develop opposite each other, creating the appearance of one gall. Galls growing in shade are usually yellow-green, while those more exposed to the sun are red-purple. These galls measure up to 70 mm long by 20 mm in diameter. The top usually tapers into the stem, while the base is abruptly swollen. As galls age and dry, they shrivel considerably. Up to five larvae can be found in a single gall. They do not cut exit holes prior to pupation. Precut exit holes increase the

Figure 59. Galls of *Euura lasiolepis*.

potential danger of floodwater reaching the larval chambers and killing the larvae in some environments. While most species in this genus overwinter in a prepupal state, this species continues to feed and grow slowly until late January. In many parts of the Sierra Nevada, this species pupates and emerges in May, timed with development of new shoots. Some clones of willows exhibit an inherent resistance to attack by these sawflies, while other clones are susceptible. Several parasitic pteromalid wasps attack this sawfly (as well as other *Euura* species). Galls with walls thicker than the length of pteromalid ovipositor are less vulnerable to attack by these wasps.

LEMMON'S STEM-GALL SAWFLY   *Euura lemmoniae*

Fig. 60

This sawfly induces abruptly swollen, potato-shaped, integral stem galls on Lemmon's willow (*Salix lemmonii*). Fresh galls in spring are slightly striated, glossy to dull, and dark green to reddish brown. These somewhat knobby galls measure up to 60 mm long by 15 mm in diameter and occur on both sides of the affected stems. Occasionally, some galls will occur in a lopsided fashion on one side of the stem. Normal-looking buds are often found on the sides of these galls. As with other members of the genus *Euura*, larvae of this species can defend themselves when disturbed by lifting and waving their posterior while ejecting pungent fluid from their abdominal glands. Males and females emerge between late April and June. This sawfly is one of the most common gall-inducing species in high-elevation meadows in the Sierra Nevada.

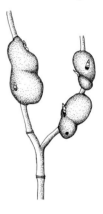

Figure 60. Galls of *Euura lemmoniae*.

SCOULER'S STEM-GALL SAWFLY   *Euura scoulerianae*

Fig. 61

This sawfly induces thick-walled, elongate, smooth, integral stem galls on Scouler's willow (*Salix scouleriana*). Galls usually taper toward the top and are usually mottled green and red when fresh; some are slightly hairy. With age, they turn brown, then bark-gray. Galls measure up to 40 mm long by 15 mm in diameter. The last-instar larvae cut exit holes near the top of the galls and then plug the holes with frass before retreating to the bottom of the galls, where they pupate later. Males and females emerge in May and June. In some areas, as much as 75% of the population of this sawfly is killed by parasites. Smith (1970) found that the moisture content of the branches influenced pupation in late spring.

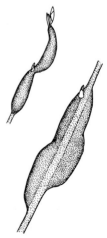

Figure 61. Galls of *Euura scoulerianae*.

PETIOLE-GALL SAWFLY   *Euura* sp. A   Pl. 361

This sawfly induces elliptical, integral petiole galls on leaves of *Salix lasiandra* and possibly other species of willows as well. Galls measure 25 mm long by 8–10 mm in diameter. The surface of the gall is generally glabrous but with distinct rounded cross ridges or furrows. As shown in the photograph, galls encompass the entire petiole into the lower midrib. These galls closely resemble those of *E. testaceipes* on *S. fragilis* in Finland. While these galls/gall-makers were briefly mentioned and pictured in Smith (1968, fig. 30), they were not identified to species.

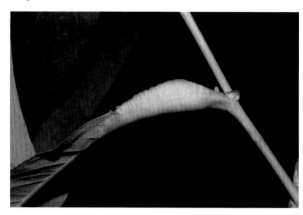

Plate 361. Gall of *Euura* sp. A on willow.

SMOOTH-PETIOLE-GALL SAWFLY   *Euura* sp. B   Pl. 362

The smooth, glabrous, monothalamous galls of this sawfly occur on the short petioles of leaves of Barclay's willow (*S. barclayi*) and perhaps other species in the subalpine environment of mountains. Galls are smooth, glabrous, and red-green, and measure 14 mm long by 3 mm in diameter. Some galls extend up into the midrib. The larval chamber is nearly the length of the gall. Larvae were still active in early September, even though some had already emerged and dropped to the ground for pupation.

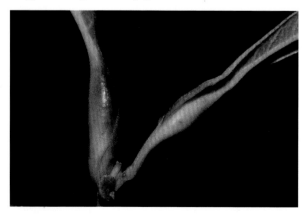

Plate 362. Galls of *Euura* sp. B on Barclay's willow.

Leaf Galls

At least three groups of organisms are associated with leaf galls that commonly occur on willows: sawflies, gall midges, and eriophyid mites. Also, an unidentified rust fungus induces galls on willow leaves. As with other hosts and gall-inducers, the taxonomy of insects on willows is complex and little understood. Several gall midges utilize willows but have yet to be identified to species level. I have also found rust, mite, and midge galls on willows along tundra streams of northern Alaska as well as subalpine meadows of mountains in Washington that are currently unnamed, even though they are abundant and common.

BEAD-GALL MITE   *Aculops tetanothrix*   Pls. 363 & 364

This mite induces irregularly rounded bead galls on both sides of leaves of several species of willow from Utah and Arizona to California. The warty bead galls measure 2–3 mm in diameter and occur singly or in coalesced groups of two or three. Hundreds of these galls can occur on a single leaf, sometimes distorting it. Galls appear between lateral veins and are often yellow-green to bright red. Depending on the species of host willow, galls may be either glabrous or covered with minute hairs. This eriophyid mite has an alternation of generations; the mites remain in the galls until fall, when the galls become dry and hard. Mites exit the galls and migrate to crevices in the bark and buds, where they overwinter. Catkins and buds on the same trees are also galled, but these galls are thought to belong to the eriophyid mite *A. aenigma*, which has also been reported in the eastern United States and in Europe.

Plate 364. Bud galls of *A. aenigma* on arroyo willow.

Plate 363. Bead galls of *Aculops tetanothrix* on arroyo willow.

POUCH-GALL MITE   Unknown #1

Pl. 365

This species of eriophyid mite induces large pouch galls on leaves of feltleaf willow (*Salix alaxensis*), diamond-leaf willow (*S. planifolia* subsp. *pulchra*), and possibly other willows in the Arctic and alpine environments of Alaska. Galls commonly coalesce into substantial masses that nearly cover the entire underside of the distorted leaf. Shapes vary; some individual galls look like clubs, arising from the leaf surface on a narrow neck, then bulging out into a globular, convoluted head. These rose-red, hairy galls measure 3–6 mm high, with a 1–2-mm-diameter neck, and a club-shaped head to 3–5 mm in diameter. The interior chamber of each tends to match the convoluted exterior surface, with multiple nooks and crannies where the mites feed. These galls have been collected along the Snake, Nome, Sinuk, and Pilgrim Rivers of the Seward Peninsula, as well as from shrub willows in open tundra near Nome, Alaska.

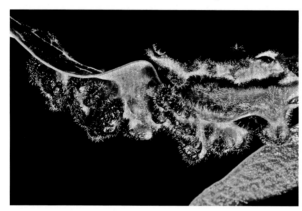

Plate 365. Galls of pouch-gall mite, **Unknown #1**, on willow.

CLUB-GALL MITE   Unknown #2

Pl. 366

The willow club-gall mite induces glabrous, stalked, club-shaped galls on the dorsal surface of leaves of Barclay's willow (*Salix barclayi*) in subalpine environments of the Cascade Mountains in Washington, and possibly occurs on other willows or elsewhere. Bright red galls on top of

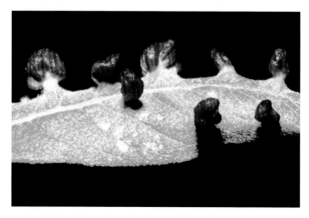

Plate 366. Galls of club-gall mite, **Unknown #2**, on Barclay's willow.

yellow stalks occur either singly or clumped together. A single leaf can bear over a dozen of these galls. Each gall has a corresponding pit on the underside of the leaf. Galls measure 3 mm in diameter by 4 mm high. This mite's galls are distinguished from those of the preceding mite by complete absence of hairs and the location on the dorsal surface. They are further distinguished from *Aculops tetanothrix* (Plate 363) by having prominent stalks.

MIDRIB-GALL SAWFLY   Unknown #3   Pls. 367 & 368

Midrib galls of this sawfly are found on leaves of *Salix* spp. in subalpine environments of the Pacific States. Galls are asymmetrical, bulging out on one side of the ventral midrib and are at least three to four times larger than the normal vein. Galls measure 4 mm wide by 12–14 mm long. The dorsal surface of the leaf shows noticeable discoloration and a pinch or convex swelling that is usually red. On the underside, the galled midrib is yellow-green. As with other sawfly larvae, the white larvae possess false legs on each segment of the abdomen (unlike moth larvae). The larval chamber is mined out along the full length of the gall. Occasionally, galls of *Iteomyia* sp. C (Plates 372 and 373) protrude out of one side of this midrib gall.

Plate 367. Dorsal view of gall of midrib-gall sawfly, **Unknown #3**, on willow.

Plate 368. Ventral view of gall of **Unknown #3**.

TOOTH-GALL MIDGE   *Iteomyia* sp. A

Pls. 369 & 370

This midge induces smooth, large, polythalamous galls mostly on the underside of leaves of arroyo willow (*Salix lasiolepis*) and related willows. Each gall is characterized by one or more slightly bent projections that look like roots of a molar tooth. Each toothy projection is correlated with a larval chamber, allowing one to count the number of larvae per gall. Larval chambers are located near the base of the galls where they are attached to the host leaf. Often, a depression surrounds the galls at this juncture, where aphids will nestle to feed on sweet cellular liquid. Galls bulge on the dorsal surface of leaves, but the majority of gall growth occurs on the underside. Galls have no openings and can be yellow-green or bright red, depending on exposure to the sun. They measure up to 10 mm long and wide, but single-toothed galls are smaller. Galls collected in August had full-grown larvae. Since gall development does not begin until summer in many locations, adults must emerge in late spring.

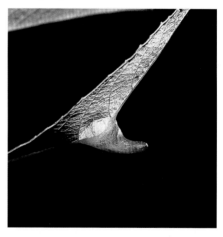

Plate 369. Multi-tooth gall of *Iteomyia* sp. A on willow.

Plate 370. Single-tooth gall of *Iteomyia* sp. A, indicating one larval chamber.

TUBE-GALL MIDGE   *Iteomyia* sp. B

Pl. 371

Plate 371. Galls of *Iteomyia* sp. B on arroyo willow.

This midge induces tubular, monothalamous galls that hang from the ventral surface of arroyo willow (*Salix lasiolepis*) leaves. The distinguishing character of these midge galls is the apical hole or depression that develops at the end of each gall. While most of the gall hangs below the leaf, there is usually a slight depression on the dorsal surface. Galls are commonly pink to red with hints of yellow and green. They measure 5 mm high by 4 mm wide at their base. These midge galls may develop singly or in coalescing groups of four to five individuals. Gall development begins in spring in the central coast area of California. This species may occur throughout the range of the arroyo willow group. Larvae appear to leave the gall by autumn and pupate in spring. Willows that retain their leaves into fall and winter may continue to support the galls of this species in some areas.

APPRESSED-TOOTH-GALL MIDGE *Iteomyia* sp. C

Pls. 372 & 373

These polythalamous–monothalamous galls occur on leaves of Barclay's willow (*S. barclayi*), and perhaps other willows, in the subalpine environment of mountains. Although superficially similar to galls of *Iteomyia* sp. A, galls of this midge differ in that they form on the ventral leaf surface flat against the leaf rather than hanging down. Individual galls measure 3 mm wide at the base by 5–6 mm long, but most often they occur in coalesced clusters along the midrib that can exceed 30–40 mm or more. On the shaded ventral surface, the galls are generally light green and hairy; on the dorsal surface the corresponding convex domes are mostly glabrous and red from sun exposure. The elongated protrusion that looks like a tooth ends in a rounded, recessed opening plugged with hair. Each tooth leads to a larval chamber. As the gall matures and larvae get ready to exit, an opening develops from the larval chamber through the tooth to its apex. Some galls occasionally form on a section of a midrib that also supports the previously described midrib-gall sawfly Unknown #3.

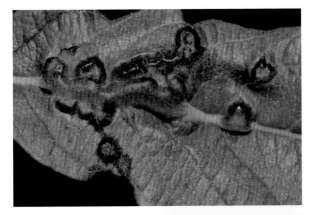

Plate 372. Dorsal view of galls of *Iteomyia* sp. C on Barclay's willow.

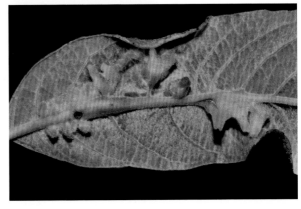

Plate 373. Ventral view of galls of *Iteomyia* sp. C.

WILLOW-APPLE-GALL SAWFLY *Pontania californica* Pl. 374 & Figs. 62–65

This sawfly induces round-ovoid, monothalamous galls that protrude on both sides of leaves of related species belonging to the arroyo willow (*Salix lasiolepis*) and Lemmon's willow (*S. lemmonii*) groups. It occurs throughout the West and as far north as the Alaskan tundra. While glabrous and generally smooth, these galls do possess minute, wart-like scales or tubercles called **LENTICELS**. This species is the only sawfly gall-inducer in the West with galls bearing such lenticels. Bright green to red galls measure up to 11 mm at their widest dimension. They occur from one to a dozen or more per leaf. Sometimes two or more galls coalesce to form much larger structures. While most galls protrude equally on both sides of affected leaves, some galls hang mostly on the underside. Gall formation begins with the injection of colleterial fluids from females. The relatively thin walls that surround the larval chamber are usually 1–2 mm thick. Prepupae drop to the ground via silken threads and encase themselves in cocoons. Adults usually emerge in spring, timed with the appearance of new leaves. While the typical life cycle involves a single generation per year, under certain environmental conditions where leaves remain on the trees throughout the year, up to six generations of this species can occur within a year. Caltagirone (1964) found a remarkable complex of inquiline, parasite, and hyperparasite species associated with this gall-maker that included six wasps, a moth, and a weevil. In some cases, it has been found that the moth alone can account for as much as 70% of the mortality of the sawfly larvae. There are other similar sawfly galls in the West, belonging to the *Pontania viminalis* and *P. proxima* groups.

Left: Plate 374. Galls of *Pontania californica* on arroyo willow.

Below left: Figure 62. Cross section of a typical gall of *P. californica* group (after Smith 1970).

Below right: Figure 63. Cross section of a typical gall of *P. viminalis* group (after Smith 1970).

Bottom left: Figure 64. Cross section of a typical gall of *P. proxima* group (after Smith 1970).

Bottom right: Figure 65. Cross section of another gall of *P. viminalis* group (after Smith 1970).

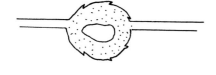

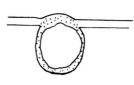

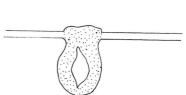

BEAN-GALL SAWFLY *Pontania proxima* Pl. 375

The bean-gall sawfly induces lenticular or kidney-bean-shaped galls on leaves of Pacific willow (*Salix lasiandra* [*S. lucida* subsp. *lasiandra*]). Galls protrude equally on both sides of host leaves and are smooth, glabrous, and red on top and yellow-green underneath. A dozen or more galls can occur on a single leaf. Galls measure 4 mm wide by 6–8 mm long and 5–6 mm deep. Adults emerge from galls in late spring and seek suitable willow hosts. By mid- to late summer, larvae drop to the ground and pupate, producing a second brood in late summer. These adults lay eggs, and the resulting leaf galls harbor overwintering pupae, which emerge as adults the following spring. However, some studies suggest there is only one generation per year. This sawfly is widespread in Ireland, Europe, the Himalayas, Argentina, South Africa, New Zealand, Australia, and North America from Alaska to Mexico. I have found it to be abundant in Washington.

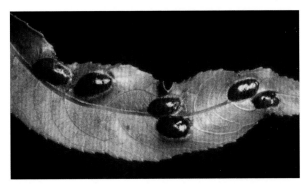

Plate 375. Leaf galls of *Pontania proxima* on Pacific willow.

FOLD-GALL SAWFLY *Phyllocolpa* sp. Pl. 376

This fold-gall sawfly is quite common on various willow species throughout the West. The simple fold occurs along only one margin of the leaves, often turning inward toward the ventral midrib in a circular manner. Sawfly females inject a fluid during oviposition thought to be responsible for leaf deformation and folding. Galls can exceed 30 mm in length by 3 mm in diameter. Multiple larvae may be found in a single fold gall. While one species, *P. bozemani*, is known to attack poplar, the taxonomy of this sawfly found on willows needs clarification.

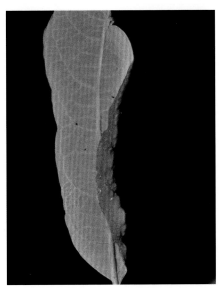

Plate 376. Leaf-fold gall of *Phyllocolpa* sp. on Pacific willow.

PEACH-GALL SAWFLY   Unknown #4

Pl. 377

This sawfly induces monothalamous, round to oblong, fuzzy midrib galls resembling a peach that terminate in a slight projection or tip. Galls occur on the underside of leaves of Sierra willow (*Salix* cf. *eastwoodiae*). Unlike galls of *Pontania* spp., these galls are light green to reddish green and covered with short, bristlelike hairs about 0.5 mm long. Galled leaves generally support only one or two galls, with some galls coalescing. Galls measure 5–7 mm in diameter. In September, at 2,134 m in the Siskiyou Mountains at Castle Lake, California, most galls found were still fresh and contained 4-mm-long larvae in the large larval chambers. These larvae leave the galls in early to mid-October to burrow deep into leaf litter or soil beneath the host, since at this elevation there can be heavy snow cover during the winter. Adult sawflies have been reared from these galls but have yet to be identified. These galls closely resemble those of *Pontania glabrifrons* on *S. lanata* in Finland.

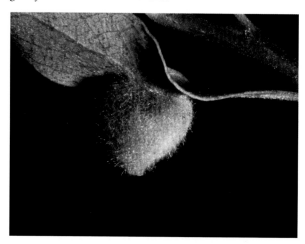

Plate 377. Gall of peach-gall sawfly, **Unknown #4**, on Sierra willow.

SHRUB GALLS

Compared to trees, especially groups such as oaks (*Quercus* spp.) and willows (*Salix* spp.), shrubs generally do not support many galls or gall organisms. For the purposes of clarity, I am defining shrubs here as those woody plants of low to medium height with multiple trunks. Most shrubs support only one or two gall organisms or none known at all. There are some notable exceptions, including creosote bush (*Larrea tridentata*), rabbitbrush (*Chrysothamnus* and *Ericameria* spp.), and Great Basin sagebrush (*Artemisia tridentata*). These widespread, multistate shrubs host a fairly large number of gall-inducing insects. Except for roses (*Rosa* spp.), thimbleberry (*Rubus parviflorus*), and chinquapin (*Chrysolepis* spp.), which host cynipid wasps, most shrubs support either mites, moths, gall midges, tephritid flies, or in one case, a leaf-mining agromyzid fly and another a new cynipid. In the case of snowberry (*Symphoricarpos* spp.), a sawfly is the principal gall-inducer. Table 15 lists some of the major gall-supporting shrubs, excluding those with five or fewer species.

The plants in this section are listed in alphabetical order by common name, even in the cases of species, such as cheesebush (*Ambrosia* spp.) and rabbitbrush (*Chrysothamnus* and *Ericameria* spp.), that are assigned to genera that also appear under other common names.

TABLE 15. MAJOR SHRUB GALL HOSTS (WITH NUMBERS OF GALL SPECIES IN THIS GUIDE)

Cheesebush	7
Coyote brush, desert broom	14
Creosote bush	15
Plum, cherry	6
Rabbitbrush	15
Ragweed, bur-sage	7
Rose	10
Sagebrush	15
Saltbush	8
Service-berry	7

Antelope Brush Galls

BUD-GALL MITE   *Aceria kraftella* Fig. 66

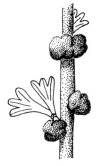

This mite induces globular, bristly, rough-surfaced bud galls along current-year stems of antelope brush (*Purshia tridentata*). Galls usually form at the base of petioles or where axillary buds occur. Galls measure 5–12 mm in diameter and are brown or gray. Galls often deform branches, but there is no evidence of stem mortality as a result of this mite. Adult mites emerge in spring to infest new branch growth. This mite and its galls have been found throughout the range of its host, from Montana to British Columbia, Oregon, Nevada, and California. Antelope brush, also called bitterbrush, is widespread throughout western rangeland from the Siskiyou Mountains and Sierra Nevada east to the Rocky Mountains.

Figure 66. Galls of *Aceria kraftella*, on antelope brush.

BEAD-GALL MITE   Unknown Pl. 378

This mite induces small, round bead galls on the upper surface of antelope brush leaves. Galls are light green and measure 1 mm in diameter. Several bead galls can occur on a single lobe of the leaves. No apparent damage appears to result from the feeding of this eriophyid mite. It has been found from Utah to the eastern Sierra Nevada.

Plate 378. Galls of bead-gall mite, **Unknown**, on antelope brush.

Barberry Galls

BARBERRY-EDGE-GALL MITE   *Eriophyes caliberberis* Pl. 379

Galls of this eriophyid mite occur along the margins of new leaves and occasionally the midrib of Oregon grape (*Berberis aquifolium*), especially the variety known as creeping barberry (*B. aquifolium* var. *repens*). Heavy galling results in an undulating appearance, as the galls are

Plate 379. Galls of *Eriophyes caliberberis* on barberry leaves.

often continuous along the entire vein or margin. Affected leaves are usually severely distorted. Galls are thin, red-purple, and measure about 1 mm wide. New terminal leaflets are galled and older leaves below unaffected. This mite has been found from Utah to California.

Bladder Sage Galls

BLADDER SAGE–GALL MIDGE *Neolasioptera* sp.   Pl. 380

This stem-gall midge induces tapered, symmetrical, monothalamous integral stem galls on bladder sage (*Scutellaria mexicana*). Galls usually occur at joints or on new growth of lateral branches. They measure up to 14 mm long by 3 mm in diameter and are the same color as host stems. Several galls can occur in close proximity to each other, one per branch, and do not appear to coalesce.

Plate 380. Gall of *Neolasioptera* sp. on bladder sage.

Box-Thorn Galls

Several species of box-thorn (*Lycium* spp.) are found in Californian and southwestern desert areas. One of the more prominent species is Cooper's box-thorn (*L. cooperi*), also called peach thorn, which occurs throughout creosote bush scrub and Joshua tree woodland in the Mojave and Colorado Deserts. Three species new to science were discovered on Cooper's box-thorn, and they may occur on other species of *Lycium* in the West, including *L. pallidum* var. *oligospermum*.

STEM-GALL MOTH *Symmetrischema* sp.   Pls. 381 & 382

This moth induces elliptical, gently tapered, integral, monothalamous stem galls on both spring basal shoots and terminal branch growth of box-thorn. Basal-shoot galls are pale green to lavender and measure up to 80 mm long by 8 mm in diameter. These fresh galls are smooth, glabrous, and sometimes asymmetrical. Terminal-shoot galls are shorter, less than 40 mm in length. Old galls harden, become light gray, and persist on the shrub for several seasons. The larval chamber is fairly large, occupying most of the gall. In April, light gray caterpillars measure 4 mm in length. Caterpillars feed until the heat of summer causes plant tissue to become woody and hardened. At this point, prepupae are thought to enter diapause until they pupate in late fall–winter. Adults emerge in November and December from galls collected in April and do not feed or drink. Adults rest on branches, rarely moving except for occasional shifts to the right or left by about 1 mm. When disturbed, they immediately jump off their perch to a lower branch, where they resume a motionless posture. Antennae are held back over the 7-mm-long body when at rest. Mating occurs in January and can last as long as six hours. Considering the adults' emergence and life span of 2–3 months under winter conditions, it is thought that these moths possess a cryoprotectant to keep them from freezing. The DNA barcode of this moth has been registered under a new species name that cannot be used here until it is formally published.

Plate 381. Gall of *Symmetrischema* sp. on box-thorn.

Plate 382. Adult moth of *Symmetrischema* sp.

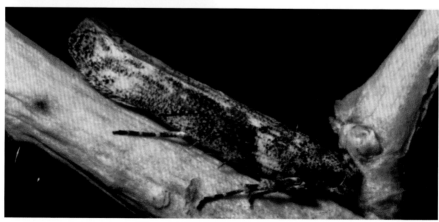

CABBAGE-GALL MIDGE   *Contarinia* sp.   Pl. 383

The polythalamous, round, axillary bud galls of this midge appear at swollen stem nodes on box-thorn in spring. The relationship between the developing bud gall and the older-appearing swollen stem node just below it is not clear. New galls have a round central larval chamber with an extremely hard, 1-mm-thick outer shell surrounded by broad, hairy, leafy bracts that resemble cabbage leaves. Short, bristly, sparse white hairs cover the entire gall. Galls reach 12–14 mm in diameter. The outer leafy bracts measure 5 mm wide by 9 mm long. The central rounded chamber measures 6–7 mm in diameter. Larvae crawl through the openings between the main larval chamber and the base of each of the leafy bracts and pupate at the surface. Adults exit the white exuviae (pupal skin) that is left at the surface, as seen in the photograph.

Plate 383. Bud gall of *Contarinia* sp. on box-thorn, with empty pupal skins.

LEAF-GALL ORGANISM   Unknown   Pl. 384

This organism induces integral, round to ovoid leaf and petiole galls on *Lycium pallidum* var. *oligospermum* and perhaps other species of *Lycium*. Galls often distort leaves, as seen in the photograph. The bulging galls measure 8 mm in diameter and are usually convex on the dorsal surface, with an opposing concave depression on the underside. While some galls are simple bumps on the affected leaf, occurring two or more per leaf, other galls curl the entire leaf into a ball. While moth caterpillars have been found in a few galls, the inducer has not been determined.

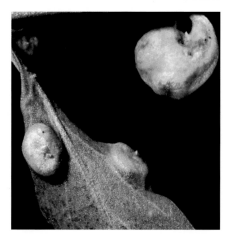

Plate 384. Galls of leaf-gall organism, **Unknown**, on *Lycium*.

Brittlebush Galls

BUD-GALL MIDGE *Asphondylia enceliae* Pl. 385

This midge induces white, woolly, globular monothalamous bud galls along the leafy stems of brittlebush (*Encelia farinosa*) and California brittlebush (*E. californica*). Galls occur at leaf axils on the main stems and are well developed by mid-March. Galls have more hairs than normal stems and leaves and measure 12 mm long by 10 mm in diameter. Each gall has a hair-lined depression at the top, from which the adults emerge the following winter, usually in February.

Plate 385. Bud gall of *Asphondylia enceliae* on brittlebrush.

LEAF-GALL MIDGE *Rhopalomyia* sp. Pl. 386

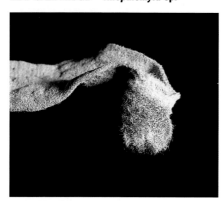

Plate 386. Gall of *Rhopalomyia* sp. on brittlebrush.

This midge induces hairy, white, conical to round, integral, monothalamous leaf, petiole, and flower galls on brittlebush (*Encelia farinosa*). Galls can show on both leaf surfaces, but often appear mostly on one side. The bottom end of each gall has a hair-lined depression in the center with a toothed margin. Galls measure 9 mm high by 6 mm in diameter and occur one to six galls per leaf. Galls examined in mid-March had mature larvae or empty pupal cases inside the gall chambers. Since the host bush retains its leaves year-round, and adults appear to emerge in spring, this species may have more than one generation per year.

California Fuchsia Galls

BUD-GALL MIDGE *Contarinia zauschneriae* Pl. 387

California fuchsia (*Epilobium canum*; also called Zauschneria), known for its long, tubular red flowers, is found on hillsides, rocky outcroppings, and chaparral environments. This gall midge induces robust polythalamous bud galls along stems of the host. Galls comprise overlapping bud scales covered in bristly white hairs. The leafy scales are rose red toward the upper half, yellow-green at the base. Galls measure 15 mm in diameter by 25 mm high. Separate larval chambers are located in the middle of the galls. Adults pupate on the outside of the galls (see white pupal skin protruding in the photo here) in September.

Plate 387. Gall of *Contarinia zauschneriae* on California fuchsia. Photo by Joyce Gross.

Catclaw Galls

Catclaw (*Senegalia greggii*) is a ubiquitous shrub of southern California and Southwest deserts to Texas. It normally produces new leaves and shoots shortly after major rainstorms. It is leafless the rest of the time. This species can easily be identified while driving, by the dark brown, 30–50-cm-wide, tight clusters of the mistletoe *Phoradendron californicum*, which readily stand out even from a distance. Otherwise, the plant galls associated with catclaw have been relatively ignored.

LEAFLET-GALL MIDGE *Contarinia* sp. Pl. 388

This midge induces monothalamous, swollen bud galls on joined pairs of leaflets before they open on catclaw. When fresh, galls are green, but because of the relatively short life of leaflets, larvae quickly mature before galls turn brown by mid-March. Galls measure 4 mm long by 2 mm across. These paddle-shaped, glabrous galls have small ridges running their

Plate 388. Galls of *Contarinia* sp. on catclaw.

length. Galls occur anywhere on any leaflet, but most seem to occur on terminal leaflets. Adults emerge in March and April in the eastern Mojave Desert, California. This relationship is interesting because of the strict timing in the emergence of adults and development of the galls during a narrow window when host leaves are available.

TUBE-GALL MIDGE   *"Contarinia"* sp.   Pls. 389 & 390

This midge induces clusters of bristle-covered, round to tubular, monothalamous bud galls on stems of catclaw. Galls measure 3–4 mm in diameter by 4–6 mm long (tubular specimens) and develop right after spring rains. Fresh galls are usually green and round with soft bristles. With age, the galls are more tubular, brown, and have stiff bristles. Each cluster may have 10 or more individual galls and occur right next to galls of other insects. In an environment that can get hot and dry soon, activities of this midge appear to be accelerated to take advantage of the host's temporary suitability. Most galls collected from a site near Henderson, Nevada, in April had already been vacated, showing exit holes at the apex of each gall. One gall was still closed and issued an adult three days after collection. This midge is close to *Contarinia* sp. and is listed in the genus provisionally.

Plate 389. Fresh galls of
"Contarinia" sp. on catclaw.

Plate 390. Old galls of
"Contarinia" sp.

STEM-GALL WASP *Tanaostigmodes howardii* Fig. 67 & Pls. 391 & 392

This wasp has been associated with two different galls on catclaw (Felt 1965). One is an integral stem gall (Plate 391) and the other a round bud gall (Plate 392, Figure 67). It is not clear whether *T. howardii* is the gall-inducer or an inquiline in either case. The first, an elliptical, sometimes lopsided, integral, monothalamous, stem gall on catclaw is a bit lopsided, measures up to 12 mm long by 5 mm in diameter, and is the same color as the stems. Adults emerge in winter and galls form on new branches in spring. The second gall is a detachable, round, monothalamous gall often found in clusters along stems of catclaw. The surface of these galls is broken into plates, with a small thorn or bristle emanating from each plate. Galls measure

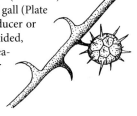

Figure 67. Gall of *T. howardii*.

5 mm across and are gray-green, similar to normal stems. Some galls have a bark-like texture. Adults had already emerged from specimens found in mid-December in southern Nevada.

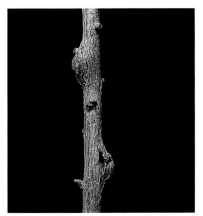

Plate 391. Integral stem gall of *Tanaostigmodes howardii* on catclaw.

Plate 392. Galls of *T. howardii*.

PETIOLE-GALL WASP Unknown Pl. 393

This petiole-gall wasp, currently thought to be a tanaostigmatid wasp, induces spindle-shaped, integral, monothalamous galls at the base of new leaf-bearing petioles of catclaw. Fresh galls collected in January were cinnamon brown and measured 7–12 mm long by 4–5 mm in diameter. These monothalamous galls protrude equally on all sides of the petiole. Leaf development

Plate 393. Two galls of petiole-gall wasp, **Unknown**, on catclaw.

does not occur once galls form. Adults have not yet been reared. This species occurs in the southwest section of Nevada near Henderson.

Ceanothus Galls

Over 40 species of ceanothus shrubs (*Ceanothus* spp.) grow in western states, along with several additional varieties and subspecies. This widespread group of typically chaparral shrubs is one of the most prominent in the West, especially in California. For the most part, the only noticeable galls occur on tobacco brush (*C. velutinus*), buckbrush (*C. cuneatus*), deer brush (*C. integerrimus*) and related forms. The inducers are an eriophyid mite, a moth, and three gall midges.

BEAD-GALL MITE *Eriophyes ceanothi*   Pl. 394

This mite induces green bead galls on the underside of ceanothus leaves, particularly tobacco brush. They usually occur in large numbers and can cause distortion of affected leaves. Galls measure 1 mm in diameter, unless they coalesce. Galls appear scattered in a random pattern between veins and along leaf margins. Each gall has a corresponding dimple on the dorsal surface, with a hole that allows escape of the adults. The mites and their galls have been found from Colorado to British Columbia and California.

Plate 394. Leaf bead galls of *Eriophyes ceanothi* on ceanothus.

STEM-GALL MOTH *Periploca ceanothiella*   Pl. 395

This moth induces integral, spindle-shaped galls on stems of several species of ceanothus, especially deer brush. Under heavy infestation, this moth and its galls can cause serious damage to branches, stunting the overall growth of the host shrub. As many as 20 galls have been found per branch. Galls measure up to 20 mm long by 5–7 mm diameter and are the same color as normal stems. Larvae overwinter inside their monothalamous galls, pupate, and emerge during spring and early summer. Adult moths lay eggs directly on the

Plate 395. Stem gall of *Periploca ceanothiella* on ceanothus.

stems, and newly hatched larvae burrow into buds and stems. Larvae appear to induce formation of the galls. There is one generation per year. This species has been reported from New York, Kansas, Texas, Oregon, and California.

BUD-GALL MIDGE *Asphondylia ceanothi*

Fig. 68 & Pl. 396

This midge induces round, monothalamous, leafy rosette bud galls on several species of *Ceanothus*. When fresh, these compact bud galls are green to rose red, with linear, toothed, pointed, leafy bracts, which are arranged hemispherically. Galls measure 12–40 mm in diameter. Each has a central larval chamber. Like other members of the genus *Asphondylia*, this species probably has a fungal associate inside the larval chamber. After the larvae leave in June and July, galls turn brown. Winter rains hasten decomposition of the gall's leafy bracts. This species has been recorded in Oregon and California.

Figure 68.
Bract of gall of
A. ceanothi.

Plate 396. An aging gall of *Asphondylia ceanothi* on ceanothus.

VEIN-GALL MIDGE *Asphondylia* sp.

Pl. 397

This midge induces globular, monothalamous to polythalamous galls along the ventral midrib on leaves of tobacco brush. Galls have sparse hairs and nearly obliterate the midrib. They may superficially resemble the galls of the midrib fold-gall midge (*Contarinia* sp.) presented next. Galls measure 7 mm long by 5 mm wide and bulge out more noticeably than those of the midrib fold-gall midge. Each gall has a corresponding lip or slit on the leaf's dorsal surface. Larvae leave the galls in July to cocoon in leaf litter and emerge the following spring.

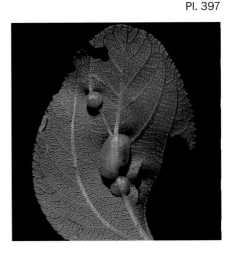

Plate 397. Galls of *Asphondylia* sp. on ceanothus.

MIDRIB-FOLD-GALL MIDGE *Contarinia* sp.

Pl. 398

This midge induces densely hairy midrib galls on the underside of leaves of deer brush and tobacco brush in California and Oregon. Monothalamous galls often coalesce to form what

appears as a single linear fold (polythalamous). The midrib remains prominent along the bottom edge of the galls. Single galls measure 3–5 mm in diameter, while clustered galls may extend 15 mm in length. One or more corresponding dimples on the leaf's dorsal surface mark the pinch-point along the midrib. Occasionally, galls appear on main lateral veins. Full-grown larvae leave the galls in July to build cocoons in leaf litter and overwinter until spring. There is one generation per year.

Plate 398. Fold gall of *Contarinia* sp. on ceanothus.

Chamise Galls

Chamise (*Adenostoma fasciculatum*) is one of the most common indicator species of chaparral in California and parts of southwest Nevada. Chamise supports a difficult-to-find gall midge (*Asphondylia adenostoma*) that galls the host's seeds without substantively altering their form. There is also an unknown organism that induces leafy, rosette bud galls. One gall mite is described here.

POUCH-GALL MITE *Phytoptus adenostomae* Pl. 399

This mite induces globular pouch galls on the tiny leaves of chamise. The galls can severely distort the linear leaves, even though there is rarely more than one gall per leaf. These pouch galls have an irregular surface and are usually 1–2 mm in diameter. Leaves that are in shade tend to be most frequently attacked by this mite. Galls are light green, turning brown with age. This mite exhibits an alternation of generations.

Plate 399. Pouch galls of *Phytoptus adenostomae* on chamise.

Cheesebush Galls

Cheesebush (*Ambrosia salsola*), also called winged ragweed or burrobrush, is a common scraggly shrub in washes, sandy flats, and disturbed areas, particularly along roads in creosote bush scrub, Joshua tree woodland, and shadscale scrub habitats of the Mojave Desert, California, and throughout the Southwest and northwestern Mexico. The peak photosynthetic period for this shrub, like most others in the desert, is in spring when it has new leaves. Gall insects associated with this shrub take advantage of this seasonal growth spurt with development of their galls in spring and summer. Six midges are known to induce galls on cheesebush, even though identification to species level has not yet been accomplished for all. A seventh gall-inducer is a moth belonging to the family Tortricidae.

STEM-GALL MOTH *Eugnosta* sp. Pl. 400

This new species of tortricid moth induces integral, gently tapered, symmetrical, monothalamous stem galls on upper sections of cheesebush. Galls measure 18 mm long by 8 mm wide. These galls are green when fresh but by midsummer the stems and galls turn light beige. Galls are striated, and shoots and buds often emerge from their sides. Larvae cut exit holes to the outside, where they later cocoon and pupate. Most galls are empty in late November, suggesting a fall emergence. The empty pupal case is often seen protruding from the exit hole, which is true for all moths in this family. Some specimens collected in November released adults 10 days later. Adults are hard to see as they fold their light gray wings back when remaining motionless on stems. Females lay eggs soon after emergence.

Plate 400. Gall of *Eugnosta* sp. on cheesebush.

SMOOTH-BUD-GALL MIDGE *Asphondylia* sp. A Pl. 401

This midge induces green, smooth, glabrous, monothalamous bud galls on cheesebush. These galls occur singly on lateral buds and are sessile. Some are pointed while others have an obtuse apex. Galls measure 6 mm long by 2–3 mm in diameter. They develop rapidly in February and March. By mid-March, adults have emerged from tiny holes in the apex of the galls.

Plate 401. Gall of *Asphondylia* sp. A on cheesebush.

WOOLLY-BUD-GALL MIDGE *Asphondylia* sp. B   Pl. 402

This midge induces round, white, woolly, monothalamous bud galls on cheesebush. These galls measure 5–7 mm in diameter and are found on axillary buds. Galls occur singly, although two or more can occur on a branch. Adults emerge in May, and egg deposition and gall development soon follow. Galls of this species lack the reddish-brown projections of *Asphondylia* sp. C, but evaluation by use of DNA sequencing is needed to make sure these are different species.

Plate 402. Galls of *Asphondylia* sp. B on cheesebush.

MEDUSA-GALL MIDGE *Asphondylia* sp. C   Pl. 403

This new species induces white, woolly, monothalamous bud galls on cheesebush, with long, soft, reddish-brown projections protruding from the gall mass. Galls measure 17 mm in diameter. White fungus lines the larval chamber walls, which may be eaten by the larvae. This species is distinguished from *Asphondylia* sp. B by the presence of the long reddish-brown projections, but as mentioned, DNA evaluation is needed for taxonomic clarification.

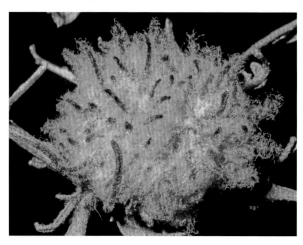

Plate 403. Gall of *Asphondylia* sp. C on cheesebush.

STEM-GALL MIDGE   *Neolasioptera* sp. A

Pl. 404

The monothalamous, integral, spindle-shaped galls of this midge occur at the base of major stems of cheesebush. The gently tapered galls usually have stunted leafy bracts covering the surface. Most galls appear the same color as new stems. Some growth occurs beyond the galls, but these branches often die. Older galls develop a hard, lacquer-like coating during summer, which might help retain moisture in the gall. Galls measure 13–15 mm in length by 3–4 mm in diameter. Adults emerged from galls in August in the laboratory, which may not match their emergence in the field under normal summer conditions. This species has been found in Arizona and California.

Plate 404. Stem gall of *Neolasioptera* sp. A on cheesebush.

ROSETTE-GALL MIDGE   *Neolasioptera* sp. B

Pl. 405

This midge induces large, monothalamous, leafy rosette galls on lateral branches of cheesebush. Galls measure 25 mm long by 15 mm in diameter. The numerous thin, undivided, leafy bracts radiate outwardly, distinguishing this gall from others on this host. Bracts measure 13–15 mm long by 1 mm in diameter. In early April, single orange larvae are found within vertical chambers that measure to 14 mm long by 1 mm wide. The outer shell of the gall is firm and covered with leafy bracts.

Plate 405. Gall of *Neolasioptera* sp. B on cheesebush.

LEAFY-BUD-GALL MIDGE   Unknown

Pl. 406

The elliptical monothalamous bud galls of this new species, found on cheesebush, are covered with long, leafy, divided bracts that mask the gall bodies beneath. The vibrant green galls measure 10–15 mm long by 3 mm in diameter minus the bracts. The branched or lobed bracts are 20 mm or more long. The central larval chamber is linear, with thin walls. These galls may look similar to those of *Neolasioptera* sp. A (on which the bracts are stunted or nonexistent) or *Neolasioptera* sp. B (bracts undivided). Recent research has shown that polymorphism exists among some gall midges. Based on this possibility, adults of these galls must be compared to determine whether they are separate species or simply one with different gall forms.

Plate 406. Gall of leafy-bud-gall midge, **Unknown**, on cheesebush.

Chinquapin Galls

Two species of chinquapin: giant chinquapin (*Chrysolepis chrysophylla*) and bush chinquapin (*C. sempervirens*) occur in coniferous forests and chaparral environments of the Pacific States. Both appear to support at least four gall-inducers, three of which are described below. The fourth species, the cynipid wasp *Dryocosmus rileypokei*, is considered a nut-galler, with its bisexual-generation galls hidden among the sharp spines of the plant's nuts.

FLOWER-GALL WASP   *Dryocosmus castanopsidis*

Pl. 407

This wasp induces large, round, monothalamous galls on male flowers of both chinquapin hosts. The deep red galls have a golden bloom that easily rubs off. Galls measure 15 mm in diameter. The flesh of the gall is also red, surrounding a greenish larval chamber. Galls are easily detached and often litter trails and roadsides. Usually only one gall occurs per staminate inflorescence. These galls have been found in several divergent locations and likely occur throughout the range of the host plants.

Plate 407. Flower gall of *Dryocosmus castanopsidis* on chinquapin.

LEAF-GALL WASP *Dryocosmus juliae* #1

Pl. 408

This wasp induces round, integral, monothalamous leaf galls on both species of chinquapin. Galls appear to have a raised collar or ring around the outer edge of the gall. The thin-walled galls have a larval cell (2 mm in diameter) inside a slightly larger cavity (4 mm in diameter), which becomes free floating (detached from outer wall) once larvae stop feeding. Galls measure 11 mm in diameter by 6 mm thick. Late spring galls usually occur one per leaf and are green when fresh but turn fawn brown by August. Weld (1957b) mentioned this gall without naming it. The asexual generation induces nondescript round galls on the staminate flowers of chinquapin in early spring. Recent research by Nicholls et al. (2018a) has shown that the DNA from this species is the same as the inducer for the next gall, both of which are from the bisexual generation. This situation,

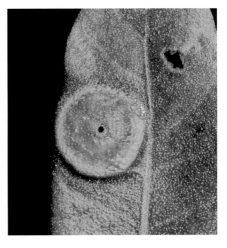

Plate 408. Leaf gall of *Dryocosmus juliae* #1 on chinquapin.

where one generation (bisexual) creates different types of galls on different plant organs, is, so far, most unusual among cynipid wasps. With increased use of DNA sequencing, we may see more relationships like this in the future. This gall is found throughout the range of this host.

BUD-GALL WASP *Dryocosmus juliae* #2

Pl. 409

This cynipid wasp's sexual generation also induces fleshy, monothalamous galls among axillary buds on chinquapin in summer. Galls are globular to pear-shaped and reddish-green to maroon, with a slightly mealy-granular texture when fresh. In July and August, galls are glossy and plump, but they shrivel and turn brown by the end of September. Galls measure 10 mm in diameter. The larval chamber is large, comprising most of the thin-walled gall. This species has been found at 2,134 m in the Siskiyou Mountains, California, with *D. juliae* #1 galls nearby, at the same time. It has also been found in Humboldt County, along the California coast.

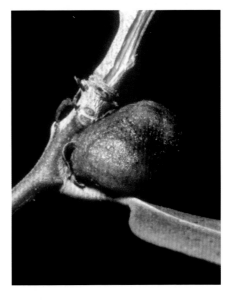

Plate 409. Bud gall of *Dryocosmus juliae* #2 on chinquapin.

Coffeeberry Galls

MIDRIB-GALL MOTH *Sorhagenia nimbosa* Pl. 410

Plate 410. Fold gall of *Sorhagenia nimbosa* on coffeeberry.

This moth induces swollen, monothalamous, midrib galls on leaves of California coffeeberry (*Frangula californica*) and Sierra coffeeberry (*F. rubra*). These are not classic fold galls, as seen in other species, but are instead the result of a significant expansion of cell tissues in and around the midrib. The rigid, thick-walled galls consume most of the affected leaf, leaving only the basal and apical portions unaffected. The sides of the leaf appear pinched together, as the swelling involves much of the leaf. Galls measure 30 mm long by 8 mm in diameter. They are usually a lighter green than normal leaf tissues. The caterpillars are brown with darker heads and are 6 mm long. Galls appear in mid-May along the California coast on *F. californica*, but later in the Sierra Nevada on *F. rubra*.

FLOWER-GALL MIDGE *Asphondylia* sp. Pl. 411

The rounded, polythalamous flower galls of this midge develop in late spring along with the normal flowers of coffeeberry (*Frangula californica*). Fresh galls are spongy and light green, with small red spots or broken red lines, and terminate in a small point. These fleshy galls measure 6–8 mm in diameter (larger than ungalled flower buds). By late June, normal fruits, which are round, solid, and dark green or purple-black, can be found at the same time as these persistent flower galls. Galls turn brown with age. The larvae of a *Dasineura* sp., a possible inquiline, have also been found in the galls of this midge.

Plate 411. Two galls of *Asphondylia* sp. on coffeeberry with smaller ungalled flower buds.

Coyote Brush and Desert Broom Galls

In the United States, at least 21 species of gall midges occur on hosts in the genus *Baccharis*. Coyote brush (*B. pilularis*), also called "chaparral broom," is one of the most interesting shrubs entomologically. Tilden's (1951) monumental study of this shrub identified 221 species of insects associated with it, as well as eight species of mites. The associated insects, in turn, hosted an additional 62 species of parasites, for a total of 291 species. Coyote brush is a hardy and dominant plant of the coastal chaparral community that exists in California; it extends into foothill areas, with a range from northern Mexico to southern Oregon, and is used in landscapes in a variety of places. Both the prostrate and erect forms of this wind-pollinated shrub host the same gall organisms. There is no evidence of any discrimination between galling agents and male and female plants as host sites for galls. The gall organisms associated with coyote brush include a rust fungus, a mite, a moth, and two gall midges.

A second species of *Baccharis*, desert broom (*B. sarothroides*), extends from southern California into Nevada, Arizona, New Mexico, and Texas. This shrub supports numerous gall-inducing insects, including moths, a tephritid fly, several gall midges, and a new cynipid wasp. One midge gall found in Texas on *Baccharis* spp. is also thought to occur in southern California.

RUST-GALL FUNGUS *Puccinia evadens* Pl. 412

This fungus induces large, elliptical, swollen stem galls and witches' brooms on coyote brush and desert broom. This rust has also been reported on *Baccharis emoryi* in California and *B. thesioides* in Arizona. As galls mature they become fissured, usually revealing orange uredinial spore areas during spring and summer. Galls can exceed 18 cm long by 4 cm in diameter and are usually found on old wood. In autumn, spore areas are covered with a white, powdery material. Through its galling activity, this rust fungus disrupts the flow of nutrients and water to outer sections of branches and leaves, which often die. This fungus also produces witches' brooms, emanating from the integral stem swellings. The brooms are composed of compact clusters of small branches up to 20 cm long that often conceal the stem swelling beneath. Brooms usually die after the first season. A gall midge, *Mycodiplosis pritchardi* (a non-gall-inducer), feeds on the spores produced in the stem galls by the fungus has a significant impact on the number of viable spores remaining.

Plate 412. Stem gall of *Puccinia evadens* showing orange spores on coyote brush.

LEAF-BLISTER-GALL MITE *Eriophyes bacch_aripha*

Pl. 413

This mite induces swollen blister galls on leaves of coyote brush. Galls are round to irregular in shape. The greenish-yellow to brick-red, pimple-like swellings are 1–2 mm in diameter and occur on both sides of leaves in spring. Exit holes usually occur on the underside of leaves or opposite the main swellings. Each infected leaf may have one or more blister galls. Some leaves are severely distorted. A related mite, *E. baccharices*, causes wart-like, irregularly shaped galls on leaves of seep willow or mule fat (*Baccharis salicifolia*).

Plate 413. Blister galls of *Eriophyes bacchariha* on coyote brush.

STEM-GALL MOTH *Gnorimoschema baccharisella*

Pl. 414

This gelechiid moth induces hard, integral stem galls on coyote brush throughout its range. These monothalamous galls are usually well developed as early as June in some areas. Galls measure up to 35 mm long by 15 mm in diameter and are generally smooth, green, and hollow. While some galls are more elliptical, tapering gradually, others are abrupt swellings. Gall development begins after overwintering eggs hatch in spring and the larvae burrow into new terminal shoots. Occupied stems swell around the larvae, leaving large cavities within which the larvae feed. In April in coastal counties of California, larvae are usually 5–7 mm long. They nearly double their size by July, though by this time, many of the moth larvae have been parasitized or lost to other predators. Usually from late May until mid-July, surviving larvae cut exit holes through the gall walls and drop to the ground to pupate. Adults emerge in August and September. Eggs are laid in fall on outer branches. The frass that accumulates inside the gall serves as a culture medium for various fungi,

Plate 414. Integral stem gall of *Gnorimoschema baccharisella* on coyote brush.

which in turn are eaten by several fungus insects after departure of the moth. Tilden (1951) found at least 10 parasites associated with this moth in addition to 17 other insects that were connected to the gall or moth in some manner. The intricacies of these complex relationships stagger the mind for such a common, yet so disregarded, shrub.

STEM-GALL MOTH   *Gnorimoschema powelli*

Fig. 69

The integral stem galls of this moth develop on spring growth of desert broom. These bark-colored, monothalamous galls are stout and spindle-shaped. They measure 17 mm long by 12 mm in diameter. The walls of the galls are 1–1.5 mm thick. Larval frass is usually tightly packed in the upper end of the larval chamber (a characteristic of many gall-inducing moths) and held in place by a frail silken mesh. Mature larvae leave the galls through a 1 mm hole excavated in the middle of each gall and drop to the ground for later pupation. Adults are nocturnal and fly in November and December.

Figure 69. Stem gall of *Gnorimoschema powelli* on desert broom.

LEAF-GALL MOTH   *Gnorimoschema* sp.

Pl. 415

This gelechiid moth induces monothalamous, terminal leaf galls on desert broom in the northern Mojave Desert, California, and likely throughout the range of the host. Galls are composed of tightly bound, swollen leaves that are held together like the staves of a barrel, similar to galls on rabbitbrush (see Plate 489). These dark green galls measure 40 mm long by 7 mm in diameter and are twisted at the apex. The larval chamber is large, nearly the full length of the gall. By mid-March there are 4-mm-long whitish caterpillars in the galls, with frass packed at the basal end. I have seen shrubs near Red Rock Canyon State Park, California, with nearly every terminal shoot galled. Pupation occurs outside of the galls.

Plate 415. Folded terminal leaf gall of *Gnorimoschema* sp. on desert broom.

DESERT BROOM GALLFLY   *Aciurina thoracica*

Fig. 70

This tephritid fly induces club-shaped to elliptical, integral, monothalamous stem galls on desert broom in southern California. Galls are usually smooth and yellow-green when young. As galls mature and reach full size, they develop red streaks and ultimately turn brown. Vegetative shoots and flower stalks project out of the galls. Fully developed galls become somewhat corky and rough with age. Eggs are laid near terminal and axillary buds in early spring. Fly larvae feed mostly on sap

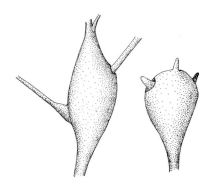

Figure 70. Galls of *Aciurina thoracica*.

from parenchyma cells. Adults emerge from January to March and live from 60 to 85 days. While this species is generally considered to have a single generation per year, late-season rains may induce a second growth spurt among host plants and sometimes a possible second generation.

STEM-GALL MIDGE   *Rhopalomyia baccharis*   Pl. 416 & Fig. 71

This midge induces integral, twisted and bent, striated, polythalamous stem galls, initially at the tips of new shoots of coyote brush in spring (a fall crop of galls also develops). By midsummer, fast-growing spring shoots have elongated well beyond the location of the early spring galls. Galls are green in spring but look similar in color to older branch sections by midsummer. Mature galls measure 50–90 mm long by 5–8 mm in diameter. Each linear gall can contain several individual larval chambers, which are usually located just below each of the bends in the gall. A single gall can bend two or three times, which makes them stand out from normal straight shoots. Larval chambers are linear, 5–10 mm long by 1–2 mm wide, and located just inward of the cambium layer of the stems. In some areas, fresh galls with orange larvae can be found in fall, suggesting that this midge has two or more generations per year. Based on this, it is presumed that adults from spring galls emerge in late summer and oviposit in the slower-growing branch tips, where fresh green, fall galls are found through winter. Studies during fall have shown that galls develop elliptical holes to the outside at the top of the larval chambers just above branch nodes. The rounded-edged holes are not typical of the normal sharp-edged, circular exit holes created by emerging insects and do not appear to have been chewed open. These convenient exit holes appear to be created by the plant after larvae have stopped feeding and before larvae change into pupae. Sometime after the holes are created, pupae develop and remain at the bottom of the chambers for a short period. Pupation occurs inside the galls, and adults emerge in November and December. These circumstances make this species stand out from most of its relatives, in which pupae partially push their way out of the gall before the adult forms. Two similar galls induced by other gall midges develop on aspen petioles and shoots.

Plate 416. Bent gall of *Rhopalomyia baccharis* on coyote brush.

Figure 71. Cross section of gall of *R. baccharis* showing position of larval chambers with preexisting exit holes (right); and stem detail showing exit hole with its atypical shape (left).

BUD-GALL MIDGE *Rhopalomyia californica* Pl. 417

This midge induces polythalamous terminal bud galls on both the erect and prostrate forms of coyote brush. The galls are round to lobed with lumpy protrusions across the surface. The spongy, green to red-purple galls measure up to 20 mm in diameter. Galls often have leaves emerging from them. Female midges lay clusters of eggs on terminal buds. While on the exterior of the host, the eggs are often heavily parasitized by the wasp *Platygaster californica*. Eggs that survive unparasitized produce larvae (generally in spring) that burrow between bud scales and commence feeding. Gall tissue swells around each of the larvae. Complete development of this midge can occur in as few as 30 days but often as many as 70 days or more. When fully grown, larvae burrow to the surface of the galls, where they develop their partially protruding white cocoons and pupate. This species represents one of the rare situations among gall insects where fresh galls and

Plate 417. Terminal bud galls of *Rhopalomyia californica* on coyote brush.

emergence of adults occur throughout the year, depending on location and environmental circumstances, even though there is a pulse of growth and gall activity in spring. Studies have found seven parasitic wasps associated with this gall, including the species mentioned above. Competition for hosts among parasites seems to impact total parasitism effectiveness on the host. In combination, some parasitism effectiveness rates exceeded 80% loss of the gall midge. Parasite influence appears to have a major impact on population control for this midge species.

TUBE-GALL MIDGE *Rhopalomyia sulcata* Pl. 418

This midge induces columnar or tubular, glabrous, monothalamous leaf galls on several species of *Baccharis*, particularly desert broom in the Mojave Desert, California. These blunt-tipped galls are usually found growing at an oblique angle out of the middle of the long, linear leaves or from the tips. There is usually some swelling or broadening of the leaf at the point of adult emergence. Shallow furrows mark the surface of the galls. Galls measure 3 mm high by 1 mm in diameter. Color varies from solid green to beige with vertical purple stripes. These midges have been reported inducing galls on various species of *Baccharis* from California, the Southwest, and Mexico.

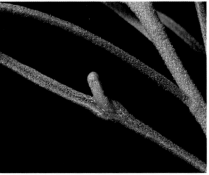

Plate 418. Tube gall of *Rhopalomyia sulcata* on desert broom leaf.

TEARDROP-GALL MIDGE *Rhopalomyia* sp. A

Pl. 419

This midge induces round, pointed, monothalamous leaf galls in spring on desert broom. These colorful galls are yellow, pink, or wine red, with a slightly granular surface. A thin, sharp point at the apex gives them the appearance of small teardrops. Galls measure 3 mm high by 2 mm wide and emerge from the leaf at oblique angles. Galls usually occur one per leaf and can be found on the same branches and leaves as galls of the tube-gall midge (*R. sulcata*).

Plate 419. Leaf gall of *Rhopalomyia* sp. A on desert broom.

BUD-GALL MIDGE *Rhopalomyia* sp. B

Pl. 420

This gall midge species induces clustered, monothalamous terminal bud galls on desert broom. Each gall cluster comprises two to four individual galls. These teardrop or pear-shaped galls are normally covered with bristly hairs but marked by nearly glabrous rounded projections at the apex of each gall. Parasitized galls are glabrous, lacking the bristles of inducer-occupied galls. Each gall measures 3–5 mm in diameter, with the entire cluster reaching 10–15 mm across. Galls examined in April at one location were heavily parasitized, leaving few gall midge larvae intact. During spring of 2008, for example, of 56 galls examined, 53 (95%) were parasitized.

Plate 420. Cluster of *Rhopalomyia* sp. B galls on desert broom.

BLACK-STEM-GALL MIDGE *Asteromyia gutierreziae*

Pl. 421

This midge initiates monothalamous, slightly swollen stem galls on desert broom, matchweed (*Gutierrezia microcephala*), and broom snakeweed (*G. sarothrae*). The occurrence of this species' galls on two unrelated genera is interesting, in that it does not happen often among cecidomyiids. Galls are easily recognized by their stark black color; if not for the color, they would be hard to find, as there is little swelling. Galls measure 12 mm long by 2 mm in diameter and are usually widely scattered, occurring several per bush. Galls of this midge have been found throughout the Mojave Desert, California; Escalante Desert, Utah; and into New Mexico.

Plate 421. Gall of *Asteromyia gutierreziae* on desert broom.

Plate 422. Galls of rosette-gall midge, **Unknown**, on desert broom.

ROSETTE-GALL MIDGE   Unknown   Pl. 422

This midge induces dark green, monothalamous bud galls on desert broom. Galls are firm and covered with stiff, waxy, pointed, green, leafy bracts that radiate outwardly. Bracts measure 7 mm long by 2 mm in diameter at the base, and whole galls measure 12–14 mm across. Galls occur in spring on axillary and terminal buds and sometimes occur one after the other along the length of the stem. Larval chambers are lined with a white fungus while the larva is alive, which is typical for galls of *Asphondylia* spp. Galls similar to these were described as *Asphondylia baccahriola* on *Baccharis pteronioides* in Texas and Arizona (Gagné 1989). While the galls pictured here may prove to be *A. baccahriola* on a new host species in the deserts of California where they were found, adults will be required to clarify their identity.

BALL-GALL WASP   Unknown   Pl. 423

This interesting cynipid wasp induces glossy, round, polythalamous galls just below the flowers of desert broom in October. The relatively smooth, glabrous gall is 8 mm in diameter. Under magnification, the surface of the gall has micro-pits, giving it the look of an orange rind. The hard, outer wall of the gall is only about 1 mm thick. The inner flesh is brown and pulpy and generally has several individual tunnels—each occupied by a single large white larva in October. The tunnels do not appear to intersect, maintaining the independence of each larva. Outside of roses,

Plate 423. Stem gall of ball-gall wasp, **Unknown**, on desert broom.

chinquapin, and oaks, where the bulk of gall-inducing cynipid wasps are found, it is rather rare for a cynipid wasp to induce a gall on any vascular plant. This new species is quite common on desert broom shrubs in the southern half of Arizona, from Phoenix south.

Crabapple Galls

GALL RUST   *Gymnosporangium nelsoni*   Pl. 424

This rust gall occurs on fruit of Pacific crabapple (*Malus fusca*) in late spring. Affected fruit can measure 20 mm long by 7 mm in diameter. During the spore-producing **AECIAL** stage of this fungus, galled fruit with bright orange spores readily stand out from normal fruit nearby. Leaves and normal fruit may be dusted with these spores. Rusts are common on crabapple, especially in some areas where intermediate hosts like junipers, hawthorns, and mountain ash occur. This rust, sometimes known as cedar-apple rust, has been found in Alaska and Washington.

Plate 424. Rust gall of *Gymnosporangium nelsoni* on crabapple, with ungalled fruit to the right.

Creosote Bush Galls

Creosote bush (*Larrea tridentata*) is the dominant shrub in much of the desert regions of southern California, Nevada, Utah, Arizona, Texas, and Mexico. When driving through these desert areas, you can see endless miles of nearly pure creosote bush. This species is remarkable for its habit of growing outwardly from the parent plant, producing clonal rings, some of which measure up to 9 m across, genetically identical to the original parent. One of these giant "fairy ring" structures has been dated to be 11,700 years old, which, if accurate, may make creosote bush one of the oldest living plants on earth (Vasek 1980). Surprisingly enough, creosote bush hosts at least 16 species of gall midges, making it a critical host plant for gall insects, including their parasites and inquilines. Nearly all the gall midges known to date on creosote bush are from the genus *Asphondylia*, whose members are also known to have symbiotic relationships with fungi. There is also a single species of *Contarinia* that induces a gall, but adults have yet to be reared for species determination. One critical study of creosote bush indicated a higher number of galls and gall-inducing species on plants growing in nutrient- or water-stressed circumstances. Galls of 15 of the 16 known species are described here.

GALL MIDGE *Asphondylia apicata*

Pl. 425

This midge induces monothalamous bud galls, with either a straight or slightly bent projection emanating from the apex of the main gall body, on creosote bush. Galls are green when fresh but turn chocolate brown with age. Old galls often have yellow or pale orange pupal cases projecting from the gall. Galls measure 7 mm long overall, with the lower swollen segment about 4 mm long by 2 mm in diameter. The thin projection is usually 3 mm long and less than 1 mm in width. Galls are usually found on terminal buds. Larvae and pupae have been found both in spring (March) and early autumn (September), and pupae have been found in November. The season of adult emergence may be stretched over a long

Plate 425. Gall of *Asphondylia apicata* on creosote bush showing a pupal case projecting from the gall.

period of time, or there may be two generations per year for this gall midge. This species has been found from Arizona to Death Valley and the southern Mojave Desert, California.

STEM-GALL MIDGE *Asphondylia auripila*

Pl. 426

This midge induces large, round, leafy, polythalamous galls on stems of creosote bush. The golf-ball-size cluster of smaller galls can measure up to 25 mm in diameter and be easily seen from the road. The entire cluster is green when fresh and is composed of hundreds of thin, 10-mm-long bracts arranged in multiple, small rosette patterns. The bracts arise from each of the individual club-shaped to pyramidal galls comprising the larger gall mass. These individual galls measure 7 mm high by 3 mm wide at the base. Fresh green galls can be found almost year-round but are most likely after major rain events. Each individual gall within the cluster has a terminal

Plate 426. Fresh gall of *Asphondylia auripila* on creosote bush.

plug through which the larvae emerge to build their white cocoon at the surface. Adults emerge from spring to late summer, although there may be some variation in different regions. Over 17 species of parasites have been associated with *Asphondylia* spp. galls; 9 of these apparently account for 98% of the parasitism. Research has shown that parasites attack this creosote bush stem-gall midge through all stages of its development. The Seri people of Sonoran Desert in the Southwest smoked the dried galls like tobacco.

LEAF-GALL MIDGE *Asphondylia barbata* Pl. 427

This midge induces small, ovoid, slightly hairy, nondetachable, monothalamous galls, often in clusters, on the underside of leaves of creosote bush. Galls are usually green, sometimes with a dark brown spot near one end, and measure 2 mm long by 1 mm in diameter. They are often found side by side on the small leaves. Larvae and pupae have been found in spring and early fall. Adult emergence is presumably in spring.

Plate 427. Cluster of galls of *Asphondylia barbata* on creosote bush.

CLUB-GALL MIDGE *Asphondylia clavata* Pl. 428

Plate 428. Club gall of *Asphondylia clavata* on creosote bush.

This midge induces green, glabrous, club-shaped, monothalamous galls on leaves of creosote bush. Galls measure 4 mm long by 1 mm in diameter at the widest point and turn brown with age. They occur singly or in pairs and usually extend off the ventral midrib. Galls resemble those of the leaf club-gall midge (*A. pila*), except for the absence of hair. Galls of this species often terminate in a more pronounced swollen larval chamber than those of the leaf club-gall midge. Occasionally, you can find both species' galls growing on the same leaf. As with other *Asphondylia* spp., this species' larvae and pupae have been found over a wide period in spring and early fall.

ANTLER-GALL MIDGE *Asphondylia digitata* Pl. 429

Plate 429. Antler-like galls of *Asphondylia digitata* on creosote bush.

This midge induces monothalamous, antler-like leaf galls on creosote bush. These green galls have noticeably toothed margins that look like moose antlers. Galls measure 5 mm across and are the thickness of normal leaves. As with the normal paired leaflets, two galls often form close together. Fresh larvae-containing galls have been collected in January. Pupation occurs inside the galls. Females deposit eggs directly into leaf tissues with their short ovipositors.

PADDLE-GALL MIDGE *Asphondylia discalis*

Pl. 430

This midge induces paddle-shaped, mono–thalamous galls that usually grow at right angles from the ventral midrib on creosote bush leaves. When fresh, galls are green, but they turn dark brown with age. Galls measure 4 mm long by 1.5 mm wide. They are flat and leaflike and occur singly or in pairs. The larval chamber is located in the center of the gall. Larvae and pupae have been found at several times of the year from spring through fall. This species may have more than one generation per year.

Plate 430. Paddle gall of *Asphondylia discalis* on creosote bush showing the exit hole.

GALL MIDGE *Asphondylia fabalis*

Pl. 431

This midge induces stringbean-shaped, monothalamous galls that protrude from the underside of leaves of creosote bush. Galls occur singly or sometimes two or three per leaf and measure up to 5 mm long by 1.5 mm in diameter. These galls are somewhat round in cross section, not laterally flattened as related galls are. Some galls are slightly bent. Galls have a mealy-granular surface and are green to brown. Larvae and pupae have been found in spring and fall. As with other members of this genus, the larvae have three instars, are usually white to yellow, and pupate inside the galls, with pupal cases usually protruding.

Plate 431. Gall of *Asphondylia fabalis* on creosote bush.

FLOWER-GALL MIDGE *Asphondylia florea*

Pl. 432

This midge induces club-shaped monothalamous galls at the base of flowers and fruiting bodies of creosote bush. Galls are easily missed, as they superficially resemble the plant's hairy seed pods. Galls are 4 mm long by 1 mm in diameter and are covered with long white hairs. Larvae and pupae have been collected mostly in spring. Pupae

Plate 432. Gall of *Asphondylia florea* on creosote bush showing an exit hole.

emerge through holes at the apex of the galls. Galls examined in November were empty. They have been found from Arizona to the southern Mojave Desert, California.

LEAFY-BUD-GALL MIDGE   *Asphondylia foliosa*   Pl. 433

This midge induces round, monothalamous, single stem galls on creosote bush. Galls do not occur in clusters, as do other species. When fresh, presumably in spring, the galls have numerous slender, green, leafy bracts that do not completely cover the base of the gall body. The bracts tend to be rather short. The entire gall measures 7 mm in diameter. Most galls in January are brown. Pupation occurs inside the gall.

Plate 433. Gall of *Asphondylia foliosa* on creosote bush.

LEAF-CLUB-GALL WASP   *Asphondylia pila*   Pl. 434

This midge induces monothalamous, club-shaped galls that stand erect on ventral midrib of creosote bush leaves. These galls have fine white hairs and occur singly or in pairs. Galls measure 7 mm high by 1.5 mm in diameter at the widest point—the larval chamber. Galls are beige near the base and dark gray on the upper section. A similar species, the creosote bush club-gall midge (*A. clavata*), has galls that are smooth and glabrous; otherwise they can be difficult to distinguish.

RESIN-GALL MIDGE   *Asphondylia resinosa*   Pl. 435

This midge induces small, round, monothalamous stem galls on creosote bush that are usually covered with hardened, glossy brown resin. Some galls are round and have appressed leafy bracts around the base. Other variants have protruding leafy bracts, arranged in clusters of four. Galls measure 3 mm in diameter and are usually olive-green. These galls have been collected fresh in January.

Plate 434. Galls of *Asphondylia pila* on creosote bush.

Plate 435. Round gall of *Asphondylia resinosa* on creosote bush.

CONE-GALL MIDGE *Asphondylia rosetta*

Pl. 436

This midge induces leafy, monothalamous, cone-shaped galls on stems of creosote bush. These galls are distinguished from those of the leafy bud-gall midge (*A. foliosa*; plate 433) by the recurved bracts that cover the entire gall body. Bracts have sparse hairs over the surface. Galls are green when fresh and brown in winter. They measure 10 mm high by 4 to 5 mm wide. Larvae have been collected in August and September, and pupae collected as late as April. Pupation occurs in the galls in spring. Emergence and reproduction occur shortly thereafter.

Plate 436. Bud gall of *Asphondylia rosetta* on creosote bush.

LEAF-POD-GALL MIDGE *Asphondylia silicula*

Pl. 437

This midge induces pod-like, pointed, laterally flattened, monothalamous galls on the underside of leaves of creosote bush. Galls hang from the middle of the leaf or from along the margins, with one or more galls per leaf. Galls measure 3 mm long by 1 to 2 mm wide and are green to brown. As with other members of this genus, larvae and pupae can be found from spring through fall.

Plate 437. Galls of *Asphondylia silicula* on creosote bush.

SCIMITAR-LEAF-GALL MIDGE *Asphondylia* sp.

Pl. 438

This midge induces flat-sided, sword-shaped, striated, monothalamous bud galls on creosote bush. These galls are green when fresh but turn brown with age. The laterally flattened sides are furrowed with shallow ridges. The apex of the galls is usually obtuse, and the whole gall is arched. These distinctive galls

Plate 438. Gall of *Asphondylia* sp. on creosote bush.

are almost always found on terminal buds and stand out from normal leaves. Adults have not been reared for identification to species level. Their behavior is likely similar to that of other *Asphondylia* adults.

CLASPING-LEAF-GALL MIDGE   *Contarinia* sp.   Pl. 439

Plate 439. Gall of *Contarinia* sp. on creosote bush.

This midge induces monothalamous galls composed of two leaves joined together to create flat, circular galls on creosote bush. These galls are green and look almost like normal leaves except for their broader, swollen nature. The galls actually look like green wings on terminal branches. Galls collected in January were either green or brown, indicating either multiple generations per year or a delay in the development of some of the galls. They measure 8 mm high by 6 mm wide and occur in pairs or clusters of several. This species appears to be the only gall-inducer on creosote bush that is not a member of the genus *Asphondylia*.

Desert Tea Galls

STEM-GALL MIDGE   *Lasioptera ephedrae*   Pl. 440

This midge induces dimpled integral stem galls, usually just above the nodes, of desert teas *Ephedra californica*, *E. nevadensis*, and *E. trifurca*, and perhaps other western *Ephedra* species. These monothalamous galls measure 10–15 mm long by 5 mm in diameter. Galls are stem green, taper gently, and show a dimple of thinner, beige tissue about midway along their length, where the larval chamber is located. Larvae feed in the pithy center of the stems. Pupation occurs in the galls, and adults emerge the following spring through the thin wall of the dimple. There is one generation per year. This midge has been found from New Mexico to California.

Plate 440. Gall of *Lasioptera ephedrae* on desert tea.

STEM-GALL MIDGE *Lasioptera ephedricola*

Pl. 441

This midge induces wrinkled or furrowed integral stem galls on desert teas *Ephedra californica*, *E. nevadensis*, and *E. trifurca*. These monothalamous galls measure 10–30 mm long by 4 mm in diameter. Galls are normally darker green than the rest of the stems when fresh and appear like dead tissue with age. Larval tunnels are lined with a fungus. Pupation occurs inside the galls, and adults emerge in February and March. This midge occurs from New Mexico to California and is common in the southern Mojave Desert.

Plate 441. Gall of *Lasioptera ephedricola* on desert tea.

Everlasting Galls

STEM-GALL TEPHRITID *Trupanea signata*

Pl. 442

Galls of this tephritid fly are elliptical, gently tapered stem swellings that occur near the tips of shoots of pearly everlasting (*Anaphalis margaritacea*) in summer in Washington. Galls are covered with white, appressed hairs, similar to stems and the underside of leaves, and measure to 18 mm long by 8 mm wide. Gall development appears to terminate normal flower growth, though shoots and leaves emanate from the sides of the galls. Each gall chamber holds three to six black-brown, hardened and sticky pupal cases in late August. Adults emerged in late August in the laboratory. Nearly half of the galls collected were parasitized. These gall insects are widespread from near sea level to at least 1,250 m on the slopes of Mount Shuksan, Washington, and are also known to occur in Oregon, Arizona, and Texas.

Plate 442. Gall of *Trupanea signata* on pearly everlasting.

False Azalea Galls

LEAF-GALL FUNGUS *Exobasidium vaccinii* Pls. 443 & 444

This fungus produces fleshy, white, bladderlike pockets on leaves of false azalea (*Menziesia ferruginea*) in spring. Besides causing swollen, deformed leaves, the fungus can induce stem galls and witches' brooms and also attacks buds and flowers. The leaf galls are usually bowl- or cup-shaped bags consuming part or all of the leaf. They bulge out on the lower surface, with a corresponding deep depression or pocket occurring on the dorsal surface, and measure up to 25 mm long by 13 mm wide. Galls found in June were sporulating from the exterior surface, giving the galls a powdery-white appearance. Spores produced in summer overwinter among bud scales until the following spring. This fungus is found throughout the United States and Canada. It has also been recorded on western azalea (*Rhododendron occidentale*), rhododendron (*Rhododendron* spp.), bearberry (*Arctostaphylos uva-ursi*), manzanita (*Arctostaphylos* spp.), blueberry and huckleberry (*Vaccinium* spp.), cranberry (*Vaccinium macrocarpon*), gaultheria (*Gaultheria* spp.), bog laurel (*Kalmia microphylla* subsp. *occidentalis*), madrone (*Arbutus menziesii*), bog rosemary (*Andromeda polifolia*), and Labrador tea (*Ledum groenlandicum*). It has been reported that Native Americans along the British Columbia coast ate these fungus galls.

Plate 443. Dorsal view of fungus gall of *Exobasidium vaccinii* on false azalea.

Plate 444. Ventral view of fungus gall of *E. vaccinii*.

Goldenbush Galls

Several species of goldenbush (*Ericameria* spp.) occur in the West. California goldenbush (*E. ericoides*) and Palmer's goldenbush (*E. palmeri* var. *palmeri*) are common shrub inhabitants of coastal sage scrub communities. Cliff goldenbush (*E. cuneata* var. *spathulata*) is common among rock outcroppings in the Mojave Desert, California.

ROSETTE-BUD-GALL MIDGE *Rhopalomyia ericameriae* Pl. 445

This midge induces rosette bud galls with flaring and slightly recurved bracts on California goldenbush and Palmer's goldenbush. At first leafy bracts are erect, but they recurve and turn brown with age. These galls measure 7 mm long by 5 mm wide and are green when fresh; bracts are 1—2 mm wide. Larvae develop during spring and early summer. The midges pupate inside the galls. Adults emerge in April to oviposit in new buds.

Plate 445. Gall of *Rhopalomyia ericameriae* on goldenbush.

GALL MIDGE *Rhopalomyia* sp. Fig. 72 & Pl. 446

This midge induces a knobby, sticky, polythalamous, terminal bud gall on cliff goldenbush. Numerous blunt projections or knobs extend from the top of the gall. Larval chambers are arranged radially near the surface of the gall. Galls measure 7 to 10 mm high and wide. Fresh galls in late November are round and extremely sticky. On some shrubs, nearly every terminal bud is galled. Presumably the adults emerge in spring. This species was found in the Mojave Desert, California.

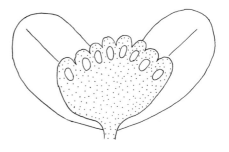

Figure 72. Cross section of gall of *Rhopalomyia* sp. showing the position of the larval chambers.

Plate 446. Gall of *Rhopalomyia* sp. on cliff goldenbush.

BUD-GALL MIDGE *Prodiplosis falcata*

Pl. 447

This midge induces round to slightly elongate, cone-shaped, monothalamous bud galls on California goldenbush. Fresh galls in May are green and have broad leafy bracts with outwardly pointed tips. Fine, white hairs show along the edges of each bract. Old galls look more like closed cones, with the bracts appressed. The tips of the bracts apparently break off with age. Some elongate galls measure 10 mm long by 7 mm wide, but most old, brown galls are 8 mm by 8 mm. Bracts measure 5–8 mm wide at the base. This species is particularly prominent in the dunes of the San Luis Obispo, California, coastline.

Plate 447. Gall of *Prodiplosis falcata* on California goldenbush.

Golden Yarrow Galls

STEM-GALL MIDGE *Neolasioptera sp.*

Pl. 448

This midge induces integral, round to oval, monothalamous stem galls near the tips of golden yarrow (*Eriophyllum confertiflorum*). Galls are covered with fine, white hairs, as are the stems and leaves of the host plant. Some galls are abrupt swellings, while others are slightly tapered. Round galls measure 5–7 mm in diameter, while the tapered versions are usually 10 mm long by 7 mm across. The inner flesh of the galls is green. The large larval chamber is lined with a white fungus. Orange larvae have been found in galls in May, though some had already exited the galls through holes near the top. This gall may also occur on the related seaside woolly sunflower (*E. staechadifolium*), which shares similar habitats. This gall was initially found in Morro Bay, California.

Plate 448. Stem gall of *Neolasioptera* sp. on golden yarrow.

Gooseberry and Currant Galls

RUST-GALL FUNGUS *Puccinia caricina* Pl. 449

This rust gall fungus occurs on fresh spring leaves of *Ribes* spp. While several leaves on a single branch can have galls, there is usually only one gall per leaf. Galls are noticeably swollen and are convex on the dorsal surface and concave on the ventral side. They measure 4–6 mm in diameter. Host plants are infected in spring by spores just as new leaves are unfurling. Under magnification, one can see the reddish-orange **SPERMAGONIA** on the upper surface. Aecia form several days after infection in depressions underneath. Several other rusts infect gooseberry, but no others form the spermagonia and aecial stages as does *P. caricina*. This rust also infects sedges (*Carex* spp.) and common nettle (*Urtica dioica*).

Plate 449. Rust gall of *Puccinia caricina* on gooseberry.

LEAF-ROLLING APHID *Macrosiphum euphorbiae* Pl. 450

This aphid induces swollen, leaf roll galls on some gooseberries (*Ribes* spp.). These galls can completely obliterate terminal leaves, rolling both edges in toward the middle. The veiny galls appear lighter green than normal leaves. The offspring develop within the rolled leaves. This aphid is also known as the potato aphid, as it infects numerous vegetable crops as alternate hosts in summer, including gooseberry, honeysuckle (*Lonicera* spp.), and crabapple (*Malus* spp.). This aphid is common throughout the United States and Canada.

Plate 450. Roll galls of *Macrosiphum euphorbiae* on gooseberry.

BUD-GALL MIDGE *Rhopalomyia* sp.

Pl. 451

This midge induces green, monothalamous bud galls on gooseberries in spring. Galls have numerous, thin bracts that flare out in an open rosette pattern and completely conceal the gall body. They measure 10–12 mm across. These are spring galls that turn brown by August, indicating a cessation of larval activity. Adults probably emerge in spring as new buds swell.

Plate 451. Old gall of *Rhopalomyia* sp. on gooseberry.

LEAF-FOLD-GALL MIDGE *Dasineura* sp.

Pl. 452

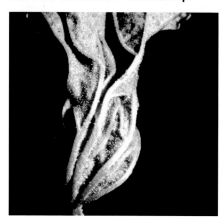

This midge induces galls on red-flowering currant (*Ribes sanguineum*). Affected leaves are completely distorted and folded inwardly, revealing on their undersides larger than normal, swollen veins. Galls are polythalamous, with several light orange larvae hidden among the interior folds. Adults emerge through openings created by the folds in late May and early June.

Plate 452. Twisted fold gall of *Dasineura* sp. on red-flowering currant.

Gumweed Galls

STEM-GALL MOTH   *Gnorimoschema grindeliae*   Pl. 453

This gelechiid moth induces large, integral, monothalamous stem galls on gumweed (*Grindelia hirsutula*). Galls occur only on lower branches, usually close to the ground and near the center of the host plant, and sometimes cause a clustering of branches above. Galls are ovoid, measure 20–22 mm long by 12–14 mm in diameter, and are composed of overlapping leafy bracts. One or more normal leaves protrude from the gall body. Most galls grow in the shade, although a few receive sunlight. They are usually green, but those exposed to sun may be red-purple. These thick-walled, succulent galls have a rather large larval chamber, up to 14 mm long. Larvae develop rapidly, reaching full size in April. Most larvae cut an exit hole near the top of the gall and drop to the ground by the end of April. Larvae create large cocoons, up to 15–30 mm long, in the sand and leaf

Plate 453. Stem gall of *Gnorimoschema grindeliae* on gumweed.

litter under their host plants. This is a host-specific moth whose life cycle is keyed to the habits of its host. These perennial shrubs usually die back by end of summer, and it is presumed that the adult moths deposit their eggs near the base of the plants, where they may overwinter.

FLOWER-GALL MIDGE   *Rhopalomyia grindeliae*   Pl. 454

This midge induces sticky, hard, capsule-like, monothalamous galls among flowers of gumweed (*Grindelia hirsutula*). Galled florets usually stand out from those unaffected by the midge. Individual galls are green when fresh in early spring and measure 5 mm long. Whole clusters can exceed 25 mm across. Galls have a hole at the apex. Adults emerge and lay eggs in October. Since the host plant dies back by fall, the eggs most likely overwinter. This gall may appear on other gumweed hosts in California and adjoining states.

Plate 454. Gall of *Rhopalomyia grindeliae* on gumweed.

LEAFY-GALL MIDGE   Unknown   Pl. 455

This midge induces large, polythalamous bud galls on gumweed (*Grindelia hirsutula*). These rosette galls are composed of numerous thin, long, green leafy bracts. The overall size of the galls can reach 40 mm across, with bracts that measure 1 mm wide by 25 mm long. Galls form in spring on terminal and lateral buds as they begin to swell. Because host plants tend to die back in fall, it is presumed that the adults emerge in fall. This species occurs in central California.

Plate 455. Rosette gall of leafy-gall midge, **Unknown**, on gumweed.

Hazelnut Galls

BUD-GALL MIDGE   Unknown   Pl. 456

This midge induces globular, monothalamous bud galls on hazelnut (*Corylus cornuta*). Galls are aborted buds that never develop or open. During the growing season in spring, galls are 7–10 mm in diameter and a normal bud green. By fall, the buds turn brown and dry. At this time the larvae have ceased feeding and enter diapause. The larvae of both a *Contarinia* species and a *Dasineura* species have been associated with these galls. Adults have yet to be reared, which is necessary to determine the species. It is presumed that they emerge in spring, timed with the development of spring buds. This bud gall is common in California.

Plate 456. Gall of bud-gall midge, **Unknown**, on hazelnut.

Honeysuckle Galls

Several species of honeysuckle (*Lonicera* spp.) occur in the West, including introduced ornamental varieties. One of the more common native species is *Lonicera subspicata*, which occurs in dry habitats and chaparral slopes along the coast from central to southern California. It supports two distinct bud galls—both induced by gall midges. A second honeysuckle, *L. hispidula*, common in the central-western part of the state, supports a distinctive bud gall made by another gall midge. The three midges described here are closely related species. Finally, two new species found on twinberry (*L. involucrata*), an aphid and a midge, are described here.

FOLD-GALL APHID   *Hyadaphis* sp.   Pl. 457

This aphid induces fold galls along the leaf margins of twinberry. There is usually only one gall per leaf. Galled tissue is swollen, distorted, and folded in toward the underside of the leaf. Galls are tightly closed and difficult to open. They measure 10–20 mm long by 3–4 mm in diameter and are reddish on the dorsal side and light green below. A single, light gray stem mother is found in the innermost fold in late May. There are several *Hyadaphis* aphids that attack *Lonicera* spp., and their taxonomy is complex. These aphids overwinter as eggs among buds. Galls are found in lowland areas of the Pacific Northwest.

BUD-GALL MIDGE   *Lonicerae lonicera*   Pl. 458

This midge induces ovoid, succulent, monothalamous bud galls on *L. subspicata*. Spring galls are green and measure 10–15 mm in diameter. Bud scales often flare out at the tips of the otherwise smooth galls. Larvae overwinter and pupate inside the galls, and adults emerge in February and March.

Plate 457. Fold gall of *Hyadaphis* sp. on twinberry.

Plate 458. Galls of *Lonicerae lonicera* on honeysuckle.

CABBAGE-BUD-GALL MIDGE *Lonicerae russoi* Pl. 459

Plate 459. Galls of *Lonicerae russoi* on honeysuckle.

This midge induces conical, leafy, monothalamous bud galls on *L. hispidula*. While these rosette galls can occur singly, they usually appear in congested clusters that can reach 30 mm across. Individual galls measure 10 mm high by 8 mm in diameter, including the leafy bracts. The bracts of these galls are oval or tongue-shaped with rounded tips. Long white hairs protrude from the edges of each bract. Each gall has a dense arrangement of white hairs filling its center, marking the entrance to the larval chamber, which measures 4 mm high by 2 mm wide. In February, galls appear fresh and green. Those exposed to direct sunlight often turn wine red. Half of the galls examined in late February contained larvae, while the other half contained pupae. Adults emerge in late February and March. Female midges are relatively large and have a dark brown thorax and orange abdomen. Males have smaller, thinner abdomens. It is not clear when galls begin development, given the apparent freshness of galls in winter. This gall-inducer was initially placed in the genus *Rhopalomyia* sp. B (Russo 2006); following thorough examination of adults, a new genus and species was assigned by Gagné (2016).

LEAFY-ROSETTE-GALL MIDGE *Lonicerae* sp. Pl. 460

This midge induces monothalamous, leafy rosette terminal bud galls on *L. subspicata* and possibly other species. The tips of galled shoots have from one to four galls clustered together, looking like one large gall. Galls are leaf green and measure 14 mm wide by 5 mm high. The leafy bracts covering the exterior are large, broad bud scales up to 7 mm wide. Larval chambers are large, reaching 3 mm in diameter. The inner wall is smooth and bright green, except for a small white patch of fungal material at one end of the chamber. Pupae begin to develop in January along the central coast of California.

Plate 460. Gall of *Lonicerae* sp. on honeysuckle.

ROLL-GALL MIDGE *Dasineura* sp.

Pl. 461

This midge induces monothalamous roll galls encompassing terminal leaves of twinberry. Galls are thick, dense, fleshy, and contain numerous larvae. Most galls are rosy red and measure 13 mm in diameter by 35 mm long. The surface of the galls is covered with short, sparse, white, bristly hairs (seen under magnification). The larvae live among the interior tightly folded leaf tissues, where the walls are covered with a dense coat of what appear to be glandular-tipped hairs. The white larvae are found between each of the swollen, distorted leaf layers comprising the gall. This new species was found on the slopes of Mount Shuksan, Washington, in the subalpine environment at 1,250 m in August.

Plate 461. Gall of *Dasineura* sp. on twinberry.

Horsebrush Galls

There are several species of horsebrush (*Tetradymia* spp.) in the West. The species covered here are cotton-thorn (*T. axillaris*), Mojave horsebrush (*T. stenolepis*), and *T. glabrata*. Horsebrush species are some of the more prominent desert plants through the Joshua tree woodland and creosote bush scrub communities. Horsebrush supports a stem-gall-inducing moth (described here). A coastal species, *T. comosa*, supports a woolly, ovoid, lateral bud gall induced by the gall midge "*Mayetiola*" *tetradymia* (not described here).

STEM-GALL MOTH *Scrobipalpopsis tetradymiella*

Pl. 462

This gelechiid moth induces white, woolly, globular to ovoid, monothalamous, integral stem galls on cotton-thorn, Mojave horsebrush, and *T. glabrata*. Galls generally occur at the base of new shoots in spring, and fresh galls often have leaves and spines emerging from the sides. Galls are symmetrically tapered toward the tip, from which the shoot continues, rarely extending more than 70 mm in length, far short of normal shoots (greater than 140 mm). Galls measure up to 15 mm long by 8 mm in diameter. The walls of the

Plate 462. Gall of *Scrobipalpopsis tetradymiella* on horsebrush.

galls tend to be thin (1 mm), as the larval chamber is quite large, occupying most of the available space for larval feeding and growth. A 15-mm-long gall, for example, had a 13-mm-long larval chamber. Galls initiated prior to normal, rapid shoot elongation tended to be smaller than those initiated during bursts of spring growth. One study revealed that galls were more abundant on plants growing at lower elevations in the Mojave Desert, California. Plants on the edges of washes or roads seem to have more galls than those farther away competing with other desert shrubs for limited water. Old galls may remain on the shrub for two or three seasons. Pupation occurs within the galls. Adults emerge during June and July, are gray mottled, and measure 8–10 mm long. They remain active primarily during morning hours through mid-August. A second generation of larvae feed from late June to mid-September, and adults emerge in late September. Egg deposition occurs through November or until onset of cold weather. Overwintering eggs hatch in April, and stem gall development continues through June.

Huckleberry and Blueberry Galls

Blueberry, huckleberry, and cranberry belong to the genus *Vaccinium*. Six species found in the West extend all the way into southeast Alaska: dwarf blueberry (*V. caespitosum*), black or highbush huckleberry (*V. membranaceum*), evergreen huckleberry (*V. ovatum*), red huckleberry (*V. parvifolium*), grouse whortleberry (*V. scoparium*), and bog blueberry (*V. uliginosum*). Four gall-inducers occur on various species of *Vaccinium*, a fungus, an unknown moth, and two gall-inducing midges.

RUST FUNGUS   *Pucciniastrum goeppertianum*   Pl. 463

Plate 463. Witches' broom of *Pucciniastrum goeppertianum* on huckleberry.

This fungus induces witches' brooms on evergreen, red, and black huckleberry and dwarf blueberry plants in western states. The stems comprising the witches' brooms are glossy, swollen, and mahogany brown, and twist and turn in a compact cluster. Several clusters of brooms can occur on a single shrub. Affected branches die after the growing season. Galled branches are usually 15–17 cm long and bear leaves. The fungus is systemic and perennial. The telial stage of the fungus is responsible for the broom galls on blueberries and huckleberries. This fungus has no uredinial stage, as do some other rusts. This rust has been called the "fir-blueberry rust," because in its aecial stage it uses a variety of fir trees as alternate hosts. Spores produced on the brooms infect fir needles, allowing development of the aecial stage. This rust fungus is found in the northern United States, including nearly all of the western mountains from Alaska south to Mexico.

LEAF-ROLL-GALL MOTH   Unknown

Pl. 464

This moth induces roll galls along the edges of huckleberry leaves, especially black huckleberry. Roll galls usually range from 10 to 15 mm long by 2 mm in width. These galls are the same color as host leaves when fresh, turning brown with age. Larvae develop through late spring and summer. Adults may emerge in late summer to deposit their eggs on branches for overwintering. There is one generation per year.

Plate 464. Gall of leaf-roll-gall moth, **Unknown**, on huckleberry.

BUD-GALL MIDGE   *"Dasineura"* sp.

Pl. 465

This midge induces red, succulent, pea-size, monothalamous bud galls at the base of the petiole or where the petiole and leaf join on dwarf blueberry and perhaps other *Vaccinium* spp. as well. Some galls encompass the entire petiole. Galls generally show the bud tip protruding from the swollen gall itself. These bud galls measure 5–10 mm in length by 5 mm in diameter and are usually bright red on the side exposed to sunlight and yellow-green on the shady side. Larvae appear to belong in the genus *Dasineura*.

LEAF-ROLL-GALL MIDGE   *Dasineura* cf. *oxycoccana*

Pl. 466

This midge induces tightly rolled leaf galls on black huckleberry and perhaps other related species. Galls generally occur only on the terminal two leaves of a shoot, with the uppermost

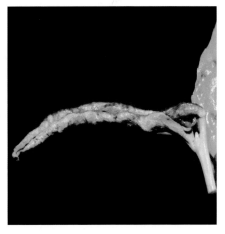

Plate 466. Leaf-roll gall of *Dasineura* cf. *oxycoccana* on huckleberry.

Plate 465. Galls of *"Dasineura"* sp. on blueberry.

leaf completely encompassed by the lower leaf. It appears that the female deposits eggs in the top leaf buds before the two leaves unfold and separate. The polythalamous galls measure up to 30 mm long and are often filled with a clear fluid. They are normally green but if exposed to direct sunlight may be rose-red. Larvae are usually found within the tightest, innermost roll of the affected leaves. So far, I have found this species only in the subalpine community of Mount Shuksan, Washington, but it has been recorded in several eastern states. Although this gall most likely belongs to *D. oxycoccana*, its name here is provisional until adults can be reared and examined.

Indigo Bush Galls

LEAF-GALL MIDGE **Unknown**   Pl. 467

Plate 467. Galls of leaf-gall midge, **Unknown**, on indigo bush.

This desert midge induces fleshy, round to ovoid, monothalamous galls on petioles or leaflets of indigo bush (*Psorothamnus arborescens* var. *arborescens*). Galls are beige-yellow or light green with three to four red dots near the base. Some galls are easily detachable, while others are integral, enveloping more than half of the leaflet. Galls measure 3–4 mm in diameter. There is no clear opening to the outside. Parasitism rates were extremely high for specimens of these galls collected in the northeastern Mojave Desert, California. Unfortunately, larvae alone are so different from other known species that a generic determination could not be made without seeing adults.

Lupine Galls

Over 70 species of lupine (*Lupinus* spp.) are endemic to western states. Of all the species examined, two coastal shrub species appear regularly to support midge galls: yellow bush lupine (*L. arboreus*) and blue bush lupine (*L. chamissonis*). Three gall midges and a nitrogen-fixing bacterium are described here. This bacterium is common to all lupines, as well as several other plants (see Table 5).

NITROGEN-FIXING-GALL BACTERIUM *Rhizobium* sp.   Pl. 468

This bacterium induces small, irregular, globular root galls (nodules) on all lupines (shrubs and herbaceous plants). These root nodules are 3–10 mm in diameter but may vary greatly in size, depending on host species and age. The gall surface appears smooth and usually light beige. This nitrogen-fixing bacterium has a symbiotic relationship with its host, extracting atmospheric nitrogen, storing it within the galls, and making it available to the host as well as other plants in the area.

Plate 468. Root galls of *Rhizobium* sp. on lupine.   Plate 469. Gall of *Dasineura lupini* on bush lupine.

BUD-GALL MIDGE *Dasineura lupini*   Pl. 469

This midge induces large, globular, polythalamous, hairy bud galls on yellow bush and blue bush lupines in spring. Galls occur singly or in small clusters with several adjoining buds galled. Composed of greatly expanded bud scales, galls are covered with short silver hairs and have dwarfed petioles with tiny leaflets emerging. Tips of bud scales recurve from the main body of the gall. Galls exposed to direct sun are usually red or purple, while galls completely shaded are green. Some galls reach 30 mm in length by 20 mm in diameter, but galls are typically smaller. The larval chamber is located centrally near the base of the gall. Melon-orange larvae occupy galls in July and remain in the gall through fall and winter, pupating the following spring, timed with new bud development. Adults emerge in May.

LEAF-FOLD-GALL MIDGE *Dasineura lupinorum*   Pl. 470

This midge induces monothalamous midrib fold galls on leaflets of yellow bush and blue bush lupines, and several other lupine species, from Oregon to southern California. The galls may be small mid-leaflet swellings or they can encompass an entire leaflet or all leaflets on a petiole. In this circumstance, leaflets are completely folded together from edge to edge at the gall site. Galls measure from 3 to 15 mm in length by 2–3 mm in diameter. They are either wine red or gray-green. In some cases, particularly during summer, as many as 80% of the

Plate 470. Leaf fold galls of *Dasineura lupinorum* on bush lupine.

leaflets on a host shrub are galled. As with many other *Dasineura* species, the larvae complete development inside the gall and remain there through pupation. This midge produces several generations per year. Fresh, larvae-containing galls can be found nearly year-round. Females lay their eggs on unopened leaflets in growing buds. Newly hatched larvae crawl between the closed halves of the leaflets and begin feeding, stimulating formation of the swollen galls.

STEM-GALL MIDGE   *Neolasioptera lupini*   Pl. 471

This midge induces polythalamous, integral stem galls on yellow bush lupine, among other *Lupinus* spp., from Washington to California. These galls can be evenly tapered and elliptical on a straight stem, or they can bend the stem. Galls reach 30 mm in length by 10 mm in diameter. They are usually stem-colored. Leaves and stems may emerge from their sides. Most galls, depending on the host species, have sparse hairs. As with the leaf fold-gall midge (*Dasineura lupinorum*), larvae remain in the galls, and adults emerge the following spring.

Plate 471. Stem gall of *Neolasioptera lupini* on bush lupine.

Manzanita Galls

LEAF-GALL FUNGUS   *Exobasidium vaccinii*   Pl. 472

The western states have over 50 species of manzanitas (*Arctostaphylos* spp.). On many species of these manzanitas, this fungus induces large, bright red, swollen, convex galls on the dorsal surface of leaves. There is a corresponding depression on the underside of the leaf where the spores are produced. The round to oval galls measure 15 mm long by 12 mm across—though

Plate 472. Gall of *Exobasidium vaccinii* on manzanita.

larger specimens may occur—and can encompass half to three-fourths of the affected leaf. The spores produced by this fungus are distributed by air currents and germinate on wet surfaces of host plants. New infections are caused when hyphae directly penetrate new leaves. The hyphae of this fungus spread throughout the entire host, and galled leaves can appear all over the infected shrub. The fungus, which can also induce witches' brooms, is found across the United States and Canada. It also occurs on cranberries and huckleberries (*Vaccinium* spp.), mountain heather (*Cassiope* spp.), rhododendron (*Rhododendron* spp.), and Labrador tea (*Ledum groenlandicum*).

FOLD-GALL APHID *Tamalia coweni*

Pls. 473 & 474

This aphid induces two kinds of galls: one, a common and widespread fold gall along the margins or midribs of leaves, occurring on many species of glabrous-leaved manzanitas; and the second, an uncommon convoluted swelling or baglike structure on the inflorescences of manzanitas. Sometimes new leaves are completely galled by fundatrices (stem mothers) of this aphid. Galls are succulent and pink-red and measure 10 mm long by 5 mm across. Although most galls turn brown by fall, after the aphids have left, fresh, occupied galls can be found almost any time of year. Galls often occur singly or in pairs on opposite sides of the affected leaf. Shrubs have been found with nearly every leaf galled by this aphid. The process begins in spring when the stem mother selects a row of cells, stinging the row in a pattern that causes the leaf to swell and fold over her. A single gall can contain several stem mothers. Once enclosed, stem mothers produce offspring that fill the gall and mature into alates. These winged females seek developing inflorescences in June and July (which would blossom the following late winter–spring), producing within them a brood of wingless females. The wingless females, which resemble stem mothers, induce globular galls, converting flower buds into large, pink-red, swollen bags. When several flower buds are galled, they look like red grapes. These wingless females mate and deposit eggs that overwinter in bark crevices at the base of shrubs. *Tamalia coweni* is widespread in Colorado, Nevada, and Pacific Coast states, as well as British Columbia. The inquilinous aphid

Plate 473. Leaf gall of *Tamalia coweni* on manzanita.   Plate 474. Flower gall of *T. coweni* on manzanita.

Tamalia inquilina, also found in these galls, is considered a commensal insect; it appears not to significantly impact survival rates of the fold-gall aphid even though it does reduce its reproductive success. The inquiline, found only in California and Baja California, enters occupied as well as abandoned galls and reproduces successfully.

Matchweed Galls

Matchweeds (*Gutierrezia* spp.) are, unfortunately, among those plants that are often ignored in the desert. Matchweed occurs from Colorado and Texas west through the desert systems of California and northern Mexico. Three species, *G. californica*, *G. microcephala*, and *G. sarothrae*, are known to support gall-inducers and appear to support the same ones: a moth and two gall midges (with a third gall midge described under desert broom).

STEM-GALL MOTH   *Epiblema rudei*   Fig. 73

This moth induces spindle-shaped, integral, monothalamous stem galls on matchweeds. Galls are bark-colored and measure 23 mm long by 7 mm in diameter. Larvae are thought to overwinter; pupation occurs in early spring. Each caterpillar prepares an escape hatch near the top of the gall, leaving a thin window through which the pupa exits. Exit holes measure 2.5–4 mm in diameter but close over soon after the pupae exit. Empty galls are indistinguishable from those still occupied. In some areas, galls are heavily parasitized by braconid and chalcid wasps.

FLESHY-GALL MIDGE   **Unknown**   Pl. 475

These fleshy, monothalamous, light green to rosy bud galls on matchweeds measure 8 mm in diameter. Galls are wrinkled, soft, and ovoid. Larval chambers are ovoid-elliptical and hard. Pupae were present in old galls found in January. Since new bud galls swell a few months later,

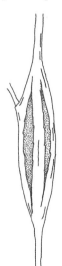

Left: Figure 73. Gall of *Epiblema rudei*.
Above: Plate 475. Gall of fleshy-gall midge, **Unknown**, on matchweed.

it appears that this species has a single generation per year. Parasitism rates appear to be high, at least in the area of original discovery near Red Rock State Park, California.

BUD-GALL MIDGE *Rhopalomyia sp.* Pl. 476

Galls of this new species found on matchweed buds are quite unlike the preceding in that they are firm and smooth. These rose-pink, polythalamous galls are smooth, glabrous, thin-skinned, and measure 8–10 mm long by 3–4 mm in diameter. Several galls can occur on successive apices of leaf clusters. The interior flesh is bright green and holds from one central larval chamber to three or four lateral chambers. This midge and its fresh galls occur in March in the eastern Mojave Desert, California, and the southwestern desert near Las Vegas, Nevada. With further study, this midge may turn out to be *R. gutierreziae*, which is currently known to gall only the inflorescences of matchweeds, though never seen by me. See also desert broom, for *Asteromyia gutierreziae* (Plate 421), which induces black-stem galls on matchweeds.

Meadowsweet Galls

ROLL-GALL MIDGE *Dasineura salicifoliae* Pl. 477

This midge induces monothalamous, midrib fold galls and occasionally leaf-margin roll galls on mountain meadowsweet (*Spiraea splendens*) and steeplebush (*S. douglasii*) in California and much of the Pacific Coast to British Columbia. These long, swollen galls are usually pink to rose red and quite noticeable. They measure up to 25 mm long by 3 mm in diameter. Those on the ventral midrib protrude. Each gall has a single large chamber within which several orange larvae feed and grow. Galls form during early summer and are fully developed by July. Larvae exit through a longitudinal slit and pupate in leaf litter the following spring. Another midge, *Parallelodiplosis* sp., is considered an inquiline in the galls of *Dasineura* spp.

Plate 477. Roll galls of *Dasinuera salicifoliae* on meadowsweet.

Plate 476. Gall of *Rhopalomyia* sp. on matchweed.

BUD-GALL MIDGE *"Contarinia"* sp. A

Pl. 478

The round, axillary, monothalamous bud galls of this midge occur on steeplebush (*Spiraea douglasii*) at low elevations in the Pacific Northwest. These galls measure 3–5 mm in diameter and are surrounded by open bracts at the base. The main section of the gall is composed of overlapping green bud scales, with the innermost fused together, leaving large, pointed, leafy edges around the sides and apex. Galls are usually green during summer. Larvae exit through a separation of the bracts at the apex and drop to the ground, where they overwinter as prepupae. This midge is provisionally placed in *Contarinia* (based on larvae) until adults can be examined.

Plate 478. Bud gall of *"Contarinia"* sp. A on steeplebush.

BUD-GALL MIDGE *"Contarinia"* sp. B.

Pl. 479

The leafy, tubular, monothalamous bud galls of this midge occur on mountain meadowsweet (*Spiraea splendens*) at high elevations or in the subalpine community of mountainous areas. These galls measure 12 mm high by 5–7 mm in diameter. They are most noticeable in fall once the host shrub's leaves drop. Galls can be red or maroon with undertones of green. Fresh galls are often found in clusters of old galls. Galls of this midge are distinct from those of the previous midge in being tubular, with bracts flaring away from the main gall body, and having an open apex, through which larvae exit by mid-September. Larvae burrow into the soil to overwinter, often beneath several feet of snow. This species can be found from northern California to Alaska.

Plate 479. Gall of *"Contarinia"* sp. B on mountain meadowsweet.

Monkey Flower Galls

STEM-GALL MIDGE *Neolasioptera diplaci*   Pl. 480

This midge induces integral, elliptical, monothalamous stem galls on bush monkey flower (*Mimulus aurantiacus*). Galls occur mid-stem or at bud nodes. Node galls measure 7 mm long and wide and are abrupt swellings, while mid-stem galls measure 15 mm long by 7 mm diameter and are gradually tapered. Galls are either brick red or pale green. Node galls usually have leaf petioles or buds protruding. Adults emerge in fall. This midge has been found only in California.

Plate 480. Gall of *Neolasioptera diplaci* on bush monkey flower.

Osoberry Galls

ROLL-GALL MIDGE *Dasineura* sp.   Pl. 481

This midge induces monothalamous leaf- margin roll galls on osoberry (*Oemleria cerasiformis*) leaves in spring. Leaf edges roll inward, creating an extremely tight and difficult-to-open gall. Galls can be 50 mm long by 10–20 mm wide. Only new, terminal leaves are affected. Thrips and other small insects are occasionally found in the innermost chamber along with midge larvae. Adults have yet to be reared for this new species.

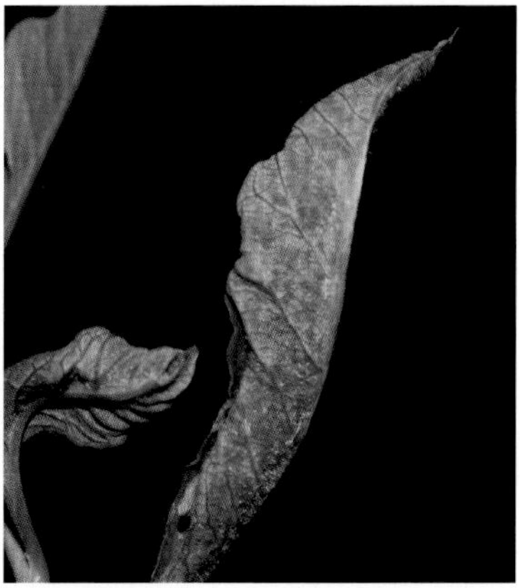

Plate 481. Galls of *Dasineura* sp. on osoberry.

Plum and Cherry Galls

The West has several species of native shrubs in the genus *Prunus*, including western choke cherry (*P. virginiana* var. *demissa*), holly-leafed cherry (*P. ilicifolia*), Sierra plum (*P. subcordata*), and bitter cherry (*P. emarginata*). Some species share the same gall organisms, while other species have their own unique gall-inducer. Galls normally found on wild plums in the West include eriophyid mites and three ascomycete fungi in the genus *Taphrina*. A different ascomycete fungus, black knot-gall fungus (*Apiosporina morbosa*), distorts stems of several species of *Prunus*. An unknown rust is also described, while an unknown gall moth that induces large, midrib fold galls, showing mostly on the underside of choke cherry leaves in mountain areas, is not included.

WITCHES'-BROOM-GALL FUNGUS   *Taphrina confusa*   Pl. 482

This fungus induces massive witches' brooms on several species of *Prunus*, but most particularly western choke cherry and Sierra plum in the West. These brooms are easily seen from the road, as clusters of compact branches exceed 25 cm across. Each broom has dozens of branches with scattered, stunted leaves. Even though this fungus has been reported across the United States, it appears to have localized concentrations. The area around Mount Shasta, California, for example, has a significant concentration of broomed *Prunus*. The taxonomy of this fungus changes among authors. The name used by Westcott (1971) is adopted here.

Plate 482. Witches' broom of *Taphrina confusa* on western choke cherry.

LEAF-CURL FUNGUS   *Taphrina flectans*   Pl. 483

This fungus induces leaf-curl galls on new spring leaves at the tip of branches and witches' brooms on bitter cherry and holly-leafed cherry. One or more leaves may be galled in a cluster, severely distorting and discoloring them. Galled leaves are normally swollen, yellow-green, and turned under at the edges. These leaves usually turn brown before the end of the normal growing season, shortly after the asci (spore-producing sacs) have released their ascospores. This fungus goes through a saprophytic stage. Some spores survive winter on bud scales and germinate in spring as new leaves unfold.

Plate 483. Leaf-curl gall of *Taphrina flectans* on holly-leafed cherry.

PLUM-POCKET-GALL FUNGUS *Taphrina prunisubcordatae* Pl. 484

This fungus induces "plum pockets," also called "bladder plums," on Sierra plum. Plum pockets are infected fruits that expand and elongate into large, soft, hollow, furrowed, light green bags that are round to potato-shaped. The surface of the galls is somewhat mealy-powdery with a waxy bloom. Under the influence of this fungus, normal fruit measuring 10–12 mm across swells into galls measuring 45 mm long by 20 mm wide. In spring these galls might be mistaken for fruit, as they hang in clusters like fruit. With age, galls turn beige and shrivel. While the fungus appears to abort attacked fruit, it does not appear to eradicate the entire fruit production on a single affected shrub. This fungus occurs from the Rocky Mountains west and throughout the Pacific States. The fungus *T. pruni* produces enlarged fruits on *P. americana* and *P. domestica* in the West.

Plate 484. Plum-pocket galls of *Taphrina prunisubcordatae* on Sierra plum.

BLACK-KNOT-GALL FUNGUS *Apiosporina morbosa* Fig. 74

This fungus induces massive eruptions or knot galls on stems of several species in the genus *Prunus*, both native and ornamental. These integral stem galls can be found any time of the year in various conditions. They range in size from 60 to 160 mm long by 30 mm in diameter. The elongated, bent, sometimes twisted black galls make their first appearance on branches in fall after initial infection the previous spring. Full development is hindered by winter until the next spring, when normal growth resumes. The fungus secretes indoleacetic acid and other growth-regulating compounds that stimulate the development of the knot gall. In early summer of the second season of development, galls are olive green and covered with spores for a short period. As the galls mature and release spores, the surface becomes pitted, cracked, and knobby.

Figure 74. Black-knot gall of *Apiosporina morbosa*.

Generally, branches and leaves beyond the galls die. New shoots often develop below old galls. Most infections in new wood appear to come from ascospores. This fungus can cause serious damage in orchards. This fungus is host to several mycoparasitic fungi and various predaceous insects and mites. It has been found on *Prunus* spp. across the United States and Canada.

RACEME-GALL RUST   Unknown

Pl. 485

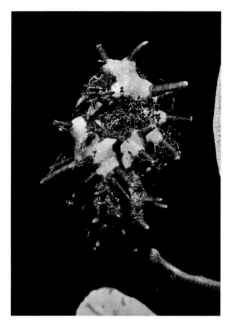

Galls of this rust fungus occur on the racemes (flower clusters) of western choke cherry in mid- to late summer, depending on elevation. When fresh, galls are green, somewhat succulent, and round to ovoid with stiff radial projections. These projections measure 4 mm long and are easily dislodged from the main gall body, revealing white sacs at the base that hold orange spores. Galls measure 10–20 mm long by 10 mm in diameter. Inquilinous insects have been found feeding on the fresh flesh of this gall in summer. While studies have yet to isolate the inducer, it seems most likely that it is a rust fungus. The growth period for these galls is extremely short, beginning in July and ending by late August. Old galls persist on affected shrubs for more than one year. This species was found at 1,829 m in the Siskiyou Mountains, California.

Plate 485. Gall of raceme-gall rust, **Unknown**, on choke cherry.

CLUB-GALL MITE   *Phytoptus emarginatae*

Pl. 486

This mite induces club-like pouch galls on leaves of several species of *Prunus*, especially bitter cherry. These blunt-tipped, somewhat hairy spring galls measure up to 5 mm high by 1 mm in diameter. Galls occur on both surfaces of leaves, and several dozen galls per leaf are common. Microscopic openings lead into the gall chambers on the side of the leaf opposite the erect clubs. When fresh, the club galls are beige, green, or red, depending on their exposure and age. While most galls stand erect, some bend over or twist. There is a single generation of these mites each year. Females retire to crevices in terminal branches by late summer. After contacting males, females carry sperm through winter and induce galls the following spring that contain both males and females. This mite is widespread across North America and Europe. Damage to leaves and shrubs appears to be negligible, although some browning of leaf tissues may occur under heavy infestation.

Plate 486. Multiple galls of *Phytoptus emarginatae* on bitter cherry.

Poison Oak Galls

Poison oak (*Toxicodendron diversilobum*) may be the scourge of hikers and campers, but it is a boon to wildlife, including some gall organisms. Its delicate leaves of three decorate hillsides in brilliant hues of red, orange, and purple in fall. Two galls occur on poison oak with regularity: eriophyid mite pouch galls on leaves, and a large, antler-shaped fasciation gall on terminal buds that is of unknown origin. Additionally, a chocolate-brown rust fungus, *Pileolaria effusa*, attacks the petioles, causing significant swelling and bending, but is not included here. The mite and fasciation galls are described.

LEAF-GALL MITE   *Aculops toxicophagus*   Pl. 487

This eriophyid mite attacks leaves of both poison oak and several species of *Rhus*: including: *R. radicans*, *R. aromatica*, and *R. vernix*. These mites induce bright red bead or pouch galls on the dorsal surface of leaves. Galls occur in a scattered, random manner across the surface of leaflets. The leaflet underside reveals corresponding pits in which the mites feed. Most pouch galls measure 1–2 mm across, but some coalesce to form masses 5 mm or more wide. New spring leaves and re-sprouts in wildfire areas are often so covered with these pouch galls, the leaves are almost beyond recognition. This species is known to occur in Europe, the East Coast, Texas, Utah, and northern California. See also skunk bush (*Rhus aromatica*) for this mite.

FASCIATION GALL   Unknown   Pl. 488

Antler-shaped fasciation galls of terminal buds of poison oak are of unknown origin. Galls measure up to 25–30 cm long by 15 cm wide and bend and twist in ways that tease the

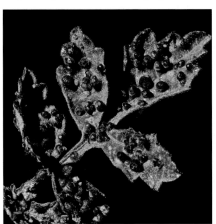

Above: Plate 487. Galls of *Aculops toxicophagus* on *R. aromatica*.

Right: Plate 488. Fasciation gall, **Unknown**, on poison oak.

imagination. They often show small, distorted leaflets at the tips. During the second growing season, new shoots will elongate but also produce fasciations at terminal buds. This process seems to continue for three or four seasons before the branches die. Whatever the cause, entire patches of dead poison oak can be found after three or four seasons of fasciation. This may prove to be a simple "noninfectious" fasciation or a genetic anomaly specific to isolated clones of poison oak or an organism we are unaware of at present.

Rabbitbrush Galls

The plant species considered here include rubber rabbitbrush (*Ericameria nauseosa*), yellow rabbitbrush (*Chrysothamnus viscidiflorus*), and rabbitbrush (*C. humilis*). These species decorate arid landscapes of the West with flowers at a time of year (late summer–fall) when few other plants are in bloom. These important small shrubs host several species of gall midges, tephritid fruit flies, and a gelechiid moth. Several new species have yet to be scientifically named. Many of these gall insects initiate gall formation during fall and winter when most other galls have stopped growing. Unlike galls of cynipid wasps, galls induced by tephritid flies can vary in shape from one region to another and from one species of rabbitbrush to another.

BENT-GALL MOTH   *Gnorimoschema octomaculellum*   Pl. 489

Plate 489. Gall of *Gnorimoschema octomaculellum* on rubber rabbitbrush.

This moth induces pointed, monothalamous galls in terminal leaves of new shoots in spring on rubber rabbitbrush. Galls are typically bent at a 45-degree angle to the supporting stem. They are composed of swollen, succulent, distorted terminal leaves that are tightly bound together like staves of a barrel. There is no growth beyond the galls. In some areas, caterpillars emerge by late spring through exit holes in the sides of the galls. In the substrate below the host shrub, these caterpillars form sediment-covered cocoons that measure 10–15 mm long and 2–3 mm wide. Rearing experiments indoors showed adults emerging in late May. Under natural conditions, the timing for these events may be much later. Old, brown galls remain for several months on dead stems.

COTTON-GALL TEPHRITID   *Aciurina bigeloviae*   Pl. 490

This tephritid fly induces woolly, monothalamous bud galls on rubber rabbitbrush. These compact clusters of white hairs measure 12–15 mm in diameter. Galls occur singly or in pairs at axillary buds and appear as puffs of cotton attached to the stems. Galls are found on the current year's growth. Old galls persist on branches for a year or more. Fresh galls in the eastern Sierra Nevada have been found in September and October with larvae. Adults emerge in spring. Galls of this species are used by the gall midge *Rhopalomyia bigeloviae* to create its own endogalls, as it does with the bubble-gall tephritid (*A. trixa*; see Plate 493).

Above: Plate 490. Bud galls of *Aciurina bigeloviae* on rubber rabbitbrush.

Right: Plate 491. Gall of *Aciurina ferruginea* on yellow rabbitbrush.

MEDUSA-GALL TEPHRITID   *Aciurina ferruginea*   Pl. 491

This fly induces monothalamous bud galls on stems of yellow rabbitbrush. The galls are characterized by numerous long, thin leafy bracts, which appear to develop in fascicles. When fresh, galls are green, but turn brown after the larvae stop feeding. Individual galls range from 3 to 18 mm long. Galls sometimes coalesce into one long, leafy mass on the side of a stem, reaching 60 mm in length. Larvae cut a tunnel to the outer skin of the gall, leaving a thin layer of skin at the surface to cover the hole. Pupation occurs within the galls. Adults break through the thin skin to emerge and then push aside the filamentous leaves to gain access to the outside in July and August. Adults mature within 10 days or so, and eggs are deposited shortly thereafter. A single egg is deposited on each axillary bud. Gall formation begins after eggs hatch and larvae commence feeding. Adults live up to 105 days, though on average about 44 days. Fresh galls have been found in September in the eastern Sierra Nevada. This tephritid overwinters in the first-instar larval stage, and there is one generation per year. This species has been found in all western states. Two species of wasps in the genus *Halticoptera* are the primary parasites of this tephritid.

LEAFY-CONE-GALL TEPHRITID   *Aciurina idahoensis*   Pl. 492

This tephritid fly induces monothalamous, hairy bud galls on yellow rabbitbrush. Galls have numerous relatively thin, leafy bracts (bud scales) that stick out and sometimes recurve from the main gall body. The galls are usually green, with white hairs on the leafy bracts. Galls occur singly or in rows bunched together along the length of the stem. Individual galls measure up to 20 mm long by 8 mm in diameter. The exterior leafy bracts measure 10 mm long by 1 mm wide but can be much longer, based on local variation. The central larval chamber is vertical and measures up to 8 mm long by 2 mm wide. Pupation occurs in the galls, and the adults emerge in spring through the gall apex by pushing apical tissues aside. Adults live up to 22 days. Egg deposition occurs shortly after emergence and mating. There is one generation per year. Several

Plate 492. Galls of *Aciurina idahoensis* on yellow rabbitbrush.

hymenopteran parasites are associated with this fruit fly, including *Eurytoma chrysothamni*, *Platygaster* sp., *Halticoptera* sp., and *Torymus* sp.

BEAKED-GALL TEPHRITID *Aciurina michaeli*   Fig. 75

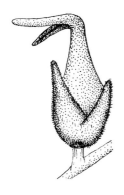

Figure 75. Bud gall of *Aciurina michaeli*.

This fly induces monothalamous, pear-shaped, smooth bud galls on the current year's growth of rubber rabbitbrush and yellow rabbitbrush. Galls are composed of numerous undeveloped bud leaves that are incorporated into the main body of the gall tissue. Usually, a few leafy bracts on the outside come to a point at the tip of the galls, which may be bent or straight. A subtle covering of hairs may occur on the surface of exterior leafy bracts. Galls measure 10–12 mm long by 4–6 mm in diameter and are leaf green when fresh. Toward the end of larval growth, larvae concentrate feeding in the apical end of the gall, thinning the tissues. Larvae pupate in the galls, and adults emerge in July and August, cutting through the area of thin tissue to exit the gall. There is one generation per year. This species has been reported from nearly all western states.

BUBBLE-GALL TEPHRITID *Aciurina trixa*   Pls. 493 & 494

This fly induces small, monothalamous bud galls on rubber rabbitbrush. While this fruit fly may appear on other species of rabbitbrush, it seems to prefer this species for galling. Galls of this tephritid have been reported by Wangberg (1980) to vary greatly in morphology, depending on host and locality. In midwinter in the Tehachapi Mountains, California, galls are fresh, lime green, round to oval, smooth, and glossy. Galls measure 5 mm in length by 3–4 mm in diameter and appear on the lower portions of branches. In some regions, such as Idaho and the northern Mojave Desert, California, these galls can be over 10 mm in diameter in March. Most galls are glabrous and sticky. Some have small, blunt-tipped protruberances, which are

Above: Plate 493. Gall of *A. trixa* showing the endogall of *Rhopalomyia bigeloviae*.

Right: Plate 494. Four normal galls of *A. trixa* on rubber rabbitbrush.

associated with gall midges (see below). As galls age, they turn pale green, yellow, and ultimately brown. Galls develop from axillary buds beginning in August, at the initiation of feeding larvae. By November, most galls are full size. These galls form at a time when host plants are generally not actively growing. Galls aborted after the death of the larvae will often have shoots growing through them. Many host plants have more than 75% of their stems galled by this fly. Larvae create an exit tunnel before pupation. Adults emerge in spring. Single eggs are placed near the base of leaves. Larvae are active in galls by August and overwinter in the third instar. Pupae are found from March to June. This fly may be found throughout the range of its host plant in several western states. Sixteen species of insects have been found associated with galls of this fly. One of the associates represents an unusual case, in which one insect galls the galls of another species, creating endogalls. The blunt-tipped protuberances mentioned earlier are actually the endogalls of the gall midge *Rhopalomyia bigeloviae*. Galls of this midge protrude 1–2 mm, look like knobs or fingerlike projections, and are glabrous and sticky. The gall midge and tephritid larvae proceed with their growth and development without any apparent impact upon each other. Both species pupate and emerge about the same time. While several tephritids have been known as inquilines of midge galls, this is a rare situation and one of the more intimate relationships between gall-inducing insects known.

LEAFY-BUD-GALL TEPHRITID *Procecidochares* sp. A

Fig. 76 & Pl. 495

This fly induces leafy, hairy, monothalamous galls on buds of *Chrysothamnus humilis* and yellow rabbitbrush. Galls of this species are normally associated with the *Procecidochares minuta* group and occur singly or in rows along the length of stems. Broad-based, leafy bracts with long tapering tips distinguish this species from other related forms; bracts measure 10 mm long by 8 mm wide at the base. Galls can measure up to 31 mm long but average around 17 mm long by 15 mm wide. They are composed

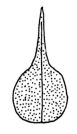

Figure 76. Bract of gall of *Procecidochares* sp. A.

Plate 495. Bud galls of *Procecidochares* sp. A on rabbitbrush.

of overlapping bud scales converted into large leafy bracts that are basically attached to the main gall body; some galls look like small artichokes. Galls are green with sparse hairs and are often sticky. Once the larvae stop feeding, the galls turn brown. Adults emerge in spring, during the morning hours, through the thin apical tissue of the chambers and by pushing through leafy bracts at the apex. Females oviposit directly into axillary buds, one egg per bud. There is one generation per year. Nine insect associates have been recorded for this tephritid fly's galls: two beetles, two moths, a gall midge, and four wasps.

HAIRY-BUD-GALL TEPHRITID *Procecidochares* sp. B   Pl. 496 & Fig. 77

This fly induces monothalamous to polythalamous galls similar to those of the leafy-bud-gall tephritid (*Procecidochares* sp. A), but the galls of this species are gray-green and densely covered with white hairs. These galls have shorter bracts and usually occur only on terminal buds of rubber rabbitbrush. This species has also been associated with the *P. minuta* group. These galls can measure up to 20 mm long by 10 mm wide, but most are 12 mm long by 5 mm wide. Bracts have a short apex, not long and pointed as in the leafy-bud-gall tephritid. In addition, a distinctive, fibrous mesh of hairs connects the

Above: Plate 496. Bud galls of *Procecidochares* sp. B on rubber rabbitbrush.

Right: Figure 77. Bract of gall of *Procecidochares* sp. B.

leaf bracts along the margins and at the tips. Gall development begins in spring in concert with new leaves. As the galls grow, the immature leaves composing the galled buds fuse together at the base, forming the rigid larval chamber. Prior to adult emergence and after larvae have stopped feeding, galls begin to desiccate and turn brown. The drying process causes the tip of the leafy bracts to separate, which allows easy escape for the emerging adults later. By the end of summer, the vacated galls have withered, and most have dropped off the host plant. Adults are usually found in June and July and mate soon after emergence. Females usually oviposit in buds nearest to the one they emerged from but rarely deposit eggs in more than four buds before interruption by ants and spiders. Eggs appear to overwinter, and hatching occurs in spring. Larvae are within newly formed gall tissue by late April. Each gall contains from one to three larvae with as many as six in a gall. There is one generation per year. Eight species of insect associates have been found in these galls, as inquilines, parasites, or hyperparasites.

ELLIPTICAL-STEM-GALL TEPHRITID *Valentibulla californica* Pl. 497

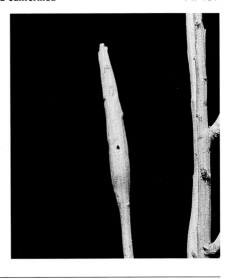

This fly induces barely swollen, polythalamous, integral stem galls on rubber rabbitbrush. These stem-colored galls may taper gently or expand abruptly and may be symmetrical or lopsided. Galls measure 30 mm long by 6 mm in diameter and are only slightly larger than the stem. Lopsided galls may have random bulges, which correspond to feeding larvae. Each larva occupies its own chamber and excavates a tunnel to the surface, leaving the epidermis as a shield from the outside prior to pupation. Most of the year is spent in larval stages. Adults emerge in June in some areas. These flies have a single generation per year.

Plate 497. Gall of *Valentibulla californica* on rubber rabbitbrush.

STEM-GALL MIDGE *Rhopalomyia chrysothamni* Pl. 498

This midge induces small, conical-tubular monothalamous galls that project out at right angles to the stems of rubber rabbitbrush. Tubular clusters of white hairs protrude from the galls. The galls occur singly or in groups. They are 3 mm long by 2 mm in diameter. There is generally some swelling at the base where the galls emerge from the stems. Often several galls protrude in different directions

Plate 498. Galls of of *Rhopalomyia chrysothamni* on rubber rabbitbrush.

from the same section of the galled stem. In other cases, several galls emerge from the same side of the stem, causing the stem to bend in the opposite direction. Old galls remain on the dead stems. These midges have been found from Utah to southern California.

JELLYBEAN-GALL MIDGE   *Rhopalomyia glutinosa*   Pl. 499

This midge induces globular, shiny, lime-green or black, monothalamous stem galls near the base of new spring growth, just above the connection with last year's branches, on rubber rabbitbrush. These hard, flat-topped, glutinous blobs measure 3 mm high by 4 mm wide. Some galls have small beige protuberances over the top. The gall body is light olive-green in March. Specimens found in late November were glossy black. Several galls may occur in close proximity to each other but apparently do not coalesce, as do galls of other species. This midge has been found from Utah west into the Tehachapi Mountains and the Mojave Desert, California.

Plate 499. Fresh green gall of *Rhopalomyia glutinosa* on rubber rabbitbrush.

COTTON-GALL MIDGE   *Rhopalomyia utahensis*   Pl. 500

This midge induces oval, monothalamous galls covered with white cotton-like hairs along stems of rubber rabbitbrush. Galls develop on axillary buds in spring. These galls measure up to 26 mm long by 12 mm wide. Galls are normally covered with numerous recurved leaflets, which are tips of the bud scales or leaflets. When fresh, galls are usually green with white hairs between the recurved leaflets. Some galls are purplish but with age turn brown. Pupation occurs in the galls, and adults emerge in April or May, depending on location. Adults mate soon after emergence and live for only one or two days. Either the eggs or first-instar larvae overwinter in diapause until the following spring. This midge has been found in Idaho, Utah, and California but could occur elsewhere within its host's range.

Plate 500. Bud gall of *Rhopalomyia utahensis* on rubber rabbitbrush.

SPINY-CONE-GALL MIDGE   *Rhopalomyia* sp. A.   Pl. 501 & Fig. 78

This midge induces glabrous, purple-rose, cone-shaped stem galls on rubber rabbitbrush and perhaps other related species. Galls can be either monothalamous or polythalamous. The flat top and green, pointed, recurved bracts, which are sparsely arranged along the sides, distinguish this gall. While these galls may superficially resemble those of the cotton-gall midge (*R. utahensis*), they lack the white hairs. Galls measure 7 mm high by 5 mm in diameter. Coalesced galls (see Figure 78) measure 15 mm in diameter by 10 mm high. Galls of this species begin development in early spring and are fully formed by mid-March. Pupae develop in a hole in the center of the flat-topped surface. By July these extremely hard galls are brown. They may remain on the stems for a year or more.

Plate 501. Fresh gall of *Rhopalomyia* sp. A on rubber rabbitbrush.

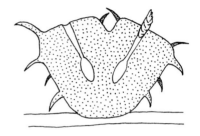

Figure 78. Cross section of two coalesced galls of *Rhopalomyia* sp. A, showing position of two larval chambers and where pupa forms (right).

COTTON-FLOWER-GALL MIDGE   *Rhopalomyia* sp. B   Pl. 502

This new species induces polythalamous flower galls on rubber rabbitbrush and perhaps other related species. These terminal galls look like tufts of cotton surrounded by long leafy bracts,

Plate 502. Flower gall of *Rhopalomyia* sp. B on rubber rabbitbrush.

which distinguish this gall from normal vegetative parts. The galls encompass all the disc flowers and are covered by dense, soft, white cotton-like hairs. Beneath the hairs are vertically arranged oval larval chambers with pointed apices. Chambers measure 2–3 mm long by 1 mm in diameter. The entire galled flower head measures 10–12 mm across; the six or more bracts measure up to 40 mm long by 9 mm wide at the base. Gall growth usually commences about mid-July, and the first visible larvae appear in mid-August. Last-instar larvae are present in early October. Specimens collected April 7 issued adults on April 12. Two species were reared from these galls—one, the gall-maker; the second, a guest—both in the genus *Rhopalomyia*. It took four years of field visits to a site in the Siskiyou Mountains, California, and multiple rearing experiments to gather this information. These galls have also been found in the Tehachapi Mountains in California and could occur elsewhere.

BUD-GALL MIDGE   *"Rhopalomyia"* **sp. C**   Pl. 503

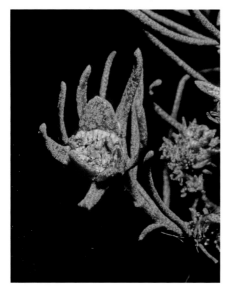

This midge induces monothalamous terminal bud galls on an undetermined species of rabbitbrush (*Ericameria* or *Chrysothamnus* sp.). Galls appear as distorted terminal flower buds composed of short, sticky, leafy, broad-based bracts sparsely covered with small white hairs. Galls measure 6–7 mm wide by 12 mm high. Bracts measure 12–14 mm long and appear hardened. Fresh galls found in January are difficult to cut open because of their hardness and a viscous material that seems concentrated around the galls. Among the several galls found on the single host shrub, only one was not parasitized. This new species and its host were discovered at Short Canyon in Owen's Peak Wilderness in the southern Sierra Nevada.

Plate 503. Gall of *"Rhopalomyia"* sp. C on rabbitbrush with old galls to the right.

Ragweed and Bur-Sage Galls

The West has over 50 species of ragweed and is botanically known as the center of ragweed diversity. Ragweeds occur in a variety of habitats from coastal dunes to deserts and are famous for their allergenic pollen. The species covered here include: western ragweed (*Ambrosia psilostachya*), white bur-sage (*A. dumosa*), woolly bur-sage (*A. eriocentra*), annual bur-sage (*A. acanthicarpa*), and common ragweed (*A. artemisiifolia*).

RAGWEED-GALL MITE   *Aceria boycei*   Pl. 504

This mite induces round-ovoid, convoluted bead galls on the dorsal surface of terminal leaves of western ragweed. Exit holes are located on the ventral side of leaves corresponding to the bead galls above. Galls occur singly but will coalesce to form larger, warty clusters on leaves, sometimes distorting the leaves severely. Galls measure 2–4 mm in diameter and are usually yellow-green. This mite is found on hosts in southern California but could be elsewhere.

Plate 504. Galls of *Aceria boycei*
on ragweed.

STEM-GALL MOTH   *Eugnosta beevorana*   Pl. 505

This desert tortricid moth induces spindle-shaped integral stem galls on white bur-sage. These monothalamous galls have ruptured bark, with green tissue showing through on fresh galls in spring. Galls measure 30 mm long by 13 mm in diameter and usually occur on two- to three-year-old growth. Although galls can occur on nearby stems, there is usually only one per stem. Larvae pupate in galls in late autumn, and adults emerge after the first winter rains. Eggs are deposited on leaves, and neonate larvae move to sections of stems suitable for burrowing and larval growth. This moth has been found throughout the Mojave Desert, California, and may occur wherever the host plant lives.

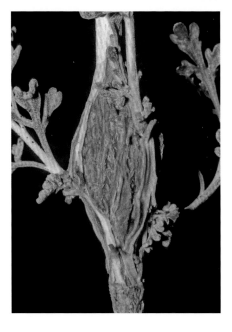

Plate 505. Gall of *Eugnosta beevorana* on white
bur-sage.

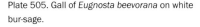

BUD-GALL TEPHRITID   *Procecidochares kristineae*   Pl. 506

This fly induces leafy, hairy, monothalamous bud galls on white bur-sage. Galls measure 10 mm high by 7 mm in diameter and are gray-green, often with hints of pink near the base. Galls are covered with a uniformly dense coating of short white hairs, like the host plant. Gall development is usually timed with vegetative growth induced by substantive seasonal rains during winter and summer. Gall development and larval growth may be arrested if inadequate rains occur during the season. One study (Goeden and Teerink 1997a) showed that first-instar larvae entered a "quiescent period" for over five months (April–September) during the absence of rainfall but resumed growth within 10 days after a major rainstorm. Adults usually mate and lay eggs within three days of emergence. Normally there are two generations per year, but there can be one during arid periods. Nine species of parasitic wasps have been reared from these galls. Spiders and birds eat the adult flies, and rodents chew through the galls to get at the larvae. A similar tephritid gall induced by the woolly-flower-gall tephritid (*P. lisae*) occurs on woolly bur-sage in southern California.

Plate 506. Gall of *Procecidochares kristineae* on white bur-sage.

WOOLLY-FLOWER-GALL TEPHRITID   *Procecidochares lisae*   Pl. 507

Plate 507. Bud gall of *Procecidochares lisae* on woolly bur-sage.

This fly induces round, white-haired, monothalamous galls on woolly bur-sage in the Mojave Desert, California, and likely elsewhere in the range of this host. Galls form just below the pale yellow flower heads, and some leafy bracts emerge from the sides of the galls or from normal axillary buds. These galls measure 12–14 mm high by 10 mm in diameter. Larval chambers are rather large, occupying most of the thin-walled, hard galls. In April, mature white larvae measure 4 mm long. By the end of April, black pupae have formed, and adults emerge soon after.

BUD-GALL MIDGE   *Asphondylia* sp.

Pl. 508

This midge induces polythalamous, terminal bud galls on annual bur-sage, common ragweed, and white bur-sage. These rather large, globose, integral swellings measure 20 mm long by 17 mm wide. They are gray-green, similar to normal stems and leaves of the host. Galls have more hairs than normal plant parts and are composed of several over-lapping bud leaves with leaf petioles emerging from the tip of the gall's leafy bracts. The larval chamber wall is lined with a white fungus, as with many *Asphondylia* galls. Several pale orange larvae are found inside galls in mid-May. Pupation occurs within the galls. Adults emerge the following spring, mate, and oviposit. Galls are well formed by mid-May.

Plate 508. Gall of *Asphondylia* sp. on annual bur-sage.

TRUMPET-GALL MIDGE   *Contarinia partheniicola*

Pl. 509

This midge induces small, green, trumpet- or funnel-shaped, monothalamous galls at the base of leaves and in bud axils of several species of ragweed, especially white bur-sage. Galls are covered with fine hairs, particularly around the rim. Galls measure 5 mm high by 3–4 mm wide at the top. These galls are often concealed among crowded new leaves, but the open funnel shape usually gives them away. Adults have been found in spring and fall. This gall midge has been recorded in Florida, Texas, and California.

WOOLLY-BUD-GALL MIDGE   *Rhopalomyia* sp.

Pl. 510

This midge induces white, woolly, polythalamous, lateral bud galls on woolly bur-sage in the Mojave Desert, California. These spring galls bear stiff brown spines or modified leaf bracts that

Plate 509. Trumpet galls of *Contarinia partheniicola* on white bur-sage.

Plate 510. Woolly-bud gall of *Rhopalomyia* sp. on woolly bur-sage.

protrude through tufts of white hair. Galls measure 15 mm high by 20 mm in diameter. Galled shrubs can have several dozen galls, with all the buds of some branches affected.

Rose Galls

Several species of native rose shrubs are found in the West and treated here, including: California rose (*Rosa californica*), wood rose (*R. gymnocarpa*), interior rose (*R. woodsii* subsp. *ultramontana*), pine rose (*R. pinetorum*), and Nootka rose (*R. nutkana* subsp. *nutkana*). There are also two European species naturalized in the West: dog rose (*R. canina*) and *R. eglanteria*. For the most part, the gall organisms associated with roses are cynipid wasps in the genus *Diplolepis*, whose larvae are responsible for gall formation, as with other cynipids. I am sure there are more species of *Diplolepis* wasps, and their galls, in the West than are described here. An isolated patch of roses I found among pines in the eastern Sierra Nevada, for example, supported seven species of *Diplolepis* galls, and in the summer of 2019, I found a new species in our garden in northwest Washington.

MOSSY-GALL WASP *Diplolepis bassetti* Fig. 79 & Pl. 511

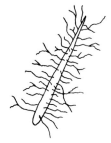

Above: Figure 79. Distinctive bract of gall of *Diplolepis bassetti* showing long, sometimes forked hairs.
Left: Plate 511. Gall of *D. bassetti* on wild rose.
Photo by Sheri Russo.

This wasp induces large round, detachable, polythalamous stem galls on Nootka rose, pine rose, and interior rose, among other species and hybrids. The galls look like balls of moss or hair. They are covered with hundreds of hairy bracts that distinguish these galls from those of the pincushion-gall wasp (*D. rosae*) (compare Figures 79 and 82). Galls measure up to 50 mm in diameter and have soft, mosslike hairs up to 20 mm long around the hardened core of the gall itself. In June, larval chambers are 3 mm long, with plump, white larvae clustered centrally, like a nestful of eggs. The bushy clusters of bracts are brick red, red, yellow, yellow-green, or moss green. Adults emerge in February and March, depending on elevation. Mating and oviposition occur soon thereafter. Well-developed galls have been found at 1,200 m in northern mountains in May. This species has been found in several locations in the central and northern Sierra Nevada and the Cascades in Oregon and Washington.

SPINY-BUD-GALL WASP *Diplolepis bicolor* Pl. 512

This wasp induces round, monothalamous bud galls along stems of several species of wild rose. Stiff spines are scattered across the gall surface in an open arrangement and mostly concentrated on the upper half of each gall. Galls measure 10–12 mm across with spines. Color ranges from reddish to yellow-green, depending upon exposure to sun. In late summer and fall, galls turn beige or dark brown. Galls can persist on the stems for more than one season. These galls look similar to those induced by the spiny leaf-gall wasp (*D. polita*) on the upper surface of rose leaflets. Adults of the spiny bud-gall wasp emerge in spring to oviposit in buds.

Plate 512. Galls of *Diplolepis bicolor* on wild rose.

LEAFY-BRACT-BUD-GALL WASP *Diplolepis californica* Pl. 513

This wasp induces green, leafy, polythalamous bud galls in spring on several species of wild rose. Galls of this wasp are distinguished from others by the flat, leafy lobes that emanate from the main gall body and look like aborted leaflets. The lobes are up to 12 mm long by 2 mm wide at the tip. The entire gall mass measures 25–38 mm in diameter. When green and fresh, galls are soft and non-brittle. Each can contain up to eight larval chambers surrounded by the white flesh of the gall. Adults emerge in February to April, mate, and oviposit into spring buds.

Plate 513. Leafy gall of *Diplolepis californica* on wild rose.

TEARDROP-GALL WASP   *Diplolepis inconspicuis*   Pl. 514

These teardrop-shaped axillary, polythalamous bud galls are fleshy, smooth, and terminate in a long point. This species occurs on interior rose and likely other related species. These galls occur in the axils of leaflet-bearing petioles and are often found on several axillary buds in a row. Galls measure 20 mm long by 10 mm in diameter and are often red-blushed on the side exposed to sunlight. Galls have larval chambers arranged along the sides of the gall opposite one another. This species was found at 2,134 m, along the edge of Castle Lake in the Siskiyou Mountains, California.

Plate 514. Gall of *Diplolepis inconspicuis* on interior rose.

LEAF-GALL WASP   *Diplolepis nebulosa*   Pl. 515

Galls of this wasp normally occur on the underside of leaves of interior rose and usually form on the midrib. Galls are globular, smooth, and monothalamous. Individual galls measure 5–7 mm in diameter; two or three coalesced galls can reach 15–20 mm long by 10 mm in diameter. Galls remain on old leaves throughout fall, and some persist until the following spring. Adults emerged in fall in the laboratory but are expected to emerge in late spring in time for new leaves at the elevation of 1,524–1,829 m in the Siskiyou Mountains, California, where they are found.

STEM-GALL WASP   *Diplolepis nodulosa*   Pl. 516 & Fig. 80

This wasp induces tapered, monothalamous, slightly swollen stem galls on wild roses and hybrids. These galls are usually located at the lower end of the affected stem, and shoot

Plate 515. Galls of *Diplolepis nebulosa* on interior rose.

Plate 516. Inquiline-modified gall of *Diplolepis nodulosa* on wild rose.

elongation occurs beyond the galls. Galls often have stunted leaf-lets scattered around the periphery. Galls measure 12–15 mm long by 3–4 mm in diameter. While these small galls are difficult to locate, galls modified by the common inquiline cynipid *Periclistus pirata* are easily seen because they are larger, more abrupt swellings (Plate 516), measuring up to 20 mm in diameter. These inquiline-altered galls are round to ovoid, smooth, and glabrous, and look like potatoes, with dimples and creases. Over half of the galls of *D. nodulosa* examined in one study (Brooks and Short-house 1997) had been modified by the inquiline *P. pirata*, which forms multiple larval chambers, unlike its host. The larvae of the rose stem-gall wasp are killed when *P. pirata* deposits its eggs. Both insects overwinter as prepupae, emerge in spring, and have one generation per year. Adult inquilines usually emerge two weeks later than the emergence, egg deposition, and beginning of gall development of the rose stem-gall wasp.

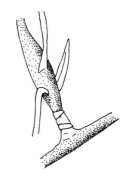

Figure 80. Normal gall of *D. nodulosa*.

SPINY-LEAF-GALL WASP   *Diplolepis polita*   Pl. 517 & Fig. 81

This wasp induces round, pea-size monothalamous galls on the dorsal surface of leaves of California, wood, and interior rose. These detachable spring galls measure up to 5 mm in diameter and have several scattered spines emanating from the sides and top. Galls occur singly or in large numbers per leaflet. Some galls coalesce, forming paired oblong galls. Sometimes all the leaflets on a branch are galled, leaving little evidence of the leaflets themselves, and the galls then look like stem galls. When fresh, galls are wine red, green, and yellow-green, and their spines are erect and flexible. With age and by late summer, galls turn brown, and spines are stiff and brittle. Normal galls have a fairly large, central larval chamber, with thin outer wall tissue surrounding it. Parasitized galls usually have either several small larval chambers or a single chamber with an irregular inner wall. Adult emergence occurs in spring over a two- to six-week

Above: Plate 517. Galls of *Diplolepis polita* on wild rose.

Right: Figure 81. Clusters of galls of *D. polita*.

period, sometimes longer if the weather is cool. Reproduction is occasionally parthenogenetic for this and other species of *Diplolepis*, as a result of infection by *Wolbachia* (a bacteria-like organism), which causes the wasps to lay eggs that produce females only. This wasp species has been found all over California and may also occur in Oregon and Washington. Five species of parasites and inquilines are associated with galls of this species, including the inquiline *Periclistus pirata*, mentioned earlier. The others are *Eurytoma longavena*, *Glyphomerus stigma*, *Torymus bedeguaris*, and *Habrocytus* sp.

PINCUSHION-GALL WASP *Diplolepis rosae* Fig. 82 & Pl. 518

This wasp induces round to ovoid, bristly, monothalamous galls on the dorsal surface of leaflets of several European rose species and hybrids. These gall wasps have been introduced from Europe, where their galls are commonly known as "rose bedeguar" or "robin's pincushion" galls. In Europe, this wasp galls over 14 rose species, while in North America it is currently known from only a few naturalized European species, including dog rose and *Rosa eglanteria*.

It could occur on other species and hybrids. Galls cover a portion or all of a leaflet (the similar galls of the mossy-gall wasp [*D. bassetti*] are not on leaves but form on stems). The "hairs" or bristles of the galls of *D. rosae* are 8 mm long and have barely detectable, short side bristles, in contrast to those of the mossy rose-gall wasp (compare Figures 79 and 82). This large mass is actually composed of several small, 4-mm-long galls that develop closely together, creating the appearance of a single large gall 25–30 mm long. When fresh, the bristles are yellow-green, beige, soft, and flexible. By late summer, galls dry and turn brown, and hairs are brittle. Adults emerge in spring and deposit several eggs in each leaflet. Galls of this species appear to be more abundant on stressed plants. They have been found in the eastern Sierra Nevada and are common in Ontario, Canada.

Above left: Figure 82. Bract of gall of *Diplolepis rosae* showing shortness of marginal hairs.

Plate 518. Gall of *D. rosae* on rose.

BLISTER-GALL WASP *Diplolepis rosaefolii*

Pl. 519

This wasp induces integral, swollen, blister-like, monothalamous galls that show on both sides of leaves of several species of rose. Galls are lenticular when viewed from the side and usually measure 2–3 mm in diameter, but some can reach 5 mm. Color ranges from green to yellow and dark red. Each leaflet can have one to several galls. Several galls can coalesce to completely distort the host leaflet. These gall-inducers overwinter in a prepupal state. Pupation occurs from April to early June, and the emerging adults are known to be the smallest in the genus. Galls are usually found from June through September. While I have found this species only in the eastern Sierra Nevada on interior rose and in southern Utah on *Rosa* sp., it has been found throughout the north-central United States and in several other western locations. It is the most common cynipid gall wasp in Canada.

Plate 519. Galls of *Diplolepis rosaefolii* on wild rose.

BRISTLY-GALL WASP *Diplolepis* sp.

Fig. 83 & Pl. 520

Galls of this wasp protrude equally on both sides of leaves of Nootka rose. These monothalamous–polythalamous galls measure up to 25 mm across with bracts; the main gall body measures 7–9 mm across. Individual bracts are 10–12 mm long, and side branches are nearly as long. Between the bract's main side branches are smaller 3–4-mm-long, glandular-tipped filaments.

Above: Figure 83. Bract of gall of *Diplolepis* sp.

Right: Plate 520. Gall of *Diplolepis* sp. on Nootka rose.

All bracts and divisions have very short, fine hairs. Bracts are generally lime green, but those exposed to sunlight are often rosy. Galls can cover half or more of the leaflet, and one or two galls occur per branchlet. There are one to two larvae per gall. These galls are quite unlike those of *D. rosae*, which occur on the leaf's dorsal surface, and *D. bassetti*, which are 50 mm or more across. The bracts of all three species' galls are different (compare Figures 79, 82, and 83).

Sage Galls

LEAF-GALL MIDGE *Rhopalomyia audibertiae*   Pl. 521

This midge induces somewhat tubular, hairy, undetachable, thick-walled, monothalamous leaf and petiole galls on both black sage (*Salvia mellifera*) and white sage (*S. apiana*). Galls can protrude from either side of leaves, showing a shallow, convex lump on the opposing side of the tubular gall, with a hair-lined depression at the apex. Galls are gray-green, or sometimes reddish or maroon. They measure 8 mm wide by up to 12 mm long; some coalesce to form larger masses that severely distort the leaves. Some galls may appear globular or aborted (see photograph) and could be the result of attack by inquilines, altering the normal tubular shape. Galls begin development as early as February. These spring galls usually produce adults in April and May. Adults emerge through the hair-lined apical openings.

TUBE-GALL MIDGE *Rhopalomyia salviae*   Pl. 522

This midge induces tubular, hairy, monothalamous galls on leaves and stems of black sage (*Salvia mellifera*) and perhaps other sage species. Stem galls appear to be more common than leaf galls. The cylindrical galls project out, usually at right angles to the stems, and are often found singly just below petioles. Galls measure 5 mm long by 2 mm in diameter and are reddish green. Unlike galls of the leaf-gall midge (*R. audibertiae*), galls of this midge are straight-sided and occur only on one side of the stem. Fresh galls have been found in early February. Larvae pupate inside the galls, and adults emerge through a hole in the gall apex.

Plate 521. Galls of *Rhopalomyia audibertiae* on black sage.

Plate 522. Gall of *Rhopalomyia salviae* on black sage.

Sagebrush Galls

Sagebrush (*Artemisia* spp.) occupies vast areas of coastal, foothill, and arid regions in the West. There are two principal species dealt with here: the wide-ranging Great Basin sagebrush (*A. tridentata*), and California sagebrush (*A. californica*), found in the coastal sage-scrub community from northern Baja California to central-western California. In contrast to sage (*Salvia* spp.), this group of shrubs supports more than 32 species of gall midges, two tephritid fruit flies, and an eriophyid mite. Only a few are described here. A large network of gall midges (28 species) and fruit flies and their associated inquilines, parasites, and hyperparasites depend on Great Basin sagebrush throughout its range of millions of acres in the West. Most of the galls associated with these shrubs in this guide are covered with three-forked plant hairs. Polymorphism has been found with midge galls (*Rhopalomyia* spp.) in Japan. Because of this, when you find two different but similar galls, as with *Rhopalomyia medusa* and *R. medusirrasa*, the galls' physical features as well as the morphology of adults may not provide reliable diagnostic features for species identification without DNA sequencing. The basic biology of all gall midges in this group is similar: larval and pupal development takes place within the galls. Larvae overwinter in the galls and pupate in spring at the surface, and adults emerge by June. While males mate repeatedly, females mate once and oviposit within a few hours after mating. The bulk of the species' reproductive activity appears to occur in the morning. Galled leaves often drop by August.

GALL MITE *Aceria paracalifornica*   Pl. 523

This mite induces swollen, pit galls with a central depression (erineum) on the thin, needle-like leaves of California sagebrush. These round to irregularly shaped galls occur singly or in clusters in the middle of leaflets, often distorting and bending them. Individual galls measure 2 mm in diameter. The erineum is usually lined with brown hairs. Mites attack spring needles and remain in their erineum depressions throughout summer and fall. These mites likely overwinter as eggs among bud scales. Severe infestations can stunt plant growth.

Plate 523. Galls of *Aceria paracalifornica* on California sagebrush.

STEM-GALL TEPHRITID *Eutreta diana* Pl. 524

This tephritid fruit fly induces spindle-shaped, integral, monothalamous galls in terminal stem tissues of new shoots of Great Basin sagebrush and perhaps other related species. These hairy galls usually have leaves emerging from the sides. Galls measure 10–12 mm long by 8–10 mm in diameter. They are usually gray-green and often have a rose-purple flush. It has been suggested that certain inquilines and parasitoids influence the development of the red-purple tones, even though sun exposure is usually the cause. With age, galls turn brown. While small amounts of whitish, frass-like material are found inside the larval chamber, usually no solid feces are present. Sometimes the apical bud of the galled branch is killed by larval activity, and no further stem elongation occurs. Galls apparently begin development in fall, remain small during winter, and resume growth and reach maturity in spring. Adult emergence occurs in May, and nearly all adults emerge within a week. Their dark wings are thought to absorb additional heat, which facilitates early morning activity. As with other tephritids, the courtship and mating activities of these flies are elaborate. Females deposit eggs directly into axillary and terminal buds. This stem-gall tephritid usually produces one generation per year. It also occurs on *Artemisia filifolia* in Texas, but its life cycle there is different than in California. One study of Great Basin sagebrush found 147 galls of *Eutreta diana* on the same individual shrub (Goeden 1990). This species is the most common gall tephritid from east of the Sierra Nevada to the Front Range of the Rocky Mountains. Its galls can occur on the same shrub with those of other tephritid flies and gall midges. Larvae are heavily parasitized by *Eupelmus* sp., *Pteromalus* sp., *Eurytoma* sp., *Rileya* sp., *Tetrastichus* sp., and *Torymus citripes*. A weevil (*Apion* sp.) is an inquiline. The more common predators of larvae and pupae appear to be insectivorous birds, namely bushtits (*Psaltriparus minimus*), which peck holes in the galls to get at the insects.

URN-GALL MIDGE *Rhopalomyia ampullaria* Pl. 525

This midge has two different generations, each inducing distinct galls on Great Basin sagebrush. The overwintering generation develops in small, nondescript flower bud galls. The second, summer generation develops in small, urn-shaped, monothalamous leaf galls. These

Plate 524. Gall of *Eutreta diana* on Great Basin sagebrush.

Plate 525. Leaf galls of the summer generation of *Rhopalomyia ampullaria* on Great Basin sagebrush.

tubular galls may occur singly or in coalesced clusters of two or three, usually protruding at right angles from the host leaf. Individual galls measure 3 mm long by 2 mm wide. Pupae protrude from the membranous apices of these galls. Adults emerge in July and August, coinciding with the development of next year's flower buds. The chalcid wasp *Torymus koebelei* has been reared from these urn galls.

LEAFY-BUD-GALL MIDGE   *Rhopalomyia anthoides*   Pl. 526

This midge induces monothalamous bud galls on Great Basin sagebrush that are composed of numerous compact, narrow bracts. The outer bracts are usually longer than the interior ones. Bracts are covered with three-forked, gray-green hairs. Galls reach full size by winter, measuring 12–14 mm high by 10–12 mm wide. Several galls occur on a branch. Galls may persist on the host shrub for a year or more. Immature larvae are found in summer. Larvae reach full development by November in some areas. Adult midges emerge in early April, mate, and deposit eggs in undeveloped buds. The tephritid fruit fly *Oxyna palpalis* is a common inquiline in these galls. Larvae of this fruit fly are known to be predators of the gall midge *R. florella* and may function the same way in galls of *R. anthoides* and *R. nucula*. The chalcid wasps *Torymus aeneoscapus* and *Tetrastichus* sp. have also been reared from these galls.

Plate 526. Galls of *Rhopalomyia anthoides* on Great Basin sagebrush.

Below right: Plate 527. Gall of *Rhopalomyia calvipomum* on Great Basin sagebrush.

PLUM-GALL MIDGE   *Rhopalomyia calvipomum*   Pls. 527 & 528

This midge induces ovoid monothalamous leaf galls that protrude mostly from the lower surface of leaves of Great Basin sagebrush. Egg-like mature galls hang from the underside of leaves. The surface is smooth and glabrous. The flesh of this species' gall is firm unlike the soft, spongy flesh of *R. pomum* (Plate 536). Galls measure 9–26 mm long by 8–20 mm wide. Early galls appear in March and April and are often wine red or violet.

Plate 528. Cluster of *R. calvipomum* galls.

LEAF-GALL MIDGE *Rhopalomyia clinata* Pl. 529

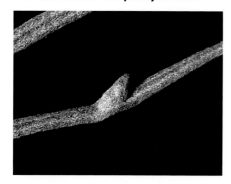

This midge induces small, tubular, thin-walled, monothalamous galls on leaflets of California sagebrush. These galls protrude at an oblique angle from the leaflet. Galls measure 1 mm in diameter by 2 mm long and are minutely hairy. Some are pointed at the apex, while others are obtuse. Galls are yellow-green or reddish brown. Adults are known to emerge in spring.

Plate 529. Gall of *Rhopalomyia clinata* on California sagebrush.

GALL MIDGE *Rhopalomyia floccosa* Pl. 530

This midge induces white, woolly, monothalamous bud galls on California sagebrush. These galls often occur continuously along main stems. Galls measure 5 mm in diameter unless they coalesce, and then a continuous mass may reach 30–40 mm long. When the long, white hairs are stripped off, the gall bodies measure 2 mm in diameter and are difficult to detach. Adults have been reared in November. Gall formation does not begin until the following spring.

Plate 530. Galls of *Rhopalomyia floccosa* on California sagebrush.

BEAD-GALL MIDGE   *Rhopalomyia hirtibulla*   Pl. 531

This gall midge induces small, hairy, monothalamous, round to slightly conical bead-like galls on leaves of Great Basin sagebrush. Most of these galls protrude from both sides and are conical on both ends. Galls measure 1.5 mm in diameter by about 1 mm in length. They are well developed in May. Larvae can be found at nearly any time of year, but adults emerge the following spring, through holes at the top of the galls.

APPLE-GALL MIDGE   *Rhopalomyia hirtipomum*   Pl. 532

This midge induces round, densely hairy, solitary, monothalamous galls on either surface of leaves of Great Basin sagebrush. Mature pale green galls measure 12 mm in diameter. These galls seem to first appear in late summer–early fall, measuring about 3 mm in diameter, and remain small until spring, when they resume growth (immature larvae overwinter). By mid-May, galls measure 7 mm in diameter in many areas. Galls reach maturity quickly and begin dropping in July and August. Adults emerge in April. Initial stages of gall formation are slow, as gall development is delayed for as long as four months after oviposition. The weevil *Apion sordidum* is an inquiline in this gall.

Plate 531. Galls of *Rhopalomyia hirtibulla* on Great Basin sagebrush.

Plate 532. Gall of *Rhopalomyia hirtipomum* on Great Basin sagebrush.

MEDUSA-GALL MIDGE   *Rhopalomyia medusa*   Pl. 533

The axillary, monothalamous or polythalamous bud galls of this midge occur on new stems of Great Basin sagebrush. Often several galls are in a row. A subtle characteristic of these galls that separates them from galls of *R. medusirassa* (Plate 534) is the reddish-brown, curled leafy bracts that stand above underlying hairs covering the gall body. These multiple bracts create a Medusa-like quality in the general appearance of the galls. Galls measure 12–15 mm in diameter, though some larger specimens reach 29 mm. Gall development appears to begin in early fall, slows or stops in winter, then resumes in spring. Adults emerge from April to June, depending on

Plate 533. Galls of *Rhopalomyia medusa* on Great Basin sagebrush.

location. DNA sequencing should help determine whether this species is separate from the next, or if the two galls are an example of polymorphism in a single species.

WOOLLY-BUD-GALL MIDGE   *Rhopalomyia medusirrasa*   Pl. 534

This midge induces hairy, polythalamous galls on buds of Great Basin sagebrush. These large galls are composed of numerous leaflike structures covered with long forked hairs, which give the galls an overall white-green color. Galls begin development in October, rest during winter, and reach full size in spring. Mature galls measure 20–25 mm in diameter and contain up to four larvae. Adults emerge in April and May. The larvae, pupae, and adults of this species are basically indistinguishable from those of *R. medusa* (Plate 533), which suggests that polymorphism may exist here, and just one species is responsible for two slightly different galls. DNA sequencing would help clarify this situation.

Plate 534. Gall of *Rhopalomyia medusirrasa* on Great Basin sagebrush.

HAIRY-BUD-GALL MIDGE   *Rhopalomyia nucula*   Pl. 535

This midge induces monothalamous or polythalamous, hairy, white bud galls on Great Basin sagebrush. Galls measure 9 mm long by 6 mm wide. While some are round, others are pear-shaped; both possess liplike openings at the apex. Some galls combine to form masses surrounding the stems. The surface of the galls is covered with a dense mat of three-forked hairs. Galls begin development in summer and reach full size in winter. Immature larvae are found from summer through winter to early spring; mature larvae appear in mid-April. Adult midges emerge in late spring to mate and deposit eggs in undeveloped axillary buds. The tephritid fruit fly *Oxyna palpalis* is an inquiline in the galls of this midge (see *R. anthoides*; Plate 526). The parasitic chalcid wasps *Torymus aeneoscapus* and *Tetrastichus* sp. have been reared from these galls.

Plate 535. Gall of *Rhopalomyia nucula* on Great Basin sagebrush.

SPONGE-GALL MIDGE *Rhopalomyia pomum* Pl. 536

This midge induces large, irregularly shaped, hairy, spongy galls on Great Basin sagebrush. This species is noted for inducing two forms of leaf galls: one is monothalamous and uniform; the second is polythalamous and deeply fissured or multilobed. The number of lobes has been found to be associated not with the number of gall midge larvae but instead with the number of parasitoids present (Hufbauer 2004). Parasitoids may contribute to lobe formation by disrupting chemical cues from the host gall midge larvae. Both forms of galls can occur on the same host shrub. Gall color varies from reddish brown or purple to completely green. Galls occur either mid-leaf or at the leaf tip; they hang from one side of the leaf, and a corresponding dimple shows on the opposite surface. Galls measure up to

Plate 536. Two monothalamous galls of *Rhopalomyia pomum* on Great Basin sagebrush.

45 mm in diameter. Larval chambers are located near the base of the galls. Gall development begins in October and follows the pattern of other species, with winter rest and full growth attainment in spring. Some galls and host leaves shed in August, while others remain on the shrub for over a year. Pupae form partially extended from the surface of the galls. Adult emergence takes place May to June. Females emerge before dawn. Males emerge soon thereafter and collect into large groups that hover over galled shrubs, searching for females. Females mate once, and oviposition occurs within hours. Eggs are deposited on buds. In most cases,

individual galls produce either all males or all females; less than 6% of the galls produce both males and females. The weevil *Apion sordidum* is an inquiline in these galls, and the harvester ant *Pogonomyrmex owyheeli* is a major predator of emerging adults. Several parasitoids, including *Platygaster* sp., *Torymus* sp., and *Tetrastichus* sp., have been reared from these galls, but their relationship to the host is not clear.

BLISTER-GALL MIDGE   *Rhopalomyia tumidibulla*   Pl. 537

This midge induces small, integral, lenticular, monothalamous galls in leaves of Great Basin sagebrush. Galls measure 3–4 mm long by 2 mm wide. Galls are gray-green, similar to the host leaves. Swellings protrude slightly from each side of leaf. Galls occur one or two per leaf. Adults emerge in March and April.

STEM-GALL MIDGE   *Rhopalomyia tumidicaulis*   Pl. 538

The integral, polythalamous stem galls of this midge develop on new growth of Great Basin sagebrush in summer, reaching maturity in early fall. Galls can measure 23 mm long by 3–5 mm in diameter. They often have stunted leaves protruding. Several galls may occur in close proximity on separate branches, reflective of the behavior of egg-laying females. Adults emerge in late September or October.

Above: Plate 537. Two galls of *Rhopalomyia tumidibulla* on Great Basin sagebrush.

Right: Plate 538. Stem gall of *Rhopalomyia tumidicaulis* on Great Basin sagebrush.

Saltbush Galls

Over 30 species of saltbush (*Atriplex* spp.) are known in the West. Those covered here include: four-wing saltbush (*A. canescens*), shadscale (*A. confertifolia*), desert-holly (*A. hymenelytra*), allscale saltbush (*A. polycarpa*), and spiny saltbush (*A. spinifera*). For the most part, shrubs in this genus play host to either gall midges or tephritid flies as gall-inducers. A rare leaf-mining agromyzid fly induces galls on two saltbush species. At least eight species of gall midges, seven of which are described here, are known to use saltbush in the West. In one study, researchers found that 12 species of gall-inducers on two species of saltbush supported 37 species of parasites, predators, and inquilines (Hawkins and Goeden 1984).

SALTBUSH AGROMYZID FLY   *Ophiomyia atriplicis*   Pl. 539

This leaf-mining fly induces leafy, monothalamous, lateral or terminal bud galls on allscale saltbush and four-wing saltbush. Large galls measure up to 30 mm in diameter, but individual galls are usually 10–15 mm across. Galls are composed of dense clusters of gray-green, elongate, thin leaves that radiate outward. Prior to pupation, each larva scrapes the chamber wall near the apex of its gall, leaving a small, thin area of tissue, like a window. Pupation occurs within the gall, and the adult exits through this thin window. Eggs are laid at the base of buds, and larvae enter the gall after gall development begins. New galls develop between fall and spring. Old galls may persist for a while. Research indicates that this fly may go through two or three generations in a year. Galls that began development in January issued adults in March. A second round of gall development commenced almost immediately, and adults left these galls in May. During the following fall, new galls began development in November, accounting for three generations in 12 months. This species is a rarity among leaf-mining flies, which are generally stem- and leaf-miners (a few species mine seeds). Only a few species of leaf-mining flies are known as gall-inducers worldwide. *Ophiomyia atriplicis* is a southern California gall-inducer.

STEM-GALL MIDGE   *Neolasioptera willistoni*   Pl. 540

This midge induces integral, monothalamous stem galls on allscale saltbush, desert-holly, and four-wing saltbush. There are two forms

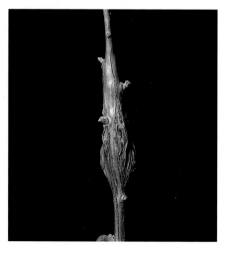

Plate 539. Gall of *Ophiomyia atriplicis* on saltbush.

Right: Plate 540. Gradually tapering stem gall of *Neolasioptera willistoni* on desert-holly.

of these galls: one occurs near the tip of fruit-bearing branches, is somewhat fissured, and has an abrupt base; the second is a smooth, gradually tapered stem-swelling. Galls measure 25–30 mm long by 5 mm in diameter. Pupation takes place inside the galls. Adults may be found emerging nearly year-round, suggesting multiple generations per year. This species occurs from New Mexico to California.

TUMOR-STEM-GALL MIDGE *Asphondylia atriplicis* Pl. 541

Plate 541. Gall of *Asphondylia atriplicis* on four-wing saltbush.

This midge induces soft, fleshy polythalamous stem galls on four-wing saltbush and shadscale. These large, sometimes potato-shaped galls measure from 7–15 mm in diameter and up to 50 mm long. Although the surface of the galls is relatively smooth and shiny, there are randomly scattered, shallow pits and whitish blotches. Galls vary from olive green to red. As many as 70 larvae have been found in one large gall mass. Larval chambers are lined with white fungus. Because larval chamber walls lack the nutritive layer characteristic of cynipid wasp galls, it is thought that larvae of all *Asphondylia* spp., as well as some other generic groups, feed on the fungus or fungal by-products. While this relationship seems to be obligatory, it is not yet clear how the fungus is transported to new galls. There is also an inquilinous eulophid, *Tetrastichus cecidobroter*, whose larvae induce endogalls within galls of this midge species. While the inquiline does not prey on the gall midge directly, the midge larvae are often crushed by the developing endogalls (see the bubble-gall tephritid, *Aciurina trixa*, Plates 493 and 494). This gall midge is known from New Mexico, Arizona, and southern California.

BLISTER-GALL MIDGE *Asphondylia atriplicola* Pl. 542

Plate 542. Blister galls of *Asphondylia atriplicola* on saltbush.

This midge induces swollen, integral, monothalamous leaf blisters on four-wing saltbush, spiny saltbush, and possibly other species. These galls occur along the midrib or leaf margins. Some galls also occur on the petiole, bending it radically. One to several galls may occur on a single leaf, sometimes distorting the leaves. Galls measure 4 mm long by 2 mm wide, are smooth, and have appressed small hairs. This gall midge can be found in nearly all stages of its cycle year-round. It has been recorded from New Mexico to California.

BUD-GALL MIDGE   *Asphondylia caudicis*   Pl. 543

This midge induces round to oval, gray-green, monothalamous bud galls on four-wing saltbush and possibly other related species. Galls measure 4 mm in diameter and have short hairs. Galls are usually found at the base of petioles, though a few were found attached to the base of galls of the tumor stem-gall midge, *Asphondylia atriplicis*. Adults emerge by March. This species has been found from New Mexico to California.

Plate 543. Galls of *Asphondylia caudicis* on four-wing saltbush (with gall of *A. atriplicis* to the right).

WOOLLY-STEM-GALL MIDGE   *Asphondylia floccosa*   Pl. 544

This midge induces large, white, cotton-like gall masses on stems of allscale saltbush, spiny saltbush, and shadscale. Galls cover most of one side of a branch and sometimes completely encircle it. White hairs are tightly compressed and often have a pink tinge near the base, particularly in young specimens. These galls can be monothalamous or polythalamous. They are often oblong, measuring about 30 mm long by 15 mm in diameter. Galls appear during two distinct periods of the year: a "spring" period from December to June, and a "fall" period from July to December. Newly developing galls can be found just about any time of year, depending on locality. Small (less than 15 mm) spring galls form near the top of the host shrub, while larger galls (more than 30 mm), forming in fall or winter, occur farther down among the branches. Pupation occurs at the surface of the galls, and black pupal cases are left behind after adults emerge. This midge likely has several generations per year. This species has been collected from the Mojave and Colorado Deserts of California to the Sonoran Desert of Arizona.

Plate 544. Gall of *Asphondylia floccosa* on saltbush.

NODULAR-STEM-GALL MIDGE   *Asphondylia nodula*   Pl. 545

This midge induces rough, fissured, monothalamous, integral stem galls on allscale saltbush and desert-holly. These galls appear as eruptions of the stem and may be round to elongated; they are the same color as the stem. Small galls measure 4–10 mm in diameter, but when coalesced, galls can be significantly larger and contain hundreds of larvae. Galls begin appearing in January, and development of new galls continues through March in southern California.

Plate 545. Stem galls of *Asphondylia nodula* on desert-holly.

POM-POM-BUD-GALL MIDGE   *Asphondylia* sp.   Pls. 546 & 547

This midge induces woolly, round, monothalamous bud galls on desert-holly. Some galls are dusty pink, while others have white-tipped red hairs or are bright reddish pink, resembling pom-poms. Hairs are dense and do not rub off easily. These undetachable galls begin development in fall (pink), measuring 10–15 mm in diameter, and do not reach full size until spring. Spring galls become creamy white, almost dirty-looking, and measure 25 mm long by 15 mm wide and high. The central larval chamber is surrounded by bright green flesh. The walls of the chamber are smooth except for a patch of white fungus at one end. Young larvae are found in fall and reach full size by March. Adult emergence likely takes place in late summer or fall.

Plate 546. Fall, pink-color phase of gall of *Asphondylia* sp. on desert-holly.

Plate 547. Spring creamy-color phase of gall of *Asphondylia* sp. on desert-holly.

Scale-Broom Galls

SCALE-BROOM-GALL MITE *Eriophyes lepidosparti* Pl. 548

This mite induces polythalamous, compact clusters of expanded buds along branches of southern California scale-broom (*Lepidospartum squamatum*) and possibly *L. latisquamum*, which also ranges into Utah. In spring, these galls are fresh and look like clusters of tiny green cabbages. Each individual gall measures 4 mm in diameter. Clusters can reach 12–15 mm across. Individual galls are composed of a small rosette of leafy bud scales. New galls often develop at the sites of old galls. These galls and their mites tend to have a stunting effect on new growth. Some have numerous stunted shoots emerging from the galls. The mites live among the bud scales.

Plate 548. Galls of *Eriophyes lepidosparti* on scale-broom.

STEM-GALL MOTH *Scrobipalpopsis* sp. Pl. 549

This gelechiid moth induces gently tapered, integral monothalamous stem galls on scale-broom. Galls measure 20 mm long by 5 mm in diameter and are mostly green, except at the apex, which turns brown. There is no growth beyond the gall. These smooth, glabrous galls are fresh in March and April, containing moth caterpillars 3–4 mm long. Caterpillars pack frass in the top of the galls, which may be related to the color change and the prevention of growth beyond the gall. Pupation occurs in the galls. Galls collected in April issued adults in early June.

Plate 549. Stem gall of *Scrobipalpopsis* sp. on scale-broom.

Service-Berry Galls

The tooth-edged, dull green leaves of service-berry (*Amelanchier* spp.) distinguish this shrub in its mountainous habitat among pines, incense cedar, and other conifers and shrubs. For reasons not well understood, service-berry has become host to an array of related gall midges whose taxonomy is challenging. The midge galls described here are currently considered to belong in the genus *Blaesodiplosis*. Until further research clarifies the taxonomy of this complex group, each has an alphanumeric label. This shrub also supports a sac fungus and an aphid that induce galls. Two service-berry species, *Amelanchier alnifolia* and *A. utahensis*, are found from the Pacific Coast to Montana, Utah, and Colorado.

WITCHES'-BROOM-GALL FUNGUS *Taphrina amelanchierii*   Pl. 550

This fungus induces compact witches' brooms at tips of shoots of both species of service-berry in spring. These witches' brooms are quite noticeable because of the dense collection of short branches and the associated swelling in the immediate area. These brooms can easily exceed 20 cm across (see the discussion on sac fungi in "The Gall-Inducers"). These massive, congested collections of branches serve as excellent hiding and feeding places for a broad variety of spiders, scale insects, and other secondary invaders.

Plate 550. Witches' broom of *Taphrina amelanchierii* on service-berry.

LEAF-ROLL-GALL APHID   Unknown   Pl. 551

This aphid induces monothalamous roll galls on terminal leaves of service-berry. Both edges of the leaves are usually rolled up and inward. More often than not, all terminal leaves of a particular spring shoot are affected by this aphid. Roll galls measure 20 mm long by 3–4 mm in diameter. Leaf tissues are swollen and distended. Large, black ants are often seen walking over these galls. Many leaf-rolling aphids have alternate hosts.

Plate 551. Galls of leaf-roll-gall aphid, **Unknown**, on service-berry.

WOOLLY-LEAF-GALL MIDGE   *Blaesodiplosis* sp. A   Pl. 552

This midge induces triangular monothalamous galls on the upper surface of leaves of both species of service-berry. These red-tipped galls are often in such close proximity to each other, they appear as a single, hairy white mass. Galls occur near the midrib at the base of the leaf, sometimes incorporating the entire leaf. Individual galls measure 6 mm high by 3–4 mm wide at the base. There is a slight protrusion on the corresponding lower side of the leaf. Given the snow-covered winters throughout much of the range of these host plants, this midge most likely has one annual generation limited to late spring and summer.

Plate 552. Galls of *Blaesodiplosis* sp. A on service-berry.

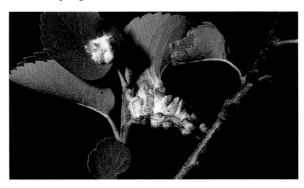

TOOTH-GALL MIDGE   *Blaesodiplosis* sp. B   Pls. 553 & 554

This midge induces glabrous, triangular, monothalamous, flat-sided galls that hang from the underside of leaves of both species of service-berry. These galls are characterized by a corresponding slit or opening on the opposing side of the galled leaf. These galls are usually yellow-beige at the base near the leaf but bright red at the narrowed tip. Individual galls measure 4 mm high by 2 mm wide at the base. The galls occur singly between lateral veins. Sometimes both the woolly-leaf-gall midge (*Blaesodiplosis* sp. A) and the tooth-gall midge can be found on the same leaf.

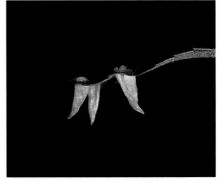

Plate 553. Galls of *Blaesodiplosis* sp. B exposed to sunlight on service-berry leaf.

Plate 554. Shaded view of galls of *Blaesodiplosis* sp. B.

RED-KNOB-GALL MIDGE *Blaesodiplosis* sp. C   Pls. 555 & 556

This midge induces monothalamous, columnar, round-topped, knobby galls on the dorsal surface of leaves of both species of service-berry in spring. The glabrous galls are recessed on the underside of the leaf, where a slit opening shows. These integral galls are usually bright wine red on the dorsal side and light green on the underside. Galls measure 2–3 mm high by 1–2 mm wide. A top-down view reveals an oblong shape that reaches 2–3 mm long. These galls occur in large numbers per leaf and often flank both sides of the midrib. They can occur with other species of *Blaesodiplosis* on the same host leaf.

Plate 555. Dorsal view of galls of *Blaesodiplosis* sp. C on service-berry leaf.

Plate 556. Ventral view of galls of *Blaesodiplosis* sp. C.

PURSE-GALL MIDGE *Blaesodiplosis* sp. D   Pls. 557 & 558

This midge induces small, lumpy, reddish galls on the dorsal surface of service-berry leaves. Each of these monothalamous galls is marked with a white-haired slit on the dorsal surface. The portion of the gall that protrudes on the leaf underside is covered with short, white hairs. These

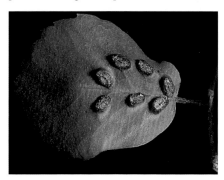

Plate 557. Dorsal view of galls of *Blaesodiplosis* sp. D on service-berry leaf.

Plate 558. Ventral view of galls of *Blaesodiplosis* sp. D.

galls can be round and measure 1–2 mm high and wide. Some forms are oblong and may reach 3 mm long by 1 mm wide. These conspicuous galls usually occur in large numbers per leaf and often in tight clusters. A similar species has been recorded on the East Coast.

RED-LIP-GALL MIDGE *Blaesodiplosis* **sp. E**   Pls. 559 & 560

This midge induces a monothalamous, oblong leaf gall similar to that of the purse-gall midge (*Blaesodiplosis* sp. D). These red-lipped galls have a noticeable slit on the dorsal surface of the leaf and are 1 mm high by 2 mm long. Galls protrude on the underside in a bulging, smooth, light green, glabrous knob form. This latter feature distinguishes these galls from those of the purse-gall midge, which are hairy-white on the underside. In the Sierra Nevada, galls are well formed by mid-June.

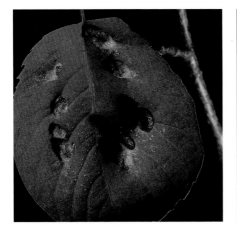

Plate 559. Dorsal view of galls of *Blaesodiplosis* sp. E on service-berry.

Plate 560. Ventral view of galls of *Blaesodiplosis* sp. E on service-berry.

Silk Tassel Galls

KNOT-GALL BACTERIUM   **Unknown**   Pl. 561

The tumorlike galls of this unknown bacterium occur along the stems of silk tassel *Garrya fremontii*. The branches beyond the galls usually die after a period of time. Galls appear as ruptured, knobby, integral outgrowths measuring 15–20 mm in diameter; some exceed 40 mm wide after several years of annual growth. Galls often occur in long

Plate 561. Galls of knot-gall bacterium, **Unknown**, on silk tassel.

chains, with several lined up one after another. Galls show fresh yellow-green growth rupturing under older bark usually in spring and early summer. Several attempts have been made by a specialist to isolate and identify the bacterial strain, while also eliminating other potential agents, without success.

FLOWER-GALL MIDGE *Asphondylia garryae* Pl. 562

Plate 562. Gall of *Asphondylia garryae* on silk tassel.

This midge induces round, fleshy, monothalamous galls on axillary buds and catkins of silk tassels *Garrya buxifolia* and *G. fremontii*. Galls are composed of greatly expanded, overlapping bud scales and bear a sparse arrangement of tiny hairs across the surface. Galls are green, red, or purple and occur singly in axillary buds, but one or more may be found on the tassel-like catkins. Some catkin galls coalesce to form larger masses. Galls measure 18 mm long by 14 mm in diameter, and the central larval chamber measures about 3 mm in diameter. The flesh surrounding the larval chamber is soft and spongy. The galls of this midge develop during early summer and are mature by July. Adults emerge the following spring.

Skunk Bush Galls

LEAF-CURL FUNGUS *Taphrina purpurascens* Pl. 563

This sac fungus causes severe distortion, swelling, and discoloration particularly of new terminal leaves of skunk bush (*Rhus aromatica*) in spring. The curling is quite similar to leaf curl on

Plate 563. Leaf curl caused by *Taphrina purpurascens* on skunk bush.

peach trees and other members of *Prunus* spp., becoming reddish to purple when fresh. The leaves' deeply incised veins are accentuated by swelling of surrounding tissues. Under proper conditions, this fungus can curl terminal leaves of every branch on a shrub, creating a rather distressed and stunted appearance. This fungus has been found on *Rhus* spp. in Europe, the East Coast, Texas, Utah, and northern California. See also, in poison oak galls, mite-induced bead galls *Aculops toxicophagus* (plate 487), which also occurs on skunk bush.

Snowberry Galls

There are at least four species of snowberry (*Symphoricarpos* spp.) in the West, but only two species are covered here: common snowberry (*S. albus*) and creeping snowberry (*S. mollis*). Distinctive white, fleshy berries help identify this shrub genus. Snowberries support three primary gall-inducers in the West: an eriophyid mite, a gall midge, and a sawfly. A common, widespread tephritid fruit fly (*Rhagoletis zephyria*) feeds inside the white fruit in summer and fall but does not create a true gall.

ROLL-GALL MITE *Phyllocoptes triacis*   Pl. 564

This mite induces fleshy, swollen roll galls along the margins of leaves of common snowberry and, presumably, other related species. The affected leaf margins roll up from the undersurface toward the midrib of the dorsal side. The thick roll galls are hard and usually a lighter green than the dorsal surface of the leaf. Galls can incorporate a portion or all of the affected leaf's margins. Galls can measure 10–20 mm long by 1–2 mm in diameter. Heavy galling by this mite may deform host leaves, but there appears to be no serious damage. This mite has been found galling snowberry in Alaska, Montana, Washington, Oregon, and California.

ROLL-GALL MIDGE *"Dasineura"* sp.   Pl. 565

This midge induces compact, linear, glossy, smooth, monothalamous roll galls along the leaf margins of common snowberry and creeping snowberry. Galls roll in from the edge toward the

Plate 564. Gall of *Phyllocoptes triacis* on snowberry.   Plate 565. Galls of *"Dasineura"* sp. on snowberry.

dorsal midrib and are very hard and somewhat brittle. They can be green or reddish purple. Galls measure 20 mm long by 2–3 mm in diameter. In some cases, the rolls extend from the leaf's basal attachment to the petiole all the way to the tip of the leaf. Galls appear in spring and continue to support active orange larvae well into October. Up to four orange larvae can be found in each roll gall; they later drop to the ground for pupation. While some adults have been reared in August, specimens found in October still had active larvae, suggesting a later emergence for adults. There are two midges associated with these galls: one, the gall-inducer; the other, an inquiline. This gall is assigned here to *Dasineura* provisionally, based on larval characteristics, until it is determined which midge is the inquiline and which is the gall-inducer. These gall midges are locally abundant in California, Oregon, and Washington

BASAL-STEM-GALL MIDGE *"Lonicerae"* sp.   Pl. 566

Galls of this new species occur on the stems of common snowberry just below the surface of the leaf litter. Galls occur singly or in small groups of two to four and measure 14–19 mm wide by 11–14 mm deep. These polythalamous galls are green throughout, fleshy, with a fibrous, pithy center. The galls' outer surface appears somewhat like a muted rosette gall, with several blunted, thick, appressed bud scales surrounding the dense interior flesh. There are fine short white hairs near the tips of the bud scales and at the center of the gall. Elliptical larval chambers are arranged around the center, with six to eight chambers per gall. Each larval chamber is slightly larger than the white larva in July. Older chambers appear to have a light brown fungus lining the walls. Galls near the surface appear clean and green, where the leaf litter is loose and allows access by adult midges, while those deeper down closer to soil are white with soil particles. While the larvae appear to be close to genus *Lonicerae*, their assignment is provisional pending confirmation by examining adults. This species has been found in the Pacific Northwest.

Plate 566. Three near-surface galls of *"Lonicerae"* sp. on common snowberry.

BULBOUS-GALL SAWFLY *Blennogeneris spissipes* Pl. 567

This sawfly induces large fleshy, globular, monothalamous bud galls on common snowberry and creeping snowberry. These light green to pinkish red galls can be round, or multilobed when individual galls coalesce. Some galls have the edges of leaves protruding from the mass. Galls of this sawfly vary greatly in size from one region to another. Galls examined in the San Francisco Bay Area measured 10–20 mm in diameter, while galls found on creeping snowberry in the Sierra Nevada were 35 mm across. Larval chambers are large and usually filled with frass by late July. Galls that form on common snowberry are less vulnerable to predators than the galls forming on creeping snowberry in the mountains. In one area, I found more than half of the galls on creeping snowberry had been gnawed open by chipmunks (*Neotamias* spp.) and golden-mantled ground squirrels (*Spermophilus lateralis*) to get at the larvae and pupae. Given the accessibility of this available protein, these rodents may be major predators.

Plate 567. Gall of *Blennogeneris spissipes* on snowberry.

Thimbleberry Galls

POUCH-GALL APHID *"Masonaphis"* sp. Pl. 568

This pouch-gall aphid is thought to be responsible for dark wine-colored monothalamous pouches on new leaves of thimbleberry (*Rubus parviflorus*). The tissues are distinctly swollen

Plate 568. Pouch galls of "*Masonaphis*" sp. on thimbleberry.

and distorted and have a convoluted, brain-like appearance on the dorsal surface of the galls. Galls measure 10–50 mm long by 10 mm wide and occur on the midrib and lateral veins. Infestations of this aphid are extremely localized, with adjoining plants completely free of this aphid. Eggs overwinter in the humus under the shrubs. These galls have been found in Washington and British Columbia and could occur elsewhere. This species assignment is provisional until the identity can be confirmed through DNA sequencing.

FOLD-GALL MIDGE   *Dasineura* sp.   Pl. 569

This fold-gall midge induces swollen, twisted, monothalamous galls among terminal buds or at the base of petioles of thimbleberry. The affected leaf's midrib and lateral veins are swollen and distorted with folds tightly bound together. Galls are 10–20 mm long. Larvae are gregarious, and more than a dozen can be found among the convoluted folds of the walls in the large gall chamber. More than one generation may occur per year. This midge has been found in Oregon and Washington.

Plate 569. Twisted fold gall of *Dasineura* sp. on thimbleberry.

STEM-GALL WASP   *Diastrophus kincaidii*   Pl. 570

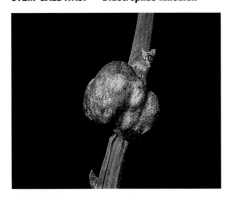

This wasp induces large, globular, polythalamous stem galls on thimbleberry that often bend the branch. Galls occur on new spring growth, reaching 80 mm long by 35 mm in diameter. They often have short bristles or spiny hairs that are pliable when fresh but brittle by fall. When fresh, galls are green to reddish brown. Some galls are round, while others are potato-shaped with numerous knobs. The number and location of larvae

Plate 570. Gall of *Diastrophus kincaidii* on thimbleberry.

have a major influence on the length and shape of galls. Larval chambers are arranged radially around a thick central core. Occasionally, larvae chew through the walls of their particular chambers, breaking into larval cavities of others. They then apparently coexist in a common chamber, as two pupae have been found sharing the same space. Galls first begin to show about 10 days after egg deposition. Larvae enter diapause in fall, and adults emerge in spring. Studies show that males emerge before females. After mating, females deposit several eggs close together into the new, soft spring growth. Wangberg (1975) found that several females deposit eggs close together, and the resulting larvae are incorporated within one large gall. Populations of this gall wasp are extremely localized, with hundreds of galls occurring in one area but completely absent from another area where the host plant flourishes. This species has been found in California, Oregon, Washington, and Alaska. At least nine species of parasitic wasps and one weevil, as an inquiline, have been associated with the galls of this cynipid.

Toyon Galls

BERRY-GALL MIDGE *Asphondylia photiniae* Pl. 571

Galls of this midge develop in berries of toyon (*Heteromeles arbutifolia*). The aborted berry galls are slightly swollen, sometimes fluted or furrowed, sterile, and for most of winter remain green instead of turning the normal bright red. These monothalamous elliptical galls measure 6–7 mm long by 5 mm in diameter. Each gall generally contains a single white larva. Well-formed pupae have been found in mid-February. Adults emerge in late spring. Populations of this midge are often localized, with some shrubs bearing dozens of branches of galled berries, while other shrubs nearby are unaffected. Galls appear to have a white fungus lining, which may or may not be eaten by the larvae.

Plate 571. Galled berries of
Asphondylia photiniae on toyon.

MISCELLANEOUS GALLS

Native Plant Galls

Several plants that do not fit into the previous two categories (trees and shrubs) support known gall organisms and are worth mentioning. Among them are ferns, fireweed, grasses, violets, lilies, and wild grapes. Each of these plants supports an interesting gall organism.

BLACKBERRY-STEM-GALL BACTERIUM   *Agrobacterium tumefaciens*   Pl. 572

The integral stem galls of this wide-ranging bacterium occur on canes of blackberry (*Rubus ursinus*) and perhaps other species of *Rubus*. Galls are convoluted and cracked, with some undulating lobes. They are hard to find when the plant is leafed out, but in fall and winter the large knobs of dark brown and black stand out. These knot galls measure up to 80 mm long by 50 mm in diameter. Older canes may have several eruptions along their length. Infected canes usually die after the growing season. This bacterium is associated with a number of other canker-like galls on various hosts including Douglas-fir trees (*Pseudotsuga menziesii*) and has been found in New York, Pennsylvania, Wisconsin, Oregon, and Washington. This bacterium is much more widely known as the cause of the famous **CROWN GALL** that infects commercial roses and fruit trees.

CAMAS-FLOWER-GALL MIDGE   *Dasineura camassiae*   Pl. 573

This midge induces melon-shaped polythalamous galls in the flower ovaries of camas (*Camassia quamash* subsp. *breviflora* and *C. leichtlinii* subsp. *suksdorfii*) in Oregon. The flowers are

Plate 572. Knot-like stem gall of *Agrobacterium tumefaciens* on blackberry.

Plate 573. Gall of *Dasineura camassiae*, with emerged larva at top, on camas. Photo by T. Barosch, courtesy of Gagné et al. (2014).

aborted without forming seeds. Galls measure 10–25 mm long and can be either lemon yellow or purple like the petals of the flowers. As many as 40 larvae exit the galls in rapid succession and drop to the soil, where they enter diapause and overwinter. Adults emerge in spring in time for developing flower buds.

PIPESTEM CLEMATIS GALL RUST   *Puccinia recondita*   Pls. 574 & 575

This fungus induces deep pocket galls on leaves of pipestem clematis (*Clematis lasiantha*) and perhaps other species. These pockets are noticeable depressions on the upper surface of leaves, with corresponding bulges on the lower surface. There is usually one pocket gall per leaf. In March, the inner lining of the depression is smooth and bright orange, while the bulge on the lower leaf surface is covered with small orange bumps or pustules. Galls measure 12 mm across by 5 mm deep. The rusty pustules that break through the epidermis of the lower surface of the leaves increase water transpiration. This fungus is found worldwide. Apparently, several varieties of this fungus affect different host plants, including columbine (*Aquilegia* spp.), larkspur (*Delphinium* spp.), and buttercups (*Ranunculus* spp.). Some of these rust varieties use wheat and wild ryegrass as alternate hosts.

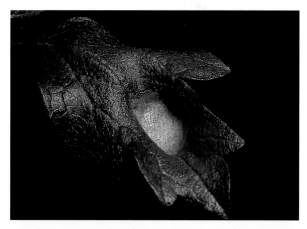

Plate 574. Dorsal view of gall of *Puccinia recondita* on pipestem clematis.

Plate 575. Close view of ventral pustules showing aecial spores of *Puccinia recondita*.

WOOD FERN SAC FUNGUS *Taphrina californica* Pl. 576

Plate 576. Gall of sac fungus *Taphrina californica* on wood fern.

This sac fungus induces fleshy, gelatinous, swollen galls at the tip of pinnules of wood fern (*Dryopteris arguta*). These succulent, emerald-green galls measure 10–20 mm wide by 5 mm thick. They are convex on one side, concave on the other. Galls form along the margins of the pinnules but can also encompass leaf tissue to the midrib and beyond. Galls originate in the epidermis of the fern. The fungal hyphae actually develop in the outer walls of surface cells. These spring galls are quite noticeable once you spot the first one. Usually by fall, the galls have dried and turned brown. This sac fungus species has been found in Mexico, California, and Oregon. A related species, *T. faulliana*, has been reported on western sword fern (*Polystichum munitum*) in Oregon and Washington. It may also occur in elsewhere.

FIREWEED STEM-GALL MOTH *Mompha "unifasciella"* Pl. 577

The fireweed stem-gall moth induces abruptly swollen, monothalamous integral galls often just below the flowers of tall fireweed (*Chamerion angustifolium* subsp. *circumvagum*) in the subalpine environment at 1,200–1,500 m in the Cascade Mountains, Washington. Galls measure 20 mm long by 15 mm in diameter and are smooth, glabrous, sometimes furrowed, and often have reddish tones. Development does not appear to interfere with normal flower growth. One or more white, sticky, silken sacs hang from the tops of the larval chamber in late August, containing fully grown caterpillars. Adults emerge in September. They live for about three weeks

Plate 577. Stem gall of *Mompha "unifasciella"* on fireweed.

without food or water. The timing of this emergence, given the cold temperatures and snow coverage in the subalpine environment, suggests that adults lay eggs prior to the full onset of winter. This moth belongs to a complex suite of moths that can be separated only through DNA analysis. Numerous parasites and a cecidomyiid inquiline are found in these galls stuck to the larval cocoons' threads.

FIREWEED FLOWER-GALL MIDGE   *Dasineura* sp.   Pl. 578

This midge induces polythalamous galls along the raceme (inflorescence) of tall fireweed (*Chamerion angustifolium* subsp. *circumvagum*) in late spring and summer throughout the range of this host plant. Galls are swollen and aborted flower buds that are round or ovoid and measure 7 mm long by 4–6 mm in diameter, standing out from normal, unopened, linear flower buds. Fresh galls are fleshy, pink to deep rose, and form at the tips of normal pedicels. Each gall contains three to nine larvae that feed on floral parts. Upon exiting the galls in late September, the larvae burrow into the soil and overwinter there. Pupation occurs the following spring–early

summer, when host plants are developing young racemes with flower buds. This new species was discovered in the subalpine environment at 1,300 m on the slopes of Mount Shuksan, Washington, and then later found near sea level.

Plate 578. Flower gall of *Dasineura* sp. on fireweed.

GOLDENROD LEAF-BLISTER-GALL MIDGE   *Asteromyia carbonifera*   Pl. 579

There are nine species of goldenrod (*Solidago* spp.) in the Pacific States and other parts of the West. East of the Rocky Mountains, goldenrods are known for hosting numerous species' galls, including those of several midges and moths. On hundreds of goldenrod plants, especially *S. elongata* and *S. multiradiata*, examined from Alaska to California, only one gall-inducer, described here, was found. This

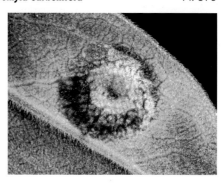

Plate 579. Leaf-blister gall of *Asteromyia carbonifera* on goldenrod.

midge induces blister-like leaf galls on many species of goldenrod across North America from coast to coast. Galls show on both sides of leaves, one or more aligning along the midrib, some coalescing into larger masses. Individual galls measure 5–10 mm in diameter. Most appear as yellow-beige with rust-red tones around the margins. From one to ten larvae can occur in each gall. Development is rapid, taking from four to five weeks from egg to adult. There can be as many as three generations per year. A black fungus can be found inside galls but is apparently not eaten by larvae. This species was collected in California.

GRAPE-LEAF ERINEUM MITE   *Colomerus vitis*   Pl. 580

This mite induces erineum galls on leaves of wild grape (*Vitis californica*) and cultivated grape (*V. vinifera*). These mites produce dozens of lumpy, blister-like, green to red, irregularly shaped galls on the leaf's dorsal surface. Each lump has a 2-mm-deep corresponding hairy depression on the leaf's underside, comprising the hair-lined erineum pocket. The hairs can be beige, pink, or fuchsia. On the upper surface, galls measure 5–10 mm in diameter; some coalesce into larger masses. This mite causes three forms of galls, each doing a different kind of damage. In addition to the leaf-erineum form, another form attacks flower buds, preventing flowering and grape development. A third form attacks young leaves, causing leaf curl. This species is widespread.

LILY-STEM-GALL MIDGE   *Lasioptera* sp.   Pl. 581

This midge induces integral, monothalamous stem galls just below the flowers of the lily Ithuriel's spear (*Triteleia laxa*). This gall-inducer has also been recorded on *Brodiaea californica* in Napa County, California. Even though I have found unaffected blue dicks (*Dichelostemma capitatum*) and ookow (*D. congestum*) growing right next to galled Ithuriel's spear, this midge may gall other related species. Galls can be smooth and symmetrically tapered or abrupt and

Above: Plate 580. Galls of *Colomerus vitis* on grape.

Right: Plate 581. Gall of *Lasioptera* sp. on Ithuriel's spear.

somewhat knobby. They measure up to 60 mm long by 15 mm in diameter. Spring galls stand out because of their size and are usually locally abundant. The central larval chamber is large and filled with a dozen or more orange larvae. Larvae pupate inside the galls and emerge in spring as adults at the time of the development of a new season's growth of Ithuriel's spear.

VERVAIN-STEM-GALL MIDGE   *Neolasioptera* sp.   Pl. 582

The integral stem galls of this midge occur just below the flowers of Dakota mock vervain (*Glandularia bipinnatifida*), a common, widespread native plant in Arizona. These large monothalamous galls measure 30 mm long by 10 mm wide. They are distinguished by the prominent raised vertical ridges running up the exterior of the gall surface and connected to new shoots emerging from the gall itself. Galls have sparse long, scraggly, white hairs. Several bright orange larvae share the large chamber. In October larvae are found inside the gall in silk cocoons, side by side like canned sardines. The interior of these galls is lined with a black-gray fungus, which may or may not be eaten by the larvae.

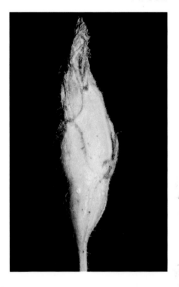

Plate 582. Gall of *Neolasioptera* sp. on Dakota mock vervain.

VIOLET-ROLL-GALL MIDGE   *Prodiplosis violicola*   Pl. 583

This midge induces a fleshy, swollen monothalamous roll gall along the margins of leaves of violets (*Viola* spp). These galls occur on numerous species and varieties of both native and ornamental violets. In response to feeding larvae, edges of leaves roll in toward the dorsal midrib. One or both margins can be rolled inward, distorting the affected leaf. Galls measure 25–30 mm long by 5–7 mm in diameter. Eggs are laid while leaves are still in bud form. Full-grown larvae drop to the ground, where they pupate. Several generations can occur per year. This midge was regarded as a major pest of ornamental violets until pesticides were applied. Although it can severely distort the host plant, it does not kill its perennial hosts. It has been found in several locations in the East as well as in the West.

Plate 583. Galls of *Prodiplosis violicola* on violet.

Ornamental and Introduced Plant Galls

Several galls and gall organisms occur on ornamental plants used in private gardens and public landscaping. Some galls also occur on introduced weedy plants found in the West. No attempt will be made here to describe these species in detail, as with the native species previously mentioned, except for two grasses. Further information on these species can be obtained from local or county Agricultural Pest Control Adviser offices or several of the cited references.

KNOT GRASS-GALL MIDGE   *Edestochilus allioides*   Pl. 584

This midge induces large, polythalamous, globular, integral galls on stems of knot grass (*Paspalum distichum*), a worldwide species. In spring, these galls are fleshy, green, and about 10–15 mm in diameter. The outside of the galls is covered with overlapping leafy bracts. Once this seasonal grass dries, the galls become extremely hard. Larvae remain in galls and overwinter in diapause until spring, when they pupate. Adults lay their eggs near the tip of new grass stems. Knot grass galls are relatively unknown since little research has been done in this area. Many species of grass galls are out there, and with more time and curious naturalists, our knowledge and the number of identified species of grass-galling midges will certainly grow.

Plate 584. Galls of *Edestochilus allioides* on knotgrass.

Below: Plate 585. Galls of *Anguina pacificae* on annual bluegrass.

GRASS NEMATODE   *Anguina pacificae*   Pl. 585

These tiny nematode worms induce small, round, yellow bead galls on leaves of annual bluegrass (*Poa annua*), a European native used in golf courses, landscaping, and home lawns. The smooth, glabrous galls measure 1–2 mm in diameter and occur singly or in compact clusters like kernels on a corncob. Each gall contains a single, white-beige, hair-like nematode worm that measures 1 mm long. This worm is considered a pest of golf courses in some areas. Other nematodes damage roots and seeds.

PLATES OF ORNAMENTAL AND INTRODUCED PLANT GALLS

Top left: Plate 586. Leaf curl caused by *Taphrina deformans* on peaches, nectarines.

Top middle: Plate 587. Stem gall of *Pseudomonas syringae* on olive or oleander.

Top right: Plate 588. Pit galls of *Calophya rubra* on pepper tree.

Right: Plate 589. Bead galls of *Aceria hibisci* on hibiscus.

Bottom left: Plate 590. Pit galls of *Trioza eugeniae* on Australian brush-cherry (or Eugenia).

Bottom right: Plate 591. Peduncle gall of *Phanacis hypochaeridis* on cat's ear.

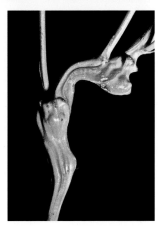

PLATES OF ORNAMENTAL AND INTRODUCED PLANT GALLS *continued*

Top left: Plate 592. Leaf-roll galls of **Unknown** mite on English hawthorn.

Top right: Plate 593. Bead galls of *Vasates quadripedes* on red maple.

Middle left: Plate 594. Nail galls of *Phytoptus tiliae* on American linden.

Middle right: Plate 595. Leaf galls of *Andricus quercuslanigera* on southern live oak (*Q. virginiana*).

Bottom left: Plate 596. Bud galls of *Aceria genistae* on Scotch broom.

Bottom right: Plate 597. Stem gall of *Urophora cardui* on Canada thistle.

AFTERWORD

Throughout the years I have been studying plant galls, I have found over 140 new species, and I still continue to find new ones to this day. I am sure you will, too, if you look carefully. Imagine what may be out there that has yet to be seen or perhaps holds a secret that may surprise us. I hope that you have found in this guide examples of the depth of intricate relationships that exist on this earth, the likes of which we still don't fully comprehend. All these complex chains and webs of bacteria, fungi, mites, and insects help hold the fabric of life together that may start with a single oak tree and yet reach so far beyond. The discovery of new species of galls, mushrooms, wildflowers, or any of the other treasures found on this planet is that intangible element that fuels our hope, drives our inspiration, and defines our humanity. It is, as Dr. Evans said, "a bright flash in the darkness" for each of us. All these years, I have felt like a child lost in a "magic kingdom," filled with awe, joy, and curiosity. I hope this will be the start of your own grand adventures!

GLOSSARY

ADELGIDS: Insects related to aphids in the family Adelgidae.

AECIAL STAGE: The stage in the rust fungus life cycle that produces cuplike or blister-like asexual fruiting structures, called *aecia*, with light yellow to orange *aeciospores*, which are wind-dispersed.

AGAMIC: Refers to the asexual or unisexual generation of females only, which reproduce *parthenogenetically* (without sexual union).

ALATE: An aphid in the winged stage of its life cycle.

ALTERNATION OF GENERATIONS: A reproductive cycle that involves alternating between a spring bisexual generation and a summer–fall unisexual generation, typical of cynipid wasps and some aphids.

AMBROSIA: Originally, the fungi eaten by certain beetles. In this guide, it refers to galls of certain midges associated with ambrosia fungi that line the walls of larval chambers. The midge larvae may eat either the fungi or its by-products.

ANTAGONISTIC: Refers here to insects such as ants and yellow jackets that are aggressive and will defend space from all intruders.

APPRESSED: Parallel or nearly parallel and often in contact with the surface of origin.

ASCOMYCETES: One group of fungi known for having eight *ascospores* in each spore-producing sac, or *ascus* (plural, *asci*). This group produces sac fungi.

AUXIN: growth-regulating plant hormones.

AXILLARY: Between a leaf and stem or petiole and stem.

BISEXUAL: Refers to a generation that has males and females.

CATKIN: A long floral spike of clustered flowers, typical of oaks, willows, alders, and cottonwoods, among others.

CECIDOLOGY: The study of gall organisms and their interactions with host plants.

CF.: Used between a genus and species name to indicate that the described specimen is close or extremely similar to the named species.

CHALCID: Refers to the superfamily Chalcidoidea, which includes many parasitic and hyperparasitic species, including gall-inducers in families Chalcididae and Tanaostigmatidae.

CHAPARRAL: an association of plants that live with full exposure to sunlight on slopes of coastal and foothill ranges where the annual rainfall is low, soil is well-drained, and summer temperatures are hot. Particular to California.

COLLETERIAL FLUID: fluid produced by a glandular organ, the colleterium, in insects.

CONVOLUTED: Refers to tissues that are rolled and folded or in a "brain-like" pattern.

CRENATE: Refers to a margin with rounded teeth.

CROWN GALL: Gall caused by a widespread bacterium, *Agrobacterium tumefaciens*, responsible for millions of dollars of damage to orchard trees and commercial roses; occurs on native plants as well.

CRYOPROTECTANT: A chemical or combination of chemicals developed by some insects to prevent freezing. These insects are referred to as "cold-hardy."

DIAPAUSE: A state of dormancy that interrupts complete development in a life cycle, or a period when growth is arrested and metabolism is low.

DORSAL: Refers to the upper surface (e.g., of a leaf).

ENDOGALL: A gall induced by an invading species within another species' gall.

ERINEUM (plural, *erinea*): The hairy, velvety, or pile-like depression on the surface of leaves caused by eriophyid mites.

EXUVIAE: The skin that surrounds a pupa, which is left behind when the adult emerges.

FASCIATION: An abnormal enlargement or flattening of plant stems or flower stalks.

FRASS: The solid fecal material produced by feeding insects and composed of digested plant material.

FRUGIVOROUS: Refers to feeding on fruit, in this guide generally in reference to tephritid fruit flies.

FUNDATRIX (plural, *fundatrices*): A female aphid that initiates gall formation; also called a "stem mother."

GALL: An abnormal plant growth, swelling, or tumor induced by another organism, including fruit and buds altered or aborted by gall organisms. An alteration of the normal expression of plant genes.

GALL-INDUCER: An organism responsible for initiating gall development.

GLABROUS: Refers to the absence of hairs.

HETEROGONY: The reproductive process that involves an alternation of a spring sexual generation with a summer–fall unisexual generation, typical of many cynipid wasps and some aphids.

HONEYDEW: A sweet liquid material produced by some aphids and scale insects as a by-product of their feeding. Also refers to the sugary material that accumulates on the surface of certain cynipid wasp galls, especially those of the genus *Disholcaspis*.

HYPERPARASITE: A parasite that specializes in attacking other parasites.

HYPHA (plural, *hyphae*): An individual fungal strand that forms after spores germinate.

INQUILINE: An insect that specializes in eating the plant tissue of a gall induced by another insect. Inquilines often kill and eat other insects confronted inside the gall.

INSTAR: The stage of a larval insect between molts. Gall midges usually have three instars, while cynipid wasps have five.

INTEGRAL: Refers to a undetachable bulge or swelling of a stem, petiole, or leaf.

KEYSTONE SPECIES: Refers to a species or group that is at the center of a complex association of other dependent organisms.

LARVA (plural, *larvae*): An immature stage in the life cycle of an insect between egg and adult form, also referred to as caterpillar, maggot, or grub.

LEAF CURL: Refers to leaf distortion where the tissue is swollen, curled, and discolored, usually in response to the invasion of a fungus.

LENTICEL: A wart-like scale or tubercle found on the surface of some galls.

LENTICULAR: Having the shape of a double convex lens; lentil-shaped. Used often in reference to clouds.

MERISTEMATIC TISSUE: Plant tissue with cells capable of frequent division and responsible for the first phases of growth.

MIDRIB: The central vein of a leaf.

MONOTHALAMOUS: Refers to a gall with a single larval chamber or cavity.

MYCELIUM: A mass of fungal strands (hyphae) forming the main body of a fungus from which fruiting bodies are produced.

OAK APPLE: Refers to cynipid galls that are characterized by a thin outer skin with a central larval chamber supported by radiating fibers through which nourishment is provided to the larval chamber and larvae.

OVIPOSITION: The act of a female depositing eggs.

OVIPOSITOR: The external, egg-laying, tubular apparatus of a female insect.

PARASITE: An animal or plant that lives off the tissues of another living organism during all or part of its life cycle.

PARENCHYMA TISSUES: Plant tissue with thin-walled cells that often store food.

PARTHENOGENESIS: Reproduction by a female (agamic) without fertilization or genetic exchange with a male.

PEDICEL: The stalk of an individual flower in an inflorescence.

PETIOLE: The slender stem that supports the blade of a leaf.

PHLOEM: Tissue made of sieve cells and sieve tubes of the inner bark used for conducting food that with age becomes bark.

PHOTOTACTIC: Turning toward the strongest direction of sunlight.

PILOSE: Bearing soft and straight, spreading hairs.

PIONEER PLANTS: Plants able to invade barren habitat, including bare rock faces, gravel bars, outwash plains, and exposed soil. These plants include mosses, ferns, alder, willow, and lupines. They provide a foothold or amend the soil to allow the growth of other plants.

POLYMORPHISM: In reference to plant galls, when one species induces morphologically different galls, as possible with the gall midges in *Rhopalomyia* spp.

POLYTHALAMOUS: Refers to a gall that contains two or more larval chambers or cavities.

PUPA (plural, *pupae*): The transitional stage between larva and adult in insects that undergo complete metamorphosis.

RACEME: A simple, elongated inflorescence.

SAPROPHYTE: Refers to a plant that derives its nourishment from nonliving organic matter.

SCLERENCHYMA TISSUES: strengthening plant tissues composed of thick-walled, elongated cells (fibers).

SCORCH: A condition caused by the gall wasp *Dryocosmus dubiousus* where leaf tissue beyond galls of certain live oak trees turns brown, making a tree look as if it is dying.

SESSILE: Refers to a leaf without a petiole or stalk.

SHOT HOLES: Refers to holes in leaves usually caused by leaf-eating beetles or other insects.

SIGNATURE HAIRS: Refers to the individual hairs of cynipid woolly gall species that are of a specific design or pattern.

SPATULA: A hardened epidermal structure found on some full-grown gall midge larvae used to push grains of soil out of the way when burrowing or to vault a few centimeters once larvae have dropped to the ground. *Neolasioptera* and *Asphondylia* spp. larvae, among others, use spatulas in cutting exit holes from galls.

SPERMAGONIA: A small receptacle in which small spores of asexual reproduction develop.

SPERMATOPHORE: A slender stalk bearing a sperm sac at the apex. In eriophyid mites, the females carry spermatophores through winter after contact with males.

STELLATE: Referring to a star-shaped or sunburst form found in some plant hairs or organs.

STEM MOTHER: In aphids, the female that initiates gall formation and the production of several generations of offspring. See also **Fundatrix**.

STYLET: A needlelike, piercing-sucking structure in the mouthparts of an insect or mite.

TANNINS: Bitter, astringent, organic substances found in certain plant tissues, which can repel some insects and other invaders.

TELIAL STAGE: The sexual stage in the rust fungus life cycle, which comes after the uredinial stage and produces *teliospores* of various colors that are dispersed short distances, generally not by wind. Many rust fungi survive winter as teliospores.

TERPENES: Substances produced by trees during good growth years that repel invaders, insects, fungi.

TUBERCLE: A small, wart-like prominence or nodule.

UMBO: A conical projection or small bump.

UNISEXUAL: Refers to the generation/stage in the life cycle of an insect species (generally cynipid wasps) composed of females only.

UREDINIAL STAGE: The stage in the rust fungus life cycle that produces asexual blister-like pustules with orange *urediniospores*, which are wind-dispersed.

VENTRAL: Refers to the underside of a leaf or other body.

WITCHES' BROOM: An abnormal cluster of shoots or twigs emanating from a common focal point on stems and branches, caused by either mechanical injury (not a gall) or by the invasion of an organism (a true gall).

REFERENCES

Abrahamson, W. G., M. D. Hunter, G. Melika, and P. W. Price. 2003. Cynipid gall wasp communities correlate with oak chemistry. *J. of Chem. Eco.* 29(1):209–23.

Abrahamson, W. G., G. Melika, R. Scrafford, and G. Csoka. 1998. Gall-inducing insects provide insights into plant systematic relationships. *Amer. J. of Bot.* 85(9):1159–65.

Alleyne, E. H., and F. O. Morrison. 1977. Some Canadian poplar aphid galls. *Can. Entomol.* 109(3):321–28.

Al-Saffar, Z. Y., and J. C. Aldrich. 1998. *Pontania proxima* (Hymenoptera: Tenthredinidae): Natural enemies and defensive behavior against *Pnigalio nemati* (Hymenoptera: Eulophidae). *Ann. Entomol. Soc. Am.* 91(6):858–62.

Arthur, J. C. 1962. *Manual of the Rusts in the United States and Canada.* New York: Hafner Publishing. 438 pp.

Ashmead, W. H. 1897. Descriptions of new cynipidous galls and gall wasps in the United States National Museum. *U.S. National Museum Proceedings* 19:113–36.

Bagatto, G., and J. D. Shorthouse. 1991a. Accumulation of copper and nickel in plant tissues and an insect gall of lowbush blueberry, *Vaccinium angustifolium*, near an ore smelter at Sudbury, Ontario, Canada. *Can. J. Bot.* 69(7):1483–90.

Bagatto, G., T. J. Zmijowskyj, and J. D. Shorthouse. 1991b. Galls induced by *Diplolepis spinosa* influence distribution of mineral nutrients in the shrub rose. *Hort. Sci.* 26(10):1283–84.

Baldwin, B. G., D. H. Goldman, D. J. Keil, R. Patterson, T. J. Rosatti, and D. H. Wilken, eds. 2012. *The Jepson Manual: Vascular Plants of California.* 2nd ed. Berkeley: Univ. of Calif. Press. 1,568 pp.

Barrett, S. A., and E. W. Gifford. 1953. Miwok material culture. *Yosemite Nat'l History Assoc.* 2(4): 192 pp.

Bassett, H. F. 1881. New Cynipidae. *Can. Entomol.* 13(5):92–113.

Bowers, N. M., R. Bowers, and S. Tekiela. 2008. *Wildflowers of Arizona.* Cambridge, MN: Adventure Publications. 423 pp.

Briggs, C. J., and J. Latto. 1996. The window of vulnerability and its effect on relative parasitoid abundance. *Eco. Entomol.* 21(2):128–40.

Brooks, S. E., and J. D. Shorthouse. 1997. Biology of the rose stem galler *Diplolepis nodulosa* (Hymenoptera: Cynipidae) and its associated component community in central Ontario. *Can. Entomol.* 129:1121–40.

———. 1998a. Development morphology of stem galls of *Diplolepis nodulosa* (Hymenoptera: Cynipidae) and those influenced by the inquiline *Periclistus pirata* (Hymenoptera: Cynipidae) on *Rosa blanda* (Rosaceae). *Can. J. Bot.* 76:365–81.

———. 1998b. Biology of the galler *Diplolepis rosaefolii* (Hymenoptera: Cynipidae), its associated component community, and host shift to the shrub rose Therese Bugnet. *Can. Entomol.* 130:357–66.

Buffington, M. L., and S. I. Morita. 2009. Not all gall wasps gall oaks: The description of *Dryocosmus rileypokei*, a new, apostate species of Cynipinae from California. *Proc. Entomol. Soc. Wash.* 111(1):244–53.

Burdick, D. J. 1967. Oviposition behavior and galls of *Andricus chrysolepidicola* (Ashmead) (Hymenoptera: Cynipidae). *Pan-Pac. Entomol.* 43(3):227–31.

Burnett, J. A. 1974. A new cynipid wasp from California. *Pan-Pac. Entomol.* 50(3):298–302.

Caltagirone, L. E. 1964. Notes on the biology, parasites, and inquilines of *Pontania pacifica* (Hymenoptera: Tenthredinidae), a leaf-gall incitant on *Salix lasiolepis. Ann. Entomol. Soc. Am.* 57(3):279–91.

Chestnut, V. K. 1974. Plants used by the Indians of Mendocino County, California. *Contrib. U.S. Natl. Herbarium* 7:343–44.

Collier, M. E. T., and S. B. Thalman. 1991. Interviews with Tom Smith and Maria Copa-Isabel Kelly's ethnographic notes on the Coast Miwok Indians of Marin and southern Sonoma Counties, California. *Miwok Archaeol. Preserve Marin Mapom Occ. Pap.* 6:100–211.

Dailey, D. C. 1969. Synonymy of *Dryocosmus attractans* (Kinsey) and *Callirhytis uvellae* (Weld) (Hymenoptera: Cynipidae). *Pan-Pac. Entomol.* 45(2):132–34.

———. 1972. Contiguous areas of Arizona and Pacific Slope floras in northern Baja California, Mexico. *Pan-Pac. Entomol.* 48(1):74–75.

———. 1977. Elevation of *Loxaulus brunneus* variety *atrior* (Kinsey) to full species status (Hymenoptera: Cynipidae). *Pan-Pac. Entomol.* 53:145–46.

Dailey, D. C., and L. Campbell. 1973. A new species of *Diplolepis* from California (Hymenoptera: Cynipidae). *Pan-Pac. Entomol.* 49(2):174–76.

Dailey, D. C., and A. S. Menke. 1980. Nomenclatorial notes on North American Cynipidae (Hymenoptera). *Pan-Pac. Entomol.* 56(3):170–74.

Dailey, D. C., T. Perry, and C. M. Sprenger. 1974. Biology of three *Callirhytis* gall wasps from Pacific Slope Erythrobalanus oaks (Hymenoptera: Cynipidae). *Pan-Pac. Entomol.* 50(1):60–67.

Dailey, D. C., and C. M. Sprenger. 1973a. Unisexual generation of *Andricus atrimentus* (Hymenoptera: Cynipidae). *Pan-Pac. Entomol.* 49(2):171–73.

———. 1973b. Synonymy of *Andricus gigas* and the bisexual generation of *Andricus crenatus* (Hymenoptera: Cynipidae). *Pan-Pac. Entomol.* 49(3):188–91.

———. 1977. Three new gall-inducing *Callirhytis* Foerster from *Quercus cedrosensis* Muller (Hymenoptera: Cynipidae). *Pan-Pac. Entomol.* 53(1):43–46.

———. 1983. Gall-inducing cynipid wasps from *Quercus dunnii* Kellogg (Hymenoptera). *Pan-Pac. Entomol.* 59(1–4):42–49.

Doutt, R. L. 1960. Heterogony in *Andricus crystallinus* Bassett (Hymenoptera: Cynipidae). *Pan-Pac. Entomol.* 36(4):167–70.

Ehler, L. E. 1987. Ecology of *Rhopalomyia californica* Felt at Jasper Ridge (Diptera: Cecidomyiidae). *Pan-Pac. Entomol.* 63(3):237–41.

Eliason, E. A., and D. A. Potter. 2001. Spatial distribution and parasitism of leaf galls induced by *Callirhytis cornigera* (Hymenoptera: Cynipidae) on pin oak. *Environ. Entomol. Soc. Am.* 30(2):280–87.

Espirito-Santo, M. M., and G. W. Fernandes. 2007. How many species of gall-inducing insects are there on earth and where are they? *Ann. Ent. Soc. of Amer.* 100(2):95–99.

Evans, D. 1967. The bisexual and agamic generations of *Besbicus mirabilis* (Hymenoptera: Cynipidae), and their associate insects. *Can. Entomol.* 99:187–96.

———. 1972. Alternate generations of gall cynipids (Hymenoptera: Cynipidae) on Garry oak. *Can. Entomol.* 104:805–18.

Felt, E. P. 1965. *Plant Galls and Gall Makers.* New York: Hafner Publishing. 364 pp.

Foote, R. H., and F. L. Blanc. 1963. *The Fruit Flies or Tephritidae of California.* Bulletin of the California Insect Survey. Berkeley and Los Angeles: Univ. of Calif. Press. 117 pp.

Force, D. C. 1974. Ecology of insect host-parasitoid communities. *Science* 184:624–32.

Fronk, W. D., A. A. Beetle, and D. G. Fullerton. 1964. Dipterous galls on the *Artemisia tridentata* complex and insects associated with them. *Ann. Entomol. Soc. Am.* 57:575–77.

Furniss, M. M., and W. F. Barr. 1975. Insects affecting important native shrubs of the northwestern United States. U.S. Dept. of Agric. For. Serv. Gen. Tech. Rep. INT-19. 65 pp.

Furniss, R. L., and V. M. Carolin. 1977. Western forest insects. U.S. Dept. of Agric. For. Serv. Misc. Publ. 1339. 654 pp.

Gagné, R. J. 1973. A generic synopsis of the Nearctic Cecidomyiidae (Diptera: Cecidomyiidae: Cecidomyiinae). *Ann. Entomol. Soc. Am.* 66(4):857–89.

———. 1975. The gall midges of ragweed, *Ambrosia* spp., with descriptions of two new species (Diptera: Cecidomyiidae). *Proc. Entomol. Soc. Wash.* 77(1):50–55.

———. 1986. Revision of *Prodiplosis* (Diptera: Cecidomyiidae) with descriptions of three new species. *Ann. Entomol. Soc. Am.* 79(1):235–45.

———. 1989. *The Plant-Feeding Gall Midges of North America.* Ithaca, NY: Corn. Univ. Press. 356 pp.

———. 2013. Four new genera of Nearctic Cecidomyiidae (Diptera) for species previously incorrectly placed. *Zootaxa* 370(2):148–58.

———. 2016. Three new genera and three new species of Nearctic Lasiopteridi (Diptera: Cecidomyiidae: Cecidomyiinae) from Asteraceae and Caprifoliaceae, and the tribe Rhopalomyiini subsumed under Oligotrophini. *Zootaxa* 4158(3):403–18.

———. 2018. Key to the adults of North American genera of the subfamily Cecidomyiinae (Diptera: Cecidomyiidae). *Zootaxa* 4392(3):401–57.

Gagné, R. J., T. Barosh, and S. Kephart. 2014. A new species of *Dasineura* Rondani (Diptera: Cecimomyiidae) in the flower galls of *Camassia* (Asparagaceae: Agovoideae) in the Pacific Northwest, USA. *Zootaxa* 3900(2):271–78.

Gagné, R. J., and P. E. Boldt. 1995. The gall midges (Diptera: Cecidomyiidae) of *Baccharis* spp. (Asteraceae) in the United States. *Proc. Entomol. Soc. Wash.* 97 (4):767–78.

Gagné, R. J. and R. W. Duncan. 1990. A new species of Cecidomyiidae (Diptera) damaging the shoot tips of yellow cypress, *Chamaecyparis nootkatensis*, and a new genus for two gall midges on Cupressaceae. *Proc. Entomol. Soc. Wash.* 92(1):146–52.

Gagné, R. J., and B. A. Hawkins. 1983. Biosystematics of the Lasiopterini (Diptera: Cecidomyiidae: Cecidomyiinae) associated with *Atriplex* spp. (Chenopodiaceae) in southern California. *Ann. Entomol. Soc. Am.* 76(3):379–83.

Gagné, R. J., and M. Jaschhof. 2017. *A Catalog of the Cecidomyiidae (Diptera) of the World.* 4th ed. Digital. 762 pp. https://www.ars. usda.gov/ARSUserFiles/80420580/ Gagne_2017_World_Cat_4th_ed.pdf.

Gagné, R. J., and D. R. Strong. 1993. A new species of *Dasineura* (Diptera: Cecidomyiidae) galling leaves of *Lupinus* spp. (Fabaceae) in California. *Proc. Entomol. Soc. Wash.* 95(4):541–46.

Gagné, R. J., and G. L. Waring. 1990. The *Asphondylia* (Cecidomyiidae: Diptera) of creosote bush (*Larrea tridentata*) in North America. *Proc. Entomol. Soc. Wash.* 92(4):649–71.

Ganaha, T. M., M. Nohara, S. Sato, N. Uechi, K. Yamagishi, S. Yamauchi, and J. Yukawa. 2007. Polymorphism of axillary bud galls induced by *Rhopalomyia longitubifex* (Diptera: Cecidomyiidae) of *Artemisia princeps* and *A. montana* (Asteraceae) in Japan and Korea, with designation of new synonyms. *Entomol. Sci.* 10:157–69.

Gassmann, A., and J. D. Shorthouse. 1990. Structural damage and gall induction by *Pegomya curticornis* and *Pegomya euphorbiae* (Diptera: Anthomyiidae) within the stems of leafy spurge (Euphorbia × pseudovirgata) (Euphorbiaceae). *Can. Entomol.* 122:429–39.

Gillette, C. P. 1893. Colorado Cynipidae. *Ento. News* 4(1):28–31.

Goeden, R. D. 1987. Life history of *Trupanea conjuncta* (Adams) on *Trixus californica* (Kellogg) in southern California (Diptera: Tephritidae). *Pan-Pac. Entomol.* 63(3):284–91.

———. 1988. Gall formation by the capitulum-infesting fruit fly, *Tephritis stigmata* (Diptera: Tephritidae). *Proc. Entomol. Soc. Wash.* 90(1):37–43.

———. 1990. Life history of *Eutreta diana* on *Artemisia tridentata* in southern California (Diptera: Tephritidae). *Pan-Pac. Entomol.* 66(1):24–32.

———. 2002a. Life history and description of immature stages of *Oxyna palpalis* (Coquillett) (Diptera: Tephritidae) on *Artemisia tridentata* (Nuttall) (Asteraceae) in southern California. *Proc. Entomol. Soc. Wash.* 104(3):537–53.

———. 2002b. Life history and description of immature stages of *Oxyna aterrima* (Doane) (Diptera: Tephritidae) on *Artemisia tridentata* (Nuttall) (Asteraceae) in southern California. *Proc. Entomol. Soc. Wash.* 104(2):510–26.

———. 2002c. Description of immature stages of *Tephritis stigmata* (Coquillett) (Diptera: Tephritidae). *Proc. Entomol. Soc. Wash.* 104(2):335–47.

Goeden R. D., and D. H. Headrick. 1991. Life history and descriptions of immature stages of *Tephritis baccharis* (Coquillett) on *Baccharis salicifolia* (Ruiz and Pavon) Persoon in southern California (Diptera: Tephritidae). *Pan-Pac. Entomol.* 67(2):86–98.

Goeden, R. D., D. H. Headrick, and J. Teerink. 1995. Life history description of immature stages of *Valentibulla californica* (Coquillett) (Diptera: Tephritidae) on *Chrysothamnus nauseosus* (Pallas) (Britton) in southern California. *Proc. Entomol. Soc. Wash.* 97(3):548–60.

Goeden, R. D., and A. L. Norrbom. 2001. Life history and description of adults and immature stages of *Procecidochares blanci*, new species (Diptera: Tephritidae) on *Isocoma acradenia* (E. Greene) (Asteraceae) in southern California. *Proc. Entomol. Soc. Wash.* 103(3):517–40.

Goeden, R. D., and J. A. Teerink. 1996a. Life histories and descriptions of adults and immature stages of two cryptic species, *Aciurina ferruginea* and *A. michaeli*, new species (Diptera: Tephritidae) on *Chrysothamnus viscidiflorus* in southern California. *Proc. Entomol. Soc. Wash.* 98(3):415–38.

———. 1996b. Life history and descriptions of adults and immature stages of *Aciurina idahoensis* (Steyskal) (Diptera: Tephritidae) on *Chrysothamnus viscidiflorus* (Hooker) (Nuttall) in southern California. *Proc. Entomol. Soc. Wash.* 98(4):681–94.

———. 1996c. Life history and descriptions of adults and immature stages of *Aciurina semilucida* (Diptera: Tephritidae) on *Chrysothamnus viscidiflorus* in southern California. *Proc. Entomol. Soc. Wash.* 98(4):752–66.

———. 1997a. Notes on life histories and descriptions of adults and immature stages of *Procecidochares kristineae* and *P. lisae* new species (Diptera: Tephritidae) on *Ambrosia* spp. in southern California. *Proc. Entomol. Soc. Wash.* 99(1):67–88.

———. 1997b. Life history and description of immature stages of *Procecidochares anthracina* (Doane) (Diptera: Tephritidae) on *Solidago californica* (Nuttall) in southern California. *Proc. Entomol. Soc. Wash.* 99(1):180–93.

———. 1997c. Life history and description of immature stages of *Trupanea signata* (Foote) (Diptera: Tephritidae) on *Gnaphalium luteo-album* L. in southern California. *Proc. Entomol. Soc. Wash.* 99(4):748–55.

Goodrich, J., C. Lawson, and V. P. Lawson. 1980. *Kashaya Pomo Plants.* American Indian Monograph Series, vol. 2, no. 79. Los Angeles: Univ. of Calif. 171 pp.

Gordh, G., and B. A. Hawkins. 1982. *Tetrastichus cecidobroter* (Hymenoptera: Eulophidae), a new phytophagus species developing within galls of *Asphondylia* (Diptera: Cecidomyiidae) on *Atriplex* (Chenopodiaceae) in southern California. *Proc. Entomol. Soc. Wash.* 84(3):426–29.

Grigarick, A. A., and W. H. Lange. 1968. Seasonal development and emergence of two species of gall-forming aphids, *Pemphigus bursarius* and *P. nortoni,* associated with poplar trees in California. *Ann. Entomol. Soc. Am.* 61(2):509–14.

Harper, A. M. 1959. Gall aphids on poplar in Alberta: Descriptions of galls and distribution of aphids. *Can. Entomol.* 91(8):489–96.

———. 1966. Three additional poplar gall aphids from southern Alberta. *Can. Entomol.* 98:1212–14.

Harris, M. O., J. J. Stuart, M. Mohan, S. Nair, R. J. Lamb, and O. Rohfritsch. 2003. Grasses and gall midges: Plant defense and insect adaptation. *Ann. Rev. Entomol.* 48:549–77.

Hartman, H. 1984. Ecology of gall-forming Lepidoptera on *Tetradymia.* *Hilgardia* 52(3):1–39.

Harville, J. P. 1955. Ecology and population dynamics of the California oak moth, *Phryganidia californica* Packard (Lepidoptera: Dioptidae). *Microentomology* 20(4):83–166.

Hawkins, B. A., and R. D. Goeden. 1982. Biology of gall-forming *Tetrastichus* (Hymenoptera: Eulophidae) associated with gall midges on saltbush in southern California. *Entomol. Soc. Am.* 75(4):444–47.

———. 1984. Organization of a parasitoid community associated with a complex of galls on *Atriplex* spp. in southern California. *Ecol. Entomol.* 9:271–92.

Hawkins, B. A., R. D. Goeden, and R. J. Gagné. 1986. Ecology and taxonomy of the *Asphondylia* spp. (Diptera: Cecidomyiidae) forming galls on *Atriplex* spp. (Chenopodiaceae) in southern California. *Entomogr.* 4:55–107.

Hawkins, B. A., and T. R. Unruh. 1988. Protein and water levels in *Asphondylia atriplicis* (Diptera: Cecidomyiidae) galls. *Southwestern Nat.* 33(1):114–17.

Haws, A., A. H. Roe, and D. L. Nelson. 1988. Index to information on insects associated with western wildland shrubs. U.S. Dept. of Agric. For. Serv. Gen. Tech. Rep. INT-248. 297 pp.

Headrick, D. H., and R. D. Goeden. 1993. Life history and description of immature stages of *Aciurina thoracica* (Diptera: Tephritidae) on *Baccharis sarothroides* in southern California. *Entomol. Soc. Am.* 86(1):68–79.

———. 1997. Gall midge forms galls on fruit fly galls (Diptera: Cecidomyiidae, Tephritidae). *Proc. Entomol. Soc. Wash.* 99(3):487–89.

———. 1998. The biology of non-frugivorous tephritid fruit flies. *Annu. Rev. Entomol.* 43:217–41.

Headrick, D. H., R. D. Goeden, and J. A. Teerink. 1997. Taxonomy of *Aciurina trixa* (Curran) (Diptera: Tephritidae) and its life history on *Chrysothamnus nauseosus* (Pallas) (Britton) in southern California; with notes on *A. bigeloviae* (Cockerell). *Proc. Entomol. Soc. Wash.* 99(3):415–28.

Hepting, G. H. 1971. Diseases of forest and shade trees of the United States. U.S. Dept of Agric. For. Serv. Agri. Handbook 386. 658 pp.

Heydon, S. L. 1994. Taxonomic changes in Nearctic Pteromalidae. II: New synonymy and four new genera (Hymenoptera: Chalcidoidea). *Proc. Entomol. Soc. Wash.* 96(2):323–38.

Hildebrand, D. C., and M. N. Schroth. 1967. A new species of *Erwinia* causing the drippy nut disease of live oaks. *Phytopathology* 57(3):250–53.

Hufbauer, R. A. 2004. Observations of sagebrush gall morphology and emergence of *Rhopalomyia pomum* (Diptera: Cecidomyiidae) and its parasitoids. *Western N. Am. Nat.* 64(3):324–30.

Inouye, B. D. F., and A. A. Agrawal. 2004. Ant mutualists alter the composition and attack rate of the parasitoid community for the gall wasp *Disholcaspis eldoradensis* (Cynipidae) *Eco. Entomol.* 29:692–96.

Johnson, Warren T., and Howard H. Lyon. 1991. *Insects That Feed on Trees and Shrubs.* Ithaca, NY: Corn. Univ. Press. 560 pp.

Jones, R. G., R. J. Gagné, and W. F. Barr. 1983. Biology and taxonomy of the *Rhopalomyia* gall midges (Diptera: Cecidomyiidae) of *Artemisia tridentata* (Compositae) in Idaho. *Contrib. Am. Entomol. Inst.* 21(1):1–76.

Joseph, M. B., M. Gentles, and I. S. Pearse. 2011. The parasitoid community of *Andricus quercuscalifornicus* and its association with gall size, phenology, and location. *Biodivers. Conserv.* 20:203–16.

Keifer, H. H. 1952. *The Eriophyid Mites of California.* Bulletin of the California Insect Survey, vol. 2, no. 1. Berkeley and Los Angeles: Univ. of Calif. Press. 74 pp.

Keifer, H. H., E. W. Baker, T. Kono, M. Delfinado, and W. E. Styer. 1982. *An Illustrated Guide to Plant Abnormalities Caused by Eriophyid Mites in North America.* U.S. Dept. of Agric. Handbook 573. 178 pp.

Kinsey, A. C. 1920. New species and synonymy of American Cynipidae. *Amer. Mus. of Nat. Hist. Bull.* 42:293–317.

———. 1922. Studies of some new and described Cynipidae (Hymenoptera). *Ind. Univ. Studies* 53:3–141.

———. 1929. Gall wasp genus *Cynips. Ind. Univ. Studies* 220(7):1–575.

———. 1930. New Mexican gall wasp (Hymenoptera: Cynipidae). *Ind. Univ. Studies* 272(22):1–573.

———. 1937a. New Mexican gall wasps (Hymenoptera: Cynipidae) *Ind. Univ. Entomol. Ser.* 22:261–80.

———. 1937b. New Mexican gall wasps (Hymenoptera: Cynipidae). *Rev. de Entomol.* 7(1):39–79.

———. 1937c. New Mexican gall wasps (Hymenoptera: Cynipidae). *Rev. de Entomol.* 7(4):428–71.

Kurzfeld-Zexer, L., D. Wool, and M. Inbar. 2010. Modification of tree architecture by a gall-forming aphid. *Trees* 24:13–18.

Lalonde, R. G., and J. D. Shorthouse. 1985. Growth and development of the larvae and galls of *Uropha cardui* (Diptera: Tephritidae) on *Cirsium arvense* (Compositae). *Oecolgia* 65(2):161–65.

Lange, W. H. 1965. Biosystematics of American *Pemphigus* (Homoptera: Aphidoidea). In *12th Inter. Congr. of Entomol.*, 102–4.

Larew, H., and J. Capizzi. 1983. *Common Insect and Mite Galls of the Pacific Northwest.* Corvallis: Oregon State Univ. Press. 80 pp.

Leech, Hugh B. 1948. Elm gall aphid eaten by evening grosbeak. *Entomol. Soc. Brit. Columbia* 44:34.

Lyon, R. J. 1959. An alternating, sexual generation in the gall wasp *Callirhytis pomiformis* (ASHM) (Hymenoptera: Cynipidae). *Bull. South. Calif. Acad. Sci.* 58(1):33–37.

———. 1963. The alternate generation of *Heteroecus pacificus* (Ashmead) (Hymenoptera: Cynipidae). *Proc. Entomol. Soc. Wash.* 65(3):250–54.

———. 1964. The alternate generation of *Callirhytis agrifoliae* (Ashmead) (Hymenoptera: Cynipidae). *Proc. Entomol. Soc. Wash.* 66(3):193–96.

———. 1969. An alternate generation of *Callirhytis quercussuttoni* (Bassett) (Hymenoptera: Cynipidae). *Proc. Entomol. Soc. Wash.* 71(1):61–65.

———. 1970. Heterogony in *Callirhytis serricornis* (Kinsey) (Hymenoptera: Cynipidae). *Proc. Entomol. Soc. Wash.* 72(2):176–78.

———. 1984. New Cynipid Wasps from California (Hymenoptera: Cynipidae). *Pan-Pac. Entomol.* 60(4):289–96.

———. 1993. Synonymy of two genera of cynipid wasps and description of a new genus (Hymenoptera: Cynipidae). *Pan-Pac. Entomol.* 69(2):133–40.

———. 1996. New cynipid wasps from the southwestern United States (Hymenoptera: Cynipidae). *Pan-Pac. Entomol.* 72(4):181–92.

MacKay, P. 2003. *Mojave Desert Wildflowers.* Falcon Guide. Guilford, CT: Globe Pequot Press. 338 pp.

Mani, M. S. 1964. *Ecology of Plant Galls.* The Hague: D. W. Junk. 434 pp.

Markin, G. P., and C. J. Horning. 2010. Discovery of the gall-forming midge, *Asphondylia pilosa* (Diptera: Cecidomyiidae) on Scotch broom (*Cytisus scoparius*) (Fabaceae) *J. Kan. Ento. Soc.* 83(3):260–63.

McClure, M. A., M. E. Schmitt, and M. D. McCullough. 2008. Distribution, Biology, and Pathology of *Anguina pacificae. J. Nematol.* 40(3):226–39.

Melika, G., and W. G. Abrahamson. 2002. Review of the world genera of oak cynipid wasps (Hymenoptera: Cynipidae: Cynipini). In *Parasitic Wasps: Evolution, Systematics, Biodiversity and Biological Control*, ed. G. Melika and Thuroczy Cs,150–90. Budapest: Agroinform.

Melika, G., A. Equihua-Martinez, E. G. Estrada-Venegas, D. Cibrian-Tovar, V. D. Cibrian-Llanderal, and J. Pujade-Villar. 2011. New *Amphibolips* galls wasp species from Mexico (Hymenoptera: Cynipidae). *Zootaxa* 3105:47–59.

Miller, D. G., III. 1998. Life history, ecology, and communal gall occupation in the manzanita leaf-gall aphid, *Tamalia coweni* (Cockerell) (Homoptera: Aphididae). *J. Nat. Hist.* 32:351–366.

———. 2004. The ecology of inquilinism in communally parasitic *Tamalia* aphids (Hemiptera: Aphididae). *Ann. Entomol. Soc. Am.* 97(6):1233–41.

Miller, D. G., III, and M. J. Sharkey. 2000. An inquiline species of *Tamalia* co-occurring with *Tamalia coweni* (Homoptera: Aphididae). *Pan-Pac. Entomol.* 75 (2):77–86.

Miller, W. E. 2000. A comparative taxonomic–natural history study of eight Nearctic species of *Gnorimoschema* that induce stem galls on Asteraceae, including descriptions of three new species (Lepidoptera: Gelechiidae). Thomas Say Publications in Entomology. Lanham, MD: Ent. Soc. of Amer. 76 pp.

———. 2005. Gall-inducing lepidoptera. In *Biology, Ecology, and Evolution of Gall-Inducing Arthropods*, eds. A. Raman, C. W. Schaefer, and T. M. Withers, 431–65. Enfield, NH: Science Publishers.

Mitchell, R. G., and J. K. Maksymov. 1977. Observations of predation on spruce gall aphids within the gall. *Entomophaga* 22(2):179–86.

Mix, A. J. 1949. A monograph of the genus *Taphrina. Sci. Bull. Univ. Kan.* 33(1):3–167.

Nicholls, J. A., G. Melika, J. D. Demartini, and G. N. Stone. 2018a. New species of *Dryocosmus* Giraud gallwasps from California (Hymenoptera: Cynipidae: Cynipini) galling *Chrysolepis* Hjelmq. *Zootaxa* 4532(3):407–33.

———. 2018b. A new species of *Andricus* Hartig gallwasps from California (Hymenoptera: Cynipidae: Cynipini) galling *Notholithocarpus* (Fagaceae). *Integr. System.* 1(1):17–24.

Nicholls, J. A., G. Melika, and G. N. Stone. 2017. Sweet tetra-trophic interactions: Multiple evolution of nectar secretion, a defensive extended phenotype in cynipid wasps. *Amer. Nat.* 189(1):676–77.

Nicholls, J. A., G. N. Stone, and G. Melika. 2018. *Protobalandricus* Melika, Nicholls, Stone (Hymenoptera: Cynipidae: Cynipini) from California. *Zootaxa* 4472(1):141–52.

Nyman, T. 2000. Phyolgeny and ecological evolution of gall-inducing sawflies (Hymenoptera: Tenthredinidae). PhD dissertation, Univ. of Joensuu, Finland. 92 pp.

Oldfield, G. N., R. F. Hobza, and N. S. Wilson. 1970. Discovery and characterization of spermatophores in the eriophyoidea (Acari). *Ann. Entomol. Soc. Am.* 63(2):520–26.

Page, R. D. M. 2016. DNA barcoding and taxonomy: Dark taxa and dark texts. *Philos. Trans. R. Soc. Lond. B. Biol. Sci.* 371(1702):1–7.

Pojar, J., and A. MacKinnon, eds. 1994. *Plants of the Pacific Northwest Coast.* Edmonton, Canada: British Columbia Ministry of Forests and Lone Pine Publishing. 528 pp.

Povolny, D. 2003. Description of twenty-five new Nearctic species of the genus *Gnorimoschema* Busck, 1900 (Lepidoptera: Gelechiidae). *SHILAP Revta. Lepid.* 31(124):285–315.

Powell, J. A. 1975. Biological records and descriptions of some little known *Epiblema* in the southwestern United States (Lepidoptera: Tortricidae). *Pan-Pac. Entomol.* 51(2):99–112.

Powell, J. A., and P. A. Opler. 2009. *Moths of Western North America.* Berkeley: Univ. of Calif. Press. 369 pp.

Powell, J. A., and D. Povolny. 2001. Gnorimoschemine moths of the coastal dune and scrub habitats in California (Lepidoptera: Gelechiidae). *Holarc. Lepid.* 8(1):1–53.

Pritchard, E. A. 1953. *The Gall Midges of California.* Bull. of the Calif. Insect Survey. Berkeley and Los Angeles: Univ. of Calif. Press. 27 pp.

Pujade-Villar, J., D. Bellido, G. Segu, and G. Melika. 2001. Current state of knowledge of heterogony in Cynipidae (Hymenoptera: Cynipoidea). *Ses. Entomol. ICHN- SCL,* 11(1999):87–101.

Pujade-Villar, J., D. Cibrian-Tovar, V. D. Cibrian-Llanderal, A. Equihua-Martínez, E. G. Estrada-Venegas, M. Serrano-Muñoz, and J. R. Lomeli-Flores. 2014. A new genus of oak gallwasp, *Melikaiella* Pujade-Villar (Hymenoptera: Cynipidae: Cynipini), from the Nearctic region. *Dugesiana* 21(1):1–29.

Pujade-Villar, J., J. L. Nieves-Aldrey, A. Equihua-Martínez, E. G. Estrada-Venegas, and G. Melika. 2011. New *Atrusca* gall wasp species from Baja California, Mexico (Hymenoptera: Cynipidae: Cynipini). *Dugesiana* 18(1):23–29.

Pujade-Villar, J., A. G. Pérez-Garcia, A. Equihua-Martínez, E. G. Estrada-Venegas, D. Cibrian-Tovar, U. M. Barrera-Ruíz, and M. Ferrer-Suay. 2013. Review of *Andricus* species (Hymenoptera, Cynipidea) producing woody tuberous oak galls in Mexico and bordering areas of the United States of America. *Dugesiana* 20(2):183–208.

Rosenthal, S. S., and C. S. Koehler. 1971a. Heterogony in some gall-forming Cynipidae (Hymenoptera) with notes on the biology of *Neuroteras saltatorius. Ann. Entomol. Soc. Am.* 64(3):565–70.

———. 1971b. Intertree distributions of some cynipid (Hymenoptera) galls on *Quercus lobata. Ann. Entomol. Soc. Wash.* 64(3):571–74.

Rose, F. S. 2011. *Mountain Wildflowers of Southern Arizona.* Tucson: Arizona-Sonora Desert Museum. 201 pp.

———. 2012. *Mountain Trees of Southern Arizona.* Tucson: Arizona-Sonora Desert Museum. 104 pp.

Russo, R. A. 1979. *Plant Galls of the California Region.* Pacific Grove, CA: Boxwood Press. 204 pp.

———. 2006. *Field Guide to Plant Galls of California and Other Western States.* Berkeley and Los Angeles: Univ. of Calif. Press. 400 pp.

———. 2007. First description of the stem gall of *Rhopalomyia baccharis* Felt 1908, (Diptera: Cecidomyiidae) on *Baccharis pilularis* De Candole (Asteraceae). *Pan-Pac. Entomol.* 83(4):285–88.

St. John, M. G., and J. D. Shorthouse. 2000. Allocation patterns of organic nitrogen and mineral nutrients within stem galls of *Diplolepis spinosa* and *Diplolepis triforma* (Hymenoptera: Cynipidae) on wild roses (Rosaceae). *Can. Entomol.* 132:635–48.

Sanver, D., and B. A. Hawkins. 2000. Galls as habitats: The inquiline communities of insect galls. *Basic Appl. Ecol.* 1:3–11.

Savage, A. M., and M. A. Peterson. 2007. Mutualism in a community context: The positive feedback between an ant-aphid mutualism and a gall-making midge. *Oecol.* 151:280–91.

Scharpf, R. F. 1993. *Diseases of Pacific Coast Conifers.* U.S. Dept. of Agric. For. Serv. Handbook 521. 199 pp.

Schick, K. N., and D. L. Dahlsten. 2003. Gallmaking and insects. In *Encyclopedia of Insects*, 464–66. New York: Acad. Press.

Shorthouse, J. D. 1973a. *Common Insect Galls of Saskatchewan.* New York: Blue Jay Books. 31:15–20.

———. 1973b. The insect community associated with rose galls of *Diplolepis polita* (Cynipidae, Hymenoptera). *Quaestion. Entomol.* 9:55–98.

———. 1993. Adaptations of gall wasps of the genus *Diplolepis* (Hymenoptera: Cynipidae) and the role of gall anatomy in cynipid systematics. *Mem. Entomol. Soc. Can.* 165:139–63.

———. 2001. Galls induced by cynipid wasps of the genus *Diplolepis* (Cynipidae, Hymenoptera) on cultivated shrub roses in Canada. *ISHS Acta Hort.* 547:83–92.

———. 2010. Galls induced by the cynipid wasps of the genus *Diplolepis* (Hymenoptera: Cynipidae) on the roses of Canadian grasslands. In *Ecology and Interactions in Canadian Grassland*, eds. J. D. Shorthouse and K. D. Floate, 1:251–79. Biological Survey of Canada.

Shorthouse, J. D., and S. E. Brooks. 1998. Biology of the galler *Diplolepis rosaefolii* (Hymenoptera: Cynipidae), its associated component community, and host shift to the shrub rose Therese Bugnet. *Can. Entomol.* 130:357–66.

Shorthouse, J. D., and A. Gassmann. 1994. Gall induction by *Pegomya curticornis* (Stein) (Diptera: Anthomyiidae) within the roots of spurges *Euphorbia virgata* Waldst. and Kit. and *E. esula* L. (Euphorbiaceae). *Can. Entomol.* 126:193–97.

Shorthouse, J. D., and O. Rohfritsch, eds. 1992. *Biology of Insect-Induced galls.* Oxford: Ox. Univ. Press. 285 pp.

Silverman, J., and R. D. Goeden. 1980. Life history of a fruit fly, *Procecidochraees* sp., on the ragweed *Ambrosia dumosa* in southern California (Diptera: Tephritidae). *Pan-Pac. Entomol.* 56(4):283–88.

Sinclair, W. A., H. H. Lyon, and W. T. Johnson. 1987. *Diseases of Trees and Shrubs.* Ithaca, NY: Corn. Univ. Press. 575 pp.

Smith, E. L. 1968. Biosystematics and morphology of Symphyta. I. Stem-galling *Euura* of the California region, and a new female genitalic nomenclature. *Ann. Entomol. Soc. Am.* 61(6):1389–1407.

———. 1970. Biosystematics and morphology of Symphyta. II. Biology of gall-making nematine sawflies in the California region. *Ann. Entomol. Soc. Am.* 63(1):36–51.

Spencer, K. A., and B. A. Hawkins. 1984. An interesting gall-forming *Ophiomyia* species (Diptera: Agromyzidae) on *Atriplex* (Chenopodiaceae) in southern California. *Proc. Entomol. Soc. Wash.* 86(3):664–68.

Stone, G. N., R. J. Atkinson, J.-L. Nieves-Aldrey, G. Melika, Z. Acs, G. Csoka, A. Hayward, R. Bailey, C. Bucker, and G. A. T. McVean. 2008. Evidence for widespread cryptic sexual generations in apparently purely asexual *Andricus* gall wasps. *Molec. Eco.* 17:652–65.

Stone, G. N., K. Schonrogge, R. J. Atkinson, D. Bellido, and J. Pujade-Villar. 2002. The population biology of oak gall wasps (Hymenoptera: Cynipidae). *Annu. Rev. Entomol.* 47:633–68.

Sullivan, D. J. 1987. Insect hyperparasitism. *Ann. Rev. Entomol.* 32:49–70.

Tauber, M. J., and C. A. Tauber. 1968. Biology of the gall-former *Procecidochares stonei* on a composite. *Ann. Entomol. Soc. Am.* 61(2):553–54.

Tekiela, S. 2008. *Trees of Arizona*. Cambridge, MN: Adventure Publications. 272 pp.

Tilden, J. W. 1951. The insect asssociates of *Baccharis pilularis*. *Microentomol. Stan. Univ. Press* 16(1):149–88.

Vasek, F. C. 1980. Creosote bush: Long-lived clones in the Mojave Desert. *Amer. J. of Bot.* 67(2):246–55.

Walls, L., and B. A. Zamora. 2001. Nitrogen-fixing nodule characterization and morphology of four species in the northern inter-mountain region. In U.S. Dept. of Agric. For. Serv. Proc. RMRS-P-21, 295–301.

Wangberg, J. K. 1975. Biology of the thimbleberry gallmaker *Diastrophus kincaidii* (Hymenoptera: Cynipidae). *Pan-Pac. Entomol.* 51(1):39–48.

———. 1980. Comparative biology of gall-formers in the genus *Procecidochares* (Diptera: Tephritidae) on rabbitbrush in Idaho. *J. Kan. Entomol. Soc.* 53(2):401–20.

———. 1981a. Gall-forming habits of *Aciurina* species (Diptera: Tephritidae) on rabbitbrush (Compositae) in Idaho. *J. Kan. Entomol. Soc.* 54(4):711–32.

———. 1981b. Observation on the bionomics of *Rhopalomyia utahensis* Felt (Diptera: Cecidomyiidae), its gall and insect associates. *Cecid. Int.* 2(1):17–24.

Waring, G. L., and P. W. Price. 1989. Parasitoid pressure and the radiation of a gall-forming group *Asphondylia* spp. (Cecidomyiidae) on creosote bush (*Larrea tridentata*). *Oecol.* 79:293–99.

———. 1990. Plant water stress and gall formation (Cecidomyiidae: Asphondylia spp.) on creosote bush. *Ecol. Entomol.* 15:87–95.

Washburn, J. O. 1984. Mutualism between a cynipid gall wasp and ants. *Ecol.* 65(2):654–56.

Washburn, J. O., and H. V. Cornell. 1979. Chalcid parasitoid attack on a gall wasp population, *Acraspis hirta* (Hymenoptera: Cynipidae) on *Quercus prinus* (Fagaceae). *Can. Entomol.* 111:391–400.

Weis, A. E., R. Walton, and C. L. Crego. 1988. Reactive plant tissue sites and the population biology of gall makers. *Ann. Rev. Entomol.* 33:476–86.

Weld, L. H. 1926. Field notes on gall-inducing cynipid wasps with descriptions of new species. *U.S. Nat'l. Mus. Proc.* 68(10):1–131.

——— 1944. New American cynipids from galls. *U.S. Nat'l. Mus. Proc.* 95(3178):1–24.

———. 1952a. New American cynipid wasps from galls. *U.S. Nat'l. Mus. Proc.* 102(3304):315–42.

———. 1952b. Cynipoidae (Hymenoptera), 1905–1950. Privately published. 27 pp.

———. 1957a. New American cynipid wasps from oak galls. *U.S. Nat'l. Mus. Proc.* 107(3384): 107–122.

———. 1957b. Cynipid galls of the Pacific Slope. Privately published. 79 pp.

———. 1959. Cynipid galls of the Eastern United States. Privately published. 155 pp.

———. 1960. Cynipid galls of the Southwest. Privately published. 151 pp.

Westcott, C. 1971. *Plant Disease Handbook.* New York: Van Nostrand Reinhold. 843 pp.

Wiesenborn, W. D. 2015. Phenology of *Lepidothrips larreae* Hood, 1938 (Thysanoptera: Phlaeothripidae) in *Asphondylia auripila* Felt, 1908 (Diptera: Cecidomyiidae) creosote stem galls. *Pan-Pac. Entomol.* 91(2):203–6.

Williams, J. B., J. D. Shorthouse, and Richard E. Lee Jr. 2002. Extreme resistance to desiccation and microclimate-related differences in cold-hardiness of gall wasps (Hymenoptera: Cynipidae) overwintering on roses in southern Canada. *J. Exp. Biol.* 205:2115–24.

Wood, D. L., T. W. Koerber, R. F. Scharpf, and A. J. Storer, eds. 2003. *Pests of the Native California Conifers.* Berkeley and Los Angeles: Univ. of Calif. Press. 245 pp.

Wool, D. 2004. Galling aphids: Specialization, biological complexity, and variation. *Annu. Rev. Entomol.* 49:175–92.

Yamaguchi, H., H. Tanaka, M. Hasegawa, M. Tokuda, T. Asami, and Y. Susuki. 2012. Phytohormones and willow gall induction by a gall-inducing sawfly. *New Phytol.* 196:586–95.

Zimmerman, J. R. 2018. A synopsis of oak gall wasps (Hymenoptera: Cynipidae) of the southwestern United States with a key and comments on each of the genera. *J. Kan. Entomol.* 91(1):58–70.

ABOUT THE AUTHOR

Ron has been a naturalist since 1963, having worked for California Department of Fish and Game; City of Palo Alto; and finally East Bay Regional Park District of Alameda and Contra Costa Counties, California, for thirty-seven years. He was Chief Naturalist for seventeen years prior to retirement. In 1989, Ron received the distinguished **FELLOW AWARD** from National Association for Interpretation, an international organization for professional naturalists and historical interpreters. In 2017, Ron also received the **OUTSTANDING SENIOR NATURALIST AWARD** and the **THOMAS SAY AWARD** for his contributions to science and education. Ron spent his vacations for eighteen years guiding natural history trips in southeastern Alaska. He has authored several field guides: *Pacific Intertidal Life*, *Pacific Coast Fish*, *Pacific Coast Mammals*, *Mountain State Mammals*, *Hawaiian Reefs*, *Plant Galls of the California Region*, *Plant Galls*, and *Field Guide to Plant Galls of California and other Western States*.

INDEX